å

BUFFALOES OVER SINGAPORE

BRIAN CULL

with Paul Sortehaug and Mark Haselden

GRUB STREET · LONDON

Published by
Grub Street
The Basement
10 Chivalry Road
London SW11 1HT

Reprinted 2004

British Library Cataloguing in Publication Data
Cull Brian
 Buffaloes over Singapore: RAF, RAAF, RNZAF and Dutch Brewster
 fighters in action over Malaya and the East Indies 1941-42
 1. Great Britain. Royal Air Force – History 2. Buffalo
 (Fighter plane) 3. World War, 1939-1945 – Aerial operations, British
 I. Title II. Sortehaug, Paul III. Haselden, Mark

ISBN 1 904010 32 6

Typeset by Pearl Graphics, Hemel Hempstead

Printed and bound in Great Britain by
Biddles Ltd, King's Lynn, Norfolk

BRIAN CULL is the author of the following Grub Street titles:

AIR WAR FOR YUGOSLAVIA, GREECE and CRETE 1940-41 with
   Christopher Shores and Nicola Malizia
MALTA: THE HURRICANE YEARS 1940-41 with Christopher Shores and
   Nicola Malizia
MALTA: THE SPITFIRE YEAR 1942 with Christopher Shores and Nicola Malizia
BLOODY SHAMBLES Volume 1 with Christopher Shores and Yasuho Izawa
BLOODY SHAMBLES Volume 2 with Christopher Shores and Yasuho Izawa
SPITFIRES OVER ISRAEL with Shlomo Aloni and David Nicolle
TWELVE DAYS IN MAY with Bruce Lander and Heinrich Weiss
WINGS OVER SUEZ with David Nicolle and Shlomo Aloni
249 AT WAR
THE DESERT HAWKS with Leo Nomis
HURRICANES OVER TOBRUK with Don Minterne
HURRICANES OVER MALTA with Frederick Galea
SPITFIRES OVER SICILY with Nicola Malizia and Frederick Galea
WITH THE YANKS IN KOREA Volume 1 with Dennis Newton

CONTENTS

4

FOREWORD

I left Wellington with three other pilots from various training camps in New Zealand, bound for the Far East. On reaching Australia we were embarked on a Dutch ship to finish our journey. Besides the four pilots, the only other passengers on board were two deported Japanese. After a leisurely trip through the islands we reached Singapore, where we were taken to Air Headquarters and then posted to 205 Squadron on Singapore III flying boats. After several weeks of being crowded into these overgrown walruses, I kept applying for postings at every opportunity and was eventually granted a transfer to a new fighter squadron being formed at Kallang, but first there was a three-week conversion course on Wirraways with the RAAF squadron at Sembawang.

On arriving at Kallang, my friend Vic Bargh and I found that we had no aircraft, and there were only six RAF officer pilots there. Vic and I were given the job of test flying all the Buffaloes as they came off the assembly line and by the time we had finished I had over 200 hours on the little plane. I really enjoyed their performance, though another three or four hundred horsepower under the bonnet would have made it a marvellous fighter. I thought it was a good little plane, certainly one that could have been improved a lot but also one that I have great affection for – and one I consider saved my life many times.

We soon found the Japanese outnumbered us by up to sixteen to one in the air, and discovered it was like committing suicide trying to dogfight with a Zero, so we devised a scheme of getting in and firing a three-to-five-second burst and getting out as fast as possible. This idea did save lives, as the Japanese never followed us down. However, my squadron lost six young fellows in a space of a few weeks – namely Butch Hesketh, Prof Rankin, Slim Newman, Russ Reynolds, Vin Arthur and Ginger Baldwin. These fellows I had been dining and drinking with for weeks. They will always remain in my thoughts.

I appreciate the efforts of the author Brian Cull [together with Paul Sortehaug and Mark Haselden] in delving through the records of the squadrons and to produce this account of the usefulness of the Buffalo and tribute to those who flew them.

Geoff Fisken DFC 243 Squadron, Singapore

THE BREWSTER B-339 BUFFALO

The forerunner of the Brewster B-339 (the B-39) was designed to a 1935 US Navy specification that called for a carrier-based single-seat fighter, and was of light alloy construction throughout, with a flush-rivetted stressed skin and metal-framed, fabric-covered control surfaces. The prototype B-139 flew for the first time in December 1937, and initial tests were disappointing, with a top speed of only 277.5mph. Following minor modifications, a speed of 304mph at 17,000 feet was obtained. On 11 June 1938, following simulated deck landings, Brewster received a contract to build 54 B-239s for the US Navy. Eleven of these were delivered promptly but the Navy requested that the final 43 aircraft be delivered with an uprated Wright Cyclone R1820-G105A engine and these were designated model B-339; the original B-239s were diverted to Finland, a country in desperate need of fighters to aid its war against the Russians.

In late 1939, Belgium ordered 40 of the improved B-339s, known as the B-339B (B for Belgium). The British Purchasing Commission followed with an order for 170 B-339Es (B-339E for England) while the Netherlands East Indies ordered 72 B-339Ds (B-339D for Dutch), and later still 20 further-improved B-439s. Finally, in May 1941, the Australian government ordered 243 aircraft, although the latter did not materialize. The US Navy also ordered 108 B-439s.

Following the collapse of Belgium in May 1940, Britain took over delivery of that country's 39 B-339s (one had been delivered, unassembled, and was believed captured, assembled and flown by the Germans). The RAF machines were allotted the serial numbers AS410-437, AX811-820 and BB450. Six of these later saw service with the Fleet Air Arm in Crete and the Middle East.

Britain's own Brewster B-339Es – named Buffalo Mk.I by the Air Ministry – began to leave the production line in late 1940, the first three (W8131-W8133) being shipped to England for handling and performance trials. Considered to be unsuitable for operations over Northern Europe, the remaining 167 aircraft (W8134-W8250, AN168-AN217) were diverted for delivery to the Far East (see Appendix V).

A FIGHTER PILOT'S RECOLLECTIONS OF THE BUFFALO IN COMBAT

Plt Off (Flt Lt) Terry Marra RNZAF
243 Squadron Singapore 1942

As a combat aircraft it was hopeless. As an aircraft to fly it was beautiful – it really was. When we first flew them there was no armour plating. After the Japs came they put a big lump of armour plating behind your head and down the back of the seat. The moment they did this it upset the centre of gravity. It was a totally different aircraft. You could put it into a dive and, if you didn't get hold of the trim tabs and start winding straight away, you had to be a real strong man to keep her there. You would have two hands on the stick, holding it in the dive, and if you had to make a grab for the trim tab, one hand wouldn't be strong enough and the stick would just flick back.

As for ceiling, 27,000-28,000 feet was the maximum and by that time you would be hanging onto your prop. One sharp turn and you would drop 5,000 feet. On a hot day, probably 22,000 feet would be as far as you could climb. The oil seals in the prop used to burst and you would get a shower of oil. It would stream back and you couldn't see where you were going. It was just hopeless. We had one aircraft on the Flight in which it wasn't the petrol that governed how long it could stay in the air – it was the oil. She used so much oil.

The main thing that caused us concern were the guns. They were .5 Colts and they just wouldn't fire. The guns worked off a solenoid – especially the two firing through the prop – and a bit of piano wire, and things used to get out of function and now and again you would punch a hole in the prop. They would cock them all on the ground before we left and there were cocking handles in the cockpit – you could cock them yourself if you were strong enough. Two guns used to fire through the prop and two were in the wings. You would depress the button and there would be one shot out of each gun and that would be all. If you managed to cock them again, you might be able to get the two in front firing through the prop, because you could put your feet against something and pull, but I don't think you could ever cock the other two. They sent two American Navy pilots out, who flew with us for months and their job was to find out why they weren't working. When 67 Squadron moved off to Burma they didn't have their guns working either.

There was a New Zealand armament officer, Phillips, who turned out to be a perfectionist. He was quite learned and a hell of a nice guy. He found out what the trouble was and the first thing they did was send him up to Burma to sort 67 out, because they thought that they were more likely to be attacked than we were. He then came back to Singapore and put ours right. I had my own aircraft and when it was serviceable it was that one I flew. I thought so little of the Colts that when the Jap war started, I asked Phillips if there was any way he could take the two out of the wings and replace them with .303 Brownings. Well, he did, and I had two Brownings. I don't know whether any of the other guys got them [they did]. I always had two guns that worked. But if the Japs had started on us a fortnight before they did, we would only have been able to fire four shots. And if you were strong enough and stayed alive long enough you could have probably fired another two. But that was it. These were faults that made you feel the aircraft hadn't been very well tested.

As I said, the Buffalo was a nice aircraft to fly but not to fight in.

AN AIRMAN'S IMPRESSION OF THE BUFFALO

LAC James Home
242 (Hurricane) Squadron, Java 1942

We found some Dutch Air Force groundstaff at the drome [Tjililitan, Java]. They had with them a couple of Buffaloes (best described as bullocks) parked near our service area. The engines had been started and run-up with no sign of any aircrew. I always said this aircraft was a disaster and now I was seeing further confirmation. It was short, fat and stunted like a beer barrel fitted with an engine, and when the engine started up it couldn't make up its mind whether to continue running or cough up its innards and report sick. The complete engine became enveloped in smoke as though attempting to hide away in shame from any onlookers. The noise from its Wright-Cyclone engine when taxiing did nothing to justify its very faltering power. Further, it reminded me of an over-affectionate bulldog loath to leave its kennel. I admit this anecdote of the Buffalo is biased, yet any groundstaff who had them thrust upon them as frontline aircraft would agree with these sentiments. I hated to think how any of our Buffalo pilots felt when they faced the Zero – one thing for sure, he needed to be brave.

Their Last Tenko by James Home

IN PRAISE OF THE BUFFALO

Kapt Pieter Tideman DFC
3-V1G-V Sumatra & Java 1942

Coming to an evaluation of the Brewster fighter, especially compared to the Zero by which it was opposed – I think that my views are not directly in line with what is generally said about the Brewster. Generally it is said that it was far inferior to the Zero. As far as speed and climb performance were concerned, the Zero might have been faster but the Japanese sacrificed everything to get a good climbing fighter. However, that meant that she was very vulnerable, even from the .303 machine-guns. On the contrary, the Brewster was a good, sturdy, fast fighter with two half-inch armour-plates behind the seat. She would take a hell of a lot of beating. My view is that our drawback during the fighter actions was not an inferior aeroplane, but that we had too few of them and also our armament was too little and too light. Only two .303s and two .50s. If only that could have been six or eight wing-mounted .50s! However, I was happy to have the Brewster. Another thing we have to bear in mind is that we were up against the *crème de la crème* of the Japanese fighter pilots.

THE DRIFT TO WAR

"Unfortunately, it has come to this, that either Japan must stop her expansion, or England must willingly give up some of what she has or hopes to have. Therein lies a cause for war."

Lt Cdr Tota Ishimaru, Imperial Japanese Navy [1]

Singapore – an island off the southern tip of the Malay Peninsula roughly the same shape and size of the Isle of Wight – had been acquired for Britain by Sir Stamford Raffles, early in the 19th century, as a trading post for Britain's eastern trade that would not unduly conflict with Dutch interests. By 1921, it housed a major city with a commercial port – Keppel Harbour. In 1925, work commenced on the construction of a naval base, incorporating a concrete dry dock 1,000 feet long by 132 feet wide, capable of housing the largest battleships. The fortification of Singapore Island alarmed many Japanese, who could not understand why Britain needed to show her military strength in the area particularly as Japan had been her ally in the Great War of 1914-18.

In the early 1920s the Japanese approached Britain for help with building a naval air service; the Japanese Navy proposed to build a number of aircraft carriers, and wished for expert guidance from the British, that would include training of its pilots. The Admiralty refused to help on the grounds that Japan might pose a threat to Britain's control of the seas. The Foreign Office, however, could see many advantages, as could the Air Ministry and the Department of Trade. A compromise was reached in so far as an unofficial mission comprising former officers and men of the Royal Naval Air Service was sent to Japan in 1921, and was led by Colonel Lord Sempill AFC. Within two years, the Japanese Naval Air Service had begun to take shape; a naval air base was being constructed and a new training programme was beginning to produce results. The young pilots were quick learners and flew with dash and élan. By 1923, plans for Japan's first aircraft carrier, the *Hoshi*, were well advanced, and some of the British team remained to give advice, but the anticipated orders for British aircraft with which to equip the new service did not materialize. Orders had been placed instead with Mitsubishi to produce the first naval aircraft designs, with British help, and eventually a former Sopwith test pilot carried out the first deck landing on a Japanese carrier. By 1930, the Japanese Navy possessed three carriers and in excess of 100 carrier aircraft.

During the next few years, as feared, relations between Britain and Japan became increasingly strained. Lt Cdr Tota Ishimaru of the Imperial Japanese Navy and author of a 1935 publication entitled *Japan Must Fight Britain*, outlined what he thought would be the likely conclusion of an Anglo-Japanese war:

"Countries when they go to war all too frequently think solely of victories, of winning battles; they do not stop to consider what they have to gain by them or what effects of the war may be. That is why so many vain and fruitless wars are recorded in history. An Anglo-Japanese war would turn to the advantage of America, of France, of Italy, of Russia, and of China, so much so that all of them would like to see it. For a war, which left these two champions exhausted, would leave the others in a stronger position than before without any effort on their part. The fall of England would be as a godsend to

America, her chief competition for it would leave her mistress of the world at no expense to herself. In other words, such a war would have the twofold effect of eliminating both Japan and England from among the Great Powers and of raising the status of the others. Unfortunately, it has come to this, that either Japan must stop her expansion, or England must willingly give up some of what she has or hopes to have. Therein lies a cause for war. We Japanese are aware of our differences with America, but very few of us realise how much more serious are our relations with England and what an element of danger they contain. Serious and irreconcilable economic and political differences are involved."[2]

Singapore

The deteriorating world economic scene in the 1930s required large financial cuts to be made by the British at Singapore, and completion of the defences was put back by five years as part of these. Nonetheless, in October 1935, the first RAF squadron arrived at Seletar, where an airfield had been constructed. Britain was not on its own as a western power in the area, however, since military aviation had reached the Netherlands East Indies as early as 1915, while the French colony of Indo-China also possessed a small air force of less than 20 aircraft.

As the fraught 1930s drew to a close, and war clouds gathered over Europe, four squadrons of RAF Blenheim light bombers were sent to Singapore, but two of these were soon redirected to Aden. By mid-1940, with war now raging in Europe, and in response to a plea to Australia for assistance, two squadrons of RAAF Hudsons arrived at Singapore, closely followed by 18 crated Wirraway[3] advanced trainers. The pilots for the latter, members of 21RAAF Squadron, followed shortly thereafter, and were commanded by Sqn Ldr F.N. Wright RAAF, who reported:

"On arrival in Singapore in August 1940, as Commanding Officer 21RAAF Squadron, it was plainly evident to me that there existed a state of affairs which was far out of line with the reports which had been received and accepted in Australia regarding the defence of Singapore. In addition to obvious shortage of aircraft and equipment, there was also an acute shortage of trained personnel. There appeared to be no prospect of obtaining additional aircraft or personnel, and neither did there appear to be any great effort made with a view to improving the efficiency of the RAF personnel who were there. Right up until hostilities broke out RAF units, with the exception of one maintenance unit, worked only from 0730 to 1230 each day, with 15 minutes break during the morning and, although RAAF units proved that working an additional two hours per day was not detrimental but beneficial, so far as efficiency was concerned, the RAF units made no effort to follow suit, and there can be no doubt that the standard of efficiency of RAAF units was far above that obtained by any RAF unit in Malaya.

"Although it is realised that there is always a tendency for units and stations to criticise higher command, it was certain that, in the majority of cases, the criticism levelled at high command in the Far East was justified. In many instances it was clear that the attitude of those responsible resulted from a general tiredness and lack of interest or determination to get on with the job. In other instances sheer stupidity and rigid adherence to Air Ministry Orders (despite obvious misapplication) prevented an improvement in efficiency.

"It is certain that the shortage of personnel in the higher command possessing up-to-date practical knowledge of the tasks allotted to them contributed to the ill-defined and half-baked schemes sent out to units and stations from time to time, and this fact, when connected with the evident lack of control exercised by senior officers at stations and units, in my opinion, resulted in the disinterested attitude which permeated the whole of the RAF in Malaya. It can be stated that the RAF pilots were very willing to carry out tasks allotted to them but they were carried out under conditions and in accordance with instructions which could only result in inefficiency."

Four airfields had been constructed on Singapore Island, at Seletar, Kallang, Tengah and Sembawang, the latter for use by the RAAF. A local unit, the Malayan Volunteer Air Force (MVAF) was formed at Kallang, which absorbed the Straits Settlements Volunteer Air Force, most of the pilots of which had been transferred to the RAF; many of them had served initially with 4 Anti-Aircraft Co-operation Unit (4AACU), which had been established with a variety of biplane types of various vintage to tow targets for the island's anti-aircraft gunners. The MVAF was formed with personnel recruited from the various civilian flying clubs. Most of the pilots qualifying were men who, on account of their age, were ineligible for operational flying duty with the RAF. In addition, the MVAF ran the Elementary Flying Training School, financed by the Malayan Government as its contribution to the Empire Air Training Scheme. Courses for 16 cadets at a time lasted ten weeks, air and ground instructors being provided by the MVAF and RAF.

The Japanese, meanwhile, gained a valuable insight as to how the Royal Air Force operated from on-the-spot observers based in London during the Battle of Britain in 1940; these included Yukio Nakano, Assistant Attaché in the Military Attaché's office in London:

"If Japan was going to fight, we had to determine what were the conditions necessary for victory. When war should be begun, or whether war should be avoided. We had to clarify the situation. Located at the very site of the battle between Britain and Germany and attacked by Germany in the very capital of Britain, we were naturally sending information that had a different perspective from the information available from the Germans who were attacking. Thus our information should be the most valuable." [4]

Another keen observer was Lt Cdr Minoru Genda, Assistant Naval Attaché and Special Air Attaché, who later returned to Japan to formulate the plan for the air attack on the US Navy base at Pearl Harbor:

"What I most wanted to see in Britain were the real capabilities of the British air force. To do this required study of British units, but under these conditions that was beyond my capability. The only way I could really grasp the air-fighting capability of the British Fighter Command was by driving in the suburbs, or playing golf and observing combat planes flying from nearby fields. By watching how they operated their fighter planes during training, I could estimate roughly how much ability their pilots possessed. In a sense this was extremely difficult, just watching in this manner, trying to estimate the whole capability of an entire air force, but with repetition it was possible to form an overall assessment of their abilities. I could roughly appraise the results of air combats between British fighters and German fighters. Using these observations I was able to estimate that the capabilities of the British Fighter Command were much lower than that of the Imperial Japanese Navy, while those of the German Luftwaffe fighters were even lower than the British. My conclusion was quite self-righteous and was criticised, but I was confident in it. And, when I observed the early combat engagements of the Pacific war, the results of Malaya, Burma, and the Indian Ocean actions bore out my assessment." [5]

While Nakano and Genda were in Britain, another senior Japanese officer, Colonel Tanikawa, Planning Chief of the Imperial Japanese Army HQ, was in Singapore, where he arrived incognito with Major Kunitake, Staff Officer of the 25th Japanese

Army. On arrival, on 10 September 1940, they were met by Mamoru Shinozaki, Press Officer at the Japanese Consulate, with whom they toured Singapore City and elsewhere on the island before driving to Johore Bahru, visiting Tinggi, Mersing and Endau. Mission completed, they returned to Tokyo four days later, where they reported that Singapore could only be attacked from the direction of Johore, from the Malayan Peninsula.

As tension mounted in the region following the outbreak of the European war, the French in Indo-China clashed with their neighbours, the Thais. With the increase in Japanese aggression, and the completion of the Singapore Naval Base and airfields on Singapore Island and construction of others on the Malayan Peninsula underway, it was decided by the Air Ministry in London that the time was right to provide a fighter force for the area, even though few could be spared from the defence of Britain and her offensive in the Middle East. Hurricanes or preferably Spitfires should have been sent, but it was not to be. However, a threat to British and American possessions in the area was not considered to be imminent, as revealed in a letter from Prime Minister Churchill to US President Roosevelt, dated 15 February 1941:

"I do not myself think that the Japanese would be likely to send the large military expedition necessary to lay siege to Singapore. The Japanese would no doubt occupy whatever strategic points and oilfields in the Dutch East Indies and thereabouts that they covet, and thus get a far better position for a full-scale attack on Singapore later on. They would also raid Australian and New Zealand ports and coasts, causing deep anxiety in those Dominions, which had already sent all their best trained fighting men to the Far East."

The new GOC Malaya, Lt General Arthur Percival DSO MC, who had previously served on the Malaya General Staff and was considered the best man available to take command now that tension was mounting in the area, wrote:

"Since I left Malaya three and a half years before, some considerable changes had taken place in the defence organisation. In the first place a Commander-in-Chief Far East (Air Chief Marshal Sir Robert Brooke-Popham DSO AFC) had been appointed with headquarters at the Naval Base on Singapore Island. He was responsible directly to the Chiefs of Staff for the operational control and general direction of training of all British land and air forces in Malaya, Burma and Hong Kong, and for the co-ordination of plans for the defence of those territories.

"Another important change which had taken place in the Far East since I had last been there was that the China Fleet, such as it was, was now based on Singapore instead of being based on Hong Kong, and the Commander-in-Chief China, Vice-Admiral Sir Geoffrey Layton, flew his flag ashore at the Naval Base. Most of the more powerful units of the China Fleet had by that time been removed to take part in the war in the West. Of more importance for the time being than the strength of the Fleet, which was almost negligible as far as major operations were concerned, was our strength in the air, and I made anxious inquiries about that.

"There were certainly more aircraft than when I had left Malaya but I was not encouraged when I was told that the same old Vildebeest torpedo-bombers as before were still there, for I knew full well that, though they might have been reconditioned and fitted with new engines, their age must run into double figures and that they could not be considered of much account in modern war. It is true also that there were fighters where there had been none before but, having seen the paramount importance of the modern up-to-date fighter in the Battle of Britain, I was far from feeling happy when I was told that our fighters were a type which I had not heard of as being in action elsewhere, i.e. the American-built Brewster Buffalo. However, a fighter was a fighter and we were in no position to pick and choose at that time. I was more disturbed to find that there were no heavy bombers, no dive-bombers, no transport and no army co-operation aircraft in Malaya." [6]

It was, therefore, to be the Brewster Buffalo that was to offer initial defence for Malaya and Singapore when war eventually came to the area.

CHAPTER I

BUFFALOES ARE GOOD ENOUGH FOR SINGAPORE

1941

"I was far from feeling happy when I was told that our fighters were a type which I had not heard of as being in action elsewhere . . . However, a fighter was a fighter and we were in no position to pick and choose at that time." [7]

Lt Gen Arthur Percival, GOC Malaya

The possibility of despatching substantial quantities of urgently needed fighters to Singapore from the United Kingdom – where the Battle of Britain had only just ended and a renewed offensive by the Luftwaffe was still anticipated – was remote. In any event the demands of the new fronts in the Middle East took priority. The answer was found by requesting that deliveries of American Brewster B-339E Buffalo fighters – originally destined for Britain, which had been ordered by the British Purchasing Commission during 1939 and 1940 – be diverted to the Far East. These aircraft had been found unsuitable for operations in the European war zone owing to their lack of high altitude performance capabilities, but were deemed to be good enough to deal with anything the Japanese might field.

Early in 1941, command of the RAF Far East Command passed to Air Vice-Marshal C.W.H Pulford CB OBE AFC, who replaced Air Vice-Marshal Sir John Babington KCB CBE DSO. Shortly before his departure, the outgoing AOC had sent the Air Ministry a memorandum, which stressed that he was in no doubt that, should the Japanese gain a foothold in Malaya, the fate of Singapore would be sealed. Consequently, he recommended not only the strengthening of the air forces, but he went further and said that the defences should include the whole of Malaya and should be based primarily on the use of air power. The day after Pulford's arrival, at a Chiefs of Staff meeting in London, the Vice-Chief of the Naval Staff advocated the despatch of Hurricanes to Malaya, but his opposite number on the Air Staff insisted that "Buffalo fighters would be more than a match for the Japanese aircraft that were not of the latest type." How the Allies could delude themselves in this manner remains a mystery. It seems that the appearance of fixed-undercarriage A5Ms of the JNAF and JAAF Ki-27s in the skies over China and Manchuria blinded the powers-that-be to the truth. Quite apart from the excellent showing of the existing Japanese fighters, a unit of the new Mitsubishi A6M Zero-Zen fighters of the JNAF had reached China as early as July 1940, where in a brief period they had virtually destroyed the remaining Chinese air strength. [8]

What Singapore needed were supplies of modern fighters – Spitfires and Hurricanes, or even P-40 Tomahawks which were on order from the United States. However, the Spitfire had not even made its appearance outside the UK at this stage, although Hurricanes were available in large numbers. At the end of August, Prime Minister Churchill rather flamboyantly offered Soviet Premier Stalin a further 200 Hurricanes in addition to the 40 already supplied, with 200 Tomahawks promised from deliveries due from the United States. As a consequence of this undertaking, Singapore was refused further proposed reinforcements when the Chief of Staff advised Air Chief Marshal Sir Robert Brooke-Popham, C-in-C Far East, that the plan to accommodate an air strength of 336 aircraft in the Far East by the end of 1941 could no longer be met, much less a recently proposed higher figure. The greater priority of both Russia and the Middle East, together with shortfalls in production in both the United Kingdom and the United States, were cited as the causes.

The *Straits Times* heralded the arrival of the Buffaloes in glowing terms, under the heading 'American Fighters in Malaya':

"Squadrons of Brewster Buffaloes, 300 mile-an-hour American made planes which are proving to be first class fighters are among new RAF reinforcements in Malaya. Malaya is the first country in the British Empire east of Suez equipped with these American fighters. They are capable of turning more quickly than any other fighter yet designed. The Buffaloes are flown by specially selected personnel, among whom are crack fighter pilots who have fought the Luftwaffe in the Battle of Britain and have been credited with destroying a large number of Heinkels and Messerschmitts. These pilots, who only a few months ago, handled Britain's marvel planes, the Spitfire and Hurricane – are taking to the Buffaloes like ducks to water. They declare that the Buffalo is a delight to handle. 'There's nothing like it for really close-quarter combat,' one of them said, 'It can turn on a cent.' The planes, which are now in service with RAF squadrons in Singapore can be assembled and take the air 24 hours after the crates have been unloaded in Singapore.

"The Buffalo started its career as a fleet fighter of the US Navy's air arm and was designed to land on aircraft carriers. Its unusually thick, barrel-like fuselage – its appearance on the ground thoroughly warrants the name 'Buffalo' – makes it an unmistakable type in the air. Its speed with the 800hp Wright Cyclone engine fitted is comparatively speaking not very great – not much more than 310mph – but speed, although ranking high among the qualities of the modern fighter, is proving by no means the only important factor in aerial fighting."

It was planned to establish two new squadrons immediately at Kallang aerodrome, the first of which was 67 Squadron, formed from a draft of five officers and 111 airmen who had arrived aboard SS *Aquitania* on 11 March. By the end of May the unit had its full complement of Buffaloes assembled and tested, and Sqn Ldr R.A. Milward DFC arrived from the Middle East to command; his flight commanders were Flt Lt D.J.C. Pinckney, a Battle of Britain veteran, and Flt Lt Jack Brandt. The rest of the pilots were predominantly members of the RNZAF sent direct from New Zealand, although Flg Off P.M. Bingham-Wallis joined the unit at Singapore when he transferred from 4AACU. One of the groundcrew, LAC J. Helsdon Thomas, wrote:

"The Squadron was equipped with Buffalo aircraft, also known as flying barrels. Maintaining these machines was a constant headache. Spot welds would break on the box section undercarriage. Rivets were discovered in the fuel lines, fuel pumps and carburettors. Big-end bearings had a habit of cracking up and depositing white metal into the scavenge filters." 9

However, 67 Squadron's stay at Singapore was to be brief and a few months later, in October, it would be despatched to Burma. The second Buffalo unit, also formed at Kallang on 12 March, was 243 Squadron. Sqn Ldr G.B.M. Bell, who had been acting as ADC to the AOC, was offered the post of squadron commander:

"We were equipped with Brewster Buffaloes, an American aircraft designed for use on carriers and at that time discarded by the US Navy as obsolete. However, we were proud to be flying the Buffalo which was, despite its obsolescence, modern when compared to the other aircraft with which the Command was equipped."

Two more Battle of Britain pilots – Flt Lt Tim Vigors DFC and Flg Off John Mansel-Lewis[10] – arrived from the United Kingdom as flight commanders, and were accompanied by Wg Cdr R.A. Chignall, who was to take command of RAF Kallang. Tim Vigors, credited with eight victories while serving in the UK, recalled:

> "John Mansel-Lewis came out on the boat with me. In fact we shared a cabin the whole way. He was, I suppose, my closest surviving friend at that time. There were six other fighter pilots who came out with us on the boat to Singapore and the only one I can remember was Colin Pinckney, who had been at school with me. As far as I can remember the remaining five of these pilots were all killed in the subsequent Japanese action."

With Vigors in charge of A Flight and Mansel-Lewis B Flight, a handful of senior pilots were transferred from resident units to assist with the training of the mainly inexperienced RNZAF pilots who began arriving. Flg Off Mowbray Garden was posted to 243 Squadron from 4AACU, while Flg Off Maurice Holder, known as Blondie due to his shock of blond hair, transferred from 36 (Vildebeest) Squadron. During his travels Holder had acquired a black flying suit, which he continued to wear once hostilities had begun, and at a time when his companions had been issued with white flying suits to assist with detection should they find themselves forced down into the jungle.

Prior to his posting to 243 Squadron, 27-year-old Garden had never flown a monoplane or an aircraft with a retractable undercarriage, and had no formal fighter training or schooling in air gunnery. When it was deemed advisable to try his hand at the latter skill, he was informed that no ammunition was available for practice. A member of the Straits Settlements Volunteer Air Force, Garden had arrived in Singapore in 1936 to take up an appointment as European assistant to a firm of solicitors. Although he had wanted to return to England to join the RAF when war broke out, he was advised that he and other members of the SSVAF would be retained. In September 1939 he was mobilised into the RAF as a VR officer. Of this period, he recalled:

> "There was friction between the European civilian personnel and the Armed Services. There were faults on both sides but, apart from officers, the two just did not mix socially. The poor troops and NCOs, when they had their pay transferred into the local currency, found it did not take them very far on a night out – even if they had been socially acceptable. This of course created jealousy and division between the European civilians on the one hand and the Armed Services on the other, which mitigated against co-operation between the two.
>
> "One of the grave shortages was aircraft of all kinds, but in the spring of 1941 a consignment of Brewster Buffaloes arrived in crated form; these were fighter aircraft, which nobody in any other theatre of war wanted – they proved most unreliable aircraft indeed. As a flying machine they handled quite nicely but as soon as a war load was installed – i.e. guns, ammunition, armour plate etc – the performance fell off very substantially. Moreover, though the guns were .50 Brownings, there were only four of them. Two of these were mounted in the fuselage, firing through the blades of the propeller, and two in the wings. The ammunition supplied was not good – it was only armour-piercing and ball, no incendiary ammunition at all. There was some tracer but it was not until the last days that we were allowed to use it because of the damage it did to the gun barrels, of which there were few replacements. The armour-piercing ammunition suffered from split casing, which meant every so often the cartridge or charges behind the bullet would split its case and jam the gun. There was a pull handle

in the cockpit by which one could try and eject the faulty round, but this rarely worked and, of course, if a wing gun jammed like this the aircraft was rendered unusable as a fighting machine because the recoiling effect of firing the opposite wing gun made the aircraft yaw to such an extent, one lost the target from one's sight."

Two more pilots arrived for 243 Squadron from 100 Squadron, also a Vildebeest unit, as New Zealander Plt Off Edgar Pevreal recalled:

"They called around the squadrons for volunteers to go to fighter squadrons. Jack Oakden and I volunteered mainly through boredom. We did very little flying with 100 Squadron because they were short of petrol, spare parts and all sorts of things – if we got one flight a week we were lucky. We only worked in the morning from 9 till 12 – and we only did four half days a week. We were bored stiff."

Another new arrival was Sgt Geoff Fisken, a 25-year-old former farm worker from Gisborne, who had arrived in Singapore in February:

"I felt my posting must have been a mistake, as I had volunteered for service in the Middle East. When I first arrived in Singapore I was posted to Seletar but found nothing to do – I filled in time flying Avro Tutors though I was then posted to 205 Squadron on Singapore IIIs – where I discovered we had more pilots than there were planes. I applied for a transfer to one of the new fighter squadrons – I had been working as a deer culler, so I knew how to shoot – and after a fortnight or so I was sent to 21RAAF Squadron with 'Kitchy' Bargh and Bill Christiansen to do a conversion on Wirraways, and on 16 March we were posted to Kallang to fly Buffaloes. It then became a job for myself and Kitchy to test and deliver Buffaloes to the RAF. Although much better than I'd flown before, no way in the world could they be considered a modern fighter plane. The hours we chalked up would help us to understand the plane's strengths and weaknesses, and prove invaluable in combat."

'Kitchy' (meaning small) Bargh was in fact Sgt Vic Bargh, a native of Carterton, who had been posted to 36 Squadron initially; he recalled:

"When we got to Singapore, we thought we'd see all sorts of modern aeroplanes, and we had the same aeroplanes [Vildebeest] flying in Singapore. We were the first ones to go; there were six of us. Three months later Buffaloes started to arrive in boxes, and they were assembled at Seletar for 67 Squadron. I thought they were terrific; they were beautiful aeroplanes. Well, we all thought they were good, you know. We didn't know they were out of date.

"We [Bargh, Christiansen and Fisken] used to fly over to Seletar in a small aeroplane and pick them up, and bring them over one by one until we'd got enough for the whole squadron, which was about 16 aeroplanes. We knew nothing else. We'd never seen a Spitfire, we'd never seen a Hurricane, we'd never seen anything else. We thought they were quite good. The guns were never satisfactory. I don't know why, but they always stopped."

When 67 Squadron was formed, Bargh and Christiansen joined it as would-be fighter pilots. Geoff Fisken, who went to the second unit to form, 243 Squadron, continued:

"Kitchy and I had a little car, a semi-racing, hill-climbing thing, a Fiat. The thing never had any brakes and often we used to cart a Flight Sergeant with us, with his feet on the seat between us and sitting on the bumblebee-like back. He had a voice like a foghorn and cleared the way from bikes and rickshaws alike for us by yelling – it certainly did the job. At one stage Kitchy and I kept a 21-feet-long python in the boot of our car, which had been caught in a pineapple patch; we believed it had swallowed a deer! We kept it for about three months but when it started to get a bit lively, despatched it with a revolver; we had the skin stretched around the walls of our quarters."

He recalled one particularly scary incident:

"Kitchy and I were heading home one day, Kitchy driving, when we hit a wobbly Chinese learning to ride a bike – he flew right over the little car, taking Kitchy's topee from the top of his head. He looked so funny with the rim of the topee on his head, just like a halo. By the time we stopped, we were 100 yards along the road. We backed quickly and, by the time the police arrived, we were within a couple of yards of the victim, rendering first aid. Out came the chalk, the policeman marking the position of the car and distance from the victim. Eventually, Kitchy was taken to court and was fined $S40. He was the quickest man I know of getting rid of his pay so consequently he had no money. I was his banker. In those days the courts had a great cage in the centre where they put the prisoners who couldn't pay and were due to go to jail. I refused to pay Kitchy's fine so he was put in the cage with coolies and thugs and what have you – but only for about ten minutes, as I suddenly found my money. The fine was paid and the court adjourned. The magistrate took both Kitchy and me out to lunch."

Another hair-raising incident occurred when Fisken and Bargh swopped seats in mid-air whilst flying a Tutor, much to the amazement of their instructor. Fisken continued:

"At this time there were about twelve pilots that had flown retractable undercarriage aircraft, so 67 and 243 Squadrons were formed, though we flew as one until more pilots arrived – mainly in twos or fours from New Zealand and, of course, on the availability of Buffaloes. I was one of the original pilots of 243 Squadron – both 67 and 243 had about five pilots each after a conversion course in Wirraways with 21RAAF Squadron.

"When the squadrons were first formed and we flew together owing to the number of pilots, Wg Cdr Chignell [OC Kallang] said he was going to teach us attacking procedure – wing over and come up under the belly of a so-called bomber – a Tutor in this case. He led in the first attack with six eager beavers following in close proximity but, somehow, as he turned over to break out, his aerial got tangled up with the wingtip of another Buffalo on the way up. He didn't wait to complete the exercise but was waiting for us in the dispersal hut, very red-faced and told us in no uncertain terms that he never wanted to see another NZ pilot as long as he lived. He never flew again with us.

"Unfortunately, I was considered a rebel as I didn't take kindly to some of the young officers, straight out of FTS, coming out and telling me what they wanted and how to fly when they had only done a few hours on the Buffalo. I used to get severely reprimanded on telling them what I thought of them and their forebears – consequently I spent some time in different parts of Malaya – Kota Bharu, Ipoh and Alor Star. The officers didn't live on the station at Kallang, which didn't improve relationships at all.

"Butch Hesketh, my great friend who was a P/O and loved dancing and visiting questionable shows, sometimes used to pick Kitchy and myself up in a taxi and, as he and I were about the same size, I'd lend him a tunic or shirt – he would then be able to visit the places in question. Officers were not allowed to frequent such places.

"Blondie Holder, whom I flew with most often, was more RAF than anyone I ever met. He always wore a black flying suit and dark glasses – who ever thought of a black suit in the tropics? Tim Vigors was a F/Lt and a really good fellow. He took a lot of trouble helping the newer pilots. The best of them all was S/Ldr Bell. He had been to New Zealand on holiday a few years before and seemed to sum us up a lot better than the others. He was one fellow you could really talk to."

Flt Sgt George Mothersdale, who had joined the RAF as an aircraft apprentice at

Halton in 1922, was Senior NCO in charge of B Flight and remembered:

> "The first aircraft we [B Flight] received was W8134/WP-M, ferried from Seletar to Kallang by Flg Off Mansel-Lewis, then B Flight's only pilot. Our Buffaloes were assembled at 151 MU (Seletar) and they arrived at Kallang with their guns harmonised to give the 'area of lethal density' at a best firing range of 200-220 yards. Some days after receipt at Kallang, Mansel-Lewis had the harmonisation set to give a spot concentration of fire at 120 yards, and then he harmonised W8134's guns to this setting himself. Together with Sgt Ginger Ransome (Fitter Armourer), I watched him doing the job. To me, his movements around the aircraft suggested lethal stealth and he spared no effort to get maximum accuracy on all four guns, continually adjusting each gun until he was satisfied, in the course of which Ransome remarked to me, 'You've got a Micky Mannock here – he intends to be lethal!'; and then Mansel-Lewis reset the horizontal bars in the reflector gun-sight with the same diligent accuracy."

Within a few days more Buffaloes arrived. Inevitably, during this training period, there were accidents, although one of the first occurred when the two flight commanders collided in mid-air, as Flt Lt Vigors recalled:

> "John [Mansel-Lewis] and I were involved in a mid-air collision when we were doing a mock attack on a Blenheim squadron with which we were having a friendly feud. I was attacking from 1,000 feet underneath them and John was coming down from about 2,000 feet above – and our co-ordination was a little too accurate in that we met about ten feet behind the tail of the rearmost Blenheim. I cut a fair bit of his tailplane off [Mansel-Lewis was flying W8134/WP-M] and in doing so lost my propeller [W8139/WP-B], but we both managed to get down safely."

A few days later, on 4 April, the Squadron suffered its first fatality when Mansel-Lewis, a 20-year-old from Pembrey, was killed in another freak accident. Of the incident, Vigors recalled:

> "On 3 April we had a party with Sqn Ldr Hackett, commander of 27 Squadron, which was stationed at Kallang with us. We got into arguments about what our respective aircraft could do, and I accepted an invitation to go up with Hackett the following day as a passenger in his Blenheim. The next morning at about 10 o'clock I got into his aircraft to make this trip but just as we were taxiing out I was called for on the radio to go immediately and attend an important meeting at Air Headquarters. Hackett started his engines and I was walking back with my parachute when I met John Mansel-Lewis, who asked if he could take my place. I handed him my parachute and he got into the Blenheim, and I went off to Air Headquarters. I had no sooner arrived there than I heard that there had been a bad accident over Singapore Harbour involving three Blenheims."

A pilot of 4AACU takes up the story:

> "The CO led the three aircraft up into a formation loop but got into a stall and went down in a flat spin into the sea on the edge of a minefield, killing the crew."

Flt Sgt Mothersdale added:

> "Mansel-Lewis baled out but his parachute tangled with the Blenheim's tail; his body was recovered the same day. On the day following the collision, RAF Vessel *Buffalo* – an RAF tug – when proceeding to locate and salvage the Blenheim, struck a mine and sank with no survivors. In the tug were Sqn Ldr Joe Farnhill and about 20 personnel of 151 MU, all of whom were key men, on an organised trip for 'a change of daily scene' as a reward for good work. The Blenheim and crew were not recovered."

In June, 243 Squadron sent a detachment of three B Flight aircraft – flown by Flg Off Blondie Holder (W8142/WP-N), Plt Off Ron Shield (W8221/WP-X) and Sgt John Oliver (W8181/WP-P) to Alor Star and Kota Bharu, to establish the suitability of fighters to operate from these forward airfields. Their detachment was brief and uneventful. A second detachment comprising Flt Lt Tim Vigors, Plt Off Edgar Pevreal and Flg Off Holder (W8137, W8155 and W8201) followed in July. A number of newly arrived RNZAF pilots now found themselves attached to 4AACU with its three Flights equipped with a variety of Sharks, ex-Royal Navy Swordfish, Tiger Moths and Queen Bees, including Sgt Tubby Saul transferred from 243 Squadron, and Sgt Peter Ballard, who recalled:

"From May onwards a number of pilots fresh from New Zealand, including myself, began to arrive. They sent me off to 4AACU and I joined A Flight, flying Sharks. The Shark was a large biplane and was fitted in the rear cockpit, with a winch from which the target drogue could be streamed at any distance up to a mile behind the towing aircraft. Relatively short tows were used for air-to-air live gunnery but for live ground-to-air shoots, drogues were generally towed at the maximum distance. A slipstream-driven propeller on the winch enabled the drogue to be recovered for examination after the shoot. The Sharks increasingly towed drogues for the newly formed fighter squadrons to practice their air-to-air gunnery, and a certain amount of frustration developed.

"The Sharks were slow aircraft with a cruising speed of around 100mph, and were hardly ideal for the kind of training needed by the fighter pilots. Unfortunately Blenheims, which had been tried as target-towing aircraft, proved unsuitable for the job. Ironically, their higher cruising speed – in the vicinity of 180mph – made satisfactory use of the winch impossible. Fighter pilots usually made their attacks on the drogues from right angles to the course of the towing aircraft. If their judgement in gauging their angle of attack was less than desirable, they frequently finished in making their run from almost dead astern, and received a red Aldis lamp signal from the alarmed towing aircraft crew, which meant they had to break off the attack. Then, with undercarriage down to reduce speed, the Buffalo would fly alongside the Shark, with the Buffalo pilot shaking his fist in frustration!"

More trainee pilots arrived from New Zealand in July, one of whom was Sgt Rex Weber, a native of Palmerston North, who maintained a diary:

"The selections of the men for the various squadrons was rather a joke, and strangely enough I nearly got what I wanted – flying boats. So eventually I finished by volunteering for fighters, but I might say that I have little faith in myself as a fighter pilot. We had a look at a Wirraway today [24 July], and per usual I was dismayed to see the numerous controls etc. Couldn't help wondering if I would make the grade. Yet again I am afraid the first solo will be quite a trial.

"Started flying Wirraways yesterday [29 July]. After a long interval I was pretty rough, and my cockpit work was very faulty. However, today I was far better, and even managed one perfect landing, but the rest were awful. It appears that I have very little judgement when it comes to landing. Moreover I am quite incapable of doing two things in an aeroplane at the same time. These crates are very nice to handle and it is a pity the controls are so manual. Actually I am not very happy at the thought of my first solo."

Weber continued to have problems with his flying but gradually began to master the intricacies of the Wirraway. Comments in his diary about his flying ability included: "My flying today [31 July] showed a fair improvement – felt pretty happy with the crate, and yet my landings were rotten"; then, a few days later:

> "First landing was from 30 feet and the instructor mentioned the fact that a stall from
> such a height was rather liable to have a detrimental effect upon the plane. However,
> the next circuit and landing was pretty good. Most of the lads finished their conversion
> courses, and some will be flying Buffaloes after only approximately 15 minutes on the
> conversion machine."

By now 243 Squadron was beginning to take shape as pilots completed the Wirraway
course and made their first flights in the Buffalo. As each qualified he was assigned
to a Flight. Following the death of Mansel-Lewis in April, 28-year-old Yorkshireman
Flt Lt Ronald 'Bertie' Bows, who had been flying Blenheims with 34 Squadron at
Tengah, was posted to 243 Squadron as commander of B Flight.

243 Squadron
Sqn Ldr G.B.M. Bell RAF

A Flight	**B Flight**
Flt Lt T.A. Vigors DFC RAF	Flt Lt R. Bows RAF
Flg Off M. Garden RAF	Flg Off M.H. Holder RAF (Blondie)
Plt Off G.L. Bonham RNZAF (Snowy)	Plt Off T.B. Marra RNZAF (Veg)
Plt Off F.W.J. Oakden RNZAF	Plt Off J.M. Cranstone RNZAF
Plt Off G.L. Hesketh RNZAF (Butch)	Plt Off R.S. Shield RNZAF
Plt Off E.A. Pevreal RNZAF	Plt Off D.R.L. Brown RNZAF
Sgt R.J. Newman RNZAF (Slim)	Sgt V. Arthur RNZAF
Sgt C.B. Wareham RNZAF	Sgt N.B. Rankin RNZAF (Prof)
Sgt M.A. Greenslade RNZAF	Sgt P.L. Elliott RNZAF {Shortie)
Sgt R.A. Weber RNZAF	Sgt J.B. Oliver RNZAF
Sgt G.B. Fisken RNZAF	Sgt B.S. Wipiti RNZAF
Sgt C.T. Kronk RNZAF	Sgt A.R.P. Saul RNZAF (Tubby)
Sgt A.R. Reynolds RNZAF	Sgt A. J. Lawrence RNZAF
Sgt C.F. Powell RAAF (Aussie)	Sgt B.K. Baber RNZAF

Plt Off Terry Marra and Sgt Bert Wipiti were both Maori, while Sgts Brian Baber and
Alan Lawrence were considered far too inexperienced for operations, although they
were allowed to fly as and when an aircraft was available. Sgt Geoff Fisken of A
Flight, on the other hand, was showing all the signs required of a fighter pilot and was
proud to have been allocated his own machine, W8147/WP-O:

> "A and B Flights being two separate identities, I was lucky in the fact that I had a very
> good and dedicated Welsh boy as mechanic, and another one as rigger, so my own plane
> had a fair amount of acquired parts from other planes on it – that kept me in the air
> when others were grounded. Humidity played a major part in the teething troubles of
> the planes – serviceable one moment, an hour later unserviceable, so it was very seldom
> we ever flew as a complete squadron. Flt Sgt Mothersdale and my mechanic and rigger
> were really lifesavers – I used to sit on the wing with them, discussing flying
> capabilities, arming my own guns and sighting them in."

Sgt Charlie Wareham from Kaikoura was one of the first of the RNZAF pilots to reach
Singapore and therefore an original member of 243 Squadron. While flying took
priority, there was time for play:

> "Being an early member in 243 I had a plane of my own, and normally you flew your

own plane and nobody else flew it. Working up as a squadron we practised formation flying, we did dogfighting, gunnery with cameras and shooting at a drogue. Sunday was a day off, Saturday and Wednesday half days. Because the city was closed down you weren't expected to fly. There was competition with soccer, hockey and rugby. I played soccer, hockey and tennis. Kallang had a team and I played those three sports as a representative at Kallang, and eventually I played rugby for the Far Eastern Combined Services and played matches against other clubs and teams all over the place. We eventually worked up a New Zealand side."

Close friends Sgts Bert Wipiti and Charlie Kronk were teamed together and, one day, while still learning the ropes, they thrilled onlookers with their flying ability, as remembered by Rex Weber:

"Bert Wipiti was a born leader, his standard of conduct was impeccable. Bert and Charlie were sent up to practice aerobatics – maybe they had ten hours flying on the Buffalo to their credit – yet that day, in the blue skies over the airport, they gave us one of the great aerobatic displays. Seasoned aces from the Battle of Britain came out from the crew room to watch, the show was so good."

But Weber, like many other colonials, was not over-keen on many of the English officers and European civilians he encountered, or life at Singapore in general, and made his feelings clear in his diary:

"The white people here are falling down on the job in not going out of their way to look after the NCO ranks. These ranks are, it seems to me, being allowed to resort to poor and low means of entertainment. It would appear that snobbishness and the old school tie are allowed to influence the white people too much – that the officers are to be treated as gentlemen, and the men as toughs, whereas if the truth was only known, the proportion of toughs is about equal in both sections of the forces.

"We so-called colonials have no members of our society who sink to the depths of grammatical depravity that the greatest majority of Englishmen attain. Yes, I may be bitter – but tell me a New Zealander who would take this insult from a Kiwi armchair soldier: 'Gentlemen and Sergeants' – and not feel bitter. Who in our place would not feel bitter to be treated as of no account, even though every day we risk our lives – and God alone knows how much I risk mine – and in the event of war in all probability lose them; whilst the armchair soldiers enjoy the privileges and rights of the élite."

He had not quite finished confiding to his diary:

"It would seem that being in Singapore one must just do without female society, or associate with coloured people. This latter alternative is of course quite impossible as far as I am concerned, but all the lads here seem to think nothing of it. Some of our boys paid a visit to a brothel last night, where they found officers and men all out for the same form of entertainment. Needless to say, after a few beers our lads were in also, and at least three of them were well satisfied, but today they were a worried group." [11]

Some took pleasure from the discomfort of others, as Plt Off Jim Cranstone remembered:

"Mowbray Garden just couldn't keep still. I remember he wanted to urinate fairly often when he was flying. They had relief tubes in the Buffaloes and the groundcrew got a bit browned off with having to flush his relief tube out, so they turned the venturi round – a venturi, in short, accentuates or concentrates a volume of air through vacuum – so anything that was introduced near its point of entry was sucked in with violence. I think Mowbray was hospitalized for a day or two."

In August, the British Government was warned by its ambassador in Tokyo that the Japanese military was preparing for a move southwards, although no word of this potential threat apparently reached Air Chief Marshal Brooke-Popham, which led the C-in-C to deliver one of his infamous public quips the following month – "it is highly improbable Japan can be contemplating war for some months." But Brooke-Popham was desperately aware of the shortfalls in his Command, as revealed in urgent signals he sent at this time:

> "At present, not only is our ability to attack shipping deplorably weak, but we have not the staying power to sustain even what we could now do. As our air effort dwindles . . . so will the enemy's chance of landing increase. I have no doubt what our first requirement here is. We want to increase our hitting power against ships and our capacity to go on hitting."

Such was his frustration, 63-year-old Brooke-Popham asked to be relieved of his command as Commander-in-Chief Far East[12]. His request was granted but his replacement (Lt General Sir Henry Pownall DSO MC) would not take up his duties until 27 December.

Mid-August saw the arrival at Singapore of a party of 143 American 'civilians', ostensibly on a sight-seeing tour but in fact they were the advance party of pilots and technicians for the newly-established mercenary air force – known as the American Volunteer Group or 'Flying Tigers' – under the command of Colonel Claire Chennault and being financed by China's generalissimo, Chiang Kai-shek, for the defence of Burma against Japanese aggression. Having booked into local hotels as students and businessmen, they departed as quickly as they had arrived, en route for Burma, no doubt their presence having been observed and reported upon by many of the Japanese spies on the island. Two members of the party quit on arrival at Singapore and were consequently discharged from the AVG.

The arrival of so many combat-inexperienced American fighter pilots in Burma led to a request to Singapore for the assistance of an RAF officer with the necessary qualifications to help with training and tactics. Newly arrived Wg Cdr George Darley DSO, a former Battle of Britain squadron commander, was duly appointed:

> "I was posted as Wing Commander Fighter Operations to AHQ, Singapore, responsible for all fighter operations in the entire Far East which entailed continuous travel including the design and construction of fighter Ops Rooms in Singapore and Rangoon; also to redesign and extend Kai Tak airfield in Hong Kong as a fighter base, although no fighters were available. I also briefed Dutch and American fighter pilots during these travels."

The first part of the newly formed 453 Squadron RAAF arrived at Singapore from Australia on 21 August and received its first Buffaloes at Sembawang five days later. Sqn Ldr W.F. Allshorn RAAF was posted to command. However, London considered him too inexperienced, and he would instead be appointed to take over 21RAAF Squadron in October, his place being taken by an RAF officer and Battle of Britain veteran, 25-year-old newly promoted Sqn Ldr W.J. Harper[13]. He arrived by air accompanied by two RAAF officers who were to command the Flights – Acting Flt Lts R.D. Vanderfield and B.A. Grace, both of whom had gained operational experience over Northern Europe flying Hurricanes with 258 Squadron. Sqn Ldr Harper immediately found it difficult to get on with some of the men under his command, and later reported:

> "I was amazed to notice amongst many of the Australian personnel on the Station the

prevalent dislike that some of them bore for the English – Englishmen were spoken of as Pommies with an air of contempt. I did not pay a great deal of attention to this, but it was this that grew into a strong dislike for RAF administration later in the war. It should be noted in turn that RAF personnel elsewhere ostracised the Australians. This matter was aggravated by the obvious – and to my mind unwarranted – dislike that the Fighter Group Controller, Grp Capt Rice, had for the two Australian fighter squadrons.

"The aircrew personnel of No. 453 Squadron, with the exception of the Flight Commanders, were pilots straight from FTS, and some of them told me when I questioned them, that they had no desire to be fighter pilots and had been given no choice in this matter. The pilots of both squadrons were put through their OTU and operational training in a remarkably short time. Everyone was extremely keen and the unit well knit."

However, Harper soon lost the respect of the Australians when he showed dissatisfaction with the quality and attitude of some of his men, particularly the Sergeant Pilots, and shortly before the outbreak of hostilities he flew to Australia to seek more suitable pilots. He reported:

"About six weeks after my arrival in Singapore, I realised that war with Japan was highly probable, and I approached the AOC in order to change some of the pilots in my Squadron – I hoped to obtain in place some experienced officers who were more suited for fighters. I was instructed by him to fly to Australia where I was to try to recruit some more pilots. Unfortunately, I was unable to achieve any results and I was told that any available experienced pilots were required to form a Fighter OTU in Australia."

This action did not endear him to the pilots of his new Squadron, several of whom he considered to be too old for fighters. Although he and Flt Lt W.K. Wells, the Adjutant, would eventually clash over a number of issues, this was not the initial reaction, as testified by Wells:

"The morale of our pilots was extremely high, they were very keen. Sqn Ldr Harper had the confidence of the pilots and personnel of the Squadron at that stage. He had come from England with a reputation of having shot down six enemy aircraft and he was very keen to get a decoration."

Meanwhile, during September, 21RAAF Squadron also converted to Buffaloes but five of the most experienced pilots, together with six of the Wirraways, were sent to Kluang to continue training activities as an OTU; this unit was designated W Flight, Y Squadron. The majority of the trainees were RAAF and RNZAF pilots converting from biplanes, on which they had trained in Australia and New Zealand, respectively, before being sent to Singapore. Training lasting at least four months was deemed necessary before pilots could be considered ready for operational flying. By late November, Sqn Ldr Donald Pearson of 36 Squadron was acting as Chief Flying Instructor following the return of the RAAF instructors to their own unit:

"I was on a conversion course myself at the time as it was rumoured that 36 and 100 Squadrons were to be issued with Beauforts in place of Vildebeest. Flt Lt Park Thompson and I had been sent to Kluang and had completed three to four hours on type when we were requested by Wg Cdr Toogood (OC Kluang) to carry on as instructors on the withdrawal of the Australians."

The lack of experience of most pilots was highlighted by the fact that between January and September 1941, Far East Command suffered 67 accidents, 22 of which resulted in write-offs and 31 in serious damage, in which 48 lives were lost. Requisition to the Air Ministry for two senior instructors was refused as none could be spared, but Air Headquarters was advised that Wg Cdr L.J. Neale, who was on his way from the UK to take command of the airfield at Ipoh, was an A1 flying instructor. It was suggested that he should test all squadron and flight commanders since many of them were themselves inexperienced.

The fatalities included two of 4AACU's senior pilots, one of whom was killed on 7 November, together with his pupil, at Kallang when their Tiger Moth was struck from behind by a landing Buffalo (W8184/WP-G) flown by Sgt Russ Reynolds of 243 Squadron. This was the most serious accident 243 Squadron suffered, but others included W8149, which Plt Off Edgar Pevreal skidded into a ditch while landing; W8194 crashed into a canal near Kallang following engine failure without injuring Sgt Tubby Saul; Plt Off Jack Oakden's W8182 ditched 70 yards off Singapore, about which Plt Off Terry Marra recalled:

> "Oakie was down over the water when his 'friend' in front quit. We had all sorts of drill about ditching the Buffalo and he was trying to reach the shore, but was not going to make it. He was doing everything according to the book and put it down nicely. He left his chute behind and got out with his Mae West, took his boots off and decided to swim as he was not that far from shore. So he dived in – and hit his head on the bottom!"

Plt Off Snowy Bonham had to face the wrath of Sqn Ldr Bell after he badly damaged WP-J in a crash-landing at Kallang; fortunately, he was not injured:

> "Aircraft likely to be u/s for a long time. Undercarriage starboard wheel through wing. CO took a dim view."

Next to be lost was W8181, which Sgt Alan Lawrence crashed on landing at Kallang following engine failure, as remembered by his friend Sgt Brian Baber:

> "The very first day they put us onto Buffaloes, we were taking off in a formation of three. I was on the flight commander's starboard and Alan [Lawrence] was on his port. We took off but Alan didn't really get airborne. He went through the end of the aerodrome. He only had a few scratches but the aircraft was a write-off [in fact, it was repaired]. It was an aircraft we could ill-afford to lose. After Alan had crashed they decided that it was better to leave operations to the experienced pilots and we were allotted various duties such as ferrying damaged planes for repairs and the like over to the Australian squadron [at Sembawang] where they had all the engineering facilities, which we didn't have."

Sgt Rex Weber, who had experienced a number of incidents while flying the Buffalo, finally managed to damage W8137/WP-C:

> "What a day. I managed to break a kite as a result of a ground loop at the end of my landing – the alternative being a trip through the fence, over the bank and into the ocean. Visibility ahead was practically nil at 300 feet and, in the heat of the moment, I forgot that brakes don't act too well in the rain on wet ground. It was no use cursing, so I just made the best of a very poor show, and thus £2,000-£4,000 was wiped off. I had the pleasant little experience of having the CO endorse my logbook for carelessness. He was very complimentary in that he put my accident down to 'stupidity' not carelessness. Nice chap!
>
> "The CO then gave us a pleasant chat on air crashes, and flying breaches. He was very brief, but decidedly to the point; the main point seemed to be that pilots were three a penny but Buffaloes were very rare. In fact, it seems that one Buff is worth three

pilots, so in future we must be very careful that if we must write something off, it must be ourselves and not the aircraft!"

67 Squadron also experienced a number of accidents before it departed for Burma, including W8146 which Sgt Kitchy Bargh belly-landed at Kallang following engine failure; W8153, W8185 and W8191 all suffered damage during June, and W8177 was damaged the following month. W8143 flown by Sgt Colin McDonald crashed on landing and W8168 (Flg Off John Lambert) crashed on landing three days later; neither pilot was hurt. This was followed by Flt Lt Jack Brandt crash-landing W8148; both W8190 and W8144 were written off while in the hands of Sgt Pedersen during September, the latter during a night landing. Then Flg Off John Wigglesworth failed to return from a training sortie. A search was carried out and the Buffalo (W8161) was located on the coast, having force-landed following a collision with a Blenheim. Wigglesworth was not hurt and soon rejoined his colleagues. Rex Weber noted:

"F/O Wigglesworth managed very successfully to ram a Blenheim – he made a crash-landing on a beach. The pilot of the Blenheim baled out, but the rest of the crew, two in number, were killed. No doubt there was a certain degree of negligence on the F/O's part, but very understandable negligence, with planes dashing about all over the skies, as they are in these practice attacks. My word, the more I see and hear about these Brewsters the more firmly I become convinced that they are grand machines to bring men out alive, no matter how serious the crash. In the case of [Wigglesworth's] Brewster, it ploughed right through the rear portion of the Blenheim, but still carried out a forced-landing on the nearest beach."

He added:

"We were doing attacks this morning, but I would have been well shot down in actual practice. However, I will improve, despite never really feeling secure in an aeroplane. This morning I also lost myself completely and absolutely, and I was panic-striken."

Sgt Greg Board – at 20, the youngest pilot on 453 Squadron – was the first of the Australians to fly the Buffalo. Extremely keen to be the first, Board had burned the midnight oil and studied the aircraft manual thoroughly, and was thus able to convince the CO sufficiently to fulfil his aim. He handled the Buffalo without too many problems, although he later commented:

"The Buffalo wasn't exactly what the British might have planned for the air defence of Singapore and the surrounding area. The Buffaloes either had no radio, or were afflicted with radios that wouldn't work. The mechanics lacked even a single page to guide them in servicing and maintenance, and for the pilots – well, the handbook stopped very far short of what was needed. We could only guess as to the limitations we were to observe in flying the aeroplanes – a sort of guide to keep the wings from tearing off in the wrong manoeuvre. The absence of these aids certainly gave us lots of practice." [14]

There followed the inevitable spate of accidents including one by Plt Off Leigh Bowes in W8202 when he forgot to lower his undercarriage on landing back at Sembawang during his first flight in a Buffalo, although the damage was superficial; next the undercarriage of Sgt Alf Clare's aircraft (W8188) collapsed at the end of his landing run and the aircraft was a write-off. Three days later Sgt Harry Griffiths force-landed W8197 following engine failure. The aircraft was written-off but Griffiths escaped with minor abrasions and shock, and was admitted to hospital for a week:

"At one stage two of us were sent off to record the difference between the behaviour of the two aircraft, one having been slightly modified. The exercise completed, we were down to approximately 1,000 feet and heading to Sembawang when my motor quit. After carrying out everything possible to rectify the problem I was down to about 500 feet. Being too low to bale out all I could do was to tighten the harness until I could hardly breathe, turn off the ignition and fuel and attempt to splurge the aircraft on top of the jungle canopy. The noise and buffeting were extreme and finally the aircraft hit the ground with a sudden stop. The canopy slammed shut and my knees capitulated into the instrument panel, but the canopy hadn't jammed and I was able to wrench it open and climb out. As I tried to get away from the aircraft, fearing it may burn, my left knee gave way and I finished up in a black smelly puddle.

"I had only just missed a native kampong, which could not be seen from the air, by no more than 20 feet. Had I landed on the main building where they were cooking on charcoal fires I hate to think what would have happened. However, the natives helped me up and sat me on a log of wood. I observed water coming through a piece of cane protruding from a clay embankment, but when I attempted to quench my thirst a woman cried out "Tudda! Tudda!" and pulled me away, whereupon two young males dashed off into the jungle and eventually returned with two bottles of soft drink. The first person I saw from our unit was Sgt Greg Board, who came slashing through the undergrowth, wielding a machete. He immediately climbed into the cockpit and sat down. I could not see what he was doing but imagined he was trying to find out what had caused the crash – although I was asked sometime later if I knew what happened to the aircraft clock. He apparently wasn't concerned for my welfare!

"Next to arrive was S/Ldr Cumming, the MO, hurrying up a jungle track with a couple of his orderlies. As he approached he was looking at the aircraft and did not notice me sitting on the log. As he passed me he dropped a large canvas bag (body bag), a short-handle shovel, and also a short-handle rake. When he looked in the cockpit and saw it empty, he spoke to someone who pointed towards me. I was soon assisted along a jungle track until we arrived at a clearing where stood a staff car and I was returned to Base Hospital. I was so bruised and sore that I was unable even to feed myself for the first few days. I believe the salvage people eventually located the starboard mainplane, which was over 200 metres away from the rest of the aircraft."

The Squadron's first fatality occurred on 8 October when 27-year-old Plt Off Max Irvine-Brown became lost and was killed attempting to force-land W8208 on the Dutch island of Pulau Buntang, about 50 miles south-east of Singapore. Another Buffalo, W8226, was extensively damaged following an overshoot, Sgt Keith Gorringe escaping injury on this occasion.

In October 67 Squadron finally departed for Burma, leaving its Buffaloes behind. On arrival at Mingaladon it took over the Buffaloes that had been delivered for the defence of that country and which had been tested and flown by pilots of 60 Squadron, the resident Blenheim squadron, pending the arrival of the new unit from Singapore. Shortly before 67 Squadron's departure, a number of RAF officers including Peter Bingham-Wallis exacted revenge on the island's over-zealous Provost Marshal, who had caused them a few headaches over the previous few months. The unsuspecting army major was waylaid one night and unceremoniously dumped into the harbour.

The Buffaloes left behind at Kallang would be used during the following month to equip a further new unit, 488 Squadron RNZAF, which had formed in New Zealand in September. On arrival at Singapore, the pilots first were sent to Kluang for Wirraway conversion. One of the trainee fighter pilots, 23-year-old Sgt Rod MacMillan from Timaru – another who had been flying Vildebeest with 36 Squadron – recalled:

"I always remember Peter Gifford's definition of a Wirraway – it was just a Harvard made dangerous! It wasn't a docile aircraft like the Harvard was. If you put it into a spin you were a bit lucky if you came out of it. We only flew five or six hours there [at Kluang] until the Australian instructors thought we were competent enough to handle them, and then we were sent back to Kallang in dribs and drabs."

Sqn Ldr W.G. Clouston DFC[15], a New Zealander in the RAF and Battle of Britain veteran, arrived from the UK to take command, as did his flight commanders, fellow New Zealanders Flt Lts J.N. Mackenzie DFC[16] (also a Battle of Britain pilot) and J.R. Hutcheson RNZAF, an experienced Hurricane pilot. One of the new arrivals from New Zealand, when asked by a journalist why he had joined up, replied: "We want to be left in peace and the only way to do that is to fight." Most of the pilots had come straight from flying training schools in New Zealand, their only experience of modern aircraft having been a short conversion course on Harvards. The RNZAF's initial report was not encouraging:

"Facilities for the repair and maintenance of these machines were sadly lacking. Such as did exist were concentrated in the workshops at Seletar on Singapore Island. These workshops, although equipped only to deal with the requirements of two squadrons at the most, were called upon to service the whole air force in Malaya; the magnitude of their task may be gauged from the fact that twenty-seven modifications had to be made in the Brewster Buffalo fighter before it could be used in battle.

"Our squadrons were seriously short of trained and experienced pilots. Many of those serving in Malaya had come straight from flying training schools in Australia and New Zealand, where most of them had never flown anything more modern than a Hart and had no experience of retractable undercarriages, variable pitch propellers or flaps. Furthermore, when the Japanese attacked, the Buffalo fighter squadrons had only been formed a few months and half of them had not reached full operational efficiency.

"The situation as regards airfields was also far from satisfactory although great efforts had been made to improve matters in the year before war came. Of the airfields that had been built, fifteen possessed no concrete runways but were surfaced with grass, a serious matter in a country where tropical rains are frequent and severe. Several, such as that at Alor Star, were out-of-date, with congested buildings close to the runways and few facilities for dispersal. Very few were camouflaged. Ground defences were inadequate or non-existent. Because of the rugged and difficult nature of the territory in Malaya many airfields had to be built on the exposed east coast, and several were sited in places where their defence proved well nigh impossible. For example, the landing grounds at Kuantan and Kota Bharu had been built next to long and excellent sea beaches, a fact of which the Japanese were to take full advantage.

"Another serious feature, especially for the fighter defence, was the lack of radar units to detect the approach of hostile aircraft and ships. On the east coast of Malaya only two were operational, the remaining five still being under construction. On the west coast one had been completed and two others were approaching completion. Only on Singapore Island itself were there three posts in working order. At some stations there was no more effective warning system than that provided by an aircraftsman standing on the perimeter and waving a white handkerchief on the approach of hostile aircraft." [17]

The Commanding Officer, Sqn Ldr Clouston reported:

"No.488 Squadron took over Buffaloes from 67 Squadron. Approximately 27 aircraft were signed for but out of these only 18 were serviceable or temporary unserviceable, the balance being write-offs which had not been struck off charge by Air HQFE. These aircraft had already been used to train the pilots of 67 Squadron and the majority were in a poor state of repair. Spare parts were extremely difficult to obtain. In some cases it was necessary to manufacture locally.

"The pilots received from the RNZAF were all extremely young and, while being exceptionally keen to learn, were hampered by the fact that their service training had been done on obsolete aircraft such as Vildebeest. This necessitated Air HQ forming a combined conversion course and OTU at Kluang. Owing, however, to shortage of instructors and aircraft, this course was not a great success and actually delayed the training of the pilots. Eventually the majority were brought back to Kallang and their training completed under F/Lts Mackenzie and Hutcheson and myself."

He added, having had the opportunity to fly the Buffalo:

"All of us who had been on decent aeroplanes – Spitfires and Hurricanes – thought Buffaloes were terrible things. They didn't have the climbing ability. It was a very pleasant aeroplane to fly but not to fight. They were too slow to get up to altitude and were cumbersome things. I would always liken them to a London bus. They were designed by the US Navy and certainly couldn't be called a modern fighter plane. It was a good aeroplane, but not for fighting. The gun platform was particularly poor."

The Squadron diarist noted:

"Today F/Lts Mackenzie and Hutcheson 'diced' for the first time in the mighty Buffalo. They found it, as reported by the Squadron Leader, 'a nice old gentleman's aeroplane."

Clouston continued:

"The technical staff supplied by the RNZAF were of a very high standard. They were all hand-picked men and their selection was subsequently justified by their skill in servicing the Buffaloes. The Squadron operated from Kallang, which, while being an excellent civil airport, did not readily lend itself to the operation and training of fighter squadrons. The main reasons for this were that the use of the aerodrome by civil aircraft continued . . . and the initial training of pilots of the Volunteer Air Force in Tiger Moths interfered considerably with operational flying in the aerodrome circuit. Also, the lack of adequate dispersal facilities, both for aircraft and aircrew, made conditions more arduous.

"The groundcrew made a reputation for themselves in Singapore second to none. I wouldn't like to say they were better than the ones we had in England but they were certainly better than anything else in Singapore. They showed so much initiative, and if we couldn't get spare parts they went round to where the spare parts were and then took them. There was no shadow of doubt about it."

One of the new pilots, Sgt Perce Killick, added:

"67 Squadron left the day we arrived there and we took over their machines. They had left no tools behind, nor instruction books. Our guys – Andy Chandler and his crowd – went into town, brought themselves a spanner and screwdriver and couple of bits and pieces, came back and had the aircraft all serviceable again in about 48 hours. Our groundcrews were bloody magnificent – I never had any gun stoppages – in fact, I had no maintenance problems with any aircraft I flew there."

When news reached 243 Squadron of the arrival of 488 Squadron, New Zealanders Sgts Bert Wipiti and Charlie Kronk decided to pay their fellow countrymen a visit, as recalled by LAC Paddy Moulds:

"Bert and Charlie saw this as an opportunity to show them just how good they were, by way of a 'shoot-up', but unknown to them Sqn Ldr Bell was paying an official visit and caught the two boys. Result – grounded for a month and given Duty Pilots' tasks in the control tower on alternate days."

488 Squadron RNZAF
Sqn Ldr W.G. Clouston DFC RAF

A Flight	B Flight
Flt Lt J.N. Mackenzie DFC RAF	Flt Lt J.R. Hutcheson RNZAF
Plt Off F.W.J. Oakden RNZAF	Plt Off G.L. Hesketh RNZAF (Butch)
Plt Off J.C. Godsiff RNZAF	Plt Off W.J. Greenhalgh RNZAF
Plt Off K.J. McAneny RNZAF	Plt Off N.C. Sharp RNZAF
Plt Off H.S. Pettit RNZAF (Bunt)	Plt Off F.S. Johnstone RNZAF
Plt Off G.P. White RNZAF (Snow)	Plt Off E.W. Cox RNZAF (Tony)
Plt Off P.D. Gifford RNZAF	Plt Off L.R. Farr RNZAF
Sgt E.E.G. Kuhn RNZAF	Sgt D.L. Clow RNZAF
Sgt T.W. Honan RNZAF	Sgt V.E. Meaclem RNZAF
Sgt W.R. De Maus RNZAF (Bunny)	Sgt P.E.E. Killick RNZAF
Sgt H.J. Meharry RNZAF	Sgt J.F. Burton RNZAF
Sgt W.J.N. MacIntosh RNZAF	Sgt C.D. Charters RNZAF
Sgt R.W. MacMillan RNZAF	Sgt A.G. Craig RNZAF

Plts Offs Butch Hesketh and Jack Oakden had transferred from 243 Squadron to assist with training, while Plt Off Pete Gifford had arrived from 100 Squadron and was among the first to complete the Wirraway course. Buffalo training commenced in early October, several machines being damaged or written off within the first few weeks, as noted by Sgt Don Clow in his diary:

"Deryck Charters turned on quite a display. Here, your approach is made over a rubber plantation – you have to judge it fairly carefully to get into the field – he stalled through stretching his glide. Eddie Kuhn put up quite a show just above the aerodrome. He fell out of several slow rolls and on his next solo he lost himself. When he got back he blurted this out in front of the CO, who nearly had a fit. There was a hell of a stink and after that we were supposed to go only a few miles from the drome. Alex Craig dug a wing in up at Kluang and they made him get his eyes tested. Sharp dug a wing in through having to ground loop at the fence. Len Farr skidded into the fence once at the end of his run, and then hit the fence another time while coming in. Eddie Kuhn broke the actuating rod in the undercart and Jack Meharry dug in a wing through having to ground loop to avoid running into a stationary plane. Terry Honan broke the undercart and dug in a wing after a heavy landing. By Jove! I must say I suffer from the jitters every time I think of it. It isn't as though you'd get hurt. It's the idea of busting a kite that worries one."

Of this period of intensive training, the Squadron diarist noted:

"So far, B Flight leads A Flight in the effort to get rid of aircraft. Both Flights did quite a bit of formation and also some aerobatics. P/Os Sharp and White were the heroes who aerobated. P/O Gifford shook everyone by landing down-wind in rotten visibility. However, he got away with it. P/O White carried out an ack-ack co-operation flight. The guns fired at him but the shells were fused to burst about 2,000 feet below his machine. Apparently no one added 2,000 feet on for luck when fusing! P/O Godsiff, deciding that tailwheels were unnecessary, left his on the fence when taking off. He was informed of its absence and made quite a good landing at Seletar."

In an effort to instill some confidence into their charges, Flt Lts Mackenzie and Hutcheson decided to show what could be done, as the diarist noted:

> "The 'Flight Loots' decided to shoot a line and do some really close formation. The formation was close. Mac hit the tailplane of Hutch's machine and Hutch thought he had been hit by ack-ack."

The first loss of a 488 Squadron Buffalo occurred on 11 November when Plt Off Tony Cox in AN199 force-landed at Seletar after damaging his propeller during low flying off Johore Bharu. Don Clow reported:

> "Since my last lot of scribblings there has been quite a lot of excitement. There have been another eight or nine kites written off. The other day we didn't have six serviceable machines between the two squadrons. Two of 243 smashed up in a taxiing accident. On the same day Terry Honan smashed the oleo leg in the tailwheel. Then, before that wreck was off the drome, came word from Seletar that Tony Cox had crashed there. He was all right but the crate was a complete write-off. It happened by low flying over water – getting so low that his prop touched. This caused the thing to be thrown out of balance and the engine seized up. Tony misjudged his approach and had to haul her over some buildings, after which he stalled and flicked into the deck.
>
> "Then, the day before yesterday, Hutcheson [W8153] came in and hit the concrete wall along the extension, wiped off both wheels and then did a belly landing. Quarter of an hour later, a chap from 243 came in, dropped his kite, wrote off the undercart and looped on one wingtip. Quite a fair effort. The upshot of the whole business was that the CO gave us a pep talk and assured us that one of their bloody mangles is worth three of us pilots, and that if he caught any of us breaking flying rules, he would have us court martialled and would do his best to have us chucked out."

A second RNZAF Buffalo was written-off two weeks later when Sgt Eddie Kuhn's aircraft (AN198) struck the wind tee on the aerodrome boundary when approaching to land. The Buffalo nose-dived into the ground. Kuhn was fortunate to survive uninjured. He was severely reprimanded for his crash. According to the diarist, the one-sided conversation went something like:

> "Hell Kuhn! What the bloody hell do you mean by coming in so bloody low, with no bloody speed, bloody nose in the bloody air, can't see a bloody thing in front of you? The number of times I've told you . . ."

Requests by Air HQ for a few long-range Hurricanes fitted with cameras for reconnaissance work went unfulfilled. It was therefore decided to equip two Buffaloes drawn from the fighter reserves for this task. The selected aircraft were stripped of guns and armour plate; one, W8136, which had previously served with 67 and 243 Squadrons, was equipped with a single F.24, sighted simply through a downward observation window in the cockpit floor. The other, W8166, was fitted with additional fuel tanks to allow four hours' duration, giving an additional radius of 700 miles, and with three F.24 14-inch cameras; this aircraft was delivered to the unit just before Christmas. Sqn Ldr C.R.G. Lewis, Air HQ's Chief Photographic Officer, was posted to command this new unit, designated 4PRU, with Flt Lt A.D. Phillips joining the unit from 4AACU while Sgt Charlie Wareham was transferred from 243 Squadron; the latter was destined to fly the single-camera aircraft and explained the operating procedure:

> "I was taken away from 243 Squadron and put onto the very secretive photo-reconnaissance unit. I had a plane [W8136] allocated to me, which was kept under

wraps except when I was flying it to test it. A camera was fitted in it and nobody out in Singapore knew very much about camera work. To take my photographs I had a trap door cut into the bottom of the plane, which I had to lift up with a sling. There were guide-wires positioned – cross-wires, two pairs – and by trial and error the camera was eventually set up so that once the cross-wires were over a target and I pressed the button, a photograph was taken of the place where the cross-wires were. The whole process was hand-operated. That was all done over a period of perhaps three or four months.

"The method was to fly up to the target area; then I opened the trap door and had a look down to see what I wanted to photograph and simply pressed the button to take the photograph; perhaps I would take three photographs at that particular stage, usually from 25,000 feet, which was the normal photographing height, then come back and take another run of perhaps a different area. From memory it was eight or nine seconds between photographs that I had to wait. It was all taken by hand, of course: I had to press the button by hand to take the photographs. All the guns were taken out of my aircraft, and all the armour plating from around the petrol tanks and around the wings, so as to make the aircraft lighter. That plane would travel at about 250-260mph on the clock, which was considered a little bit above what the normal Buffalo would do with armour plating and guns."

During one practice flight in W8136, Sgt Wareham became lost while flying over Sumatra. Fortunately for him, he spotted a group of Dutch soldiers on the ground upon whom he dropped a message, requesting assistance. The soldiers formed a human arrow giving him the direction of Singapore and he returned safely without further incident. He was congratulated by the AOC for his initiative.

The daily aerial activity, with Buffaloes, Blenheims and Vildebeest carrying out practice flights, inspired confidence amongst the civilian population including newly arrived Ian Morrison, Far East Correspondent for *The Times*, who wrote:

"I came to Singapore in October 1941, two months before war broke out in the Pacific. Previously I had lived in China and Japan. I had travelled in parts of the East, which had recently been the scenes of bloody battles. I had known Chungking, a city which Japanese bombers were still trying to bomb into submission. I had lived for two years in Shanghai. Living there was like living on a volcano. At any moment the Japanese might seize upon one particular act of terrorism and make it an excuse for marching into the International Settlement. In other words, I thought of the East as being a troubled part of the world where one could not expect security of any sort. Having lived in Japan I had an inkling of the passions and frustrations that were seething in the breasts of eighty million people.

"Singapore, alone of cities in the Far East, gave its inhabitants the illusion of security. Aeroplanes droned overhead during the day. The little Buffalo fighters looked beautifully speedy and manoeuvrable. There was hardly an hour of the day when one looked up into the sky and failed to see an aeroplane of some description – a Blenheim bomber, a Wirraway, a Catalina flying boat, a torpedo-carrying Vildebeest. There was frequent fire practice, when the big naval guns that protected the island would hurl their shells many miles out to sea. After nightfall powerful searchlights played over the water or shone upwards into the sky. There were occasional blackout practices. Every Saturday morning the sirens would be tested and would wail piercingly over the city. With all these superficial indications of power, it is easy to see how people could feel safe and happy in Singapore. They saw many different uniforms in the streets. They saw aeroplanes in the sky. Therefore we were strong in the air. We have a marvellous Naval Base. Therefore we had nothing to fear at sea. By October 1941 the Singapore legend was well and truly established." [18]

However, it was not long before Morrison had assessed Singapore's true position:

"A few people, after they had been in Singapore a short time, began to realise that Singapore's strength was potential rather than actual. Amazing strides had admittedly been made during the past 18 months. If Japan had come into the war at the time of the fall of France, we should not have been in a position to contest a Japanese advance down the mainland at all. We could only have attempted to defend the island. That dangerous moment passed. Both troops and equipment began to flow into Singapore in a steady stream. Nevertheless, in October 1941 there were still certain grave deficiencies. There were virtually no ships. Despite the continuous drone of aeroplanes over Singapore Island, there were not enough aeroplanes. There were no tanks. There were very few anti-tank guns. There were not enough anti-aircraft guns. But we hoped, and indeed assumed, that these things would come." [19]

General Percival was equally worried about the lack of modern aircraft and the large numbers of inexperienced pilots who were to fly the few obsolete aircraft his Command did possess:

"To make matters worse, there were few reserves and a great shortage of spare parts as a result of which flying had had to be curtailed during the greater part of 1941 at a time when it was of the utmost importance to train pilots as quickly as possible, for many of the pilots had no experience in flying operational aircraft. Few of the fighter pilots, for instance, had had any previous experience in flying fighter aircraft. They were made up of pilots drawn from other squadrons and of men straight from the flying training schools – many of them Australians and New Zealanders.

"To sum up, there was in fact no really effective air striking force in Malaya, there were none of the aircraft which an army specially requires for close support or for transport purposes, and the fighters were incapable of giving proper support to such bombers as there were or of taking their proper place in the defence. The blame for this state of affairs cannot be laid on the Air Officer Commanding, Air Vice-Marshal Pulford, who was as concerned as we all were about the weakness of the forces at his disposal and repeatedly represented the position to higher authority." [20]

*   *   *

An indication that all was not well as far as the civilian population was concerned, occurred on 3 October when 600 Japanese residents of Singapore were evacuated aboard the *Fuso Maru* to their homeland; a second evacuation occurred the following month when a further 450 Japanese departed aboard the liner *Asama Maru*. But many of the well-heeled European residents hardly gave the departure of so many Japanese a second thought. Life at Singapore was good and they continued enjoying it to the full. CBS's Cecil Brown wrote:

"At a press conference, this afternoon, General Percival appealed to the Asiatic population to volunteer for military service. He said at least a thousand were needed and explained that their response thus far 'was very disappointing.' He urged a reduction in food wastage and suggested that the hotels cut down their menus to three courses instead of six. The hotels are not taking very kindly to the idea. The management at 'Raffles' said: 'We don't think our patrons would like it.' And the luxurious 'Seaview', six miles outside the city, said: 'We don't think it's fair to compare the hotels in England with the hotels here. We don't have any difficulty in getting supplies of food. When it does become difficult, then we will cut down.'" [21]

The *Malayan Tribune* described General Percival's appeal as "an attempt to shake

Malaya out of the stupor it has been in since the beginning of the war." It gave this description of Malaya: "Malaya is in the drowsy, languid interval between sleep and awakening. We in Malaya are metaphorically still in bed." Brown continued:

> "I think the real pinch of the war will be felt by the people of Singapore at the end of the month when the drinking hours are going to be restricted between 11.30am and 2.30pm, and between 5.30pm and midnight. It is going to play hell with the famous Singapore Saturday nights, which end on Sunday morning. The reason the authorities give is that it will reduce liquor consumption and thus cut down on shipping space. In all probability what will happen is the people will simply drink faster before midnight. In any event, everyone I have talked to is outraged that anyone should attempt to restrict the drinking hours." [22]

The attitude of many was understandable when such erroneous and totally misleading articles, such as the following penned by Leonard Mosley of the *Daily Sketch*, appeared in the local and UK press with the apparent blessing of the censor:

> "As the first war correspondent to be allowed to see our secret air bases in the Malayan jungles, I bring to you good news. There is no need to worry about the strength of the air force that will oppose the Japanese should they send their army and navy southwards. The air force is on the spot and waiting for the enemy – clouds of bombers and fighters are hidden in the jungle and ready to move out camouflaged tarmacs on our secret landing fields and roar into action at the first move of the Japanese toward this part of the world. Yes, landing grounds are here – modern landing grounds with tarmac runways capable of handling everything up to Fortress [B-17] bombers – but so cleverly camouflaged that they look like paddy fields and forest glades from the air.
>
> "Planes are here tucked away in the jungle and consist of the most modern planes Britain, Australia and America are producing. Constantly on the alert, standing beside their machines are veteran pilots and crews, newly arrived from the battles of Britain and Germany and just itching to try out the tricks they have learned . . . one aerodrome not far west of Penang that was torn of the jungle and this aerodrome, like all others I visited, is as modern as the best in America and Europe, and anything can land on it." [23]

Of the defences at Kota Bharu, he wrote:

> "Japanese naval convoys and parachute troops will undoubtedly try to make a landing for possession of Kota Bharu, which would bring the 'Yellow Air Force' within range of Singapore. So Kota Bharu is magnificently defended both from the ground and in the air. Since the new crisis came, its bomber strength has been increased and formations of planes take off from it to scour the Gulf of Siam and China Sea day and night, watching for planes or ships of the Rising Sun that would herald an invasion." [24]

Other war correspondents were furious when they read the article, including Cecil Brown, who wrote in his diary:

> "I think that is as fine a piece of fake and dangerous writing as I have encountered. The keynote of British propaganda here is to present to the world the idea that Singapore is so strong that the Japanese would be fools to attack. The British seem to be forced to use that bluff game because of the heavy demands on their forces elsewhere. But it does seem a bit silly for two reasons. The first is that it prevents American correspondents from showing how desperately American help is needed out here. The second is that British bluff about the strength of Singapore has no effect in Tokyo. The Japs have too good an espionage service here to be fooled by that propaganda. But the British do

think these statements have frightened the Japs. As a matter of fact, Sir Robert Brooke-Popham told an American military officer who was here on a special mission: 'The greatest value of Singapore is the illusion of impregnability built up in the Japanese mind.'" [25]

Daily Express correspondent O'Dowd Gallagher also wrote about a visit to Kota Bharu, in more realistic terms:

"Kota Bharu was Malaya's most advanced air striking base. It was the base for a squadron of Australian-manned Hudsons, some Brewster Buffalo fighters, and Vildebeest torpedo-bombers. The men there would be the first to go into action in any war with Japan. Their job would be to attack the Japanese Navy and troop transports.

"It was an airfield that lacked every amenity. The RAF and RAAF men exiled to this outpost of Singapore led the bleakest life imaginable. I found a sodden, cold encampment. The ground squelched underfoot. Water dripped from the palm trees. It was so wet that I saw groundcrews going about their duties in bathing-trunks, rubber boots, and caps. In the midst of all that liquid waste there was no good drinking water. I had some lemon squash in the Officers' Mess, and they said if it tasted queer I wasn't to mind as they had to chlorinate the water. Lunch consisted of two boiled potatoes with a thin layer of watery stew, a mug of tea, and bread and jam. Food was the chief complaint. They swore that lunch was a typical meal. They said everyone on the station had stomach trouble of some sort." [26]

The correspondents complained about Mosley's report to the censor's department, only to receive the response:

"That's cracking good stuff. That's the kind of thing we want out here." [27]

The first casualty of war is invariably truth. While these totally false statements were emanating from Singapore – with the supposed idea that somehow they would scare the Japanese from invading Northern Malaya en route to attacking Singapore – the reality of war moved a step nearer. On 20 October, Colonel Masanobu Tsuji, Chief of Operations and Planning Staff of the 25th Japanese Army, departed Saigon as an observer in a fast, high-flying Ki-46 reconnaissance aircraft flown by Capt Ikeda, to undertake a special clandestine sortie over Southern Thailand and Northern Malaya. On arrival over the target area heavy cloud obscured the RAF's most northerly airfield at Kota Bharu on the east coast of Malaya and the sortie was aborted when fuel ran low. Two days later they tried again, initially flying over Singora and Patani in Thailand. Colonel Tsuji later wrote:

"I immediately came to the conclusion that if the British made good use of the Kota Bharu aerodrome then disembarkation at Singora would be impossible, and that therefore, come what might, we would have to capture Kota Bharu simultaneously with our landings at Singora and Patani. This at any rate was one request I would press upon the Navy, as the necessity of simultaneous landings was immediately firmly fixed in my mind.

"Before long our plane passed directly over Singora and we found ourselves looking down upon the Thai airstrips – they were indeed poor affairs. Forgetting the possibility of being attacked by an enemy plane, we kept our eyes on the ground. A little later we flew over the mountain range on the Malayan frontier. Fortunately for us it appeared that because of the rain the British Air Force was resting and, unperceived, we rose to a higher altitude and continued flying south. Soon we saw another large aerodrome – Sungei Patani – and still farther on at Taiping yet another. Obviously our enemies would be able to employ all their available air strength on these aerodromes.

At any sacrifice we had first of all to capture the enemy aerodromes at Kota Bharu and Alor Star, for use by our own air force." [28]

The British authorities were first aware that their aerodromes in Northern Malaya were being overflown when advised so by 8RAAF Squadron based at Kota Bharu, although they were initially less than interested, as testified by Wg Cdr Frank Wright, former CO of 21RAAF Squadron:

"The attitude adopted by Air HQ staff concerning matters which, to us, appeared to be of great importance, was amazing. During November 1941, strange reconnaissance aircraft were sighted and reported flying over RAF Station Kota Bharu. Application was made to RAF HQ for fighter aircraft to be stationed at Kota Bharu, but the first interest displayed by Air HQ was a signal asking whether we needed their help to identify the aircraft and a query as to whether we required better binoculars. In reply to this facetious signal, CO 8RAAF Squadron made a complaint to Air Staff, and some weeks later three Buffaloes were stationed at Kota Bharu."

The three Buffaloes were detached from 243 Squadron and were flown by Flg Off Blondie Holder, Plt Off Ron Shield and Sgt John Oliver – the same three pilots who had visited the two airfields in June. They had been on detachment to Alor Star, where they remained for about a week before moving over to Kota Bharu. Their orders were to attempt to persuade any intruding aircraft to land in Malaya, although they were not allowed to open fire on any such aircraft they might intercept. Following a lack of success, they were ordered back to Alor Star on 20 November to try their luck from that aerodrome but again to no avail.

21RAAF Squadron, now under the command of Sqn Ldr Bill Allshorn RAAF and having completed its Buffalo training without any serious problems, was declared operational on 19 November. However, one Buffalo (W8214) had been lost when its engine caught fire, but Flg Off Wallace baled out safely. The Squadron was inspected by the AOC who congratulated it on its efficiency, an assessment not reached by its former CO, Wg Cdr Wright, who wrote:

"Just prior to being despatched to their war station, 21RAAF Squadron had been completely disorganised owing to (a) change over in command, (b) change over from Wirraway to Buffalo aircraft, (c) change over of more than 50 per cent of their pilots, (d) the remaining 50 per cent of Squadron pilots detached from the Squadron and engaged on instructional flying at RAF Station Kluang."

Nonetheless, four days later the Squadron was ordered to Sungei Patani and the movement of its 18 Buffaloes was completed by the 28th, of which 13 transferred initially. One of the two Hudsons which assisted with the move then flew three of the pilots back to Sembawang, from where they picked up more Buffaloes and flew these to Sungei Patani in company with another two.

21RAAF Squadron RAAF
Sqn Ldr W.F. Allshorn RAAF

A Flight	B Flight
Flt Lt F.H. Williams RAAF	Flt Lt J.R. Kinninmont RAAF (Congo)
Flg Off A.M. White RAAF (Max)	Flg Off G.M. Sheppard RAAF
Flg Off R.A. Kirkman RAAF	Flg Off B. Hood RAAF
Flg Off C.R. McKenny RAAF	Flg Off R.H. Wallace RAAF (Dainty)
Flg Off H.V. Montefiore RAAF (Monty)	Sgt H.W. Parsons RAAF

Flg Off D.M. Sproule RAAF   Sgt N.R. Chapman RAAF
Flg Off J.B. Hooper RAAF   Sgt G.T. Harrison RAAF

Flg Off Montefiore had transferred from 8RAAF Squadron Hudsons, having completed the Wirraway course first. Sqn Ldr Allshorn was not completely happy with his Squadron's detachment to Sungei Patani, nor was he satisfied with the Buffalo, and later reported:

"The Brewster Buffalo undercarriage once retracted gave frequent trouble on being lowered again, in as much as the undercarriage used to stick up in the locked position and the manual release devices were not efficient. The Squadron, however, had less trouble in this regard than some other similarly equipped units because the Commanding Officer published a definite cockpit drill for lowering and raising the wheels which seemed to get rid of most of the trouble.

"The armament is four .50-inch calibre machine-guns, two of which were synchronized to fire through the airscrew. The armourers found great difficulty in ridding the electrical system of heavy corrosion and rusting in the short time which we had to become operational, and the Squadron as a result never ever had efficient armament in spite of the fact that these guns on occasions tested well on the ground."

The senior Flight Commander, Flt Lt Fred Williams, added:

"Finally the only way we could get over the trouble was to replace the .5s with .303 calibre guns. We did that with the engineering facilities we had down on Singapore Island. But even then we couldn't win. We got our first issue of Buffaloes into good shape, only to have them re-issued to fly in Burma. So we lost them for another assignment of unmodified Buffaloes. But not only that, we were ordered immediately to Sungei Patani without doing the modifications. These aircraft were now the problem. If we could not depend on our guns we were in real trouble. Up there in the north, we had to use Penang engineering firms' workshops. They were simply not capable of doing the work. Our unhappy armourers never did get the guns serviceable although their efforts were admirable." [29]

Incredibly, the removal of five aircraft from 21RAAF Squadron was part of a plan to create a British version of the AVG comprising a squadron each of Buffaloes and Blenheims to operate under General Chennault as part of the International Air Force in China. From July 1941 onwards, the Chinese Government made repeated requests for greater British support against the Japanese. Initial British responses were muted for fear of provoking the Japanese, although attitudes hardened as Japanese intentions became apparent. By mid-November 1941, approval had been granted for the creation of a British Volunteer Group and, by the end of the month, eight Buffaloes, five from 21RAAF Squadron and three from 453 Squadron, had been allotted to the unit. However, the plan was overtaken by events. With the Japanese attack on Malaya, the need for a British Volunteer Group evaporated and the aircraft were reallocated to operational squadrons on Singapore.

21RAAF Squadron shared Sungei Patani with the Blenheim IFs of 27 Squadron, the latter unit tasked with the rôle of day and night fighter defence. One of 27 Squadron's airmen, AC2 Geoffrey Rex Collis, remembered the arrival of the Buffaloes:

"I don't think any of us had set eyes before on the American-built radial-engined Buffalo, sometimes referred to as the flying beer barrel. We could see the likeness, as the squadron buzzed noisily across the drome before landing; rather like a swarm of bees, escorted by the queen bee in the shape of a [Hudson]. From the racket their single engines made, considerably more decibels than our twin-engined Blenheims, I could see we were going to enjoy little peace while they were around.

"I suppose that the Brewster Aero Company had designed the Buffalo as a fighter plane, but it had no great speed, with its short stubby wings and body to match. It was something like a monoplane version of the venerable Gloster Gladiator, with its radial engine that kicked up such a din on take-off. I would think that the US Department of War was quite glad to get them off their hands." [30]

Under the control of NORGROUP, 21RAAF's primary duty was to support III Indian Corps responsible for the defence of Malaya north of Johore and Malacca. It was the rainy season, hence the airfield was in a very bad condition: there were no hangars and all maintenance work had to be done in the open. Effective dispersal of aircraft was impossible because of the boggy nature of the field. Wireless communication at Sungei Patani was very poor, and there was a serious lack of operational control. Besides this, there was no observer organisation to give warning of the approach of enemy aircraft. The only operational radar units were centred on the defence of Singapore Island. Despite the theoretical advantage radar provided, operating staff were inexperienced as were fighter controllers at Singapore.

21RAAF Squadron was kept busy at its new base since, during the week leading up to the invasion, Sungei Patani was regularly overflown by photographic-reconnaissance Ki-46s operating from Saigon. Flt Lt Williams recalled:

"What they were doing was obvious to us. We signalled to Singapore Headquarters asking what we should do about the flights. They replied, to our astonishment, that we could intercept them with fighters and force them to land if we could, but on no account were we to fire on them! How we were to force them down without firing was anyone's guess, but by policy Britain and America were careful not to risk any provocative action." [31]

The Australians were ordered to put up two aircraft daily in an effort to intercept or at least prevent the unwanted intruders, but no sightings were achieved. Meanwhile, 453 Squadron, under the temporary command of Flt Lt Tim Vigors on attachment from 243 Squadron while Sqn Ldr Harper was in Australia, was also declared operational, on 20 November.

453 Squadron RAAF
Sqn Ldr W.J. Harper RAF
Flt Lt T.A Vigors DFC RAF (temporary CO)

A Flight
Flt Lt R.D Vanderfield RAAF (Van)
Plt Off F. Leigh Bowes RAAF (Curly)
Plt Off D.R.L. Brown RNZAF
Plt Off G.L. Angus RAAF (Gus)
Sgt V.A. Collyer RAAF (Wild Bill)
Sgt J. Austin RAAF (Tozzler)
Sgt A.W.B. Clare RAAF (Sinbad)
Sgt M.N. Read RAAF (Mac)
Sgt W.R. Halliday RAAF (Wop)
Sgt H.H. Griffiths RAAF (Griff)
Sgt S.G. Scrimgeour RAAF
  (Gentle George)

B Flight
Flt Lt B.A. Grace RAAF (Mad Mick)
Plt Off R.W. Drury RAAF (Droopy)
Plt Off T.W. Livesey RAAF (Desert Head)
Sgt K. Gorringe RAAF (Keith)
Sgt R.R. Oelrich RAAF (Docum)
Sgt E.A. Peterson RAAF (Pete)
Sgt G.R. Board RAAF (Blondie)
Sgt J. Summerton RAAF (Barrel Bum)
Sgt K. Ross Leys RAAF (Strangler)
Sgt M.D. O'Mara RAAF (Shamrock/Matt)
Sgt G.E.G. Seagoe RAAF (Ocker)

Plt Off David Brown RNZAF was attached to the Australian unit from 243 Squadron. Nicknames are shown since they were frequently used in the Squadron's secret and unofficial 'war diary', in which pilots aired their grievances, impressions and aspirations. It contains many humorous and light-hearted entries and commenced on 20 November 1941, when Sgt Mac Read wrote:

> "Much surreptitious brushing of hair as official photographer does the rounds on the day we become operational. Great line-shooting on the R/T but source unfortunately withdrawn though Ocker featured prominently in the running commentary. Van is reported to be a little camera shy after the 'Australian episode'. The men were entertained by the pilots and NAAFI later. Great interest was aroused by stirring renditions of folk songs and dances by Flight Commanders and other ranks."

Next day Plt Off Geoff Angus followed up with:

> "The Admiral's house was a special target in the Army and Navy operations today. Complaints of low flying over his house gave us cause for special attention. Squadron pilots had a celebration dinner at the 'Airport Hotel'; the first time we have all got together to let off steam. All was well until Ocker called his favourite oath. The whole dining room floor bustled and you could have heard a few bricks fall. After one or two toasts to our success, we took over the bar with Wild Bill doing the part behind the counter. Mad Mick and Gentle George were the ring-leaders of popular classical songs. What happened to the three bottles of wine that appeared from nowhere? Ask the boss!"

Apparently the celebration was a roaring success, as Sgt Wop Halliday noted:

> "Today memorable for several things (1) first day of three days leave; (2) pilots starting their leave as from today, the first three being Sgts Read, Peterson and Collyer; (3) getting over the night before. The pilots' dinner broke up at midnight as the bar then closed. A few got away in taxis, but the rest took over a bus, requesting the natives to leave. At the terminus we changed to a trolley but soon abandoned this as Sgt Board, at the wheel, drove it away from the overhead wires. Back again to a motor-bus which we left after a few minutes when Sgt Griffiths tried his hand at rickshaw-pulling. Blissfully sleeping natives outside buildings were rudely awakened. The party started to break up at this time, some going home, but the rest had better answer for themselves. Most pilots spent Saturday in bed, Desert Head being so sick he has sworn off for the first time in his life."

And so it went on, one entertaining entry following another as the Australian pilots made the best of the last few days of peace.

> "Friday – raining cats and dogs. Daring pilots – those that could be found amused themselves madly by playing at boats in the drains, and getting very wet. Notice! Anyone knowing whereabouts, or having pinched, one steel helmet, return at once. Blondie is here moaning dolefully that he is the owner of the said missing tin hat."

Next day, Sgt Ross Leys added:

> "Very little flying was done except to try out a new type of formation in which two machines from A Flight and four from B Flight took part. The landings of B Flight were particularly interesting. Droopy came in first, flew into the deck, bounced like f**k and only pulled up on the right side of the gutter because his brakes seized. Shamrock came next, and with a gentle side-slip, made a pansy landing in full view of the bludging B Flight pilots. Gus made a normal landing, but Docum's calls for special comment as he came in very low, narrowly missed an innocent boong [native] who happened to be

cycling by, hit the ground once, and eventually found it again about halfway up the drome. There were no casualties though."

With most pilots reasonably proficient on the Buffalo, practice combat interception take-offs became part of the daily routine. Sgt Greg Board commented:

"This went on for some three weeks or so, and it didn't take long for all the pilots to regard with great distaste those bloody practice alerts. They were a damned nuisance after a while. The natives were jumpy; they were scared out of their wits at the possibility of a Japanese attack, and every time a flock of birds appeared near the border, they would become hysterical and sound the alarm and set off every siren within ten miles. You couldn't get any sleep or any rest while all this commotion was going on. Things got so bad we had a tendency to ignore the alarms." [32]

Of this pre-hostilities period, he later wrote:

"Intelligence briefings almost daily by the most learned of men, who came from the other side of the Japanese bamboo curtain, and told us the best of the Japanese fighters were old fabric-covered biplanes which wouldn't stand a chance against the Buffaloes. With this ringing promise of slaughtering the Japanese in the air should they get too big for their breeches, we concentrated on flying and learning different methods of drinking gin and tonic. We flew with the absolute confidence in our prowess, we drank hard, and we were on top of the heap as far as we were concerned." [33]

Arrival of HMS *Prince of Wales* and *Repulse*
The arrival at Singapore on 2 December of two of the Royal Navy's capital ships was thought to be of sufficient deterrent to keep the Japanese at bay, at least until reinforcements could be made available. They were accompanied by two destroyers and were to have been joined by the new armoured-deck aircraft carrier HMS *Indomitable* equipped with Sea Hurricanes and Fulmars, but she had been damaged in an accident and was temporarily out of commission. The ships had been despatched from European waters at the insistence of Prime Minister Churchill and much against the better judgement of the Admiralty. Rear-Admiral Sir Tom Phillips arrived by air from Colombo to take command of the thus newly-formed British Eastern Fleet.

The Admiralty signalled Phillips that while he might consider cruising one of his formidable ships to the east of Singapore, ostensibly to "disconcert the Japanese", they were also concerned about the possibility of the vessels being caught in harbour by a surprise air attack and he was asked to consider whether Darwin (on Australia's northern coast) would be a better choice of base than Singapore! The Japanese were well aware of the arrival of two capital ships, as recalled by Colonel Masataki Okumiya, Staff Officer with the Japanese Air Force HQ:

"In late November 1941, we received intelligence reports stating that two British battleships had been sighted moving in an easterly direction through the Indian Ocean. Additional reports from the area indicated that the two warships had reached Singapore on 2 December. It was also determined that the commander of the newly strengthened fleet was Rear-Admiral Sir Tom Phillips, and that the two large warships were the new King George V and the fast battle cruiser *Repulse*. Subsequent to the action on 10 December, the battleship was identified as the *Prince of Wales*." [34]

On board the Prince of Wales, as one of several special passengers, was Sqn Ldr Frank Howell DFC[35], another Battle of Britain veteran, who was to take command of 243 Squadron from Sqn Ldr Bell; Howell reported:

"During the journey from England I was taken on Admiral Phillips' Staff as Fleet Aviation Officer, and so fully realised how serious was the position and expected the declaration of war almost hourly."

With the arrival of Howell, Bell was promoted to Acting Wing Commander and given command of RAF Kallang, while the incumbent Station Commander, Wg Cdr Robert Chignell, was posted to the *Prince of Wales* as Fleet Aviation Officer with the task of co-ordinating cover for the Fleet – an unenviable job due to the lack of availability of fighter aircraft. It did not take long for Howell to find out for himself just how unprepared Singapore was for war:

"Having come directly from a fighter squadron in England, my reactions to peacetime Singapore were probably more critical than those who had been stationed there for a few months, and even more so than those who had been there throughout the war. I found it very difficult to convince anyone that war was imminent, and I found 243 Squadron very little prepared.

"No arrangements had been made for the dispersal of aircraft other than around the perimeter of the aerodrome. The dispersal huts for pilots and crews were disgraceful, being aircraft packing cases joined together. There was no dispersal of workshops, first aid posts, personnel, messes, or offices. If there had been a major raid during the first fortnight of the war on Kallang, there would have been little left with which to operate.

"Flying training was still following prewar syllabus, and little advantage seemed to have been taken of experience gained in the war in Europe. Although Sqn Ldr Bell, whom I relieved, did his best in training the Squadron, he was handicapped by having no combat experience himself and, even more than this, no experienced fighter pilot in charge of training at Air HQ. The Squadron had only been up as a squadron – twelve aircraft – in an operational exercise, I think twice, before I arrived, and had little idea even of what formation to adopt. Flight or squadron attacks had not been attempted, although dogfighting was comparatively good."

Regarding other facilities, he added:

"Telephone lines were entirely inadequate, and communication up country difficult at all times. However, contact with own RDF stations was, under the circumstances, excellent. With the exception of Air HQ, the lack of any type of camouflage and air raid shelters was immediately noticeable, and none was seen at the Naval base, at Kallang Airport, or outside messes and barracks. The defence of Kallang against sabotage, Fifth Column activities, etc, was negligible."

On the eve of the outbreak of hostilities, with Japanese forces poised for the invasion of Northern Malaya, the Japanese Army Air Force had assembled 263 fighters, 234 bombers and 185 reconnaissance and army co-operation aircraft in Indo-China and Formosa, while the Imperial Japanese Naval Air Force's land-based strength in the area totalled over 400 including 151 fighters, 216 bombers and 24 flying boats – almost 1,100 front-line aircraft. Many of the Japanese fighter pilots were battle-hardened veterans of the fighting in China and during the Nomonhan Incident; for example, pilots of the Ki-43-equipped 64th Sentai had been credited with almost 150 victories before moving to Indo-China. Other fighter units including the 59th Sentai, also with Ki-43s and the K-27-equipped 1st and 11th Sentais also contained many experienced fighter pilots. By comparison, RAF Far East Command possessed the four fighter squadrons comprising a total of 60 Buffaloes, with a further 52 held in reserve. There were also 47 Blenheims (plus 15 in reserve), 29 Vildebeest (12), 24 Hudsons (seven), and three Catalina flying boats, with two in reserve – a total of 155 operational aircraft. There was also a miscellany of second-line aircraft – Wirraways, Swordfish and Sharks – which would be called into action.

Meanwhile, the Dutch were also increasing the strength of their fighter force in the East Indies, and had ordered 72 Brewster B-339Cs and Ds. The Model Cs had 1,100hp engines and were very similar to the RAF's Buffaloes, apart from a few equipment differences, while the Model Ds had the more powerful 1,200hp engines. These aircraft had also begun arriving in March 1941. With the arrival of the Dutch Brewsters, V Groep was formed, incorporating two squadrons: 1-V1G-V under Kapt Andrias van Rest, and 2-V1G-V commanded by Kapt Jacob van Helsdingen. A third squadron soon followed, with Kapt Pieter Tideman in command. The two other NEI fighter squadrons were equipped with Hawk 75s and CW-21Bs. By the eve of the Japanese invasion only 83 Dutch fighters were available to protect the whole of the East Indies. There were also 58 Glenn Martin bombers and nine serviceable CW-22 two-seater reconnaissance aircraft, together with about two-dozen FK-51 biplanes and a few Lodestar and L-212 transports.

Elsewhere in the Pacific area the Americans were also reinforcing their air strength, which was concentrated mainly in the Philippines. They were as equally unprepared for war as were the British and Dutch.

* * *

The pilots of 453 Squadron were still enjoying life at Sembawang and oblivious to what the morrow would bring. Scots-born Sgt Jim Austin wrote in the diary on the eve of Sunday 7 December:

> "Unfortunately, through lack of organisation and one thing and another, this diary has slipped a whole week in its continuity. Though many stirring deeds, both on land and in the air, will thus be denied to history, it is hoped that the thrilling escapades of No.453 will, from this date onwards, flow turbulently through the pages of this, our diary. A temporary change in the command of our Squadron has taken place through the ghost-like disappearance of The Shadow. His place has been taken by Flt Lt Tim Vigors, a wild Irishman with a long string of victories to his credit.
>
> "Today marked an epic event – the birthday of Wild Bill Collyer. The said William has just returned from leave in Malacca (lucky dog) minus his bushranger's moustache. Tis said he removed the heirloom to pander to the capricious whim of a fair AIF nurse. Oh Bill! How could you be so fickle? Anyway, the occasion was celebrated in the accepted fashion in the Sergeants' Mess, and a beery time was had by all."

But everything was about to change.

CHAPTER II

INVASION

The First Two Days: 8-9 December 1941

"No honest persons today or a thousand years hence, will be able to suppress a sense of indignation and horror at the treachery committed by the military dictators of Japan under the very shadow of the flag of peace borne by their special envoys in our midst."

US President Roosevelt

Northern Malaya – Monday 8 December 1941

For the troops stationed at Kota Bharu on the north-eastern coast of Malaya, the first part of the night of 7/8 December was relatively peaceful and quiet. The sky above, for most of the night, had been clear and bright but, just before midnight, a heavy blanket of cloud, extending to some 50 miles out to sea and almost down to sea level, descended – fortuitously, for the Japanese, obscuring three transports that had just arrived off the coast. The invasion of Northern Malaya was about to begin. The three troop-carrying transports were flanked by a cruiser and four destroyers, and soon the advance echelon of the 5,600 troops on board the transports began disembarking into numerous small landing boats and, by 0200, the first wave was under way.

The first indication defending Indian troops had of the impending landings was when three small craft were observed moving stealthily towards the mouth of the Kemassin, an area criss-crossed by creeks and streams, just north of Kota Bharu airfield. Within minutes there followed a brief bombardment by the unseen Japanese warships, shells raining down amongst the coastal defences.

Unable to react immediately owing to prior instruction, the airfield commander contacted Air HQ at Singapore (Singapore received its first air raid at 0415 – see Chapter V) for permission to scramble a Hudson equipped with flares to determine what was happening. However, before the Hudson could be sent off came news of Japanese troops landing on the beaches. All available Hudsons were at once ordered into action, aircraft taking off at two to three minute intervals with the crews briefed to make independent low-level attacks. One Hudson was shot down during the first attack, with the loss of the crew. Those remaining returned and prepared for a second strike, aircraft again taking off individually as soon as they had been rearmed. A second Hudson was shot down, with only the observer surviving and the four others returned with varying degrees of damage. A temporary halt was called to determine the serviceability of the remaining aircraft and to assess what damage had been inflicted on the enemy. Reports suggested that all three transports had been hit, and that two were on fire. Of the action, Colonel Tsuji of the 25th Army HQ wrote:

"The officers and men of the anti-aircraft detachment, although scorched by the flames, finally shot down seven [sic] enemy planes. As the fires burst through the decks of the ships, the soldiers still on board, holding their rifles, jumped over the side. Kept afloat by their lifejackets with which they had been equipped, some managed with difficulty to get into boats while others swam towards shore. For these men it was a grim introduction to war." [36]

Meanwhile, to the defenders of Kota Bharu it was apparent that the Japanese ships were withdrawing to the north-west; only one of the fiercely burning transports remained and could be seen burning by those on shore. Despite the damage that had been inflicted, the other two transports made good their escape. Seven Vildebeest were ordered off from Gong Kedah to intercept the retreating ships but with the weather rapidly deteriorating out to sea, only a Japanese light cruiser was sighted and attacked, but it was impossible to synchronise the attack and no hits were registered. As the Vildebeest approached Kota Bharu, defending troops thought they were Japanese aircraft. One soldier of the 5th Field Regiment RA, Gunner H.W. Berry, later wrote:

"Suddenly a shout went up – 'Take cover, here they come!' The faint hum of approaching aircraft grew louder, and presently we saw them. There were five, and they confirmed the impression we then held of the Jap Air Force. They were all single-cockpit biplanes . . . But as they passed right overhead we gave gasps of astonishment. They weren't Japs. They had the circular red, white and blue on their wingtips. Someone suggested they were our training planes getting away whilst the going was good, and it seemed the only reasonable explanation. Our confidence was again shattered when, a few minutes later, we saw a squadron of low-winged monoplanes approaching from the north. We stood out in the open and cheered, but rushed for cover when they started dive-bombing and machine-gunning the drome. This time it was the Japs. Before we went into action that night we saw most of the hangars on fire and all the aircraft on the ground destroyed. Our air arm had ceased to function." [37]

Hudsons continued to attack landing craft and troop concentrations on the beaches. Barges were reported being towed up the Kelantan towards Kota Bharu town, the two Buffaloes of 243 Squadron being ordered off at 0630 to deal with these. Flg Off Holder and Plt Off Shield carried out strafing attacks on the craft and the beaches, but Holder's aircraft was hit by small-arms fire, making it difficult for him to control when landing back at Kota Bharu, where he subsequently collided with a crash-landed Hudson, causing further damage to both machines. 243 Squadron's Senior NCO, Flt Sgt Mothersdale, later related details of the incident, having conversed with Sgt Bill Snell, one of the groundcrew present:

"Holder landed at Kota Bharu. The sky had clouded over and the night was dark. After touch-down his aircraft was running out along the runway when his landing lamps picked out a damaged RAAF Hudson obstructing the runway. He swung off in an attempt to avoid a collision, but his mainplane struck the Hudson. Snell said the Hudson had been on the runway for some time, and the RAAF ought to have at least pulled it clear – they had enough time to do it. The mainplane was fairly extensively damaged, and a temporary repair was required to enable it to be flown to Kallang for a permanent repair to be made."

Meanwhile, shortly after 0700, Shield (W8221/WP-X) encountered a formation of nine Ki-21s – probably from the 62nd Sentai – between Kota Bharu and Machang:

"While at 9,000 feet in pursuit of nine enemy bombers, I observed a bomb burst approximately three miles ahead. Turning sharply to port, I saw a Japanese aircraft at 2,000 feet below. I overhauled the enemy but as my windshield was covered in oil, I was able to get only occasional glimpses of him. At 350 yards, as near as I could judge in the circumstances, I opened fire. After one burst, three of my guns stopped; the remaining gun stopped after two further short bursts. I was unable to see whether the enemy returned my fire. Breaking away downwards, I returned to base."

The Japanese assault troops had landed in sufficient numbers to push the defenders back, and soon Kota Bharu airfield – the main prize – lay ahead.

As daylight came all available bombers and fighters in Northern Malaya were preparing to take up the attack on the invasion force. Seven Blenheim IFs of 27 Squadron from Sungei Patani were already in action, having been ordered off during the hours of darkness. At 0645, Ops at Kota Bharu warned Sqn Ldr Allshorn of 21RAAF Squadron of the approach of two unidentified aircraft from the west. Two sections of Buffaloes were placed on immediate readiness, but no scramble was ordered. Ten minutes later, without further warning, a formation of five Ki-21s of the 98th Sentai was seen heading for Sungei Patani at about 11,000 feet. On the airfield two pilots were already strapped into their Buffaloes, and two others were at readiness, but still no order to scramble was received. Flt Lt Fred Williams, the flight leader, telephoned Ops for instructions, only to be told by the Station Commander to do nothing and to await further orders. Allshorn recalled:

". . . the rest of the twelve pilots standing-by at the briefing room, including myself, recognised the aircraft as enemy and made for the unit's aircraft, prepared for scramble to take-off and intercept. As the pilots were putting on their parachutes and the aircraft were being warmed, I looked up to see a stick of bombs leave the enemy formation and realized it was too late for take-off."

Flt Lt Williams shouted for everyone to leave their aircraft and take cover, but Flt Lt Bob Kirkman and Flg Off John Hooper managed to get into the air through bursting bombs; they pursued the fleeing bombers for some distance but when they closed in to attack, both Buffaloes suffered total gun failure. It would seem that during the chase they had overflown positions occupied by troops of the 1/Leicesters, one of whom, Lt George Chippington, later wrote:

"I saw a seaplane, a low wing monoplane with large floats . . . It flew south slowly and parallel to the road, the heads of the pilot and navigator clearly visible in the open cockpit. Under each wing I saw a large round scarlet blob – a Japanese plane . . . Our Bren mounted on a tripod opened up, followed at once by a change in the note of the engine – an increase in revs as it banked and turned. Once more it crossed overhead, even more slowly, its engine stuttering and misfiring. We had hit it. A few minutes later two fighter planes roared up from the south. They were unfamiliar to me, but I guessed they were Brewster Buffaloes . . . Almost immediately the Buffaloes came roaring back and disappeared to the south . . . Later the seaplane was reported down in the jungle between Jitra and the Thai border." [38]

Meanwhile at Sungei Patani, bombs fell among the dispersed aircraft. Two Buffaloes were destroyed, while three others were damaged by shrapnel and two more by fire. Two Blenheims were also destroyed. The Station HQ was hit, where two airmen were killed, as were 16 nearby Chinese women labourers. A fuel dump was hit, sending flames and billowing clouds of black smoke hundreds of feet into the air. 27 Squadron's Blenheims returned shortly thereafter, as recalled by AC2 Rex Collis:

"It was a grim beacon for our returning planes which flew low across the airfield, circling round to find a clear strip between the bomb craters sufficient for landing. The seven planes all returned safely, the pilots claiming to have shot down four of the Jap bombers on the way back." [39]

Two of the bombers were claimed by Sgt Mervyn Baldwin, a 33-year-old from Sussex known as 'Ginger' to his friends and 'Buffalo Bill' by the groundcrew. He had apparently lived in Australia at some time and had only recently joined 27 Squadron.

Rex Collis continued:

> "Just how Buffalo Bill managed to enter the Royal Air Force and then persuade HQ that he could fly Blenheims, I do not know. One thing was certain: the man had guts, and this he showed on the very first day of war. He was piloting one of the planes of the dawn foray on enemy barges landing on the east coast beaches. By all accounts he lashed into them again and again for as long as his fuel supplies would allow, but still had enough ammunition to claim having shot down two Mitsubishi bombers on the return journey. How he managed to land safely was something of a minor miracle. The fuselage was liberally peppered with bullet holes; one of the engines was glowing red-hot and petrol was seeping steadily out of the port wing. His parachute, which doubled as a seat, was ripped open by enemy fire." [40]

By now a force of a dozen Hudsons and eight Blenheims from Kuantan arrived off Kota Bharu to continue the series of attacks on landing craft, the beaches and the burning troopships. All Blenheims returned safely to Alor Star where, within half an hour of being refuelled and rearmed, an estimated 27 Ki-21s of the 60th Sentai raided the airfield. Four Blenheims were totally destroyed and another five rendered temporarily unserviceable. Buildings were set on fire, a large petrol dump set ablaze, and an officer and five airmen killed. Raids on the airfields continued throughout the morning, Kota Bharu, Machang, Gong Kedah all being visited. While the fighting over Kota Bharu was at its height, Flg Off Hooper of 21RAAF Squadron had been sent up from Sungei Patani to patrol over his base. Flt Lt Williams remembered:

> "Two hours later Hooper, again in the air on a perimeter patrol, sighted seven Mitsubishi Navy Type 97 bombers [in fact Ki-21s] 2,000 feet above him. He was immediately attacked by six Zero fighters escorting them. They dived on Hooper and locked on to his tail, firing at him. They swept all over him, turned inside him. In no way could he shake them off until he rolled his Buffalo over on to its back and slid down into a dive for home, with all the engine power on that the Buffalo would take." [41]

On this occasion, however, the bombers did not attack Sungei Patani, their destination being one of the west coast airfields. Two further Buffaloes were now readied for flight, Flt Lt Kinninmont (W8232) and Sgt Norm Chapman being sent off on a reconnaissance over Singora, on the Thai west coast, where it was believed further landings had been made. As they approached the area they were intercepted by a dozen fixed-undercarriage fighters – obviously Ki-27s – which they incorrectly identified as 'Navy 96s' (A5Ms); Kinninmont later graphically recalled:

> "Then the sky seemed full of red circles and the Japs all tried to shoot us down at once. I pulled up to meet one as he dived down. I was in such a hurry to shoot something that I didn't use my gun-sight. I simply sprayed bullets in his general direction. Somebody was on my tail and tracers were whipping past my wings. Chapman was turning and shooting with four Japs. I decided to get out and yelled to Chapman. As I went down, I glimpsed the sergeant diving straight for the ground with three Japs on his tail. At 3,000 feet I had a quick shot at a four-engined flying boat [an H6K of the Toko Ku], and missed. Of the three Japs that had followed me down, one stuck like a leech; a burst of bullets splattered into the Buffalo. I was watching his guns. Each time they smoked, I slammed into a tight turn; the Jap couldn't hit me again. We raced down a valley to the Thai border and the Jap quit."

Their attackers were probably Ki-27s of the 11th Sentai, which claimed two aircraft shot down over Patani. In the event, both Buffaloes returned safely to Sungei Patani.

At 1045, with five Buffaloes standing-by, a formation of two-dozen bombers (Ki-21s of the 12th Sentai) was seen approaching from the north at about 1,200 feet. Again Sqn Ldr Allshorn requested permission to get his aircraft airborne but the Station Ops Room Controller again refused to allow the Squadron aircraft to take off. The raiders each dropped two sticks of bombs, one on the large petrol dump north of the administration block, and a second on the Station barracks; the petrol dump, holding 200,000 gallons of aviation fuel, went up in flames, whilst the aerodrome was damaged almost beyond use. 27 Squadron was reduced to four flyable Blenheims. Sgt Ginger Baldwin was again in the thick of the action, as Rex Collis remembered:

"The pilots had not long landed and were mostly flaked out on chairs in the flight dispersal hut, when the pencil-thin line of 27 bombers was sighted over Kedah Peak. 'Which of you bastards is going to lend me his plane? I don't think mine's going to take off in a hurry on one engine,' roared Buffalo Bill. 'Take mine,' was the chorus, 'if you must be a bloody hero.' 'Who's going to crew for me then?' shouted Bill, as he struggled into his Mae West and moved to the door. Not a soul spoke or stirred. 'Right, you lily-livered bastards, I'll go on my own; f**k the regulations.'

"So saying, he charged across the dispersal area to the nearest plane, signalled the groundcrew to disconnect the lead from the bowser that was refuelling, shouted to remove wheel chocks, and roared away to find a take-off path between the bomb potholes. Luck was still on his side. He had just pulled off the ground and was retracting wheels as the first of the bombs exploded. The one pilot [Sgt Michael Willows] who was shamed into following him was not so lucky, and was just starting his take-off run when a bomb exploded just in front of the Blenheim's nose, killing pilot and navigator instantly. We had heard the sickening explosion as we lay in our slit trench.

"Buffalo Bill's bravado was all in vain, for his tanks had only been a quarter filled when he took off, and there was not sufficient juice for him to gain height in order to engage the enemy, so he just had to return to base. It couldn't have surprised him that the other pilots avoided his eyes. He asked for an immediate transfer to the RAAF to pilot Buffaloes, but he was too late for that [although he did later transfer to 243 Squadron at Singapore]; the whole squadron was just leaving Sungei for the last time. I could never imagine Bill, who liked his beer and a coarse chorus or two, ever shouting out the last verse of the ditty that went, 'We would rather f**k than fight.' It was a saddening thought that perhaps the others did mean it after all." [42]

On learning that only four Buffaloes now remained serviceable, the Station Commander directed Sqn Ldr Allshorn to withdraw these to Butterworth airfield forthwith, and to despatch his surplus personnel by road to the same destination, although sufficient pilots were to remain to fly out any repairable aircraft; in the event, none were made flyable.

Immediately after these instructions to evacuate had been given to Allshorn, he received a request from the 11th Indian Division to send an aircraft to report on the situation at Singora, and to reconnoitre the Singora-Alor Star road. Flt Lt Kinninmont volunteered to carry out the sortie; at Singora he observed about 40 ships in the harbour and flying boat activity on Singora Lake, while motor vehicles were seen moving along the Singora road towards Alor Star. On the return flight he was intercepted by five 'Zero-type' fighters, but once again managed to out-manoeuvre them and escape; despite again being hit by a number of bullets, his aircraft was not seriously damaged.

To the west, Butterworth airfield had been on the receiving end of a low-level strafing attack by the 1st chutai of the 64th Sentai, as had the civil airfield at Bayan Lehas on the island of Penang. By midday sections of Japanese troops were approaching Kota Bharu airfield, and had begun sniping. A pocket of snipers was located by the defenders at the south end of the aerodrome, intermittently firing on aircraft and personnel who approached the barrack blocks in the dispersal area. The order to evacuate the airfield was given and all flyable aircraft departed for airfields further south, while most of the remaining air force personnel embarked in a fleet of trucks for Kuala Krai, where they were to entrain for Singapore. There had been much panic at Kota Bharu, where repairs to Flg Off Holder's aircraft continued up until the last moment, as Flt Sgt Mothersdale related Sgt Snell's account:

"243 Squadron Detachment personnel commenced this repair job and kept it manned all day, work only stopping when we had to take cover during enemy air attacks on the airfield. The remainder of the Detachment continued to handle the two other serviceable Buffaloes. When we mustered at their aircraft, the beaches barely two miles away were under enemy bombardment. We heard the sounds of the infantry battle at the beaches and it gradually moved through the bush towards the airfield. As the afternoon progressed, the firing in the bush was coming slowly forward on two sides of the airfield – from the airfield it looked like the beginnings of encirclement, and at times stray bullets whistled overhead.

"When the afternoon was getting on, it got around that the Japs had got through to the airfield. It turned out to be a rumour. We knew it was duff gen – the firing was still in the bush and it seemed the same. Some of us went out further on the airfield and had a look. The firing had come a bit nearer on one side. Soon afterwards all 'fly-out' aircraft were flown out. It was a mad panic. Aircrews were running around; some Hudsons had chocks-away before engines started up, and they went off like scalded cats – it was all over in minutes. There were a few stragglers – unserviceable aircraft – including a Blenheim. Its cowls and panels went back on in the fastest time ever and it was on its way – it shed two panels as it went! The two serviceable Buffaloes were the last to leave, flown out by Shield and Oliver."

Flg Off Holder stayed behind and assisted the dozen or so men of the Detachment with the repairs to his aircraft:

"We realised that the Station was being evacuated when we saw some of the buildings had been set on fire. We were feeling tensed and somewhat lonely – it seemed to us that we were the only people around the airfield. Among us, only Holder and I had weapons; we each had a .38 revolver. After some time an officer came and ordered us to leave everything and run for it. He wouldn't even let us set a fuel tank on fire, or even bash some holes in the aircraft. When we left the Station we felt certain that there was no need to have left the aircraft when we did, and thought we could have got the aircraft away. About half-an-hour and it would have been away."

All members of the Detachment including Holder eventually reached Singapore by road and rail, via Kuala Krai, as had the earlier departees. Sungei Patani airfield was also now considered unusable for further operations, the four operational Buffaloes of 21RAAF Squadron departing for Butterworth that evening. They were followed by the personnel of this unit, and the four remaining Blenheim IFs and personnel of 27 Squadron, which had to all intents and purposes been wiped out on the ground. On arrival at Butterworth, it was found that accommodation and food had not been organized, and the Australians were forced to spend a miserable night on the beach.

For the RAF in Northern Malaya it had been a disastrous first day, with the whole striking force seriously crippled. Three of the most northerly airfields were already virtually unusable, while any possibility of a forward deployment into Thailand by the ground forces to regain the initiative had all but gone. General Percival later commented:

"The rapidity with which the Japanese got their air attacks going against our aerodromes was quite remarkable. Practically all the aerodromes in Kelantan, Kedah, Province Wellesley, and Penang, were attacked, and in most cases the bombers were escorted by fighters. The performance of Japanese aircraft of all types, and the accuracy of their bombing came as an unpleasant surprise. By the evening our own air force had already been seriously weakened." [43]

Northern Malaya – The Second Day: Tuesday, 9 December
Frantic efforts were being made to get 21RAAF Squadron's four surviving Buffaloes serviceable, and by 1040, two were ready, Flg Offs Geoff Sheppard (possibly W8236) and Daryl Sproule (AN186) taking off to provide cover for a planned Blenheim raid on Singora. But, as Sqn Ldr Allshorn reported, the bombers failed to appear:

"I produced two aeroplanes which, after being briefed by Butterworth Ops Officer, took off at the appointed time, flew around for 40 minutes in the vicinity of the aerodrome at rendezvous height and reported back to me that the Blenheims had not taken off."

However, the two pilots carried out a reconnaissance sortie during which they saw about a dozen light tanks moving southwards into Malaya from Ban Sadao, and as the fighters dived to strafe these, a Japanese soldier was seen standing nearby, waving a flag; it was assumed that the soldier must have initially believed the attacking aircraft to have been Japanese. At 1530, as two more Buffaloes flown by Flg Off McKenny and Flt Lt Williams took off and circled the airfield they were engaged by fighters, as the latter recalled:

"We were jumped by a horde of Zeros and the shooting began both ways. The weather and static were so severe that our radios were only working after a fashion. The grease on the bullets of my .5s firing through the airscrew had vaporised and come back over the windshield. It made it almost impossible for me to see ahead. I fastened on to one aircraft that I thought was a Zero and fired a short burst. I nearly shot down Dick McKenny. We had taken off together, were furiously engaged, murderously outnumbered and fighting as much to save our own lives as to shoot down anyone else. 'Hey Fred! Lay off! It's me, Dick!' Thank heaven the radio had worked for once. It was all a mix-up. There were so many. We were firing blindly and trying to get away. At last we did break off and Dick and I got back to the aerodrome at Butterworth. We were practically out of fuel on landing after more than an hour and a half in the air. So we landed. It was 5pm. White and Montefiore were still flying. Two formations of Japs had just gone over the airfield before we arrived and had bombed and strafed it. We knew we had to hit back at them.
　　"There was a petrol tanker near the strip. McKenny and I went straight over to get fuel from it, but found only that some conscientious person in awe of Air Force orders had padlocked the hoses. Everyone was in the slit trenches. Who on earth had the key? We were stymied. But we could see the Japs coming back, twenty-seven bombers and twenty-seven fighters in formation. Without wasting any more time or thought on fuel, we took off again and climbed for the formations on rated power. Dick and I had little way of knowing how much fuel we had but were in no doubt that, on flying time alone,

it was precious little. The best we knew was that our tanks were self-sealing. Even if they had holed, they would not have leaked, but our fuel gauges were useless. There was no way of being sure just how we stood.

"The Jap formation flew on as we climbed. It took no notice of Penang's pitiful anti-aircraft guns until two bombers trailed smoke. Then the bombers unloaded on Butterworth again. By that time we were in the scrap, mixed up with them over the airstrip. After the bomb run, at least three Zeros peeled off and came at us, the leader firing at Dick. They separated us. Dick went to the left. I went right, and that was when he was shot down. Things were pretty desperate. Dick fired back whenever he could latch on, but soon he was hit and his aircraft [W8224] burst into flames. He parachuted and went down into the sea between Butterworth and Penang.

"I got locked in with about three Zeros and my guns jammed. I had no choice than to dive away for the airfield, but as I did I drew the Zeros through the anti-aircraft fire. They forced me to dive at such speed that I came in fast in my first approach to the strip. The Buffalo was so far along the runway and still too fast to land that I had to go round again. Only the Heavenly Father knew whether there was enough fuel in the tank. There almost was. On the second approach my engine coughed and died, out of petrol as I was coming in. I made a dead-stick landing, flung out of the cockpit on to the strip and scrambled into a bunker. They followed me down, swept the strip with machine-gun fire and got my aircraft [W8232] – blew it up on the runway. Dick and I had lost our Buffaloes and Dick was somewhere in the sea." [44]

McKenny had come down into the sea between Penang and Butterworth, suffering severe facial burns, but was able to swim to a native fish trap, to which he clung until rescued by an elderly English naval officer in a launch.

The other pair of Buffaloes was also swiftly overwhelmed by a mass of fighters. Flg Off Montefiore claimed one shot down, but was then forced to bale out of his stricken aircraft (W8236); free-falling for as long as he dared, he pulled the ripcord and floated down. During his descent he saw a parachute open from a flaming Buffalo plunging towards the sea; this was McKenny. He then saw another Buffalo diving towards Butterworth, pursued by three Japanese fighters (Williams' aircraft). Eventually Montefiore landed in a palm tree, and on releasing himself, hailed a Malay on a bicycle, borrowed the machine and cycled back to Butterworth. Flt Lt Max White's AN188 was also riddled with bullets and he was obliged to make a forced landing on Penang Island; although the Buffalo's fuel lines had been severed, its tank punctured, spars holed and control surfaces damaged, the aircraft was deemed repairable and recoverable[45]. With his parachute pack slung over his shoulder, he made his way to the ferry and arrived back at Butterworth that evening.

When this attack ended, a MVAF Rapide that had been delivering supplies to the airfield taxied out to return to Ipoh. As it gathered speed down the runway, its pilot was suddenly faced with the disconcerting experience of having a Buffalo (Williams' aircraft) make its dead-stick landing right in front of him. He just managed to lift the biplane over the smoking fighter, when a twin-engined aircraft – which he thought was a Blenheim – opened fire. Although the Rapide was hit and the instrument panel shattered, the pilot nursed the damaged aircraft to Ipoh on one engine, landing there safely. It seems likely that the Rapide was pursued by Ki-43s when on its way to Ipoh, as witnessed by Sgt Wareham in the PR Buffalo:

"I was coming back from a reconnaissance flight [to Singora] and I was due to refuel at Ipoh. Strangely, civilian aircraft were still flying and I arrived to find a Rapide, which was carrying civilian passengers, being shot at by several 'Zeros'. They saw me coming and one or two started to chase me. I had nothing in the way of guns, so I couldn't do any fighting. But I knew the terrain very well, and Ipoh has some very funny places with some very narrow ravines. One bloke was following me very closely and I went down between two very small hills. He followed me but he went into one. I was credited with that plane. One of the civilians on the Rapide happened to be an Australian reporter and I later learned they got back to Singapore."

On the outward leg of the reconnaissance sortie, Wareham had landed at Butterworth to deliver gun solenoids to 21RAAF Squadron in an attempt to make six unserviceable Buffaloes operational. A little earlier during the day, by way of coincidence, the MVAF's other Dragon Rapide was fired upon by British troops in the neighbourhood of Taiping, and this too suffered the loss of one engine, although the pilot managed to land safely at Ipoh. The gunners responsible for firing at the aircraft apparently claimed that they had shot down a machine that was in the book of silhouettes of enemy aircraft!

At the start of the raid on Butterworth, just two of the Blenheims had succeeded in getting airborne. One was attacked almost immediately and landed again, but the other continued to Singora alone, where it came under attack from several fighters. The pilot, Sqn Ldr Arthur Scarf, was severely wounded but nonetheless with the aid of his crew managed to fly the damaged aircraft to Alor Star, where a belly-landing was achieved. Sadly, Scarf succumbed to his wounds and was later posthumously awarded the Victoria Cross.

That evening, with the aerodrome in ruins, the Station Commander at Butterworth ordered an evacuation to Ipoh, including the remnants of 21RAAF Squadron and six airworthy Blenheims. Thus within two days, an initial force of some 50 Blenheims based in Northern Malaya had been reduced to ten, only two of which were in a fit state to operate. Ipoh was a very small station with few facilities of any kind, for it was nothing more than an advanced landing ground located near Penang Island; there was only a skeleton HQ staff, consisting of one Pilot Officer and six airmen. Messing and quartering arrangements had to be made, Station defences organised, trenches dug, transport acquired, a spotting system inaugurated and communications organized, the responsibility for which fell upon the personnel of 21RAAF Squadron, under the leadership of Sqn Ldr Allshorn. But all was not well, as Flg Off Barrie Hood recalled:

"We found the RAF very hostile to us at Ipoh because we had left them to it the night before when we left Butterworth. The fact remains that they were not able to do anything and had no hope of aircraft replacements . . . No one there seemed to know what to do . . . and the logical reasoning of our CO . . . was that we at least were part flyable and could get to a place where we could stand and fight back with a reasonable chance of being successful." [46]

There was also an influx of other airmen and soldiers evacuating from the north; arrangements were made with an Australian M/T unit, located about eight miles from the aerodrome, to accommodate and feed the new arrivals. The chaotic events and the uncertainty were already having a damaging effect upon morale. During the withdrawal to Ipoh there was some defective discipline amongst the ground parties of both 27 and 21RAAF Squadrons, occasioned by the constant circulation of alarming rumours, the lack of firm direction, and the obviously out-of-control conditions that they observed. Day Two of the invasion had seen almost unprecedented success for the Japanese forces – on the ground and in the air.

Back at Sembawang, when 453 Squadron learned of what was happening up country to their fellow countrymen, Sgt Greg Board commented:

"The entire 21RAAF Squadron was wiped out to a man [*sic*]. Suddenly we realised what we really had in the Buffalo – a barrel which the Zeros could outfly, outclimb, outgun, outmanoeuvre and out-do almost everything else that was in the book for a fighting aeroplane. And all this time, I hadn't yet fired my guns at a Japanese machine. The boys were taking a beating almost everywhere they tangled with the Zeros . . ." [47]

CHAPTER III

THE LOSS OF THE CAPITAL SHIPS

8-10 December 1941

"In my whole experience, I do not remember any Naval blow so heavy or so painful as the sinking of the *Prince of Wales* and the *Repulse*."

Prime Minister Churchill

At dawn on the morning of 8 December, following the first bombing raid on Singapore (see Chapter V), a JNAF C5M two-seater reconnaissance aircraft flew over that island, its crew reporting on visible effects of the bombing raid and confirming that the apparently undamaged capital ships were still in harbour. Whilst delighted with the news that they had not sailed, the Japanese High Command decided that they must not be allowed to interfere with the landings at Singora, where they would wreak havoc amongst the transports, and a torpedo-bomber attack against them was planned. The Japanese were fully aware of the threat posed by the two mighty ships, which they considered to be more powerful than their own battleships *Kongo* and *Haruna*, which were currently patrolling off the south coast of Indo-China as distant cover to the landings.

Later that same day, at 1735, the *Prince of Wales* and *Repulse* belatedly put to sea with an escort provided by four destroyers; this small but potentially powerful fleet was designated Force Z. Heading northwards at full speed, Admiral Phillips' declared intention was to intercept the large concentration of Japanese transports off Singora. He had requested that air reconnaissance of the area be made on the 9th and 10th, and that his force be afforded fighter protection while in the vicinity of Singora, where he expected to be at daylight on the 10th. The loss of Kota Bharu, Gong Kedah and Machang airfields, together with the unserviceability of Alor Star due to demolitions and Sungei Patani due to bombing, made this latter request now little more than a pious hope. Indeed, even as Force Z sailed, Phillips was advised that fighter protection was not possible. Unfortunately, the signal failed to make it clear that the lack of available fighter protection applied only to the morning of the 10th off Singora, as had been the specific request, whereas it would seem that Phillips was under the mistaken impression that fighter protection would not be available under any circumstances.

Initially luck was with Force Z when, early next morning, the crew of a JNAF reconnaissance C5M reported that *Prince of Wales* and *Repulse* were still in harbour, having mistaken two large merchantmen for the warships, but at midday a Japanese submarine signalled Japanese Naval HQ with the news that the ships were in fact at sea. All Japanese cruisers providing cover for the landing were ordered to launch their spotter floatplanes to search for the British fleet, while torpedo-armed G3Ms and G4Ms of the 22nd Air Flotilla at Saigon were scrambled to carry out a night attack. However, despite long searches subsequently carried out by the strike force, no sightings were made. The reason for the lack of Japanese success in locating Force Z was due to a sudden change of course and plan by Admiral Phillips. During the early evening the task force reached a point level with Kota Bharu when the *Prince of Wales'* aircraft-warning radar picked up blips of three approaching aircraft. Then, at 1720, the rain clouds cleared and a Japanese floatplane was seen. Before long two more floatplanes appeared. With surprise gone, Phillips decided that the risk of continuing was too high and, at 2015, set course for Singapore at top speed.

At around midnight Phillips received a signal from Singapore advising him of a reported landing at Kuantan. Force Z changed course to intercept, but the reported landing proved to be no more than a probable light reconnaissance. Meanwhile, the British fleet had been tracked by another Japanese submarine and, at 1015, was spotted by a C5M floatplane. Time was now beginning to run out for Force Z. At 1113, the first bombers and torpedo-bombers appeared – eight G3Ms of the Mihoro Ku, followed by nine torpedo-armed G3Ms of the Genzan Ku – which targeted *Repulse*. The *Prince of Wales* was the target of the next wave of Genzan Ku torpedo-bombers, two torpedoes striking the ship; one struck home on the port side aft, the other abaft Y turret: her steering failed and both propeller shafts stopped. The pride of the Eastern Fleet rapidly took a list to port, and her speed dropped. By 1230, it was all over except for the suffering of the men in the sea. Both ships had been sunk. [48]

A total of 51 torpedo-bombers and 34 bombers participated in the attacks on the two ships, two G4Ms of the Kanoya Ku and one G3M of the Genzan Ku being shot down (with the loss of all 18 crewmen), while a third G4M crashed due to battle damage on its return to Saigon. In addition, at least seven G3Ms and a similar number of G4Ms returned with varying degrees of battle damage. Although a total of 2,081 men survived the sinking of the *Prince of Wales* and *Repulse*, 840 were lost including Admiral Phillips.

Singapore was not aware of the attack until Captain Tennant of *Repulse* sent an emergency signal at 1158, and due to Force Z's radio silence and Phillips' change of plan, GHQ had no idea where the ships actually were. On receipt of the signal two Buffaloes from 243 Squadron were immediately scrambled from Kallang, as was a 4PRU Buffalo, while close behind followed ten 453 Squadron Buffaloes in two flights of five aircraft from Sembawang. First on the scene was Flt Lt Mowbray Garden of 243 Squadron:

"I received a signal from Ops on the telephone to scramble my flight and take off in pairs at intervals of 20 minutes, and fly on a bearing 10° from Kallang, which would take us into the China Sea. I did not know what to expect, but I had been told (on the telephone) that I had to look after an 'important' ship which was being bombed.

"There was a certain amount of mist but quite quickly I noticed that the sea had not only traces of oil, but increasingly was one mass of oil, and then I saw it – one large battleship floating helplessly in the choppy sea, without steerage and listing badly to one side. With its four gun turrets it could only have been one ship – the *Prince of Wales*, and she was sinking. All around her the sea, as far as the eye could see, was oil – and men were jumping off the ship into the oil, some with and some without pieces of debris, like chairs, planks, etc, with which to support themselves when in the oily sea. There were a few small Navy ships of one kind or another standing by to try to help. On my approach, the remaining workable anti-aircraft guns on the *Prince of Wales* opened fire on me, which was hardly surprising, but I was able to release the colours of the day (through the Very pistol) and the firing stopped. There was nothing I could do except to patrol the area in case of a fresh Japanese attack, and wait for my second section of Buffaloes to come and relieve me."

Garden's No.2, Sgt Geoff Fisken, commented:

"As our planes reached the rendezvous point, I could see below me a grey metal bow sticking out of the sea, surrounded by an oil slick and many bodies."

On reflection he added:

> "Could just two squadrons of Buffaloes have saved the battleships? The meandering Jap bombers and torpedo-bombers, laden down with their deadly cargo, would have been easy targets for a Buffalo."

Also in the vicinity by now was Sgt Charlie Wareham in the PR Buffalo (W8136), busily taking pictures of the carnage below, whilst close behind came the 453 Squadron Buffaloes led by Flt Lt Tim Vigors, who recalled:

> "By the time my Squadron arrived on the scene the battle was over. I just saw the *Prince of Wales* sink on the horizon, and by the time I was over the remnants, there was not a Japanese aircraft in sight."

Sgt George Scrimgeour remembered:

> "Tim Vigors went down to have a look at the ships and we stayed above to give him cover at about 6,000 or 7,000 feet. I saw one Japanese aircraft leaving as we arrived. That was the only aircraft we saw [this was probably a reconnaissance G3M that had remained behind to witness the fates of the capital ships]. Before we left both ships had turned over and one was sinking. After that we flew back to Singapore. On that particular flight we had no idea of what our mission was because the pilots did not have that much knowledge of what they would see. We were just told to take off. The time of the flight was two hours and 15 minutes and this was pushing the Buffaloes to the limit of their endurance. I was flying too high to see survivors, but I did see the destroyers and corvettes standing alongside to pick them up. If there had been Japanese aircraft about there was not a great deal that we could have done." [49]

As the Buffaloes flew over the mass of struggling men, Tim Vigors believed he was witnessing survivors waving and cheering:

> "I witnessed a show of the indomitable spirit for which the Royal Navy is so famous. I passed over thousands who had been through an ordeal, the greatness of which they alone can understand . . . It was obvious that the three destroyers were going to take hours to pick up those hundreds of men clinging to bits of wreckage and swimming around in the filthy, oily water. Above all this, the threat of another bombing and machine-gun attack was imminent. Yet, as I flew round, every man waved and put his thumb up as I flew over him. After an hour, lack of petrol forced me to leave, but during that hour I had seen many men in dire danger waving, cheering and joking, as if they were holidaymakers at Brighton waving at low-flying aircraft. It shook me, for here was something above human nature. I take off my hat to them, for in them I saw the spirit which wins wars."

In retrospect it would seem more likely that the survivors he saw waving and cheering were, in fact, shaking their fists at the belated arrival of British fighters, or that they were simply gesticulating to be seen in the vain hope of discovery and rescue by others. An entry in 453 Squadron's war diary added:

> "Both Flights were ordered into the air – first Flight [led by] Tim Vigors proceeded northwards past Mersing, and shortly afterwards came upon the scene of a major Naval disaster. Large patches of oil covered the water and two large warships were observed to be sinking – other Naval vessels were standing off picking up survivors. The Flight patrolled the area in search of enemy aircraft but none were sighted, so returned to base. The other Flight [led by] Van came along a bit later but they had no luck either. Discovered on landing that the two ships were the *Prince of Wales* and *Repulse*."

Sgt Greg Board was similarly amazed at the scene below:

"A giant warship with its long, curving wake still showing was rolling over on its side. I had never seen such a huge battlewagon before. The ship kept rolling over while it was still moving, and I saw hundreds of men scrambling frantically up along the keel. [We] cheered wildly at the sight of the Japanese battleship [*sic*] as it began to go down, and circled, watching in suspense as the bow of the huge vessel began to go lower and lower. Then the stern lifted high into the air, the propellers glistened briefly, and the monster plunged to the bottom. I saw another part of the sea filled with wreckage and the forms of men in the water. Without any Japanese aeroplanes in the air, [we] turned and headed back . . . [we] had no radios, but waved happily to each other. That must have been one hell of a fight, with the Japanese Navy taking it right where it hurt the most." [50]

On their return to Sembawang, the pilots leaped from their cockpits, cheering and laughing. They walked back in high spirits to their bamboo huts, eager to drink to the smashing defeat of the Japanese naval force. They had just filled their glasses when the intelligence officer walked in. One look at his face stopped the pilots cold in their tracks. Then the officer began to talk. Quietly, he broke the news to his audience: "Those weren't Japanese warships."

When Sgts Weber and Powell of 243 Squadron reached the area, the battle was long over; Weber wrote:

"I went on an aerial patrol from which I had my doubts about returning. We arrived only in sufficient time to see a huge slick of oil. The enemy planes had departed. Actually, we had to travel 160 miles to this point, and orbit for 20 minutes over the sea, and many miles out of sight of the land. If we had struck a fight, and it seemed very likely that we would, petrol may have been insufficient; and in any case I did not relish the idea of finding my way home after tearing round over the ocean. I am pleased to be able to say that as far as I was concerned, there was no question of fear nor even nervousness, and I enjoyed the flight out. However, I was very happy to recognise Mersing on our way back, still more happy to pancake at base."

488 Squadron also sent out pairs of Buffaloes to search the area, Flt Lt Jack Mackenzie (W8223) and Sgt Jim MacIntosh making up one section, as the former recalled:

"We went to a point we had been given and when we arrived there was nothing but a destroyer which was picking up survivors – there was no sign of anything else. Jimmy and I then escorted a destroyer that picked up some survivors; we were out three and a half hours in our old Buffaloes – a terribly long time . . . Our Buffaloes were absolutely hopeless." [51]

Sgt MacIntosh added:

"We went out as the first section to give cover to the cruiser and destroyer that were picking up the survivors. By the time we arrived there, which was about 170 miles from memory up the east coast of Malaya, and well out, both the warships had been sunk. There were just very large oil patches and a lot of debris floating around. We covered quite a large cruiser that was picking up survivors and steaming down towards Singapore. We stayed there providing cover for an hour during which time two aircraft approached from the north. They didn't come in close enough for us to recognise because once they observed us they turned away. They could have been Jap reconnaissance. It was rather a devastating experience to say the least. The times were pretty grim. It was rather devastating for morale to know that those two ships, which had been at the Naval base at Singapore just a few days before, and which we had been flying past and over, were gone. We thought that they were indestructable. It was unbelievable."

One of the tragedies of this disaster was that fighter cover could have been provided had Singapore known sooner that Force Z was operating off Kuantan. Admiral Phillips had not informed Singapore of his change of plan on the evening of the 9th. Flt Lt Vigors was bitter about the whole shambles, and later wrote:

"I reckon this must have been one of the last battles in which the Navy reckoned they could get along without the RAF. A pretty damned costly way of learning. I had worked out a plan with the liaison officer on the *Prince of Wales*, [Wg Cdr Chignell, who was left behind when the ships sailed] by which I could keep six aircraft over him all daylight hours within 60 miles of the east coast to a point north of Kota Bharu. This plan was turned down by Admiral Phillips. Had I been allowed to put it into effect, I am sure the ships would not have been sunk. Six fighters could have made one hell of a mess of even 50 or 60 slow and unescorted torpedo-bombers. As we could do nothing else, we kept virtually the whole Squadron at readiness at Sembawang while the Fleet was out. I was actually sitting in my cockpit when the signal eventually reached us that the Fleet was being attacked. Phillips had known that he was being shadowed the night before, and also at dawn that day. He did not call for air support. He was attacked and still did not call for help. Eventually it was the captain of *Repulse* who called for air support just before his ship sunk."

This was a view similarly held by Colonel Masatake Okumiya, Staff Officer at JAAF HQ in Saigon, who wrote:

"It was completely incredible that the two warships should be left naked to attack from the skies. Interception of our level and torpedo-bombers by British fighters might have seriously disrupted our attack and perhaps permitted the two warships to escape destruction. The battle of Malaya illustrated in the most forcible manner that a surface fleet without fighter protection was helpless under enemy air attack. The battleship, long the ruler of the seas, had been toppled from its dominant position and was now just another warship to be destroyed by aerial assault." [52]

243 Squadron's CO, Sqn Ldr Howell, summed up the tragic fiasco when he later reflected:

"243 Squadron was ordered to patrol an area 'about 150 miles' north of Singapore, where ships were being attacked. No position was given; no information about the number of ships, or the number or type of attacking aircraft could be obtained. Two aircraft were sent to locate the exact position, and to try to solve the riddle. They found two very large circular patches of oil on the sea and several ships including destroyers.

The distance was so great, over 170 miles from base, that a patrol of only two aircraft could be maintained for a period of a quarter of an hour only, over the area. However, no further attacks were made by the Japanese on the destroyers, which had picked up the survivors, and these were escorted south until dusk.

It is probable that if information had been given to us as soon as the ships were attacked, together with their exact position, we could have sent a Flight, at least, to their aid. It is doubtful, however, if they would have arrived in time. However, if the destroyers had been subsequently attacked, we could have been there very much sooner if we had the above information."

On his return to Singapore, the rescued Captain Tennant of *Repulse* was greeted by an equally distressed Air Vice-Marshal Pulford, who exclaimed:

> "My God, I hope you don't blame me for this. I had no idea where you were."

The loss of Force Z marked the death knell for British hopes of holding on to their Far East possessions. When informing the House of Commons of the tragedy, Prime Minister Churchill commented:

> "It is a very heavy loss that we have suffered . . . It may well be that we shall have to suffer considerable punishment, but we shall defend ourselves everywhere with the utmost vigour in close co-operation with the United States and the Netherlands Navies. The naval power of Great Britain and the United States was very greatly superior, and is still greatly superior, to the combined powers of the three Axis Powers."

The effects were profoundly psychological as well as material, creating a feeling of hopelessness and a tremendous impression of total superiority in all arms of the enemy. The general effect on British morale and confidence was disastrous. In many, the will to resist now deteriorated rapidly. Worse was to come.

CHAPTER IV

AMOK IN MALAYA – BUFFALOES OVERWHELMED

10-24 December 1941

"The initial surprise attack, with no declaration of war, and the decision of the Thai Government to offer every facility to the enemy, have made things very difficult for us. They have not gone as we hoped. But that is nothing new in the history of the British Empire." [53]

Sir Shenton Thomas, Governor of the Straits Settlements

Following the initial shock of the landings at Kota Bharu, and the virtual destruction of the RAF and RAAF units in Northern Malaya, the 11th Indian Division was moved from its assembly area, where it had been ready to implement Operation Matador – now superseded by events – partially to prepared defences around Jitra, just to the south of Alor Star. Meanwhile, after assembly in the Singora/Patani area, the Japanese 5th Division also headed southwards, crossing the border into Malaya and sending spearheads of two of its regiments down the west coast towards Alor Star, while the third made for the line of the Perak, well to the east. Two Japanese battalions with tank support struck the Jitra defence on the 11th, finding the British and Indian troops ill-prepared for a hard fight after the recent changes of plan and alarming events. They had few anti-tank and no armoured support, save for a few Bren-gun carriers. Not withstanding this, the Japanese attack was brilliantly executed and the 11th Division forced to withdraw after suffering heavy losses – in the face of a significantly less numerous opponent, for the Japanese had employed no more than the initial attacking force, which had suffered only light casualties. This defeat was a major disaster for the defence, and preceded a series of retreats of varying distances to defendable locations. 11th Division halted briefly at Sungei Kedah, but then fell back steadily until they were south of Sungei Patani.

During this initial battle, little aerial participation occurred. The RAF was reforming its battered units in the south, while the JAAF was busily moving to airfields in Thailand with all despatch. Twenty Ki-43s of the 59th Sentai arrived at Nakorn airfield on the 11th, while next day 14 Ki-51s of the 71st Independent Chutai, together with 13 more from the 73rd, flew in to Singora, the Ki-48s of the 75th and 90th Sentais joining the 59th at Nakorn on this same date.

Penang Island was the main target for the JAAF during this period, the first major raid there being made during the morning of the 11th, following a day when no major operations were undertaken by the JAAF over Northern Malaya. Now 41 Ki-21s of the 12th and 60th Sentais, escorted by 64th Sentai Ki-43s, raided the island, which was bereft of both AA defences and air raid shelters. While the 12th Sentai directed its bombs onto Georgetown, the capital, the 60th Sentai attacked ships in harbour. The bombers flew over the town, and then wheeled back in sections of three and dive-bombed it. Nearly all the bombs fell on the densely crowded native quarter, many hundreds of casualties resulting as thousands of people had come out on to the streets to watch instead of taking shelter. The fire station took a direct hit and fires continued to burn for days. During the return flight, three Ki-43s landed at the newly captured Kota Bharu airfield, where fuel was found in the tanks of abandoned British aircraft. The availability of this base allowed the rest of the unit to move forward in readiness for operations over Kuantan.

Next day (12 December), the attacks on Penang were repeated from 0900 onwards, this time by a total of six Ki-51s of the 27th Sentai, 24 Ki-48s from the 75th and 90th, with five Ki-43s of the 59th Sentai acting as escort. Aircraft from these units operated in flights of five or six throughout the late morning and early afternoon. In Georgetown Harbour and the Penang Channel a number of auxiliary patrol vessels were attacked and sunk. The raiders returned during the early afternoon and further craft were sunk. One Japanese fighter (reported to be a 'Type 96') was shot down, its pilot baling out before his aircraft crashed in the vicinity of Kulim. A message was sent from NORGROUP to Air HQ:

"Enemy pilot who baled out near Butterworth almost certainly German. At present in Penang gaol. Will be visited tomorrow by Sqn Ldr Powell [OC Kuala Lumpur] and Plt Off Lofton-Patch (slight knowledge of German) and then sent to Singapore."

Rumours abounded, which seemed to confirm German pilots were serving with the Japanese. However, on this occasion the captured pilot would seem to have been 1/Lt Tomoichiro Fujisaki of the 1st Sentai, who was posted missing. Correspondent Cecil Brown wrote:

"Lieutenant Peter Court of a Dogra regiment . . . said that one of the planes shot down had a German pilot, wearing a Luftwaffe uniform . . . everyone I talk to say there are German pilots, but I can't find anyone who's actually seen and talked with one of them." [54]

At least two German-speaking, non-Japanese pilots were alleged to have been captured[55]. There had also been a number of reports of white officers leading Japanese Army units in the fighting in Northern Malaya, suggesting to the British authorities that German nationals were fighting with the Japanese. In addition, British and Australian pilots had reported meeting 'Messerschmitts' and 'Stukas', which seemed to support this theory, although no German aircraft served with the JAAF and JNAF.

The raids on Penang, together with the threat they posed of attacks on the retreating troops of 11th Indian Division, led Air Chief Marshal Brooke-Popham to order the renewed despatch of fighters to the area on the 12th; at once a detachment of four Buffaloes from 243 Squadron flown by Flg Off Blondie Holder (who had only just returned from his adventures at Kota Bharu) and Sgts Geoff Fisken, John Oliver, and Bert Wipiti – departed for Ipoh, where they were attached to 21 RAAF Squadron. It was intended that the detachment would carry out a strafe of Japanese troops, but this was aborted owing to severe tropical thunderstorms in the area. Instead, Holder and Fisken carried out a reconnaissance of Penang, Alor Star, Singora and Butterworth, failing to meet any enemy aircraft. On returning to Ipoh the section came under fire from British AA, Fisken's aircraft (W8147/WP-O) sustaining slight damage and the pilot suffering a minor leg wound:

"There were masses of Jap planes on Singora. I flew down low over it and I didn't get fired on. However, I was shot at when I came into land at Butterworth. Evidently there had been a Jap raid about ten minutes before we came back. The Indians manned the defence force and so far as they were concerned, every plane was a Jap plane."

Meanwhile, Holder and Oliver flew to Kuantan, via Mersing, where several white smoke fires were observed to the north-east of the town. They circled the aerodrome at 500 feet: it appeared serviceable and at the south-west corner a burnt-out Blenheim was visible. Both hangars appeared undamaged but six blocks of buildings were burnt out.

On the same day as the 243 Squadron detachment arrived in Malaya, Flt Lt Tony Phillips of 4PRU attempted a sortie to Singora in Buffalo W8136; en route he encountered four twin-engined aircraft, which he believed were German Messerschmitt 110s, and then five Messerschmitt 109s, which he successfully evaded:

> "I was then attacked by three ME110s [*sic*]. I dived to ground level but they still chased me until finally I got away in some cloud. Soon afterwards, I ran into a couple of ME109s [*sic*]. They turned in my direction and we played 'tag' about the place for some time. I came down out of the cloud expecting to find my objective. It was not there but the 109s were – and plenty of them."

The interceptions, coupled with cloud in the target area, prevented Phillips from taking photographs and, after refuelling at Butterworth, he returned to Singapore. Meanwhile, following his arrival at Ipoh, 21RAAF Squadron's Sqn Ldr Allshorn had been summoned to meet Wg Cdr R.G. Forbes, OC NORGROUP, at his HQ at the Ipoh Swimming Club; he recalled:

> "During a very strained conversation, he ordered me to reform 21RAAF Squadron and said that I personally was not to fly until the job of preparation was completed. I asked for 12 replacement Buffaloes and he informed me that as far as he knew it would be some days before they would be forthcoming. I asked him how then was I to reform and said that I thought the unit personnel would be more usefully employed preparing the Ipoh defences. This did not meet with his approval. I then suggested that some medical and cooking staff should be supplied to the unit. This he informed me would be done in due course. I then made a request for food and suitable messing arrangements for the Squadron personnel.
>
> "I was directed by him to an Army unit some eight miles out of Ipoh to the west which he thought could supply the unit with rations. The Army captain in charge of this unit informed me that the unit had just moved out and had left very few rations of any sort but that he would give me what he could, which was entirely inadequate. Drinking water was a problem as we had been refused permission to drink the water in the creeks because of its highly infectious qualities."

Nonetheless, with the arrival of the 243 Squadron Detachment and the promised reinforcements, Allshorn departed for Singapore to collect some replacement aircraft but was less than pleased with the task that confronted him:

> "On arrival at Seletar I found that the six replacement aircraft [believed to have included AN172, AN179, AN205 and AN206] for 21RAAF Squadron were still in cases and would take two to three days at least to unpack and assemble. At breakfast this morning, the Commanding Officer of Seletar, Grp Capt Brown, asked me where we were from and what we were doing. I brought him up to date on what was happening. He also asked what I thought of the Buffalo in relation to the Navy Zero fighter. I stated that the Buffalo was not good enough.
>
> "Later on during the day, Grp Capt Brown called me to his office and in the presence of his second-in-command, informed me that he was of a good mind to put me under *close arrest* [authors' emphasis], that I had gone out of my way to run-down the Buffalo as a fighter to members of his unit and that I was ruining the morale of his troops. In fact, the only person that I, or any of my pilots, talked to in relation to this matter was Grp Capt Brown himself.
>
> "I told him that I did not appreciate his threat, and that if he had finished with me,

was I free to leave? He said yes, but that he was not satisfied and that as soon as each of my aircraft was assembled and operationally serviceable, I was to fly them to Sembawang and park them there until the six were ready, because he had too many aircraft on Seletar aerodrome, which was in constant danger of being bombed. I assured him that I would do this."

Unimpressed with the attitude of the RAF officers, Allshorn flew over to see Wg Cdr Wright, who was in temporary command of RAAF Sembawang in the absence of Grp Capt J.P.J. McCauley RAAF, who had yet to return from a visit to the Middle East.

"I spoke at some length about 21RAAF Squadron with Wg Cdr Wright, and he told me that he was satisfied with what we had done and that if I had any trouble while I was in Singapore getting my replacement aircraft, I was to let him know. Next morning, I paid a visit to Grp Capt Rice, who was the OC of the Fighter Organisation on Singapore Island. Grp Capt Rice was angry because he had not heard anything of the work and conditions of 21RAAF Squadron since the war had began. I told him I thought that was the job of my NORGROUP Commander, and in fact we had all been working so hard, moving so quickly and at such short notice, that this was the first opportunity I had had of going back to Singapore.

"Grp Capt Rice directed me to have the six aircraft ready to leave the following morning [14 December] because we were obviously required at Ipoh. I told him that as soon as the six aircraft were operationally serviceable I would return to Ipoh but that, in my opinion, I did not think that the aircraft would be ready the following morning. He instructed me to see that they were. On my return to Seletar I found that there was no possible hope of the aircraft being ready to depart the following morning and instructed my aircrew to assist manually where possible with assembly of the aircraft, which they did, and we worked all night. At approximately 1800 hours, Grp Capt Rice rang me and asked me what the situation was in regard to the aircraft. I told him that I thought we would not be ready to depart until the day following. I than rang Wg Cdr Wright at Sembawang and he authorized me not to leave Singapore until I was satisfied that the six aircraft were operationally serviceable."

Meanwhile, in northern Malaya, Penang was subjected to yet another attack during the morning of the 13th; an estimated 30 bombers were reported approaching Georgetown just after 0930. The raiders comprised an unescorted force of three Ki-48s from the 75th Sentai and 18 Ki-51s of the 71st Chutai. Craft in the harbour were again targeted, several being sunk or damaged. These continuous air raids on Georgetown caused extensive damage to buildings and dock installations. Many buildings burned unchecked and there was a total breakdown in municipal services; most of the native police deserted and the entire labour force disappeared, although the majority of the ARP personnel remained on duty, many taking over tasks normally associated with the police. In response to desperate pleas already made for help for the almost defenceless island, Air HQ Singapore had belatedly ordered fighters to the area. Hence, in the early morning, even as the Japanese bombers had been lifting off from their base, Buffaloes were on their way northwards, with the despatch of 453 Squadron from Singapore. The 16 fighters were to depart in two flights of three aircraft each and two of five.

The first three Buffaloes led by Flt Lt Vanderfield were sent off at 0600, the pilots briefed to undertake a reconnaissance over southern Thailand following their arrival at Butterworth, where they landed to refuel. Before they could continue with their mission however, they were ordered off to intercept the latest raid on Penang, which comprised 18 Ki-48s and three Ki-51s. Aircraftman Rex Collis recalled:

">... three Brewster Buffaloes touched down, having been sent up from Ipoh. No sooner had they landed than a squadron of Stuka-type Jap bombers began dive-bombing shipping in and around Penang harbour. Without waiting to re-fuel the Buffs took straight off again, roaring up towards some handy cloud cover. For a while we lost sight of them behind the clouds, and we held our breath, hoping the Japs had not seen them, but they were too busy concentrating on the bombing of the ships below to notice what was happening above. One, two, three, the Buffs roared down out off the clouds, and two Jap planes immediately spiralled into the water as Buffalo shells found their marks. More enemy planes had now appeared and a general dogfight developed. Heavily outnumbered and nearly out of fuel, the Buffs had to land again. Only two now; but we had seen at least three enemy planes destroyed, and one limping off with black smoke pouring from it. For us, with our grandstand view, it had been a thrilling sight, enough to raise cheers from the trenches and to raise our morale for a while from the low level to which it had sunk." [56]

Vanderfield, although unable to retract the undercarriage of his aircraft (AN185/TD-V), nonetheless led Sgts Bill Collyer [AN180] and Mac Read [W8209/TD-E] to engage the raiders, encountering the unfamiliar, twin-engined Ki-48s, identifying them as 'Mitsubishis' and single-engined K-51s which they thought were Japanese Ju87s (Stukas). The Squadron diarist wrote:

"At 0600 Van, Bill Collyer and Mac Read left base to proceed to Butterworth to refuel and thence to do a recce over Thailand. The trip to Butterworth was uneventful but no sooner had they landed than bombers were reported over Penang. The three pilots immediately took off and intercepted three Mitsubishis; Van's first attack was a wizard and his target blew up in a sheet of flame. Then six Stukas [*sic*] joined in the show and a dogfight quickly developed. Van got another Mitsubishi while Bill and Mac between them accounted for three Stukas [apparently Read was credited with two and one shared]. Five confirmed in 453's first show; a very fine piece of work Van, Bill and Mac. It is very worthy of mention that Van fought the whole of this action with his wheels down. After driving off the bombers, Van landed at Ipoh while Bill and Mac went back to Butterworth. No sooner had these two landed then over came a ground strafing raid."

Of his combats, Vanderfield – who claimed two heavy bombers and one dive-bomber shot down – recalled:

"We immediately took off and intercepted three Japanese bombers. We attacked these bombers and five or six dive-bombers came out of the clouds and attacked us. We let them have the works and definitely shot down two in the first attack. A Sergeant Pilot in my flight fired on a dive-bomber, which was trying to sit on my tail, and it rolled over and disappeared. Another went out to sea in a long dive."

Collyer added:

"Vanderfield was having trouble with his undercarriage. His wheels were still down. Read and I were line astern, with Vanderfield leading. At about 7,000 feet Vanderfield led an attack on a Betty. The port engine caught fire and the aircraft dived into the sea. No one baled out. I saw Vanderfield attack a Stuka-type aircraft and then he disappeared. I thought we had lost him. I was still flying line astern on Read. He attacked another Stuka and pulled away in a climbing turn, and the Jap aircraft was on his tail. The Jap lined himself up nicely for me, so I shot him down. At this stage I lost

Read. I attacked two more Stuka types. The second one was going downhill trailing smoke. I was out of ammo, Read caught up with me and we returned to Butterworth, to carry on with the refuelling.

"Whilst refuelling I was called to the phone. I was told that the bridge over the Alor Star river was blown, to go there and attack transport on the road held up at the bridge. So Read [whose aircraft had been shot up during the earlier fight] and I did that till we were out of ammo again. I was having trouble with my guns – a common problem. We went back to Ipoh as per instructions. I was relieved that the first bloke I saw was Vanderfield.

"Conditions at Ipoh were primitive. I must have lost contact with the rest of the team because I finished up sleeping in the aircraft. My last meal was breakfast before we left Sembawang. The following day things got a bit more organised. The Sergeants were billeted in the railway pub. There was beer, food and a bed."

It seems that one or two of the 243 Squadron detachment pilots took off from Ipoh and engaged the bombers, Sgt Geoff Fisken (W8147/WP-O) later recalling:

"My first action was over Ipoh aerodrome. I reckon a total of 13 [sic] Jap bombers were shot down here. Ack-ack must have been responsible for some, but not all, of the damage on the low-flying bombers. It was a case of flying in and out as quickly as possible. I made my first kill, a Jap bomber – an Army 97 – after diving on it from above."

Apparently Fisken was credited with a probable. Two of the twin-engined bombers fell in this action, including that flown by Capt Kunimi Hotta, acting CO of the 75th Sentai, and records would suggest that possibly two Ki-51s also failed to return. As the fight progressed, four Ki-43s from the 59th were ordered to go to the bombers' rescue, arriving 30 minutes later to find no aircraft in the air. They then strafed Butterworth where Collyer and Read had just landed, claiming to have destroyed four fighters on the ground. During the return flight to Nakorn, the CO of the 59th collided with his No.2 and crashed to his death. The Ki-43s may have strafed aircraft already beyond repair from earlier attacks – certainly they did not hit the two 453 Squadron Buffaloes.

Meanwhile, the next flight of Buffaloes were on their way from Singapore. Flt Lt Vigors led five Buffaloes to Ipoh at 0900, followed an hour later by a second formation of five Buffaloes led by Flt Lt Grace. All ten arrived safely, as recorded in the Squadron diary:

"Five Buffaloes led by Flt Lt Vigors [AN213] left for Ipoh to relieve No. 21RAAF Squadron. These were flown by Scrimmy [W8231], Curly [W8217/TD-B], Tozzler [AN175] and Geoff Angus [W8152]. They arrived at Ipoh at 1100. Shortly afterwards, B Flight, led by Mick [W8159] and consisting of Matt [W8192], Blondie [W8216], Geoff Seagoe [W8211] and Ron Oelrich [W8225] announced their arrival by a low level shoot up of the drome which caused a great rushing for 'funk holes'. After parking our aircraft in the labyrinth of dispersal pens, six were then ordered to proceed to Butterworth. Meanwhile, Geoff Seagoe and Greg kept up a watchful patrol over the drome. Tim Vigors, Mick Grace, Geoff Angus, Ron Oelrich, Jim Austin and Matthew took off for Butterworth, but Jim's undercart would not go up so he had to return to Ipoh."

The other five had just landed at Butterworth when a large formation of Ki-27s of the 1st and 11th Sentais, estimated to be 25-30 strong, suddenly appeared. Vigors painfully recalled:

"I remember when we landed there was an airman standing on the fence with a red flag – the early warning system and long before we had a chance to refuel, he waved the flag wildly before disappearing into a ditch. I told my lads to get off the ground regardless, and immediately did so myself. One other Buffalo managed to join me [Sgt O'Mara] and we climbed up over Penang, where I could see about 30 Army 97s showing their flag.

"We attacked these from above and from behind a cloud, giving us the advantage of surprise, and I told the lad who was with me that I was going into the middle of them, to try to break them up, and that he was to watch my tail while I watched his, until such time as we got the hell out of it, which wouldn't be long. The usual mêlée ensued during which time I was pretty certain that I got hits on several of the Japs, but things were far too hot to bother about the score. The Army 97 could turn right inside the Buffalo, and I was a little too long in realizing the extent of their manoeuvrability! As a result, I received a direct hit in the petrol tank, which was situated under my feet and, which somewhat naturally, proceeded to blow up in my face.

"I used the old trick which is undoubtedly the quickest way of getting out of an aircraft, of undoing my straps and kicking the stick. The only mistake I made was to pull the ripcord too early, with the result that within seconds I had what seemed like the whole bloody Japanese air force shooting at me, from 10,000 feet down to where I eventually hit the deck, on top of the Penang mountains. Fortunately for me they were rotten shots. The Japs continued to shoot at me until I made cover of some convenient jungle."

In fact, Vigors deliberately deflated his parachute three times to avoid the Japanese attacks. O'Mara's aircraft was damaged during the action but he managed to escape in cloud and force-landed at Kuala Kangsar, while Flt Lt Grace also came under attack at 700 feet; he reported shooting down one of his assailants however, before a bullet severed his oxygen and radio leads, following which he avoided further involvement and got back safely to Ipoh. The aircraft of the other two pilots – Plt Off Geoff Angus and Sgt Ron Oelrich – were still being refuelled as the raiders approached, as the fomer remembered:

"I noticed some Zeros gathering near the end of our take-off location. They would have been about half a mile from the drome. I shouted 'Enemy aircraft at end of drome – let's go!' Hopping into our aircraft, we scrambled off. Immediately, we were amongst them and from then on we never reached much above treetop height. Ron soon collected their fire and crashed, burning furiously.

"My own experiences were that I could only save myself from being shot down. Occasionally managing a burst at anything in front of me, I cannot really claim any hits because everything was so rapidly occurring that I could not concentrate on results. Eventually my aircraft was smoking badly and with no height for parachuting, I decided that it was an impossible situation. Fortunately there was a paddy field available, which I headed for. I remember that I could not lose sufficient speed soon enough so merely moved the control stick forward and splashed in, thinking that I may have cart-wheeled.

"The gunshot wound in the left ankle was not painful at that stage, nor the cut below the eye. I scrambled out into the muddy water, noticing a cannon-sized hole in the side of the cockpit, which I may have received as I was leaving. As I looked up there was at least one Zero turning into me and I was so scared that I put up my hands, thinking 'Don't shoot me!' I immediately thought this is ridiculous so I dived under the water and held my breath for as long as I could. They disappeared.

"Finally, a Malay came to my rescue. He led me to a hut where a number of natives had gathered. He organised bicycles for me and himself and guided me to Butterworth aerodrome. In the Officers' Mess I was plied with whisky – on an empty stomach. A few hours later a couple of Army officers were leaving for Taiping and arranged for me to accompany them. With no headlights – and about halfway there – the driver misjudged a turn and we ended up in a ditch at an unusual angle. They decided to walk and left me to a swarm of large mosquitoes, which continuously buzzed me. I was glad, when finally next morning, an ambulance took me to hospital."

Rex Collis also witnessed this fight:

"We saw one Buff in a shallow dive, with smoke pouring from its engine, disappear towards the trees to our right. We set off in our wagon as far as we could go over the rough ground round the perimeter of the airfield. At least the plane had not caught fire on hitting the ground, but we feared for the pilot. It took us nearly half an hour to locate the plane, not too badly smashed up, in marshy ground between some palm trees. When we reached the cockpit we were amazed not to find the pilot still in the plane, for we were sure he had not baled out; he would have been too low to attempt it anyway. By some miracle the fuselage had missed the tree trunks, which had ripped off the port wing, thereby reducing speed drastically as the pilot slid down the other wing and landed in the bog. By the time we got there an ambulance [sic] had already reached him from a shorter route." [57]

Angus' companion, Ron Oelrich, a 23-year-old from New South Wales was killed. Later retrieved from the wreck, his body was carried back by Padre Pearce to the airfield for burial. The Squadron diarist wrote:

"So our second engagement with the enemy was not so successful. Outnumbered by ten to one, and taken completely by surprise, the boys had no chance. One lesson we have learned is never attempt to leave the ground when enemy aircraft are overhead. Seven weary pilots went into the town at night and took quarters at the 'Station Hotel' and the 'Majestic'. After a good feed and a few beers, all felt slightly better but still considerably shaken by our first introduction to the real thing."

Meanwhile, up amongst the Penang mountains, Tim Vigors was in a sorry state:

"All the skin had been burnt off my hands, arms and legs, and a good lot off my face. Also I had a bullet straight through my left thigh, which somehow miraculously had missed both the bone and the main artery, having passed conveniently between the two. Having started my way down the mountain, I collapsed, and was picked up by a couple of little Malayans, father and twelve-year-old son. I told them how to make a tourniquet, and we built a stretcher out of two branches, what remained of my Mae West, and their shirts. They carried me all day through a violent thunderstorm, down a precipitous mountain path, until we eventually hit a road and managed to stop a jeep. They accompanied me to the hospital but the sad thing was that due to my being nearly unconscious by that time, I never got their names and address."

On the ground, watchers of the action believed that Vigors had accounted for three of the Ki-27s, but it seems more likely that the aircraft seen falling by these observers were the stricken Buffaloes, including Vigors' own aircraft. Vigors was evacuated from Penang that evening when it was decided to withdraw all military personnel and Europeans from the island:

"I was evacuated on a little boat which took us to the mainland. There followed an unpleasant three days, lying for the most part on the floor of a cattle truck, which eventually ended up in Singapore."

The decision to evacuate military personnel and Europeans only from Penang caused much resentment amongst the Chinese and Malays. Flg Off Barrie Hood of 21RAAF Squadron, who visited the island, wrote:

> "We saw dead civilians still lying in the streets. The telephone exchange, fire brigade and many other public buildings had suffered severely. On the roads was a line of pitiful natives trudging into the bush . . . The hospital was doing a marathon job taking care of casualties but the staff was afraid the place would be bombed again . . . Penang had fallen by the wayside, in effect, without a shot being fired in its defence." [58]

Further bad news was to follow for 453 Squadron. The final formation of three Buffaloes departed Sembawang bound for Ipoh, including one flown by 36-year-old Wg Cdr Leonard Neale, who was to take command of the Station. With him were Plt Offs Tom Livesey and David Brown, the latter on attachment from 243 Squadron. Although the Wing Commander had no experience on the Buffalo, he had volunteered to ferry one to Ipoh due to the shortage of pilots. Livesey briefed him on cockpit drill, following which Neale took off and carried out a circuit of Sembawang before being joined by the other two, as Livesey later recalled[59]:

> "We departed at 1055, and had only flown 60 miles when we hit bad weather. We edged around the storm and pressed on in deteriorating conditions, often being forced as low as 300 feet above the sea to stay visual. Any attempt to edge inland was thwarted by very heavy rain and low cloud base. I tried to maintain some sort of course as we zig-zagged along, although my main compass was acting badly. Calling the other two on the radio I asked if they recognised any landmarks or knew where they were. They didn't. We were well and truly lost.
>
> "Heading inland, we searched over very wild country with little sign of habitation. No landing fields, main roads or town. Finally, open ground was sighted below with an adjacent sandy beach. Fuel was also becoming short. Beating up the field so low that my propeller almost grazed the ground, I noted that it appeared to have wheat or corn growing on the surface. The top appeared firm enough for a wheels-down landing. Calling up the others I said I would go down first and told them to watch my efforts before trying themselves."

Touching down after a slow, low approach Livesey discovered that the flat land was no less than a paddy swamp. His Buffalo (W8180) somersaulted several times and ground to a halt on its back. He finished up with his head and shoulders rammed heavily into mud and water. Somehow extricating himself, he tried to signal to the others to land on the beach. Apparently, the waving was misunderstood and the pair began their final approach with wheels up and flaps down.

> "Wing Commander Neale hit a tree on approach, spun in and his aircraft [W8176] burst into flames. I struggled across to the fighter but could not get close due to the intensity of the fire. Turning around I suddenly noticed Pilot Officer Brown's Buffalo [W8158] a short distance away, also blazing. There were no tracks or skidmarks in the swamp and it seemed that he had stalled in at the last moment."

Livesey, after assuring himself that nothing could be done or gained by remaining at the crash sites, set out to look for natives who obviously owned or cultivated the paddy field. It was late in the afternoon and, after wading through chest deep swamp, he eventually reached firm ground. Approaching some people near a river, he was taken to their village. The natives were to prove very friendly. They washed his clothes and fed him, mostly on fruit.

Next morning the people obligingly guided him back to the crash site. He particularly wanted to recover his parachute to use as a net the following night, mainly against mosquitoes. Back at the Buffalo, just as they were about to depart, a platoon of uniformed natives apprehended them with fixed bayonets. Each was initially to mistake the other for Japanese.

"After 30 minutes of difficult explanation the matter was resolved and my gun and soggy wallet were returned by the guards. Suddenly, seemingly from nowhere, up popped another figure. This time, white. He shouted orders in a foreign language, bayonets were again levelled and once more my papers and revolver were confiscated. The white man was Dutch, spoke English and once again good sense was restored to the situation. For the second time my belongings were returned. Van der Meer was the man's name and he was the area administrator. He confided to me later that reports he had received by native runner were interpreted as a Japanese parachute landing. Hence all the drama."

Before leaving a guard was posted on the Buffalo wrecks and arrangements made for the recovery of the bodies. Each was identified by nametags and plans were made for them to be buried at Pakan Baroe. The group then travelled downriver by canoe and later by bicycle to where vehicles had been left. The drive to Van der Meer's residence was a further 50 miles. By the evening Livesey was back at Pakan Baroe. Early the following morning, only two days after departing, he boarded a Dutch Lockheed Lodestar and proceeded to Singapore to lodge his report.

Back at Ipoh, 453 Squadron suffered yet another accident late in the evening of 13 December. Returning from a dusk patrol in W8217/TD-B, Plt Off Leigh Bowes taxied into an unmarked crater, writing off the aircraft. Of thirteen aircraft dispatched from Sembawang that morning, three had been shot down, four lost to accidents, and several of the remaining machines had suffered battle damage. It had been the intention that the arrival of 453 Squadron at Ipoh would release 21RAAF Squadron for return to Singapore, but the heavy losses already suffered led to the retention of both units at Ipoh, with 21RAAF's groundcrews responsible for servicing the remaining aircraft. However, the Buffaloes of the 243 Squadron Detachment did return to Singapore next day, but not before Sgts Fisken and Wipiti had attempted to carry out an attack on Kota Bharu, as Fisken noted:

"Ipoh was a very difficult aerodrome to land at, with two big, high mountains on either side. Up on a mission to strafe the Jap troops at Kota Bharu, we were engulfed in heavy rain, so visibility was difficult and the pilot with me, Bert Wipiti, was inexperienced. He told me that he hadn't flown at night since he'd left training school in New Zealand. I reckoned he wouldn't have had a show of landing in the middle of the night in a tropical storm, with these two mountains getting in the way. I radioed my commander at the base – 'It's raining like the hammers of hell up here, I can't see the end of the aerodrome. My mate has no experience of bad weather flying,' I said. I was pretty chuffed when the boss said, 'Abort the mission!' I instructed Bert to keep close to me coming in to land."

Throughout the 14th, the Australians at Ipoh kept two Buffaloes at readiness, while groundcrews worked ceaselessly to prepare others for offensive missions away in support of the hard-pressed troops falling back towards Penang. During the morning five fighters were ordered off for a strafing attack on Japanese columns reported in a paddy field near Alor Star, Flt Lt White and Flg Off Montefiore of 21RAAF Squadron leading Sgts Seagoe, Board and Scrimgeour of 453 Squadron. Montefiore and his

No.2 (Scrimgeour) became separated from the rest of the formation in cloud, and returned to base. The other three carried out the strafe and then met three Ki-51 light bombers, part of a force from the 27th Sentai on its way to raid Ipoh. The Buffalo pilots attacked, but on this occasion the agile attack bombers proved more than a match for them. 25-year-old Max White (AN201), a native of South Australia, was shot down and killed, believed hit by the rear gunner of the aircraft he was attacking. Board, manoeuvring wildly just above the treetops, came around on the tail of another and opened fire from close range, reporting that flames "mushroomed" from the wings and almost at once a huge ball of red fire swept round it before it crashed into the jungle and exploded. Seagoe attacked another, reporting pieces falling off before it climbed away. He then dived to strafe the Japanese column when his aircraft (W8211) was hit by an explosive bullet, apparently fired from the ground; although Seagoe received a severe shoulder wound he was able to fly back to Ipoh, accompanied and protected by Board.

Later in the afternoon Montefiore led two 453 Squadron pilots – Plt Off Leigh Bowes and Sgt Jim Austin – on another strafing mission near Alor Star, but again he was forced to return early. Leigh Bowes took over command and led Austin to the target area where they successfully strafed M/T and troops without interference; both returned safely to Ipoh.

During the day three 21RAAF Squadron Buffaloes arrived at Ipoh from Butterworth, having been made airworthy by the hard-working groundcrews there. The pilots were all volunteers from 62 Squadron – Sqn Ldr C.H. Boxall, Flt Lt N.D. Lancaster and Sgt S.H. Stafford – who had driven to Butterworth from Taiping to collect the machines, even though none of the three had flown this type of aircraft before. By the end of the day however, despite the efforts of the groundcrews, no Buffaloes were fully serviceable at Ipoh, leading 453's diarist to comment:

> "Now we were in a sorry state. Six serviceable pilots and not one fully serviceable aircraft. Our guns were particularly troublesome, and there seemed to be no one at Ipoh capable of keeping them in order. In addition, we were all very tired as the six of us had stayed on readiness from dawn to dusk. No arrangements were made for supplying us with food or drink, our only meal in the day being the one at night at the pub. Someone definitely slipped up in the organising here – who?"

Patrols of Japanese fighters and light bombers continued to harass retreating British troops; two of the latter caught a group of soldiers from the 6th Indian Infantry Brigade, although one attacker was apparently brought down by ground fire. Witnesses recalled seeing a Gurkha, armed with a Bren-gun, defiantly standing his ground as an aircraft approached at treetop height, the crew of which were seen to toss hand grenades at the men below. Suddenly the plane disintegrated and burning petrol and debris showered over the sheltering troops; the brave Gurkha was amongst the casualties and later died of his burns.

Back at Singapore, Sqn Ldr Allshorn was still struggling to get the replacement Buffaloes ready for operations. During the day all six aircraft were flown over to Sembawang, where the guns had to be re-harmonised and work on brakes had to be carried out because the staff at Seletar were not available. The aircraft were finally deemed ready that evening and were prepared for an early departure on 15 December, as recalled by Allshorn:

> "I rang Grp Capt Rice that evening and told him that I had advice that weather would prevent me departing the next morning. He informed me that I was to leave *no matter what the weather was like* [authors' emphasis]. This I did, at 0600 hours. After taking

off, with Flt Lt Kinninmont as my No.2, the six aircraft left the circuit area at about 700 feet under low cloud and rain for Ipoh via Port Swettenham. Whilst forming up I called the other aircraft, but could not ascertain whether they were receiving me because my receiver had gone unserviceable. At approximately 25 miles out, having flown through rain and cloud for short periods, I lost four other aircraft. After flying around at low height for about half an hour to endeavour to pick them up, still failing contact, I decided to proceed myself with Kinninmont in company.

"The weather depreciated badly until Kinninmont and I were flying at approximately 15 feet along the beach. I decided that it was unsafe to proceed further than Port Swettenham, flew up the river, made an approach and landed on the short bitumen strip. I made a precautionary approach and managed to stop my landing run without over-running the strip. Kinninmont on the other hand made three attempts to land. On his fourth attempt he overran the strip and turned his aircraft [AN172] on its back. The local Volunteer Army Company gave us assistance and I decided to proceed by car to Ipoh and leave my aircraft for Kinninmont to return when the weather cleared. I arrived at Ipoh that evening and Kinninmont fortunately arrived just before dark."

Of the four pilots who had elected to return individually to Singapore, all returned safely apart from Flg Off Hooper who crash-landed his aircraft in a paddy field but escaped with only cuts and bruises.

By daylight on the 15th, three Buffaloes had been made available at Ipoh for operations, and the detachment was advised that more were on their way from Singapore. The whole burden of maintenance was thrown upon 21RAAF Squadron, which had neither men nor facilities to cope with the work. Furthermore, the problems with the Buffaloes' guns had not been resolved. This was again highlighted when a raid by 19 Ki-48s of the 90th Sentai was intercepted by Flt Lt Vanderfield (TD-D) with Sgts Greg Board and Matt O'Mara; three of the bombers were attacked but none of Vanderfield's guns would operate, whilst both Board and O'Mara experienced stoppages to two of their guns. Despite this they were able to claim one bomber shot down between them, as recalled by Board:

"I held the dive until a bomber appeared in my gunsight . . . I squeezed the trigger . . . the raider erupted in crimson flame and almost immediately afterward broke into large flaming chunks that tumbled earthward." [60]

Fighters then appeared and one pursued Board's aircraft:

"Fortunately, there were enough loose clouds around for us to hide in, because if you mixed in a dogfight with a Zero, the outcome was very clear. Very quickly you were a dead man." [61]

Bofors gunners of the 14th LAA Battery also claimed two bombers shot down. The 90th Sentai admitted the loss of one Ki-48, though the unit put this down to bad weather; gunners aboard the bombers mistakenly believed that one of the attacking Buffaloes had been shot down. Of the raid, the diarist wrote:

" . . . three Mitsubishis attacked the aerodrome. These were at once attacked by our three pilots . . . one bomber was brought down, but had the guns been working there is no doubt that the Japanese press, in describing the attack, would have had to report 'None of our aircraft returned'. The Japs dropped one stick of bombs and scored a lucky hit on a petrol dump. Bombs were also dropped on the town but little damage was done."

Later in the day, once the weather had settled and cleared, the three pilots who had safely returned to Sembawang set out once again as part of a formation of ten Buffaloes, led by Sqn Ldr Harper (W8160), 453 Squadron's CO (who had just returned from Australia); on this occasion all ten aircraft[62] reached Ipoh safely. On greeting the new arrivals, Sqn Ldr Allshorn recalled:

"Sqn Ldr Harper informed me that he had brought his squadron up to stop the rot."

453 Squadron's diarist wrote:

"Late in the day reinforcements arrived at Ipoh, and all the lads were relieved, and considerably cheered up to see the Shadow once more leading the Squadron. On arrival of Shadow things brightened up considerably at Ipoh; he was given control of both squadrons and instructed to prepare an operational centre and ground wireless station. Also he arranged a standing patrol of four aircraft over the aerodrome during all daylight hours, with eight aircraft standing by on the ground. Before Shadow's arrival, transport facilities for 453 pilots were nil and Van's feet were worn down about three inches in his walks backwards and forwards between HQ and the tarmac. Main transport for going to town each night was left to Blondie, who always appeared to have either a truck or car tucked away somewhere. Several three-ton transports and various cars appeared on the station after Shadow's visit to town, and solved transport problems."

Harper was not impressed by what he found on arrival at Ipoh:

"I found that the morale of both squadrons had dropped. Both units had suffered some losses and Flt Lt Vigors, who had come from Kallang to command No. 453 in my absence, had been shot down in flames on his first sortie. Several matters required immediate attention, but the most serious was the considerable losses we were suffering from our irreplaceable aircraft that were being destroyed on the ground, and I decided that if we were to be able to operate at all at the end of another seven days, we must stop this heavy drain on our numbers.

"The landing ground position was disastrous for fighter operations. There was only one landing ground and that was at Ipoh, the surrounding country was jungle, rubber, or mountainous, and we had no facilities for airfield strip construction. Ipoh airfield consisted of a usable strip with another at right angles to it at the north end, but which was too small for any but the latest types of aircraft. A narrow macadam taxi track led off from the usable strip and off this track lay the dispersal pens. However, there were no pens and no other possible means of dispersing the aircraft on the strip itself owing to the Japanese ground strafing tactics. Our only alternative was to have the aircraft either in the air or along the taxi track in their dispersal pens, as we had no warning system.

"The taxi track to the dispersal pens was exceedingly narrow and it was inviting disaster to taxi without a man at each wing tip, furthermore the track was dangerously undulating. There were no means of passing the aircraft which had become bogged through a wheel running off the track; it was necessary for all pilots to exercise extreme care, as many of the pens were a remarkably long way distant at the end of this winding track. It was nearly impossible to get a flight or squadron onto the strip for take-off in less than 20 minutes, by which time it would have been too late to intercept any enemy aircraft."

There was no warning system at Ipoh:

"The airfield was located in a valley and if no air cover was in the air while the aircraft prepared for take-off, Japanese fighters or bombers, signalled by spies located in the nearby hills, would attack our aircraft when they were on the ground or taking off. Furthermore almost invariably when our aircraft were landing, Japanese aircraft attacked if no top cover was available; in any case they usually attacked the top cover when it attempted to land.

"This problem was discussed with the Officer Commanding NORGROUP and I proposed that the only solution to operating from Ipoh lay in some form of warning system. This was agreed and I was instructed to prepare a fighter ops system. A crude observer system was available which, theoretically, gave us reasonable cover. However, there were practically no signal specialists available to us, and very little equipment. We had to rely on asking assistance from the local AA unit for our telephone equipment. The telephones, which literally must have been some of the first that were ever made, were totally unreliable. The observer system which I had to use had been organised by fighter ops Kallang, and under it we were unable to get reports on approaching enemy aircraft direct from the observer posts, but got them through the railway station master at Kuala Lumpur. Owing to the delays attendant on this system, we usually got our warnings that the Japanese were 40 miles away, just as the raid was on. I had with me in the Ops Room the colonel commanding the local AA unit and we occasionally got helpful information from him on approaching enemy raiders. Considerable delays were experienced however, through the telephone lines, which ran through the jungle, being cut by either Fifth Columnists of whom there were plenty, or by bombing."

In an effort to take some of the workload off his shoulders, Harper endeavoured to seek help from his officers, but without success:

"As soon as the operations system was completed, I tried to instruct the four Flight Commanders so that they could take a turn at controlling in order to relieve me, but they had no knowledge of controlling units and they needed supervision if we were to intercept any raiders. Unfortunately, the day after the completion of the ops system, the Army lost ground and we our observer posts.

"During the two days that were necessary to construct the fighter control system, including the provision of a suitable ground station, as there were none up to that time, I arranged for a constant cover of four aircraft from each of the two squadrons throughout daylight. This was expensive as we anticipated, on engine hours, but as we were not attacked once during that period it gave us two days' valuable respite in which to reorganise and repair the aircraft.

"The need for re-organisation was considerable. The aircraft of the two squadrons were being serviced by the groundcrews of only 21RAAF Squadron. This unit's groundcrew strength was totally inadequate for one squadron, let alone two, and the vast majority of guns in the aircraft would not fire, because of the rust which the troops had not had time to clean off. I had signalled to Singapore for armourers from my own Squadron as soon as I had reached Ipoh; these men had arrived before we retreated from the airfield and had improved the guns considerably before we left. Inspections were also not being done and the aircraft were rapidly becoming unreliable. The ex-civil airline engines on the Buffaloes were quite unsuited to the treatment they were getting in combat and on the ground, and many developed a serious loss of power.

"The re-organisation of the Station was also a serious and pressing problem. There was no appointed Station Commander. Food was an urgent need – the men were going without food and so were the pilots. There was no suitable accommodation and, as the men and pilots were sleeping without mosquito nets under any available covering, I feared malaria. I therefore requisitioned accommodation in a hotel at Ipoh and sent out the cooks with money to buy food. I also tried to introduce certainty and reliability into the organisation so that morale should be improved.

"Transport was lacking at first and caused grave difficulties. Spare parts for aircraft were usually obtained by the cannibal system, but oxygen was not available. Neither 21RAAF Squadron nor 453 Squadron were equipped with either men or equipment for the rôle they were given, and while expected to be self supporting they had neither trained cooks, M/T, nor sufficient specialist staff or equipment to do their duty as they would have liked to do it. Furthermore, nearly all-native labour on which we had to rely, had disappeared when the war became 'dangerous'. I believe, from hearsay, that these circumstances were foreseen by the RAAF Headquarters at Sembawang sometime before the war started."

Due to the recent losses of Buffaloes, further offensive sorties were now cancelled by Air HQ and the units were ordered to restrict operations to airfield defence and tactical reconnaissance flights on behalf of III Corps. JAAF aircraft meantime continued to make attacks on the aircraft abandoned on the northern airfields, 20 Ki-43s of the 59th Sentai strafing Butterworth, where they claimed seven Blenheims destroyed. Bad weather caused two of these fighters to force-land, along with three of four Ki-51s of the 27th Sentai, that had been supporting ground forces around Sungei Patani. The JNAF now returned to the attack, raiding targets in eastern Malaya, 25 G3Ms of the Genzan Ku from Indo-China bombing Kuala Trengganu.

More Army support aircraft – three chutais of Ki-51s and Ki-36s of the 83rd Independent Hikotai – moved from Singora to Alor Star to co-operate with the 5th Division's advance. When Japanese units initially arrived at Alor Star they found the airfield hardly damaged: the bomb dump was piled high and 1,000 drums of high-octane aviation fuel were found in the surrounding rubber trees. By noon the first Japanese fighters had landed and by the evening a sentai of light bombers had joined them; within hours sorties were being carried out against retreating British troops, using abandoned bombs and fuel [63].

At Ipoh, standing patrols were maintained throughout daylight on 16 December to provide warning and defence against further air attacks, although no Japanese aircraft were sighted. Wasteful in engine hours and tiring for pilots, the standing patrols were nonetheless necessary to prevent further surprise attacks of the kind that had so devastated the RAF in the early stages of the Japanese assault. On the ground, the hard-pressed maintenance staff of 21RAAF Squadron, augmented by 81 Repair and Salvage Unit, strived to get damaged aircraft operational, or at least sufficiently serviceable to enable their return to Singapore for repair at the better-equipped workshops of 151 Maintenance Unit. Japanese air attacks began to intensify on the 17th. A standing patrol of three Buffaloes was in the air during the morning when three Ki-43s from the 59th Sentai swept in to strafe the airfield. The Australians dived to intercept, and a dogfight began in which the Buffaloes were well outfought:

"While Barrel, Alf and Wild Bill Collyer were in the air three Navy 0s appeared and commenced to strafe our aircraft on the ground. They were immediately engaged by our boys, and a willing dogfight ensued. Wild Bill blazed a trail right across the drome for about two miles with a Zero right on his tail – managed to escape by getting in among the hills, and his aircraft somehow escaped damage. Both the other machines returned safely, both bearing scars of battle."

Both Sgts Clare (possibly flying AN180) and Summerton claimed to have scored hits on their opponents, while the Japanese trio reported fighting six Buffaloes and claimed two shot down, also claiming to have strafed seven bombers. Sgt Collyer recalled:

> "I was doing everything to get to cloud base when three Japs came out of the cloud right above me. My aircraft stalled before I could get amongst them. I dived at full power with one of them right on my tail. He did not open fire. I managed to lose him, and climbed back up to cloud base. I did see another Buffalo cloud-dodging. I was sure there was something different about him. I tried to find him but failed. I also failed to make contact with the Japs. They must have gone home. This was all in full view of the airstrip so I fell in for a bit of ragging of course. There was an itinerant RAF Wingco who suggested that the Jap who was on my hammer down to ground level should go home and offer a very blunt instrument to his armourer to do the hari kari bit. Very droll chaps the Brits."

Somewhat later eight Buffaloes were scrambled, giving chase to ten fighters that flew away; Sgt Scrimgeour managed to close on one but a sudden oil leak completely covered his windscreen, obscuring his vision.

> "Later in the day we had eight in the air including one 21RAAF Squadron pilot. These were decoyed away from the drome by enemy fighters who did not make any attempt to mix it. Meanwhile, five enemy bombers came over and made a leisurely attack on the aerodrome from only 1,500 feet."

A number of buildings were destroyed as a result of this latest raid, as were two grounded Buffaloes, a third being damaged. Two more raids were made on Ipoh on the 18th, the bombers waiting until the patrolling Buffaloes had just landed before attacking:

> "Blondie piled up in a hurried attempt to take off but was not hurt. Wild Bill Collyer ripped out a panel from his fuselage [W8211] when he landed on an obstruction sign. Due to the probable presence of 'Schmitt der Spy'[64] in and around Ipoh, the Squadron was put to a great deal of inconvenience and many opportunities to add to our score were lost. The bombers always waited until our patrols were landing before attacking; it happened time after time. The bloke who was passing out the information regarding our patrols would have had a very thin time if any of the boys had caught him. For instead of being up in the air spraying lead at the bombers they were always forced to go to ground, which is no place for a fighter pilot when bombers are around."

Sgt Greg Board had in fact had a lucky escape. In the mad scramble to get airborne, he realised that he was on a collision course with the other two Buffaloes. Unable to swerve away, he cut the engine and pulled up the undercarriage, whereupon the aircraft (W8216) careered into a tree and broke in half – "I shook my head in disbelief, noticed that my feet were in a creek and that there wasn't any aeroplane in front of me."

Bombs had just started to fall when one of the ground personnel, Wt Off Ballintine, arrived and half-dragged the dazed pilot into a nearby slit trench. Around midday, a MVAF Dragon Rapide approached Ipoh, carrying spare parts and ammunition, but it was at once attacked by two Buffaloes by mistake, as the diary noted with misplaced glee:

> "The one bright spot of the day was the shooting up of a Rapide by two of our pilots. This bloke apparently did not know that bombers were in the vicinity so no doubt he was surprised to hear the rattle of point fives from the nether regions of his aircraft. Fortunately he wasn't shot down."

Despite the damage to his aircraft, he was able to go in and make an emergency landing. The 59th Sentai Ki-43s and 90th Sentai Ki-48s then attacked, the fighters strafing and claiming one taxiing aircraft burnt, while the bombers claimed one large and two small aircraft in flames, plus three others damaged. Two more Buffaloes were destroyed and three damaged during the attack, while the Dragon Rapide received a direct hit. The pilot and one of the unloaders were killed and the aircraft's 'gunner' fatally wounded. Several others, who were helping to unload its cargo, were wounded. Also killed in this raid, when a bomb exploded beside his car as it approached the Rapide was Flt Lt F.W. Hordern, 21RAAF Squadron's Equipment Officer.

By dint of all-night working, six previously unserviceable Buffaloes had been made flyable by the morning of 19 December and these were flown down to Singapore:

"By working all night, six crocks were made sufficiently serviceable to be flown back to Sembawang. These left early and were brought down by Matt, Van, Mick, Wild Bill, Keith and Summerton. Nine serviceable aircraft were left at Ipoh and five of our pilots."

An operationally unserviceable Buffalo of 21RAAF Squadron was also flown to Sembawang, with Flg Off Barrie Hood at the controls. En route, he encountered heavy cloud – without the benefit of a functional artificial horizon instrument – and soon found himself upside down and heading for the ground. Fortunately, through a break in the cloud, he realised his predicament and was able to regain control and reached Singapore without further incident. Meanwhile, at Ipoh, there occurred another raid, as noted in 453 Squadron's diary:

"In the morning an alert was sounded and all took off to intercept but after patrolling for nearly an hour they came in. Just as the last one, with Scrimmy aboard, had touched down, bombs began to fall. Two of 21RAAF's aircraft were put out of commission, but little other damage was done. Later the Japs appeared again and did some more bombing, 'Shirley' [W8231/TD-G] suffering the indignity of getting a bullet in her nose."

Of the two Buffaloes written off in this latest raid, Flt Lt Bob Kirkman's aircraft had swerved into a deep drain and was wrecked; the other was caught by the blast of an exploding bomb and flung on its side, with one wing ripped off. There were, however, no casualties. Clearly, Ipoh was no longer tenable, so these aircraft were ordered to Kuala Lumpur, where 453 Squadron was to be brought up to strength.

Sqn Ldr Harper's subsequent report continued (it should be noted that dates in this report are not necessarily correct):

"On the 20th [sic – probably the evening of the 18th], the day on which our observer system fell to the Japanese advance troops, we received instructions to retreat to Kuala Lumpur at first light the following morning. Transport was borrowed but considerable difficulty was experienced through the night in preparing for the move, as we even lacked torches and the airfield was completely backed-out through lack of any form of lighting. Fortunately, a Crash and Repair unit (also retreating, I believe) reached us that evening and they were able to assist considerably with breaking up crashed aircraft and removing all valuable and transportable parts including engines."

It was a hurried departure, as recalled by Sgt Board:

"The men couldn't even bury their dead, there were too many of them. They packed the living and the wounded into trucks, buried bombs in the runway, and as soon as we got into the air, they set off the bombs and tore up the airstrip. Then drove for their lives to Kuala Lumpur, where we all began the bloody struggle over again." [65]

Harper continued:

"On the 21st morning [sic – 453 Squadron retreated to Kuala Lumpur on the evening of the 19th], I flew with the pilots of 453 Squadron to Kuala Lumpur; it had been arranged for 21RAAF Squadron pilots and groundcrew to return to Sembawang to reorganise and for me to have my own groundcrews from Singapore. Kuala Lumpur airfield was a single strip, which was being partly reconstructed. There were no dispersals and we had the aircraft spread out around the strip and covered with branches from trees. The groundcrews with tankers did not arrive until later that day, and no operations were carried out. An Operations Room and warning system were again in the course of being formed, but were not ready in time to control us successfully by the time we left for Singapore.

"It did seem at first that there was every chance of our being able to get down to some regular operations from Kuala Lumpur. The Japanese ground troops were about 100 miles away and I anticipated that we had ten clear days at least in which to operate. Our first task was to get the aircraft fully serviceable and to utilise our troops so that the Squadron was on a working basis with facilities for food and accommodation. The Group Ops organisation had been placed in the hands of an experienced officer, Wg Cdr Darley [back from his travels to Burma and elsewhere], and we were fortunately comparatively free of duties in connection with its functioning."

The new base was the peacetime home of the local flying club, and efforts were still being made to transform it into an operational airfield. Light aircraft of C Flight of the MVAF were currently based there. Sungei Patani, Butterworth and Taiping had by now been evacuated by the RAF, stores and men proceeding by road to Kuala Lumpur. Before they departed, airmen were ordered to salvage fuel and ammunition from abandoned Buffaloes, which was then loaded onto trucks heading south. With Japanese forces rapidly closing on Taiping, putting Kuala Lumpur at risk, 153 Maintenance Unit was hurriedly evacuated from the latter base, and moved to the safety of Java.

Kuala Lumpur was to be no refuge for the retreating forces, however, for the Japanese were already putting Sungei Patani into use as a forward refuelling field, from where attacks on Kuala Lumpur could be made. Despite a certain amount of stores and supplies having been successfully evacuated from vacated airfields by the retreating British forces, when Japanese troops arrived to occupy Sungei Patani and Taiping (which was the satellite airstrip for Ipoh), vast quantities of ammunition, fuel, equipment and provisions were found, as had been the case at Alor Star; so much so, that such finds were called 'Churchill aerodromes' by the grateful Japanese! Indeed, when the 27th and 59th Sentais, with the Headquarters of the 3rd Flying Battalion, began moving to Sungei Patani, 1,500 drums of aviation fuel were discovered undamaged. Events were moving fast.

Three repaired Buffaloes arrived at Kuala Lumpur from Sembawang at lunchtime on the 20th, followed by a further three aircraft that evening, just in time to help repel the renewed Japanese onslaught, which began in earnest the next day. The first standing patrol on the morning of the 21st had just landed at Kuala Lumpur when a raid was made by 14 Ki-51 and Ki-48 bombers of the 27th and 90th Sentais, and a dozen escorting Ki-43s of the 59th Sentai. Little damage was inflicted on the airfield, as noted by 453 Squadron's diarist:

"As usual, shortly after the patrol had landed, over came the bombers and laid their eggs. These went astray, the only serious damage being to our nice green lawn in front of the clubhouse. Also all the windows in said clubhouse were shattered, and it took a good stiff whisky to bring our barman back to reality again. One bomb landed on top of a bank behind the clubhouse. This would have been quite all right if it had not been for the fact that Sinbad had taken refuge at the foot of the bank. Result was that about three tons of red clay came rolling down on his venerable head, completely burying him. He quickly burrowed his way out, and emerged dirty and dishevelled, uttering horrible curses at the bloody sons of Nippon who had dealt him such a dastardly blow!"

Sgts Mac Read and Bill Collyer, on readiness duty, also had narrow escapes from death or injury, as the latter recalled:

"We jumped out of the aircraft and into the nearest slit trench. One bomb landed about five feet away from the lip of the trench. It did not do any damage, even though the aircraft were only a few feet away. The ground was very soft. The bomb made a hole about three feet deep, so I suppose all the blast was directed upwards. It made me a great supporter of slit trenches."

Although negligible damage had occurred at the airfield during this raid, a converted coaster was sunk just off the coast, with the loss of 44 of her 50-strong crew. Two Buffaloes of the airfield patrol were already in the air when the next raid came in, and these at once attacked, Sgt Ross Leys (W8206) taking on the fighter escort, while Sgt Eric Peterson went after the bombers. Leys wrote:

"We had been scrambled over Kuala Lumpur without much warning. I flew over Port Swettenham, finished our patrol, returned to the strip and had just landed when there was another sudden scramble. My good friend Eric Peterson was first off. Then I followed. I climbed to about 800 feet and ran into what I believe were three Japanese Stukas [sic]. I am sure they were Stukas. I could see the big red roundels of the Rising Sun on their wings. I didn't realise that they were as big as they were and they frightened the hell out of me. Peterson, who was now ahead of me, turned into them to make an attack. They were low down and he was above and slightly ahead of them in a good position to attack. I continued on southwards to gain height because I was expecting more Japanese aircraft to appear at any moment.

"I climbed to 4,000 feet and turned looking for the Stukas and saw a formation of Japanese fighters below me. I realised that they were Navy 0 fighters. Most pilots would have made a run for it, but before I fully realised where I was I found myself right in the middle of them. I remembered that a well-known World War I fighter tactic was that if you found yourself within a circle of attacking fighters you flew inside and in the opposite direction to it. I did this. They broke up their circle and made individual attacks on me. I could see them coming at me from every direction.

"I felt my Buffalo shudder under the impact of the Japanese cannon fire. I tried to fire my guns but before I could return their fire, a Japanese fighter turned inside of me and poured a burst of machine-gun fire into my engine. He must have also hit the hydraulics because there was an awful smell of hydraulic oil. There was fire and smoke in the cockpit. I decided the best action then was to bale out. I undid my safety harness, pulled out my oxygen tube. I pulled the nose of the Buffalo up until the aircraft was on its side and tried to fall out, but I was kept inside of the cockpit by my pistol holster, which had caught on the canopy. This later came loose and suddenly I was falling out of the aeroplane from 4,000 feet. There seemed to be Zeros coming at me from every direction.

"For a moment I thought that the parachute had become caught in the tail of the aircraft, but I eventually worked myself free and looked up and saw the parachute billowing. I saw a Zero flying in my direction and as the Japanese fighter came close to me, I could see puffs of smoke coming out of his machine-guns. I thought to myself that this was it. He made three or four attacks at me. I realised that the Japanese fighters were in earnest. One Zero flew so close I could actually see the pilot looking down at me. They were making the parachute rock with their slipstream. The Japanese fighters were firing at me from all directions. I attempted to escape the bursts of machine-gun fire by trying to make the parachute shift in all directions. I even tried to crawl up the yards of the parachute towards the top of it and for most of the time during the descent, I was hanging on to the parachute by my hands rather than by my harness." [66]

The pilots of the 59th Sentai optimistically claimed four Buffaloes shot down, one being credited to Sgt Hiroshi Onozaki of the 1st Chutai; all the claiming pilots had apparently attacked the aircraft flown by the unfortunate Leys. The diarist commented:

"Eric clean bowled one bomber and also got two probables. Good work boys! At night we were billeted at the palatial mansion of one who, tis said, amassed his fortune by devious and none too honest ways. However the lads all enjoyed sleeping in the huge double beds and partaking of the quite substantial stock of liquor."

Before dusk set in, three more replacement Buffaloes arrived from Singapore.

Air battle over Kuala Lumpur

During the morning of 22 December came the biggest air battle over Malaya yet, and the first in which the Ki-43s of the 64th Sentai were to play a major role. Following early morning standing patrols, the whole of the reinforced 453 Squadron was ordered off from Kuala Lumpur at 1000, a dozen Buffaloes taking to the air, led by Flt Lt Vanderfield (AN210/TD-J). They had reached 7,000 feet when fighters were seen and engaged. No sooner had action been joined, than a dozen more appeared, together with others identified as Type 97 fighters (Ki-27s) and 'Messerschmitt 109s'. Other Japanese aircraft including Ki-48s and Ki-51s were also reported to have become involved in the big battle, which lasted for over 30 minutes, before the intruders withdrew – probably due to fuel shortage. 453 Squadron's diary provides a graphic account of the Buffaloes' last stand in Malaya:

"Back on the job at dawn and maintaining readiness on all serviceable aircraft. B Flight went up for a patrol but saw nothing of the enemy. Shortly after, the whole Squadron was ordered to take off. The first formation of ten climbed up to 7,000 feet and there encountered Navy Zeros. A dogfight quickly developed and lead began to fly everywhere. The situation was in hand when about a dozen more Japs appeared on the scene. Some of these were Zeros and some ME109s. Things began to get very wild and woolly and our forces were disorganised. More Japs appeared and some kept top cover while some joined in the fight. The battle lasted for over half an hour and the enemy finally cleared out.

On landing it was found that Mac, Scrimmy, Blondie and Wild Bill Collyer were missing. Bob Drury had crashed on landing his aircraft [AN204] having been very badly shot about. His crash was a bad one and he had been wounded in the fight. He was taken to hospital in a very serious condition. Tom Livesey who had wiped off his undercarriage on an ack-ack post when taking off, came in and made a successful crash landing [in AN184]. He had been wounded in the leg by shrapnel. Griff brought

'Shirley' [W8231] in with more holes in her than a sieve. All the others returned safely and unhurt. It was reported that a large force of bombers which had been following the fighters had turned back."

Despite heavy damage to his aircraft and slight wounds to his head and right hand, Sgt Harry Griffiths was able to land safely with two victories to his credit:

"About mid morning our flight was scrambled, altitude being of primary importance. I was at 8,000 feet when Sgt Alf Clare formated on my starboard side and Sgt Greg Board on my port. I heard Doug Vanderfield saying 'Form up on me', but he was probably no more than 1,500 feet. It was then that I observed approximately 20 enemy aircraft coming down sun. I called up base saying that I was about to engage about 20 enemy fighters, the reply was unmistakably the voice of Harper, who said, 'Well good luck, when you have finished with that 20 there is a further 20 above them and still more above them.' Alf Clare had a big grin and gave me the thumb up, Greg Board for some reason pulled away going into a steep dive and I did not see him again that day.

"Then it was on. Aircraft were milling everywhere, everyone seemed to be getting mixed up then to my surprise an enemy aircraft appeared straight in front of me. I gave him a good burst and saw pieces break away and the aircraft starting to burn. He then went into a flatish spin. I then saw one of our aircraft, which I identified as Sgt O'Mara's, about 500 feet lower and being pursued by one of the enemy, who was firing at him from behind. I was in a perfect position but had to aim at O'Mara'a tail to allow for deflection. I pressed the button. As my bullets hit I saw a flash of flame. The aircraft spiralled upwards, rolling onto its back then dived towards the ground with smoke trailing (that evening Matt complained bitterly that one of our own aircraft had fired at him). It was then I was hit. A cannon shell hit my port mainplane, puncturing a full 90-gallon fuel tank. The fuel syphoned out, soaking me and the aircraft. Why we didn't burst into flames, I will never know. Two aircraft continued firing at me until they both ran out of ammunition. One of them formated on me very close, the pilot grinning and gesticulating with his hand at something. He was so close I fired two or three rounds at him from my revolver before he slipped away a short distance, then completed a perfect barrel-roll around me, finishing the roll-back in perfect formation, it being the first barrel-roll I had ever seen. There was little I could do so went around a hill hoping he would follow me across to the aerodrome, where the Bofors gun opened up – and when I looked behind he was nowhere to be seen, having broken off before reaching the field. The damn fool Indian gunners were firing at me.

"S/Ldr Harper was soon on the scene and told me not to take my helmet off until the doctor saw me, I asked him why, he said there was blood coming from beneath it. It was then that I observed one of our aircraft blazing fiercely and flying away from Sungei Besi. How I knew it was Sgt George Scrimgeour, I don't know, but I found myself yelling into the mike to him to bale out. Finally, at last I saw a tiny black dot and then the brolly open, but still two aircraft repeatedly dived at him, firing their guns. However, he was not hit and I believe they may have been firing at his parachute. Apparently my groundcrew were counting the number of hits my aircraft had received by putting a chalk mark around each entry. I was told they counted over seventy when Harper stopped them, telling them to stop wasting time and to get on with their work. They handed me an armour-piercing bullet, which had failed to penetrate the piece of armour plate behind my head and had fallen down behind my seat. They said, 'Keep it in your pocket, it's your lucky charm.'

"Harper started telling me what I should have done. I thought with his experience he should have been showing us. As I walked back up the field I saw one of our aircraft approaching too low. Unfortunately he clipped the top of an embankment and crashed, the engine breaking loose. There was no ambulance in sight so I jumped on the running board of a truck and went up to the Aid Post but there was not a soul to be seen. I then went out the back of the building and observed a Pilot Officer doctor, with the entire staff, huddled in a hole in a clay bank. I said 'What the hell are you doing in there, there are men dying on the strip who need you.' Nobody moved, so I said, 'Come out before I blast you out'. The doctor was the first to move, and as he did, he said, 'Alright, my man, I will have you up on a court martial over this.' I was so wild, I said that I would look forward to it (but heard no more about it). Just then they carried the pilot in. He was making a horrible gurgling sound and I recognised him as P/O Bob Drury. The doctor didn't examine him and just said take him to the hospital."

One of the many witnesses to the series of dogfights was 453 Squadron's Flt Sgt Warren Gillespie:

"We sat on the airfield and watched a fantastic dogfight that started at about 15,000 feet. The groundcrew were lying down on the airstrip firing their rifles at the Japanese fighters. There were aircraft, Australian and Japanese manoeuvring in all directions. Tom Livesey took off in a hurry to join the fight. Before he reached the end of the strip he knocked off his undercarriage on a sandbank surrounding a gun position that was at the end of the runway. Tom joined the fight with no undercarriage, except one piece of leg hanging down on one side at his aircraft. As he gained altitude, the dangling leg caused a thin vapour trail. As he pulled out of a turn to have a shot at a Jap fighter, the dangling undercarriage leg made his aircraft shudder." [67]

Of his plight, Plt Off Livesey added:

"My fighter, perhaps not delivering full power, had lost both wheels. Only the two stumps were left hanging down. Zeros seemed to be everywhere and the dogfight was mostly on the treetops, rarely above 1,000 feet. When the main battle broke up, I found that four of the enemy were giving me their undivided attention. This went on for what seemed like hours but in actual fact was probably about 20 minutes. It was twist and turn, constant violent manoeuvres, the smell of gunfire and hot oil. Eventually my pursuers gave up, either low on fuel or out of ammunition.

"Figuring I was south of base, I headed north and gained a little altitude. Later, when everything seemed okay, I had another look around. Blood on the cockpit floor! I'd been too busy to realise a hit in my leg. There had been the rattle and bump of machine-gun and cannon fire hitting my aircraft but surely not me, too! On arrival back at Kuala Lumpur, because there was no hydraulics or wheels, I switched everything off for a once-only approach. Lining up on the strip I heaved a sigh of relief and coasted in. Both friendly ack-ack guns opened up on me and kept it all the way in." [68]

Gillespie continued:

"I saw George Scrimgeour being machine-gunned by a Japanese fighter as he came down in his parachute. George had baled out at 10,000 feet, right over our aerodrome. You could see the Zero diving at him and shooting at him. We sent a truck out to pick him up when he landed. Bob Drury [one of the older pilots, he was 27-years-old and hailed from New South Wales] came in badly wounded. I waved at him because he was coming in too low. He hit the embankment at the end of the strip. The engine shot out of the front of the Buffalo." [69]

The main opponents of the Buffaloes were in fact 18 Ki-43s of the 64th Sentai, led by Maj Tateo Kato, which had taken off from Kota Bharu and approached Kuala Lumpur at between 7,000-10,000 feet. The Buffaloes were initially spotted by Lt Takeo Takayama's chutai, which immediately dived to attack; the other chutai followed and in all a total of 11 Buffaloes were claimed shot down, with another four as probably destroyed. Takayama himself was seen to account for three then, according to one of his pilots, the wings of his aircraft collapsed as he pulled out of a dive, and he was killed in the ensuing crash; however, when Indian soldiers later located the wreck, bullet holes were found in the tail section – an indication that Takayama's Ki-43 had, in fact, been hit during the combat and was also the probable victim of a collision which killed Sgt Mac Read, a 24-year-old from New South Wales. Lt Oizumi was also credited with a Buffalo shot down but the identities of the other claimants are unknown, although at least one was almost certainly claimed by Maj Kato, a seven-victory ace from the China conflict; others may have been credited to Lts Yohei Hinoki and Shogo Takeuchi, and to Sgts Yoshito Yasuda and Miyoshi Watanabe. Lt Hinoki, who was flying No.2 to Maj Kato, recalled:

" . . . Takayama formation flew at 7,000 feet, north of Kuala Lumpur airfield, at 1140 on the day. Kato formation was at 10,000 feet. [I] saw the Oscar of Lt Takayama was shaken by the sudden bursts of anti-aircraft fire. The wingmen, 2/Lt Aito Kikuchi and Sgt Major Choichi Okuyama, were thrown up by the intense burst. It seemed that [Takayama's aircraft] was hit and damaged by the AA fire. Then [we] spotted around 15 Buffaloes which were ascending. Lt Takayama and Sgt Major Okuyama attacked the right end Buffalo of the tail formation leader. They approached it from behind and above.

"Lt Oizumi's Oscars attacked left formation. The formation of Buffaloes were scattered. Capt [Katsumi] Anma caught a Buffalo but he could not fire at it due to mechanical fault. His wingman, Lt Takeshi Endo, fired at it. His machine-guns also stopped after five or six rounds. Then [I] saw another Oscar fire at the Buffalo, which spouted black smoke from the engine. Lt Takayama was chasing a Buffalo when Major Kato signalled to close the combat. Lt Takayama continued to chase it to very low altitude. Wingman Sgt Major Okuyama followed them and saw the Oscar of Lt Takayama was 'broken' when he tried to pull to avoid colliding with the Buffalo. Okuyama did not witness that Lt Takayama had collided with the Buffalo, or had been 'broken' by the heavy stress against the wing-root." [70]

Hinoki recalled that the aerial battle lasted about ten minutes, whereas 453 Squadron says 30 minutes, so it does seem likely that the bombers were encountered separately to the Ki-43s. Following the loss of Lt Takayama's aircraft, the 64th Sentai's other Ki-43s were all inspected on return to base, where six were discovered to have cracks in the wings. Maj Kato immediately requested aircraft engineers to fly out from Japan to strengthen the weak wing-root and service the unreliable machine-guns but, in the meantime, his pilots had to make allowances during combat manoeuvres.

Later in the day news was received regarding the fates and fortunes of the missing pilots, as noted in the Squadron diary:

"Scrimmy and Blondie turned up, both having baled out. Blondie was unscathed but Scrimmy had nasty burns on his arms and face. He was machine-gunned on the way down and his parachute had 16 holes in it. Incidentally, he still has his ripcord! Mac Read [AN175] rammed his opponent, crashed and was killed. Wild Bill Collyer limped back to Sembawang in a badly damaged aircraft and with shrapnel wounds in his foot. He landed safely and was taken to hospital. So the day closed and a rather sad and sorry bunch of pilots went back to the mansion at night. As far as can be estimated, our score was three confirmed, the scorers being Alf, Mac Read and Griff. In addition there are a few probables as all pilots got in many good squirts. We are hoping that many more failed to return to their bases. The full story of the dogfight cannot be told in narrative form as it is too difficult to co-ordinate all the individual stories. But many of the lads were saved by having their opponent shot off their tail. Alf shot a ME109 [*sic*] off Tozzler's tail, thus saving his bacon."

Of his part in the action, Sgt Collyer (AN189) later reported:

"I saw a Zero attacking one of the Buffaloes about 500 feet below. The pilot of the Buffalo could not get his wheels up. The Zero had made a couple of attacks and was pulling up after each one into a stall turn. Just as I made my attack on the Zero, another Zero attacked me and many of the bullets from the second Zero hit the aircraft I was attacking. I would say that between the two of us we got him. Quite a few bullets hit my aircraft, including one which flew just past my ear and hit the priming pump and went on down into my right foot. I pulled up hard to the left and found myself doing a head-on attack on another aircraft. I just kept firing at his prop spinner until I broke off below him. I heard his engine as he passed over me. I think the bugger would have rammed me if I hadn't got out of his way. However, I don't think my .50s would have done his engine any good. He might have had a bad trip from then on.

"All this happened in the first few seconds. From then on there was a general mix up. I finished up within sight of the coast. My engine had been damaged, the aircraft had been badly shot up. It was not possible to make any kind of an assessment of what damage had been done. I thought the worst thing that could happen would be a wheels-up landing on the wide mud flats, which are exposed at low tide on that part of the coast. So I just kept flying south and eventually got to Sembawang. On the approach to land I discovered that the wing flap on the left side would not work, the right flap was only partly down and came up again, and on touch down one tyre was found to be punctured. A bit of a hairy landing."

An inspection of his Buffalo following its arrival at Sembawang revealed a bullet in the crankcase and more than 70 holes elsewhere in the aircraft. Collyer was admitted to the hospital at Sembawang and was later sent to No.1 Malaya Hospital to convalesce. Of his experience, Sgt Greg Board, who claimed a bomber shot down, later recalled:

"I shoved the stick forward, rammed the throttle to the firewall, and plunged in a screaming vertical dive, I held the dive until a bomber swelled in my gunsights, then squeezed the trigger. The twin-engined Mitsubishi broke into flaming chunks that tumbled earthwards.

"Spotting a Zero below, I half rolled . . . before I could set up the fighter for the kill, all hell broke loose behind me . . . the instrument panel exploded and blew apart . . . brilliant fire gushed from the fuel tanks . . . whoever was in that Zero was good, damn good, and he had a hell of a better aircraft under his hands. He chopped that Brewster to ribbons . . . I had nothing left but to try to get out by going straight down. I was pulling with all the power the aircraft had and I shoved the stick forward and tried to save my life by diving vertically." [71]

Board felt the heat as the Buffalo [W8170] burst into flames. The fuel tanks belched fire. It was time to bale out. He rolled the aircraft onto its back and did so. He delayed the temptation to open the canopy until he had dropped clear of the action:

"It was a lovely feeling and I enjoyed it thoroughly. It was suddenly quiet after the terrific noise of combat and the scream of the engine. There was absolute silence, except for a lovely wind blowing by me. It was a relief and as I fell towards the trees, I pulled the ripcord." [72]

He came down in the jungle east of Kuala Lumpur. After wandering about for some time he came upon a village, from where he was passed on to an Army patrol, and returned to the airfield later the same day. Sgt George Scrimgeour had a similar, albeit more painful, tale to tell:

"The Buffalo was an easy target from head on because of its large belly. I was involved in a head-on attack with a Zero. We were firing into each other and the Buffalo [W8160] caught on fire. The fire flamed back from the belly into the cockpit. My face and eyelashes were burned because I had lost my goggles during a very tight turn. My wrist and fingers were burned because I was not wearing flying gloves. I decided to bale out even though I was at a low altitude. I was not keen on taking to the parachute because I had seen Japanese fighters firing at Ross Leys the day before when he had baled out. On my way down a Japanese fighter made three passes at me. I counted 25 bullet holes in the canopy. He didn't hit me because I was able to change the direction of the parachute by pulling on the ripcord. But in doing this I pulled the skin off my fingers where I had been burned. In all of our fighter actions in the Malayan campaign the Japs were always above us. The only time I got near a Japanese fighter with a good chance of shooting him down was in a dogfight over Ipoh. But there was nothing that I could do because a glycol leak had completely covered my windscreen and I could see nothing." [73]

The action and grief for the Australians had yet to end; 453 Squadron's diary continues:

"Readiness was continued for the rest of the day with the remaining serviceable aircraft and pilots. At about 1530 the signal was given to take off and the aircraft commenced to taxi out, but before they could get to the end of the runway, out of the clouds dived four Zeros with all guns blazing. Following our lesson at Butterworth, all the pilots except Pete [a native of Sydney, Sgt Eric Peterson was 24-years-old] quickly got out of their aircraft and dived for the scrub. Pete can't have seen the Zeros as they came in from behind him. He got off the deck, but they were on him immediately and he spun in and crashed from about 700 feet. Pete was killed."

No other damage was done in this attack, which was believed to have been carried out by aircraft from the 59th Sentai. 453 Squadron was again down to only three serviceable aircraft.

Initially only three of the Squadron's claims were allowed, the successful pilots being assessed as the deceased Sgt Read (by ramming), Sgt Griffiths, who in fact claimed two 'Mitsubishi 97' fighters and Sgt Clare, who apparently claimed two dive-bombers (presumably Ki-51s) and a twin-engined aircraft, but only one dive-bomber was granted as a confirmed victory. Harry Griffiths recalled:

"Regarding the two aircraft I claimed, I am convinced there is no doubt. When Harper advised me that I was only credited with one and a half as the Bofors gunner had also claimed one I was claiming, I pointed out that both aircraft I claimed were well out of range of the Bofors gun. I also pointed out that as I flew across the field at under 1,000 feet they opened up at me. They did not hit me and only stopped firing after I had violently waggled my wings. Was it me they claimed as having shot down?"

In addition, probables were credited to Flt Lt Vanderfield (one Me109F-type and one

Type 97 fighter according to his logbook) and Sgts Gorringe, Scrimgeour and Collyer, while Sgt Board was apparently awarded a victory on his return. Clare later commented:

"Everybody was shooting at everything, and there was no time to see your enemy aircraft crash if you wanted to stay alive."

Flt Lt W.K. Wells, the Adjutant, wrote:

"The Squadron claimed three enemy aircraft confirmed, and a number damaged. Following on reports received in conjunction with Military Operations, Kuala Lumpur, we understand that at least five more enemy aircraft had been shot down in this dogfight. These have not been claimed by living pilots. However, all pilots had fired bursts at enemy aircraft during the action, but, being under such pressure, they were unable to watch the effects of their fire; consequently, if these further enemy aircraft that are reported to have been shot down, actually were shot down, their destruction will be to the credit of No.453 Squadron."

As for Japanese losses, one aircraft – presumably a dive-bomber or a Ki-27 – was seen to fall at 1037 and was found completely burned out near Bahit Sungei Besi; the pilot's body was recovered and identified as Major Numo; some personal effects were removed and were presented to Clare, including a photograph of the Japanese pilot's wife and child, and a German pistol[74]. Parts of the wreck were salvaged and sent to Singapore. A second wreck was found, with the pilot still alive, as recalled by Sgt Harry Blackham of the 5th Regiment RA:

". . . we levelled our guns at him. He appeared demented, and speaking fair but disjointed English entreated us to kill him. He grabbed the muzzle of one of the rifles and put it against his chest, saying, 'Shoot! Shoot!' He apparently wished to die for his Emperor, but Captain McEwan felt he was too valuable a prize to be given that pleasure and ordered us to take him to our truck. We found his automatic pistol was under his thigh, cocked and with the safety off. It seemed his desire to die for his Emperor was not so strong as we had thought." [75]

Apparently a Ki-48 crashed in a small village 10 miles south of Kuala Lumpur, as recalled by a ten-year-old boy who witnessed the incident. He related that the villagers were watching an air battle overhead when a twin-engined aircraft fell out of formation and dived into the village, narrowly missing the small school. Some villagers ran away as the aircraft crashed and others leapt into the nearby river. None were hurt although the crew was killed. A few months later Japanese troops arrived to take away the bodies, at the same time filling in the crater made by the aircraft. To his earlier account, Harry Griffiths added:

"Another strange occurrence was an enemy fighter that crash-landed not far from the aerodrome. The pilot got out and was running for cover when one of his own team machine-gunned him, killing him. They then strafed the aircraft, setting it on fire. I did not witness this action but have no reason to doubt it as a number of groundcrew assured me they had seen it happen."

Some of the Australian pilots decided to drown their sorrows that evening, while others celebrated their survival:

"Some of the lads went into Kuala Lumpur in search of amusement while the rest sat around a table and drank old Choong's grog. Gentle George, who incidentally has been a tower of strength to us all along the line, distinguished himself by polishing off three bottles of whisky without showing the slightest effect. The transport situation at Kuala Lumpur was rather well organised, the pilots possessing between them about ten cars of various sizes and ages. The flagship was the Shadow's Super S.S. while Blondie's Riley was probably the most disreputable of the lot even though it did make more noise than any of the others. Incidentally the navigation of our convoy leader left much to be desired. Otherwise how did we come to set out for the mansion – two miles from the drome – and after meandering round for about 20 miles end up at the 'Majestic Hotel'?"

Subsequently, observers and Army personnel on the ground reported that ten or eleven Japanese aircraft had been seen falling during the course of the battle; undoubtedly these were, in the main, damaged and shot down Buffaloes. Allegedly a number of wrecks were later located in the vicinity by Army patrols, which were reported as 'Army 97s' (Ki-27s), possibly an indication that they were the result of earlier crashes but this was highly unlikely, as this was only the second raid on the Kuala Lumpur area.

There was renewed tension arising between Sqn Ldr Harper and some of his officers, who considered that he should be leading them in the air rather than remaining on the ground. It was alleged that following Plt Off Livesey's crash-landing at Kuala Lumpur, Harper drove the injured pilot away from the airfield to be safe from the raids, instead of remaining on station to see to the needs of others. According to one source, Harper was approached by Flt Lt Grace just after Sgt Peterson was killed:

"What are you doing here? You know, the blokes are beginning to think you have got a yellow streak." [76]

Apparently, Harper did not respond, although he later explained away his lack of leadership in the air in different ways. He evidently told Sqn Ldr Allshorn that he would not fly the Buffalo because it was not good enough against the enemy. To others, he said that he was either too busy organising the operational control of the Squadron, or arranging accommodation and transport. In his subsequent report, although he did not mention specifically Grace's words, Harper did comment:

"I had a considerable disagreement with Flight Commanders, who considered we ought to return and operate from Singapore under a reasonable working fighter control system, rather than lose our aircraft in penny packets for little apparent result at Kuala Lumpur. My orders however, were to stay there and, in supporting my superiors, I made myself extremely unpopular with my Squadron. This was a very unenviable position for me to be in, and as these circumstances repeated themselves before the campaign was over, I do believe the troops felt I was in league against them."

Harper had made it clear on a number of occasions that he disliked the Australians for their lack of discipline; to his pilots it soon became apparent that he was temperamentally unsuited to command an operational Australian unit. Following this latest raid on Kuala Lumpur, Wg Cdr George Darley signalled Air HQ:

"Must have more aircraft. Have only four. Pilots are down in the mouth. Only have six or seven who are reliable. Others badly shaken. Japanese 0 Type fighters appear to be vastly superior to Buffaloes. Can't get any coolie labour and therefore cannot make dispersal points."

Despite their lack of experience and proper air combat training, the Australian pilots had performed relatively well. Flt Lt Wells later noted:

> "It has been confirmed that at least ten enemy aircraft have been shot down by members of this Squadron."

This figure related to the total claims for the Squadron while operating in Malaya, although the claims for this period would seem to have been slightly higher than ten accredited by Wells (see Appendix IV).

With the effective demise of 453 Squadron, Air HQ decided to disband NORGROUP and next day the survivors were ordered to return to Sembawang. The Australians buried their dead, seven pilots – Sqn Ldr Harper (AN215), Flt Lts Vanderfield (AN206) and Grace (W8156), Sgts Board (W8237), Clare (AN180), Summerton (W8163) and Austin AN210) – flying three serviceable and four unserviceable aircraft back to the island, while Sgt Harry Griffiths set off by car with the wounded, as he recalled:

> "The following morning Harper produced a beautiful little white Jaguar Swallow car with red leather upholstry and told me to take George Scrimgeour, Tom Livesey and Ross Leys to the hospital at Malacca, the car having been commandeered from a car showroom in the city. I must admit that I never thought we would get George to hospital. He looked ghastly sitting alongside Ross Leys in the rear seat, with fluid dripping from his nose, chin and both arms. I pulled into a small village hoping to find a doctor who could give him some pain relief but there was none, so we acquired a small bottle of brandy for him but I doubt if he touched it.
>
> "Finally arriving at the 2/10 AGH Malacca, they wanted to admit the four of us. As I felt responsible and planned to leave for Singapore in the morning, I allowed them to probe for small pieces of shrapnel, which they removed. I then booked into the Government Rest House. After a clean up I went for a look around Malacca and ran into Matt O'Mara, who had a small car full of parachutes and was looking for somewhere to stay the night, so we both finished up at the Government Rest House. In the morning, having fuelled up, I said goodbye to George, not expecting to see him again, collected Tom and Ross and started off for Singapore. When Harper arrived he claimed the car as his own but that was short-lived for it received a direct bomb hit. Someone handed me the steering wheel as my share, saying that was all that was left of it."

On arrival at Singapore, the two Australian Buffalo units were amalgamated under Harper's command – which obviously did not please many:

> "On my recommendation Flt Lt Kinninmont RAAF, ex-21RAAF Squadron, took over 453 Squadron from me. This enabled me to leave all the administration and to lead both squadrons of whom I was given tactical control."

Newly promoted Acting Sqn Ldr Fred Williams was given the reins of 21RAAF Squadron, while Sqn Ldr Allshorn was posted to the Operations Room at Sembawang, under somewhat of a black cloud. He was removed from his command "because of unsatisfactory leadership in association to air operations"; undoubtedly his confrontations with Grp Capt Brown (OC Seletar), Grp Capt Rice (OC 224 Group) and Wg Cdr Forbes (OC NORGROUP) was a major factor in his removal, although apparently he was not overly-popular with his pilots. But then, nor was Harper, and he retained his position. Harper also questioned the lack of cordiality between the Fighter Controller Grp Capt Rice and the Australians under his charge, adding that it affected his own control of the amalgamated Squadron:

> ". . . this was later a distinct fillip to inducing a lack of confidence with both Nos.

21RAAF and 453 Squadrons in the controlling of the air campaign. I believe the crux of this matter was between my Station Commander Grp Capt McCauley RAAF, and Grp Capt Rice RAF, and centred on, I believe, the question of whose Headquarters should have control of my two squadrons. Whatever the cause, however, this imposed a strain on me as CO of 453 Squadron."

Following the retreat from Malaya, Harper recommended the deceased Sgt Malcolm 'Mac' Read for a DFM for his involvement in the Squadron's initial engagement on 13 December, the citation he prepared stating:

"The above-mentioned pilot has destroyed two enemy aircraft and shared with another pilot the destruction of a third. Subsequent to a fight in which his aircraft was badly shot up, he re-armed and refuelled and carried out in the same machine a dangerous ground-strafing raid over enemy lines, in company with one other pilot. Damage was inflicted to men and transports. He completed this task, returned and carried out his normal duty of stand-by for the rest of the day."

Alas, the recommendation was apparently not approved since such an award could not be made posthumously.

The two remaining Moths and one Falcon of C Flight of the MVAF, which had been working with the Australians, were also ordered back to Singapore, where they were to be absorbed into A Flight; one of the biplanes had been damaged during a recent bombing attack, and was despatched to Singapore by rail. Station HQ staff also left Kuala Lumpur for Sembawang, where they would arrive on Christmas Day. It was at this stage decided that all units should be based on Singapore Island, using Kuala Lumpur and other remaining airfields only as advanced landing grounds.

With the shambles of the evacuation of Northern Malaya shockingly fresh in the mind and thoughts of all involved, there came a written rebuke from Air Chief Marshal Brooke-Popham (one of his last unpleasant tasks before being relieved) to Air Vice-Marshal Pulford regarding the general performance of the air units under his control:

"During the last fortnight it has been necessary to order the evacuation of several RAF aerodromes. It has come to my notice that in some cases the process has been badly carried out. This has been due largely to failure on the part of those responsible to organise in advance and set a proper example of leadership.

"There have been many cases of gallantry and devotion to duty on the part of individual officers and airmen, but there have also been instances where aerodromes appear to have been abandoned in a state approaching panic. Stores have been left behind, material that is urgently required has been abandoned and a general state of chaos has been evident.

"This is utterly opposed to all traditions of the Air Force over a period of 30 years. It is the duty of every commander, whatever may be his rank, to remember his first duty is towards the officers and men who are under his command; his second duty is to see that the aeroplanes or other material for which he is responsible is safeguarded, moved, or if no other course is possible, rendered useless to the enemy. After he is satisfied on all these points, then and only then is he at liberty to think of his own safety and comfort.

"In the majority of cases the bombing of aerodromes has been on a smaller scale than that suffered calmly by women and children in London and other towns in England, and aerodromes have usually been vacated whilst still well out of range of enemy land forces. Several of the moves back were carried out in a regular and orderly manner; there is no reason why they should not all have been.

"Let us hope that there will be no further need for withdrawal, but whether this be so or not, I look to everyone to play his part, not only in ensuring that there is no ground whatever for criticism of RAF movements in future, but that we in Malaya add our full share to the high reputation being gained by the Air Forces of the Empire elsewhere."

In a little more than a fortnight the RAF had been driven from the mainland.

CHAPTER V

ALL QUIET ON THE SINGAPORE FRONT

December 1941

"The pattern of life with its regular office hours, golf, cricket and racing, bands on the
club lawn and the somewhat petty social life went on with the Japanese at the gates."

Brigadier C.N. Barclay

Singapore experienced its first taste of war at exactly 0415 on the first night of the
Japanese landings in Northern Malaya (8 December), when bombs fell on and around
Keppel Harbour, the Naval Base and the airfields at Seletar and Tengah. Most
however, actually fell on Chinatown, where 61 civilians – primarily Chinese and
Sikhs – were killed, and 133 injured. Elsewhere, 'Robinson's' newly opened
restaurant in Raffles Place received a direct hit, and the Police HQ in New Bridge
Road was shaken by a near miss. Three airmen were killed at Seletar, although no
aircraft were hit, but three Blenheims were severely damaged by bomb splinters and
debris at Tengah. The attack was carried out by JNAF bombers from Indo-China, 34
G3Ms of the Genzan Ku having set out from Saigon during the late evening of the 7th,
with Singapore as their target 600 miles to the south. However, extremely bad weather
was encountered and all were forced to turn back, as recorded by Lt Sadao Takai,
commander of the 2nd Chutai:

"Visibility was so poor that it was almost impossible to recognise the formation lights
of the two aircraft immediately behind me. The air was extremely rough; my aircraft
rocked and shook. Sheets of rain drummed on the wings and fuselage and smashed
against the cockpit windshield. Without changing course I began a descent to a lower
altitude. Behind me, some high, others low, could be seen the glowing red, green and
yellow lights of the bombers in my squadron as they struggled to maintain formation in
the rough air. Every now and then great flashes of lightning were reflected from the
whirling propeller blades of the bombers. The pilots were trying desperately to hold the
group together, so that they would not be left behind or separated from the formation,
or become lost over the sea.

"I was still losing altitude when directly below the aircraft there appeared the dull
white crests of waves streaking the black ocean surface. I pulled up from the steady
descent, and searched for the other bombers; only two of the original squadron of nine
were in sight. It seemed almost impossible to recognise the formation. I was still
looking vainly for an area of clear sky amidst the boiling clouds and rain when a
'Return to base' order was received by wireless from Lt Cdr Niichi Nakanishi, our wing
commander. All bombers returned to their take-off points." [77]

Some two to three hours later a further attempt was made, 31 G3Ms from the Mihoro
Ku departing Thu Dau Moi airfield north of Saigon, led by Lt Cdr Yagoro Shibata.
Of this formation, 14 were obliged to return early but the remaining 17 arrived over
Singapore just after 0400. These aircraft had been plotted by the Mersing RDF
station at 0320, when some 75 miles north-east of Singapore; RDF HQ at Seletar was
advised, similar plots then being reported by the Changi RDF station as the bombers
approached the coast. Despite the advance warning, Singapore City was brilliantly
illuminated as the bombers droned across the island in the moonlit sky. Such an

attack had not been anticipated and consequently the Air Raid Precautions HQ was unmanned, and sirens were not sounded until the raid was well under way. The raiders were virtually unopposed. Wild and inaccurate AA fire from the inexperienced gun crews, aided by the big guns of the *Prince of Wales* and *Repulse*, caused only minor consternation amongst the Japanese airmen, Lt Yoshimi Shirai's aircraft suffering slight shrapnel damage. Of the raid, General Percival commented:

> "Somewhere about 4am the sirens went and shortly afterwards came the well-known sound of falling bombs. Most of them were directed against the aerodromes but a few fell in the very centre of town and did some damage. For some reason the headquarters of the civil ARP organisation had not been manned and lights were still on in some of the streets when the aeroplanes arrived – not that this really made much difference for there was no mistaking the waterfront at Singapore, even at night. It must be admitted that this raid came rather as a surprise for the nearest Japanese aerodromes were 700 miles from Singapore, which was a considerable distance and we hardly expected the Japanese to have any very long-range aircraft. It was a bold enterprise on their part. It was also the first indication most of the citizens of Singapore had that war had broken out." [78]

At Sembawang airfield, three fully-armed Buffaloes of 453 Squadron stood idly in the pens, the pilots of which had been refused permission to take off. When Flt Lt Tim Vigors – who had flown night sorties in Spitfires in England, during which he had shot down a German bomber – argued that he would take off without permission, he was warned he would be placed on a charge if he did so. The reason given for the refusal was that the AA commander had requested a free field of fire for the guns, fearing his inexperienced crews might shoot down any friendly aircraft that might become involved. However, when Governor Shenton Thomas later enquired why night fighters had not been sent up, he was apparently informed that Buffaloes were unsuitable as they were day fighters, and that the only night fighters were the Blenheims of 27 Squadron, currently up country at Sungei Patani. Although Sembawang was not bombed on this occasion, the 453 Squadron diarist later wrote:

> "Rudely awakened in the small hours by the screams of air raid sirens and the roar of ack-ack guns. And in the moonlit night droned a formation of Japanese bombers. Bombs were dropped but none fell in our area. So the war in the Far East has started. Well, they've asked for it!"

Sgt Board was among those who dashed to the airfield:

> "I pedalled furiously down the dirt road leading from my hut to the airfield. Suddenly dazzling splashes of light split open the darkness. In the sudden glow of the searchlights I saw bombers roaring in my direction. Every goddamned gun on the Island started firing at the same time, and they kept right on firing. I seemed to be in the middle of the concussion waves. On top of that I saw the bombers heading for the airstrip and decided that was no place for me." [79]

He endeavoured to cycle to safety but ended up throwing himself into a ditch as a bomb fell nearby. One of the Vildebeest pilots stationed at Seletar recalled:

> "I personally expected that the Japs had come off a carrier, and that we were going to attack it with torpedoes. I also imagined that the Japs would not waste the opportunity with such a small raid, but would return later. I was wrong in both cases."

488 Squadron's diarist recorded the reaction among the New Zealanders in his imitable way:

"At 0415, F/Lt Hutcheson, who was doing Station Duty Officer, woke F/Lt Mackenzie and informed him that war had been declared and Japanese bombers were overhead. Mac was not amused at being woken at such an unheard-of hour and said 'Balls!' However, he was out of bed a few seconds later. P/O Sharp reported to F/Lt Hutcheson with a tin hat on, and said, 'OK Hutch, let's go!' Troops dashed across to dispersal and had machines warmed up."

243 Squadron's Sgt Geoff Fisken was among those who had a change of heart about the ability of the Japanese bomber crews:

"We were standing outside the swimming club [when] the Japanese planes flew over. As we watched them just flying around, showing us what they could do, we quickly realised that the prewar stories we'd been told about the Japs' flying skills were far from the truth. In fact, the early Japanese pilots were highly skilled."

At dawn, one of the 4PRU Buffaloes (W8136) in the hands of Sgt Charlie Wareham, was sent from Singapore to obtain photographs of the landings, as Wareham recalled:

"My first job was to photograph a place called Singora. There were no maps – the RAF did not have a map of any area outside of Malaya, it was not the thing to have a map of somebody else's country – so I hunted around to get some type of map, and I found a World Atlas in the town. My first flight was done from that World Atlas. I flew up to Alor Star and refuelled, and then went across the peninsula to Singora, and photographed it. The photographs I brought back were, of course, of the Japanese landings and that was also my first experience of being shot at by anti-aircraft guns. Because no one knew at that stage that the Japanese were landing there, I didn't know what to expect, but I saw that there was a lot of activity down at that particular place, so I simply photographed it."

On 488 Squadron, ground personnel were still in the throes of fitting armour plating to their Buffaloes, as LAC Max Boyd of B Flight noted in his diary:

"Started fitting armour plate to the planes today. It was cut out to shape at the Naval Base workshops. We finished two planes with all the aircraft crews working flat out, the rest of the planes being unserviceable due to the springing of seats and the bolt-holes being out of line. Stan Guiniven, our Flight Sgt, said in an emergency we could tie them in with fencing wire. We worked until dark. Our machine [W8235] is next to the only proper air raid shelter this end of the drome but it fills up with water when the tide comes in as the airfield has been built on a reclaimed swamp and the surface is little above sea level at high tide."

Two days later he wrote:

"All our Squadron planes were got serviceable today. We did have to finish attaching the armour plating on some planes with fencing wire as it is not possible to drill armour plate, and seat attachments must not be altered. The higher ups seem to be a most inefficient lot of bunglers, they will have to do a lot better when hostilities hot up. This is supposed to be a fortress but we are a little dubious already as the heads seem to be carrying on in an old colonial way."

On the evening of 9 December, 453 Squadron lost two of its aircraft in unfortunate accidents:

"Late in the afternoon came an order to disperse six Buffs at Tengah. Wild Bill Collyer's motor cut out as he was taking off and despite valiant efforts on his part, the aircraft [W8151] crashed into a dispersal pen and was wrecked. Bill was a bit shaken but otherwise uninjured. Shortly after, Eric Peterson attempted a night landing without a flarepath, and he had the bad luck to just touch a Glenn Martin as he was coming in. His aircraft [W8210] turned over and was completely wrecked. Eric got out of it with a few bruises and a shaking. Congratulations to both Eric and Bill on their escapes."

Of his lucky escape, Sgt Collyer added:

"When I commenced my run for take-off, the engine misfired quite a bit. I brought it back to the tarmac. F/Sgt Gillespie ran the engine up to full power, and it seemed to be OK. I went back to take off again. This time I had a lot of speed on the clock when the engine misfired again, so I aborted the take-off. It is appropriate to describe the aerodrome at Sembawang. In order to build an aerodrome in that area in the first case it was necessary to take the top off a hill and dump it on the slope of the hill in order to create a flat area. There was no such thing as a bulldozer. The work was done by thousands of Chinese coolies, mostly women. The downhill side of the built-up area was almost a sheer drop of about 50 feet. My choice was to go over the drop or hit a blast pen with one wing. I opted for the latter. It did not occur to me to pull up the undercarriage. Gillespie told me afterwards that he could hear the engine misfiring on the second attempt and he felt badly about it."

When the air raid sirens were sounded that night, there was a vast improvement in the reaction of the authorities to the threat posed when compared with the first night's raid; Ian Morrison wrote:

". . . when we looked down on the city from the watch-tower where we lived, there was hardly a light to be seen. Zealous Chinese volunteers, mostly young men, who formed the backbone of the ARP and all auxiliary services, threw themselves into the task of blacking Singapore out as they might have thrown themselves into some game. The slightest chink of light at a window would provoke frenzied shouts from the street below. Drivers of cars were stopped if their lights were thought to be the smallest degree on the bright side. Anyone attempting to light a cigarette in the street would be fiercely pounced upon from all sides. A few fines were imposed, but the zeal of the Chinese wardens and the desire of the population to comply with the regulations rendered these fines hardly necessary. Singapore's first air raid was not serious enough to cause panic but it served as a spur to galvanise all the civil defence organisations into wartime activity." [80]

The morning of the 12th saw the departure of four Buffaloes of 243 Squadron to Ipoh, where they were to be temporarily attached to 21RAAF Squadron for operations; they returned two days later. A reinforcement arrived at Kallang next day in the guise of 2-V1G-2, a Dutch Brewster squadron from Buitenzorg in Java, in accordance with a pre-hostilities agreement with the Dutch. In the opposite direction, one squadron of Glenn Martins returned to Java from Sembawang. The Dutch fighter pilots were:

2-V1G-V
Kapt J.P. Van Helsdingen

2/Lt A.G. Deibel	2/Lt P.A. Hoijer
Ens J.H.A. Ellecom	Ens F. Swarts
Ens R.A. Rothcrans	Ens P.R. Jolly
Ens F. Pelder	Sgt G.M. Bruggink
Sgt A.E. Stoove	Sgt A. Voorbij
Sgt J.F. Scheffer	

None of the Dutch fighters was fitted with armoured glass windscreens, and following their arrival aircraft dumps were searched for suitable screens from damaged or crashed RAF Buffaloes. All nine aircraft were swiftly fitted with the hardened glass protection. 488 Squadron's LAC Max Boyd commented in his diary:

> "The Dutch pilots are magnificent as both men and flyers. Best on the Island. Some have thousands of hours flying time logged. Leo Arden [LAC Flight Mechanic] and myself are seconded to one of their more modern Buffaloes as groundcrew until their own maintenance crews arrive. Our Squadron has supplied several groundcrews. The planes are much faster than ours and have self-sealing fuel tanks."

Next day 453 Squadron was similarly ordered to Ipoh, 16 Buffaloes departing in four flights during the morning, although three crashed en route (see Chapter II). That same morning, a Ki-46 reconnaissance aircraft ventured over the island, all of Kallang's serviceable Buffaloes being scrambled. The diarist noted:

> "Great excitement today. All machines were ordered into air as quickly as possible. Aircraft were taking off in all directions, 243 opening up from their dispersal point, the NEI Squadron doing ditto and old 488 beating them all. We had 16 aircraft off in six minutes. The groundcrews worked like hardened veterans, put u/s aircraft serviceable just for the sake of getting them into the air. P/O McAneny and Sgt MacIntosh took off without ammunition. From the spectators' point of view a Hendon display was tame after Kallang's effort. However, it turned out to be a false alarm but nevertheless we learnt a lot. We found that 488 could get into the air in record time and also that all pilots used their heads in an emergency. God help any Jap who pokes his nose into Singapore. Note. This is a diary not a line book."

During this period, when Singapore enjoyed an almost complete respite from attack, a small force of six Blenheims was despatched on the night of 12/13 December in a further futile attempt to interrupt proceedings at Singora. One aircraft crashed on take-off and a second failed to start, leaving just four to make the long trip to Singora, where three bombed the airfield. All returned safely. Early next morning Sgt Wareham was off in PR Buffalo W8136 to photograph the result of the raid. He landed at Ipoh and telephoned Sqn Ldr Lewis to report what he had seen. He was then ordered to recce the Kroh Road and thence inspect Kroh, Bannangsa, Kota Bharu and Grik, before returning to Singapore via Ipoh:

> "I carried out my recce as ordered but encountered very bad weather over the whole route. I came down to 4,000 feet over Singora landing ground and did not see any aircraft on the ground, but several transports were lying close inshore."

Japanese reconnaissance aircraft continued to intrude into Singapore's sky and, during the morning, four Buffaloes of 488 Squadron led by Flt Lt Jack Mackenzie gave chase to a lone aircraft without success:

> "The Buffalo would have made a very nice aero club machine but they were old and had passed their useful operational life . . . [they] had reconditioned engines, which gave us a lot of trouble. We had tremendous trouble with the oil pressure, especially when we tried to get a bit of climb out of them, and used full throttle. We had a lot of engine failures. But really the aircraft was just not fast enough, nor did it have a good enough rate of climb. It was difficult to even catch up with the enemy bombers – it was just too slow and completely unsuitable for the job it was given to do." [81]

On the night of 15th/16th, a Buffalo flown by Flt Lt Mowbray Garden joined a pair of Blenheim IFs in patrolling the skies. However, with inadequate radar coverage, control inefficiency and poor R/T communications, little was achieved, while the island's AA commander still would not agree to friendly aircraft operating over Singapore during night alerts! Flying a Buffalo at night was therefore an unrewarding task, as Garden recalled:

> "When the moon was at all in evidence I had to undertake to attempt night fighting. This was pretty hopeless because the flames from the exhaust stubs of the engine of the Buffalo could not be dampened, and the enemy could see me coming miles off, whilst I could not see them."

The initial bombing of Singapore, coupled with the ineffectiveness of the standard Buffalo for night fighter work, prompted Sqn Ldr Howell to initiate the modification of W8143 for night fighter duties; Howell wrote:

> "A certain number of pilots had flown Buffaloes at night, but the aircraft were considered unsuitable owing to the length of the exhaust flame. I asked Air HQ about night fighting when I arrived, and was told that there was none, and that it was unnecessary owing to the distance from any Japanese base. After the first night raid on 8 December, I flew to Seletar and saw a Wing Commander to see if he could design a flame trap for the exhausts. He was more than helpful, producing a pair within 24 hours – I think he was doubly keen, as he was injured in the knee during the first Japanese raid! After several designs had been tried, one was found to be satisfactory, showing very little light from front view. I painted two aircraft black, and these two were used at night with, unfortunately, no success. I was however officially ordered by Air HQ three weeks later to start practice night flying. This came as a great surprise to me, and the Squadron, as we had been doing so for a fortnight and even had a section at night readiness."

The following night (16th/17th), a surprise low-level raid was made on Tengah airfield by two Ki-21s; although few bombs fell on the runway none of the Blenheims was damaged. Despite the lack of damage inflicted by this small-scale attack, a Blenheim operation planned for that night was cancelled.

With news of the air actions over Malaya filtering back to Singapore, the defenders were on a knife-edge of expectancy for an aerial assault that still did not come. Nonetheless, orders were belatedly issued for trenches to be dug across the many sports fields dotted about Singapore Island, to deter and prevent Japanese aircraft from landing on these inviting open spaces. Sqn Ldr Howell of 243 Squadron was also concerned about the lack of air-sea rescue facilities at Singapore:

> "I was naturally anxious about life saving arrangements owing to the nature of the

country over which we were flying. To my surprise, I found them non-existent. I saw
Flt Lt Moore and he informed me that although he had an organisation, he had no boats,
and that the last two had been handed to the Navy."

Howell made further enquiries, successfully argued his case and within days Flt Lt
R.C. Moore had taken on strength half a dozen craft: *HSL105*, to be based at Pulau
Bukum, a small island about ten miles south-west of Singapore, Pinnaces *53* and *54*,
and Seaplane Tenders *ST257* and *ST258* to operate west of St John's Island, and
Marine Tender *MT941* to be based on the slipway at Kallang Harbour. The rescue
craft were to work in conjunction with the MVAF. Howell took steps to ensure that
his pilots and aircraft were properly equipped:

"There were only land rations and first aid kits [in the aircraft]. Owing to the most
unpleasant country over which we were flying, and lack of any organisation for a search
and rescue of pilots landing in the jungle, good kit was essential. It was difficult to get
quickly. However, in the end, all pilots of 243 Squadron carried a parang, rope, white
overalls, mosquito netting and cream, money, cigarettes, matches, Malay-English
essential phrases, pocket compass, etc, etc. Revolvers were almost impossible to obtain,
although NCOs on ground duties at Seletar were wearing them.

"To sum up, few people realised that fighter pilots and aircraft were the air force in
Singapore, and everything should have been done to maintain their efficiency,
equipment and morale at the highest possible level with minimum possible red tape.
This was done in England magnificently, and it was a very bitter pill in Singapore. The
majority [of my pilots] were New Zealanders. They were varied in their ability as pilots
(having had very little flying hours) but not in their keenness and courage, which was
magnificent."

Howell also had cause to complain, as did others, about the poor intelligence received
concerning the performances of Japanese aircraft:

"Information on the types of enemy aircraft we should meet was almost useless. No
details of speed or armament for any types were given, and very misleading rumours
were current about Japanese pilots and their capabilities. For example, we were told
that a Japanese pilot could not fly over 20,000 feet! It was a very unpleasant surprise
when we did meet them. The Buffaloes were not only out of date, but mostly in poor
condition, some having been flown for over 200 hours. Unloaded, they were a delight
to fly. Loaded, with four .5-inch guns, each with 650 rounds, 130 gallons of petrol,
armour glass and plate, they were impossible to handle."

488 Squadron suffered its first fatality during the afternoon of 18 December, when 23-
year-old Sgt Alex Craig from Christchurch hit a tree in W8175 while involved in a
formation landing at Kallang, as recalled by Flt Sgt Mothersdale of 243 Squadron:

"A vic of three nearing the eastern boundary of the airfield came into view on a
powered approach to land, heading into the sun still well above the horizon. The
formation was close and steady. The leader [Flt Lt Mackenzie] was bringing them in
over the trees with little to spare – precision judgement! The vic – trim and steady –
cleared the first line of trees and was clearing the second line when much of the No.2's
starboard mainplane went in among the branches of a higher tree and the aircraft, its
nose pulled down and round to starboard, went plunging wildly through the branches.
As it struck, a low line of yellow flame ignited; barely a moment and the wrecked
aircraft was engulfed in a mass of red flame, coning to yellow and dense black smoke
at 40 feet."

Of Alex Craig's death, Sgt Weber of 243 Squadron noted:

> "Poor chap. He was a big, jovial and kindly fellow. It really is amazing how callous we have become – a couple of minutes after the crash we were back in the dispersal hut fooling and laughing. I guess it is that we don't allow ourselves to think, but also no great bonds of friendship ever seem to be formed."

Two of the Dutch Brewsters were damaged three days later, when they collided on landing. Fortunately, neither pilot was injured but both aircraft were rendered temporarily unserviceable until repairs had been carried out.

Next morning a dozen Buffaloes of 488 Squadron were scrambled when another Ki-46 approached Singapore at high altitude. Flt Lt John Hutcheson and Sgt Don Clow actually sighted their quarry but did not have sufficient altitude to intercept the faster Japanese machine, which was also seen by Sqn Ldr Clouston and Plt Off Grahame White – the latter inevitably known as 'Snow'. One of those involved, Plt Off Peter Gifford (W8173), noted:

> "Attempt by whole squadron to intercept Jap recco plane over northern part of Singapore and southern Johore. Six sections of two spaced at intervals of 1,000 feet from 26,000 feet down. P/O Hesketh and self were to climb to 25,000 feet but W8173 suddenly sprang an oil leak at 22,500 feet and I returned to base. Recco aircraft seen but not caught."

All the squadrons were experiencing difficulty in obtaining spares, as noted by Sqn Ldr Clouston:

> "Spare parts were extremely difficult to obtain. In some cases it was necessary to manufacture locally. In this connection, even after the outbreak of war, vital spares were withheld by the Depot at Seletar on the grounds that they were 'War Reserve'. This was remedied by my Equipment Officer going direct to the Depot and helping himself to spares in order that aircraft could be used in action."

Cecil Brown sent a cable to *Newsweek*:

> "Unless additional aircraft are supplied to the British forces in Malaya, Singapore stands in grave danger (I tried to say the 'gravest danger' but the censor toned it down) from the land advance. The wishful thinking and almost countrywide conviction among the military that the Japanese would back down, as well as the underestimation of the Japanese strength, plus the suddenness of the Japanese attack, are responsible for the present situation.
>
> "There is throughout Singapore great criticism of the amazing unwillingness of the High Command to inform the people what's going on. This method of treating Asiatics as well as Europeans as children who are unable to stand bad news, is inevitably causing internal repercussions. It is believed that Sir Robert Brooke-Popham is personally writing the communiqués and determining what revelations will be allowed." [82]

To his diary he added:

> "I have never felt so insecure in my life as here in Singapore. I feel that tremendous bombings are coming on and there's not much to stop it nor, I fear, much in the way of land forces to stop the Japanese advance, incredible as that seems. I have been fairly optimistic about Singapore, but now the shadow of coming events seems to be in front of me. The realization that Singapore can and might fall is becoming more vivid almost every moment." [83]

On the evening of 22 December, a flight of four Hudsons reached Sembawang from Darwin, via Koepang and Sourabaya. On approaching Sourabaya the flight had been intercepted by Dutch fighters and a general air raid alert had been sounded; unbeknown to the Australian airmen, orders had been issued that if aircraft approached the city in formation they should be considered hostile. However, no shots were fired on this occasion. On arrival off Singapore just before 1830, the Hudsons were again challenged, this time by Buffaloes, which had been scrambled to investigate, as their arrival was not expected. The following afternoon a further flight of four Hudsons arrived from Darwin, the new aircraft being issued to the two resident RAAF squadrons.

With the remnants of the two RAAF Buffalo squadrons safely back at Sembawang following their actions up country (see Chapter III), the survivors were at least able to celebrate Christmas, as noted in 453 Squadron's diary:

"24 December: All the boys are back from Kuala Lumpur except Keith who is spending Christmas up there with 'Shirley' [Sgt Griffiths' aircraft, W8231/TD-G], and Scrimmy, who decided he liked the look of an AIF nurse at Malacca. A party was held at the 'Cathay' at night and attended by the serviceable (for drinking) pilots. Much good makan was consumed and champagne flowed like water. The Shadow [Sqn Ldr Harper] brought along two very attractive wenches and some others were incorporated. And when the ball was over they all went home to bed; but not until we had settled our small taxi bill for 254 bucks! The blackout presented a great problem; taxis were practically unobtainable. And who was it who shot up the Yellow Taxi Co? Anyway, it was a good party.

"Christmas Day in the work'ouse – 'appy Christmas folks. Nothing much doing. The Squadron is being reorganised with No.21RAAF. We are to form two Flights, one Flight 453, the other 21RAAF. The Shadow is to lead the combined Squadron and F/Lt Kinninmont of 21RAAF is to be Flight Commander of 453. By the way, we have a problem for the brains of medicine to cope with. It is a disease we contracted at Kuala Lumpur and is known as 'Nipponisis'! The symptoms of this new plague are large red spots before the eyes! Tis said there are several crates of WAAFs over at Seletar waiting to be unpacked. Mick says that just goes to show they don't organise things properly. So we appointed him as Chairman of the Committee for Organising Crated WAAFs. He's taking Van into his staff to help with the check inspections. The Shadow has the job of expert adviser to the Committee – an obvious selection for that post."

Of this period, Sgt Griffiths wrote:

"Once back at Sembawang, we flew many sorties, aerodrome defence, reconnaissance. At about this time there was considerable speculation regarding Fifth Column and sabotage, particularly after one of the Hudsons completely lost power when attempting to take off. After returning to the run up position and again checking the preflight procedure, when everything checked normal, again the aircraft lost all power and was made u/s. The Hudson CO then took the aircraft and the same thing happened. When they investigated, they found a number of squares of brown paper in the air intake, which, when under full power would rise, shutting off the air.

"I returned from a mission, dropped my gear on my bed including a map I had been using, stripped off and went for a shower, which was on the other side of our barracks. Having forgotten something, I went beck to my room. There, to my surprise, was the chap who acted as a batman. He had opened my map, which he was studying. I think he may have been Indian or Eurasian. Anyhow, I asked him what he was doing and he said he was interested to know where I had been. I felt I should report this, which I did, and that was the last I saw of him."

The New Zealanders of 488 Squadron also enjoyed the celebrations, the diarist ending his account of the day's activities with:

"De-bagging was the order of the day, F/Sgt Patterson (Senior ground NCO) being the first to lose his trousers, followed in quick succession by F/Sgt Chandler (Senior Engineer NCO), P/O Sharp, F/Lt Hutcheson and the CO. This was the culmination of a very enjoyable evening which was characterised by the good behaviour and spirit of all present."

Although there were no raids on Singapore on Christmas Day, Sqn Ldr Howell of 243 Squadron (in W8193/WP-V) was ordered off with his section to investigate a suspicious plot. It turned out to be a false alarm and they were recalled after about ten minutes. However, one of Singapore's Catalina flying boats was shot down in an action with a G3M of the Mihoro Ku during the morning; notwithstanding, its crew, most of whom suffered burns when the aircraft caught fire while two others sustained bullet wounds, survived the ordeal despite the loss of the aircraft's dinghy, when they were rescued by the Dutch submarine K-XII which happened to be in the vicinity.

Next day (26 December), shortly after 0900, Fighter Ops reported that a 'Ju88' – obviously a Ki-46 – was reconnoitring the docks, Naval Base and Kallang and ordered an interception. Although a section of Buffaloes sighted the aircraft they were unable to close. An appropriate entry in GHQ's war diary stated:

"The Ju88 [sic] was painted silver and was a good deal faster than any aircraft of ours. It was supposed the pilot was a German. He had a sense of humour and used to make vapour trails round heavy AA bursts and to play hide and seek with our Buffaloes in the clouds.
"The Ju88 recce aircraft which flew over Singapore every morning, between 8-9 o'clock, was never less than 24,000 feet and often as much as 30,000 feet. The Ju88 recce aircraft employed by the Japanese were said by the RAF to be stripped and therefore a faster edition than that normally seen on the Western Front. When attacked by Buffaloes – a very rare occurrence – it left them standing."

At 1330, Singapore's guns opened fire at what they thought were two Japanese aircraft flying over the island at 17,000 feet but which turned out to be Dutch Buffaloes from 2-V1G-V. Grp Capt A.G. Bishop, Group Captain Ops at Air HQ, ordered that Lt Col J.J. Zomer, in charge of the NEI contingent on the island, be advised of this misidentification and suggested that some sort of distinctive marking be painted on his aircraft. It was immediately agreed that the Dutch would follow the British example and have a light band painted on the rear fuselage of their Buffaloes. However, next day, three Glenn Martins returning from a west coast recce at 1600 were fired on over Johore by a Buffalo from Kallang, just after they had lowered their wheels prior to landing at Sembawang. It seems probable that at least one Glenn Martin was hit since the official report states that it was "attacked at 750 feet with wheels down and shot up by a Buffalo". The errant pilot was not identified.

The AA gunners at Port Swettenham achieved success on the 26th, when they shot down a Japanese fighter that crashed at Kuala Selangor. The pilot, 19-year-old Corporal Matsuo Matsumoto, was captured. He was sent to Singapore for interrogation and revealed that he was flying a Ki-27 of the Tanimura Buntai, operating out of Sungei Patani, when he suffered engine failure – presumably due to battle damage. The PoW report stated:

"Prisoner showed some concern that he should have permitted himself to be taken alive, though as he is at the same time very worried about the air raids, it seems apparent that he is but paying lip service to the traditions of the Jap soldier. However, he seems to have small hopes of ever being allowed to return to Japan, and is anxious to know whether he might be permitted to work in some capacity for us. Would like to be employed in an aircraft assembly works. From declining in the early stages of interrogation to disclose any information that he thought might be prejudice to his country's interests, prisoner now declares himself as being willing to answer any questions. He has become very bright and friendly and seems grateful for the treatment he receives."

Flt Lt Philips was airborne in one of the PR Buffaloes (W8166) at first light on the 27th, his task to reconnoitre Sungei Patani and Georgetown. As he approached the former at 25,000 feet he saw three 'Navy 0s' flying 10,000 feet below. They sighted the Buffalo and climbed to intercept but were unable to overtake it. Following his report – which revealed over 100 aircraft at Sungei Patani including approximately 60 fighters – the RAF went on the offensive and a small force of Blenheims and Hudsons from Tengah and Sembawang carried out a dusk raid against Sungei Patani, where aircraft of the 3rd Flying Battalion were based. Eight or nine Ki-51 light bombers of the 27th Sentai were destroyed although these losses were quickly replaced. Operations from this occupied airfield commenced next morning, shipping being attacked and sunk in the Malacca Strait and at Port Swettenham. One of three Blenheims sent from Singapore to investigate was erroneously shot down by Bofors gunners at Port Swettenham, and a second was damaged. A further Blenheim raid against Sungei Patani took place on the night of 28/29 December, when one aircraft failed to return.

Aircraft of the JAAF's 3rd Flying Battalion continued to support the ground forces during the day, whilst that night (29th/30th) a Ki-48 from the 75th Sentai bombed oil tanks on Singapore Island, after which the crew reported five fires. During the same night eight G3Ms from the Genzan Ku raided Seletar, while nine more attacked Singapore City and a dozen others bombed Keppel Harbour. The first substantial raid on Singapore Island did not cause a tremendous amount of damage, and was noted casually in 453 Squadron's diary:

"We had a few bombers over last night and naturally they dropped a few bombs. None of them landed over here but there were all kinds of shrapnel whizzing about. We didn't get overmuch sleep last night – how the hell do you go about having the moon blacked out – or did the bloke who wrote that sweet little ditty 'You can't black out the moon', really know something?"

Cecil Brown and a few friends were in 'Raffles' when the bombers came over:

"When they came we went across the street to a field where we could watch the raiders come over. There were nine bombers and the searchlights caught them going directly over 'Raffles' at about fifteen thousand feet. There was heavy anti-aircraft fire. At one point I saw what I thought were bombs coming down. I flopped into a muddy ditch in the field. When the raid was over there was a huge fire some four or five miles away and I wanted to see it. I did a very foolish thing. I got into a taxi and went racing out to the fire. They had hit an oil tank out near the Alexandra barracks. Out there some of the volunteers were not so sure that it had been hit by a bomb, but that it had been fired by Fifth Columnists on the ground.

"The idiocy of going out to the fire lay in the fact that the fire obviously would be a beacon for other raiders and probably would be attacked again. That didn't occur to me until I got to the hotel after midnight and told the other correspondents what I had seen. They were happy enough to get a report on it, but said I was a damn fool for going out. During the night the Japs came over twice again but I stayed in bed. I was too tired to get up." [84]

While Singapore braced itself in readiness for the anticipated Japanese bombing assault that would surely follow, the Buffalo pilots bided their time and some, like those of 21RAAF/453 Squadron, tinkered with their aircraft in an effort to increase performance:

"Today [28 December] marked an important event in aeronautical history: namely, the inaugural test of the Shadow's 'Super Sports Special' [thereafter referred to in the diary as the SSSS]. This remarkable piece of machinery is an erstwhile Buffalo which, to state the matter simply, has been got at. The flight surgeons have performed many major operations upon it by removing all kinds of vital equipment. In fact, all that is left is the good guts. A brilliant scene was witnessed on the tarmac where spectators eagerly took up vantage points and sat nervously masticating their tin hats in anticipation of the soul-stirring spectacle about to be witnessed. While those two daring test pilots, Blondie and Sinbad strolled nonchalantly about, casually perusing F.700s and the like, the inventor and designer was observed restlessly pacing to and fro with a very worried countenance. Of course, no such gathering would be complete without a smattering of sceptics and critics. These took up their positions.

"At last the big moment arrived and the indomitable pilots climbed into their machines, Sinbad into the SSSS and Blondie into a Buffalo Mk.I. With a roar from their exhausts and a cheer from the crowd, they flashed into the air – but what's this? For the love of Mike, look at Sinbad! He's unnatural! He's defying all the laws of gravity – up! up! up! Will he ever stop? Ah yes! He's stopped at 6,000 feet. And now comes Blondie . . . they sight each other, turn and rush head-on at each other – and miss – they turn around again, streamers flying everywhere. They're diving, turning, now Sinbad's on Blondie's tail. Blondie is flying madly, trying everything but Sinbad easily stays there. Aah! A sigh of relief from the crowd, a broad smile on the face of the tiger, excuse me I mean The Shadow, and a glum silence from the critics – the SSSS has proved herself superior in all departments to the Mk.I. Boy! What a dogfight, the flying of Sinbad and Blondie was 'banya bagoose' – now the crowd disperses. The flight surgeons go to sharpen their knives in preparation for a mass attack on the Mk.Is, while the pilots smile happily in pleasant anticipation of what they are going to do to the Zeros next time they meet them. The critics are wondering whether – if – after all!"

The modifications had been applied at the instigation of Sembawang's Station Commander, Grp Capt McCauley, who wrote:

"I [had] removed two of the guns from the Brewster Buffaloes in order to lighten them, but still retaining enough weaponry to fight against the Zero. I reduced the ammunition by half. With these two modifications alone I was able to lighten the fighter by 1,000 pounds. Wherever we could, we faired the Buffalo to reduce drag and improve its performance. We faired over the gun ports and we lightened the radio equipment. These changes were carried out by the groundcrew of the squadron. The result was that with these improvements our Buffalo fighters were able to almost match the Zeros in performance. Now our fighter pilots were gaining confidence after initially having been given a hard time in battle."

Other modifications to Buffaloes included the two .5 wing guns being replaced by two

.303 guns, thus reducing the weight of both guns and ammunition. The external radio mast was replaced by an internal aerial, while non-essential items such as the Very pistol and its bracket, cockpit heater and parachute flare bin were all removed. It was also decided that, except for long sorties, the aircraft would carry 80 gallons of fuel instead of the normal 130 gallons. Thus, by reducing the weight of the fighting machine, a much better all-round performance was achieved, increasing top speed by some 30mph and allowing for greater manoeuvrability. Grp Capt McCauley was also deeply concerned over the shortage of fighters:

> "Lack of fighter strength in Malaya was a constant cause of concern, yet the employment of fighter aircraft which were frittered away on inconsequential tasks at Army behest continued to be permitted. The loss of every fighter aircraft reduced the defences of our Navy, Army and air bases. Numerous instances of these types of Army-inspired operations can be given.
>
> "The lesson to be deduced is that squadrons must not be handed over to Army for co-operation, but their employment must remain within the veto of an Air Force officer. In Northern Malaya, it may be mentioned that the senior Army Co-op Officer was a Squadron Leader and the Senior Army Officer was a Major-General.
>
> "At no time in the campaign in Malaya was there adequate fighter cover on any aerodrome. This was due to the numerical insufficiency of fighter aircraft. Over some aerodromes an attempt was made to maintain a first light to last light fighter patrol, but this eventually broke down owing to the endurance of the small number of available aircraft, and pilots becoming exhausted."

The MVAF lost another of its aircraft on 29 December when a Moth flown by a RNZAF pilot collided over Singapore City with a 488 Squadron Buffalo which was coming in to land at Kallang; the Moth lost a wing, the wreck crashing in Lavender Street, killing both pilot and pupil, while Sgt Bunny De Maus, the Buffalo pilot, was able to land W8200 with only minor damage. This was the second such accident involving a MVAF Moth and a Buffalo. Meanwhile from Sembawang, Sgts Gorringe and Board of 21RAAF/453 Squadron were ordered to carry out a reconnaissance sortie up the peninsula. When flying at 500 feet about half a mile south of the Slim river, the Buffaloes received a burst of machine-gun fire from the ground, Board's aircraft sustaining damage to its tail, engine and windscreen:

> "Blondie had trouble with his aircraft – bits would keep falling off it! Most annoying really. So he left it at Kuala Lumpur and Keith stayed with it. We are beginning to wonder if Keith has unearthed anything up there. Blondie was followed home by a Zero but not attacked."

It would seem that Board's pursuer was a Ki-43 of the 59th Sentai from Sungei Patani rather than a Japanese Navy A6M. The 453 Squadron diarist continued:

> "Much panic in the dispersal pens tonight. A fair dinkum inter-boong war broke out with spears, stones and war cries. Things were looking far from bright but Wop [Sgt Halliday] and Tozzler [Sgt Austin] rushed in with drawn guns. While Tozzler broke up the main fight with threatening actions and the most 'orrible swear words, Wop executed a smart strategy and headed off a big batch of reinforcements who were coming up at full gallop. When peace was restored it was found that the source of all the trouble was, as usual, a female; to particularise, one of the 'concrete annies.' The brawl started between two boongs who both claimed that it was their turn next!"

Constant air and ground attacks on 30 December caused the Brigade Group defending

Kuantan to be withdrawn to prevent communications being cut by infiltrators. Kluang airfield was also raided, two Buffaloes of 243 Squadron hastily being despatched to investigate but by the time Sgts Rex Weber (W8139/WP-B) and Bert Wipiti had arrived all was quiet.

Darkness allowed two Ki-48s from the 90th Sentai to intrude over Singapore, bombs falling on Tengah where three Blenheims were slightly damaged. At least one Blenheim of 27 Squadron was airborne, Sgt Ginger Baldwin intercepting one of the bombers at 12,000 feet, which he sighted as it flew off in a northerly direction. Although he pursued it, his top speed of 200mph was no match for the Ki-48, which rapidly drew away. Baldwin returned disappointed to the patrol line, and was informed that another enemy aircraft was in the vicinity but he was unable to locate it. The two Japanese bombers landed back at Sungei Patani just as three Blenheims and two Catalinas – also armed with bombs – arrived to attack. One Ki-48 was damaged and 13 men killed on the ground, with a further eight wounded. Light AA fire was experienced and one Catalina was slightly damaged although it returned to Singapore safely.

The last day of 1941 was relatively uneventful in the air, the only action of note occurring when six H6K flying boats of the Toko Ku and five G4Ms of the Takao Ku attacked a vessel identified as a cruiser, which had been spotted in the South China Sea by a reconnaissance aircraft. Their target was in fact the Dutch flying boat tender *Helen*, which was struck by two bombs. Fierce resistance was put up by the gunners on the Dutch vessel, return fire shooting down one H6K, causing two others to force-land and damaging a further four of the raiders.

There was a further night attack on Singapore by Mihoro Ku G3Ms to bring in the New Year, Cecil Brown and his friends watching:

"Late tonight the siren sounded – a beautiful moonlight night – while we were out at our place in the country. We went out on a hill to watch the planes better. It was a beautiful sight the way the British searchlights caught and held the Japanese bombers. The anti-aircraft firing was very poor, however. The bombers were in one direction and the anti-aircraft firing must have been a full ten miles away, on the other side of the horizon." [85]

The black-painted Buffalo of 243 Squadron piloted by Flt Lt Mowbray Garden was aloft to hunt for the raiders:

"On this occasion the radar gave me a course far out over the China Sea for an interception of an approaching force of enemy bombers, and the course plotting was very accurate; but I never saw them except for a fleeting flash of aircraft below me – only feet below me – and then nothing but the black night again. I particularly remember the occasion because it was New Year's Eve and my instrument panel clock showed it was midnight – and I thought what a funny place to be spending New Year – in a Buffalo at 22,000 feet over the China Sea! Later, on looking at the chart and the plotted courses of the enemy and myself, I was told that I must have flown straight through the formation of bombers, on a diagonal course, without knowing it!"

While Flt Lt Garden was up defending Singapore all on his own, his comrades on the ground, including those of 21RAAF/453 Squadron were celebrating the arrival of the New Year:

"Strangler quaffed a little too deep of the giggle juice and after telling the world, passed out in a refined and orderly manner. Much admiration was expressed for our rendition of 'Aloha' with actions. Did we see The Shadow flit out of the door at an early stage complete with femme? Mick seemed to have things very well organised once more. Matthew and Sinbad stayed a little late to discuss a few points with some pongos but were finally persuaded to go home by Hank and Tozzler. By the way, let me introduce Hank of the NEI squadron – his chief hobby is dropping bombs on Japs, and for relaxation he drinks, smokes and goes out with bad women; so we have much in common with Hank and he is very popular with the Squadron. Where did Matthew go, and what did he do? Just picture our young Irishman riding in a rickshaw and firing his pistol into the air. You've heard of a red rag to a bull, well just show a redcap [MP] to Matthew. Did someone say there were enemy bombers overhead while we were in the 'Cathay'? Many cheers!"

CHAPTER VI

SINGAPORE – THE CALM BEFORE THE BLITZ

1-10 January 1942

"The paths we human beings race, across it they run sideways, the Anglo-Saxons after all, are only monkeys. Those hairy white apes don't have the Japanese fighting spirit."
Derogatory poetry directed at British and Dutch airmen,
popular among Japanese aircrew

During the last few days of December, a battalion of Japanese troops had advanced rapidly down the west coast of Malaya, using seven small steamers that had been captured at Penang, which in turn towed a variety of barges and landing craft; these had been carried overland by road and rail from the Singora landings. On arrival at Lumut this advance force had been strengthened by specialist troops from the 11th Regiment, and on the night of New Year's Eve the force was reported off the mouth of the River Bernam. Thus, on the morning of New Year's Day, two Blenheim Is set off from Kluang to attack these craft. Despite forewarning of the presence of Japanese fighters, both aircraft failed to return. The 3rd Flying Battalion reported that its pilots – from the 59th Sentai – shot down two Blenheims and a Glenn Martin while escorting motor launches operating on the river.

Three Glenn Martins had departed Sembawang at 0703 to reconnoitre shipping off the Bernam estuary. At 0920, four motor vessels were sighted, each towing between two and four smaller craft. The Dutch aircraft continued flying up the coastline, since their task was reconnaissance, and on the return flight the leader was seen to descend to about 100 feet apparently endeavouring to identify the vessels, but the aircraft suddenly dived into the water. The two remaining aircraft proceeded with the recce, one some 15 miles behind the other. The lead aircraft, M-597 flown by Vdg (Vaandrig = Reserve Officer Candidate) I.J. Koster, then came under attack by two fighters when near Pulau Lumut. The pilot of the other aircraft, Vdg Christian Cleef reported on his return:

"[Koster] was attacked by two aircraft which came from the direction of the mainland. All personnel [in my] aircraft identified these attackers as Brewsters. They attacked the Glenn Martin from the rear. The Glenn Martin turned left, gaining height, but later was noticed gently descending, completely circled once, and made a belly-landing on the water between the islands of Pulau Lumut. One of the attacking aircraft kept circling over the Glenn Martin and the other made several dives down towards it."

Cleef's aircraft landed at Sembawang at 1206. There is no record of Buffaloes being active in this area at the time and it would seem more likely that Kloster's aircraft was shot down by the 59th Sentai Ki-43. There were no survivors from either of the Dutch aircraft. The Blenheim attacks on the troops resulted in only a few casualties and did not prevent an assault on Port Swettenham, which rapidly smashed British resistance, forcing a further withdrawal.

Twice during the day Flt Lt Park Thompson (a New Zealander in the RAF) scrambled from Kluang in one of W Flight's Wirraways, in vain attempts to intercept Japanese reconnaissance aircraft reported to be in the area. As with two similar sorties flown the previous day, the crew failed to locate any intruders. From Singapore, patrols of Buffaloes were up throughout the day, including one pair from 243 Squadron scrambled to investigate an unidentified aircraft approaching the island along the west coast of the mainland, as Sgt Vin Arthur recalled:

"Today, at approximately 0900, Marra and I were sent out to intercept a 'bogey'. After flying at 21,000 feet for approx one hour, I saw a brown plane about ten miles to the west of us coming down the western coast of Johore. I yelled out to Marra and we set out after the Jap. As soon as we saw him, he saw us because he made a sharp right angle turn away from Singapore on a course of 230 degrees. We followed flat out but he just left us standing. The colour of the Jap machine was brick red with silver underneath [a Ki-46 from the 81st Independent Chutai]. Operations were late with their plotting of the Jap and tried to make us fly on the reciprocal course when we were following him. When we finally lost the 'bandit' we then flew the course Operations asked us to. It was a great thrill chasing that Jap and 'Marie' [W8178/WP-Y, named after a girlfriend] behaved wonderfully."

Later, he added:

"Over in the Indian quarter they are still digging out the bomb that fell off the Dutch Glenn Martin. It fell so close to an Indian soldier that it splashed him with mud when it hit the deck. Just as well the bomb didn't explode. This afternoon I gave an Indian boy 10 cents to climb a coconut tree and bring me down a coconut. Apparently he couldn't understand English because he wouldn't stop picking the nuts till he had skinned the palm-tree. As the nuts were green they weren't much use. I wasted about an hour trying to open one with an adze. Tonight, as I walked back from the mess, a Blenheim was doing a bit of night flying. When it passed over some of the houses in Katong the children began to cry. It was rather pathetic. They thought it was a Jap."

However, Japanese bombers were active over Singapore later that night, two Ki-48s of the 90th Sentai and three Ki-21s of the 98th Sentai raiding Tengah again, where three Swordfish of 4AACU were destroyed, and one other damaged. Seletar, Kallang and Sembawang airfields were also bombed by 25 G3Ms of the Mihoro Ku – and although five Blenheim night fighters of 27 Squadron were sent up, they failed to intercept the raiders. Later, in an attempt to prevent a similar fate to that which 4AACU's Swordfish had suffered, five of the unit's Sharks were flown up to Batu Pahat before dark, from where they would return at dawn, a procedure which would be repeated over the coming weeks. There was at least one casualty, a sentry at Kallang, as noted unsympathetically in GHQ's war diary:

"One Volunteer private, on sentry duty, lost an ear from a bomb splinter because he ran to take cover in a slit trench instead of falling flat where he was . . ."

The Australians at Sembawang took it all in their stride:

"We were bombed again. When I say bombed I mean we spent several uncomfortable hours in the trenches. Though now we have moved to our dispersal huts in the ooloo, the procedure is to place the old battle bowler over the head and slumber on peacefully."

Meanwhile, in the opposite direction three Blenheims carried out an attack on Kuala Pest airfield, where two Ki-21s of the 98th Sentai were burned and 20 other aircraft damaged. On the same night three more Blenheims searched in vain for Japanese transports reported off the west coast, while two Catalinas were despatched at 1830 to carry out a raid on the airstrip at Gong Kedah. So extremely keen was Air Vice-Marshal Pulford for Gong Kedah to be attacked, that he expressed his intention of accompanying one of the crews, as he considered the operation called for maximum co-ordination. In the event he was persuaded from undertaking such a flight; which subsequently achieved negligible results.

Throughout the daylight hours of 2 January, Buffalo patrols continued, albeit without success. Vin Arthur wrote:

"During the afternoon Marra and I flew for one-and-a-quarter hours trying to find a bogey. We were at 20,000 feet over Johore and Tengah. We could see the results of last night's raid on Tengah. The aerodrome was pitted with bomb holes. Two kites were also set on fire. I believe 40 bombs were dropped. A pretty serious fire was started on the Dutch islands. The Japs made a gliding attack on Tengah and then machine-gunned the drome from a low level."

Following his return to Kallang, he added:

"I went into town and bought a revolver holster and belt for my gat. I also got a very expensive set of 'Reeve's' watercolour paints and several tubes of colours. When I was coming back from town in a taxi, an air raid started. The taxi driver (Chinese) had the wind up good and proper and we almost collided with another car. All these natives are very windy of air raids, especially the Indians."

The raiders on this occasion turned out to be a flight of Ki-43s that strafed Seletar from 300 feet. Little damage was done and the Japanese fighters escaped unscathed.

That night Tengah and Singapore City were again raided and the airfield's Technical Area, including the Operations Room, was severely damaged, a number of fires breaking out. 243 Squadron scrambled two Buffaloes including W8143/'Black Bess' but Sqn Ldr Howell and Flt Lt Garden were unable to make contact. Cecil Brown wrote:

"It is amazing the way the Japanese attacks every night are carried out at almost the same time. They are usually caught by the searchlights, but they fly over to drop their bombs in perfect formation and thus far I haven't seen them break their formation in the face of anti-aircraft fire. The anti-aircraft has improved somewhat but is still far from efficient. The Japanese give the impression of complete indifference to the British defences. These bombers are evidently coming from some distance, since their bombs are rather light. They make a crater only three feet deep and four feet in diameter. People are being urged during the black-outs to wear white to avoid being struck by autos. A curious thing is that the Chinese women insist on dressing in all-black because they are convinced that then the bombs will not find them." [86]

The first reinforcement convoy (codenamed BM9A), comprising five transports carrying personnel and equipment of the 45th Indian Brigade and a pioneer battalion – all only partially trained troops – was now approaching Singapore. Throughout the daylight hours of 3 January, Buffaloes were sent out in pairs to patrol over the convoy as it neared the island, 488 Squadron commencing the patrols at 0700, handing over to 21RAAF/453 Squadron later in the morning, as noted by the unit's diarist:

"The job today was to secure the safe passage of a convoy coming to Singapore. This was done with great enthusiasm as there are said to be many 'treasures' on board the ships. Mick [Flt Lt Grace] still insists he saw many crates of WAAFs on the deck of one ship. We are sceptical but we haven't given up hope.

Griff got tangled up in some clouds and lost the formation, with the result that he had to force-land. This he did in an amusement park in some remote spot and got away with only slight personal damage [sic]. He was lucky he didn't take to the silk as not

only were inhabitants instructed to shoot any parachutists, but the surrounding waters
are reputed to be full of crocodiles."

Sgt Griffiths had in fact crash-landed AN211 at Oeroeng on Pulau Koenboer off the
east coast of Sumatra, about 100 miles south-south-east of Singapore, where he had
attempted a wheels-up landing only for the aircraft to flip over; he suffered bad facial
injuries (see Appendix I). Meanwhile, 243 Squadron took over the convoy patrols at
1600, six aircraft of B Flight including one flown by Sgt Arthur taking off to meet the
convoy as it was entering the Johore Straits; he later wrote:

> "We met it [the convoy] out in the Straits and split up into three sections. The first and
> second sections flew either side of the ships at 1,000 feet while Marra and I in the third
> section acted as top cover at 6,000 feet. We didn't see any hostile aircraft. A Flight sent
> up six planes to relieve us but they couldn't find the convoy. As a result, we had to stay
> on till the convoy was safely in port, the trip lasting two hours 50 minutes. A section
> from A Flight, Bonham and Powell, got lost in cloud and were separated from the rest
> of their Flight. All B Flight and the remainder of A Flight were trying to land at the
> same time in the dusk. Mr Bows [W8234] had his guns switched on and when he came
> into land accidentally fired a burst over 488 Squadron machines. So far no casualties
> have been reported."

While Plt Off Bonham (WP-F) returned on the last drops of his fuel, his No.2, Sgt
Aussie Powell, was still missing when darkness fell. Flt Sgt George Mothersdale, B
Flight's Senior NCO, also remembered the day's tragic events:

> "Near the end of the afternoon Flt Lt Bows came into the dispersal hut office and told
> me that one of A Flight's aircraft was long overdue. As dusk began a searchlight near
> Kallang was switched on, with its beam vertical to serve as a homing aid. We had
> noticed that when our pilots took a look they scanned the southern sky – not to the
> north. Bertie Bows came out of the hut and scanned the sky southwards. He remarked
> to me that he (Powell) may have got down on one of the islands. The sky was overcast
> with light-grey high cloud and visibility was good.
> "If the pilot could make Kallang he would be very low on fuel and would
> undoubtedly came straight in. He might come in over the fence near our dispersal, so
> we delayed spreading out our aircraft for night dispersal to give him more yards of
> airfield. The dispersal night guard arrived, and darkness came. The beam continued for
> about 30 minutes of darkness. It would be seen from an aircraft 70 miles or more to the
> south. During our waiting I gave thought to what the people of blacked-out Singapore
> would be thinking. The sirens had not sounded and a searchlight beam shining
> vertically had not happened before. For we on the airfield our standing-by ended
> abruptly when the searchlight was switched off. We dispersed our aircraft and stood
> down until dawn."

Despite the use of a searchlight as a beacon to guide back the missing Buffalo as
darkness closed in, it failed to return. Short of fuel, Aussie Powell had in fact crash-
landed AN197 on Pulau Bukum, a small island to the south of Singapore; the
Australian suffered severe burns and injuries to his face and spent the remainder of
the night wandering about, firing his revolver intermittently, endeavouring to attract
attention. Finally he reached civilisation and was taken to the local Dutch hospital,
from where he was picked up by a launch and taken back to Singapore and urgent
treatment for his severe burns. Rex Weber confided to his diary:

> "I have been promoted to lead a section but it's a doubtful honour and I only wish that
> there were more capable men in the Flight to take over. I have been out on two patrols

over convoys. Pevreal led the first and we found the convoy when it was nearly into port. The last, Flt Lt Garden led and we went miles out to sea, but didn't find it [the convoy] until we were coming home – too late. My word, when one is so far away from land it is gratifying to recall the reliability of the Buff's engine. Poor old Aussie was being led by Bonham. The plane was spread over an acre, but Aussie got out of it with severe burns about the face. It is doubtful whether he will ever fly again."

Earlier in the day Sqn Ldr Harper of 21RAAF/453 Squadron had instructed Plt Offs Tom Livesey and Leigh Bowes, together with Sgt Greg Board, to carry out a reconnaissance of islands south of Singapore to search for any signs of Japanese parachutists rumoured to have landed in that area. As they were about to take off, Harper spoke to Livesey and told him also to reconnoitre the aerodrome at Batu Pahat and strafe any aircraft seen there. Nothing untoward was seen on the islands but many aircraft were sighted on Batu Pahat, which were duly machine-gunned. All three Buffaloes returned safely.

Another Buffalo (W8223) was lost next day (4 January) in a landing accident, Plt Off Jack Godsiff of 488 Squadron being lucky to survive; Sgt Arthur commented:

"At approx 1200, a 488 chap P/O Godsiff made a ropey landing. He slammed on the throttle and the engine momentarily picked up and then cut. It did this three times. The pilot saw be would have to put her down so he made for a lawn. As he had his wheels down he misjudged and crashed on the roof of a house. The plane then fell on the ground and the engine was torn out. The pilot was unconscious when he was picked up but not seriously hurt [he did however suffer a fractured nose and forehead in addition to abrasions]. He apparently hit the reflector sight and the stick had jammed violently into his stomach. When the plane hit it made a sound like a horse and cart going through a greenhouse."

The Squadron diarist provided a more humorous version of events:

"Jack Godsiff caused quite a stir today and proved the fleetness of our CO. We were all sitting playing cards and doing no harm at all when an aircraft was observed heading directly towards our hut, with a failing motor. S/Ldr Clouston was two lengths ahead of everybody at the first door and Jim MacIntosh scrambled out a good last after nearly being trampled to death in the stampede. But W8223 ('Pettit's Pride') just cleared the roof, a few trees etc but not a housetop. There was a loud plonk, a cloud of dust and Jack Godsiff came out plus a few cuts, a broken nose, slight fracture of the forehead and little sympathy. However we were all relieved to hear Jack had come out so lightly."

Sgt Weber, who also witnessed the crash, added:

"Jack Godsiff is the luckiest man about – his motor cut just after he became airborne, and with great skill and coolness he managed to get the plane down without killing himself, although with a bit more luck the plane would not have been so much tangled about – another foot clearance would have taken him onto a clear patch. His CO was very amused because when he was pulling Jack out of the tangled heap, Jack came to and enquired: 'How the hell did I get into this tangle – sir?'"

Despite this latest accident, 488 Squadron's official historian recorded:

"The Squadron, though not fully operational, has reached a high standard for the short time we have been allowed; 90 per cent of the pilots are quite at home in Buffaloes as far as throwing the machines around is concerned, but have had very little altitude flying. One of the main reasons for lack of altitude practice is that the Buffalo engine

will not stand up to full-throttle climbs. We have had cases of engine loss of power
through drop of oil pressure and excess oil temperature. The maximum height that can
be reached is 25,000 feet."

Sadly, as will be seen, the New Zealanders' keenness and ability in "throwing the
machines around" in the air would not compensate for the limited operational training
they had received, nor for the inferior equipment with which they were to fight the
enemy.

With darkness the Japanese bombers were back over Singapore, two aircraft
dropping incendiaries on the city. The crew of a patrolling Blenheim night fighter of
27 Squadron actually sighted one intruder, but was unable to carry out an interception.
453 Squadron's irreverent diarist noted:

"Bombs fell in Nee Soon village and damaged a few boongs. Also write finis to the
budding careers of several fine pigs who had stayed out without their tin helmets etc."

The spate of accidents among the inexperienced Buffalo pilots continued, with the
loss of two more lives on 5 January: again Sgt Arthur was a witness:

"Today Shortie Elliott [from Wellington and, at 19-years-of-age, the youngest pilot on
the Squadron] went west. As I had started my training with Shortie I was very sorry to
hear of his death. The Squadron had been ordered to scramble and P/O Shield took off
in W8179, leading the section. However, his undercarriage wouldn't retract and his
engine was missing badly, so he made a quick circuit, landed and preceded to taxi
speedily across the centre of the drome. Meanwhile, Mr Bows was an aircraft short in
the formation and sent Shortie off in W8199. Shortie had just started to get airborne
when he crashed into Ron Shield [also from Wellington]. Both machines immediately
burst into flames and both pilots were burnt beyond recognition. It is just as well they
were both killed on impact. When the oxygen bottles exploded they made a sound as
loud and sharp as an anti-aircraft gun. The ammunition, of course, was bursting all over
the place and bits of jagged shell cases and oxygen bottles were picked up a long
distance from the planes. When the fire went out all that was left were two skeleton
tailplanes and a lot of twisted metal. The two machines met head-on. The time was
0710."

Next day the funeral was held for the two pilots; Arthur continued:

"We buried Shortie and Ron at 1100. Their ages were 19 and 23 respectively. The
funeral was quiet. Twelve airmen (bearers), twelve officers, and Alan Lawrence and
myself being present. After the coffins had been lowered into the graves, the natives
noisily shovelled earth on top of them while we walked away after having one by one
saluted them. I was glad when it was all over."

Before dawn on 6 January, Flt Lt Bob Kirkman and Flg Off Geoff Sheppard of
21RAAF/453 Squadron departed Sembawang to investigate reports of barges
proceeding up the Bernam. Nine troop-laden craft were located and strafed, the two
Australians believing their attacks to have been highly successful. At about 1000, a
lone Japanese aircraft arrived over Malacca and began circling, then released bombs
aimed at two large Straits steamers anchored in the roads. Neither vessel was hit but
when they later departed, heading southwards, they were attacked by a formation of
bombers. The larger of the two coasters was hit and set on fire, but with skilful
handling by her master she eventually reached Singapore safely, six Buffaloes of 488
Squadron led by Flt Lt Jack Mackenzie providing escort as she approached the island.
453 Squadron's diarist recorded that the unit's Buffaloes carried out another convoy

(codenamed BM9B) escort during the day, which brought forth the comment "not such a big one this time, but surely Mick's WAAFs will arrive now."

Another Buffalo came unstuck on the 7th, on this occasion one of the Dutch aircraft of 2-VlG-V, B-399 flown by Sgt Jan Scheffer. Sgt Weber of 243 Squadron wrote:

"Then the Dutchmen had another accident – taxiing fast across the drome one hit the spot where the two planes had burnt – which had not been cleared up properly – with the result that he burst a tyre, which caused the plane to ground loop first onto a wing and then on to the prop."

Vin Arthur added:

"There are still a lot of exploded cartridge cases around where Shortie and Ron collided . . . his right tyre was punctured by one of the jagged shell cases."

This latest accident brought the number of Buffaloes lost or damaged during the past four days to seven, with two pilots killed and four injured – and the shooting war was yet to start in earnest. In a belated attempt to curb the series of training accidents and to boost confidence within the ranks of the untested and untried Buffalo pilots, Sqn Ldr Peter Brooker DFC, yet another Battle of Britain veteran, arrived at Kallang from Air HQ, and promptly led both Flights of 488 Squadron on a convoy patrol.

Once the Japanese had targeted Singapore's airfields, key personnel were relocated off station in an attempt to avoid unnecessary casualties, particularly amongst aircrews. The pilots of 243 Squadron were accommodated in a house just outside Kallang, as Rex Weber's diary records:

"Quite a nice place, and soon we hope to run it as a Mess. We now feel quite immune from night air raids, although the feeling is very much akin to the ostrich when it buries its head in the sand to avoid danger because we are right next to the drome. But, you see, we are surrounded by trees, and that does help!"

Vin Arthur added:

"Last night a 27 Squadron air-gunner asked if he could sleep in our house. He is so scared that he is afraid to sleep at the aerodrome. Veg Marra is on night flying duties tonight. I wish I was up with him."

At this time 224 (Fighter) Group was formed under Grp Capt Rice to co-ordinate the activities of the fighters. Sqn Ldr Howell commented:

"Grp Capt Rice had completed plans for the formation of 224 Group, and I understand that the establishment (very much larger than in existence) had been approved by Air Ministry. However, owing to the lack of aircraft to warrant a large establishment, this was never brought into being. If however, reinforcements had arrived in time, the staff would have been far too small to deal with the situation, and lack of personnel with war experience would have been very serious.

"Even as it was, the only officers who had any experience of controlling an Ops Room in Malaya or Singapore were Wg Cdr Darley, Sqn Ldr Clouston and myself. Wg Cdr Chignell had been posted to the Fleet. Wg Cdr Darley was up country a great deal, so it meant that Sqn Ldr Clouston and myself had to run a squadron, and spend 8-12 hours daily in the Ops Room at the same time. Other officers did not seem inclined or willing to learn. These duties included giving the civilian and service air-raid warnings to the island."

Clouston was in total agreement, and wrote:

> "I found it impossible to combine the duties of Squadron Commander and the controlling of aircraft from the Ops Room at 224 Group. On the instructions of Grp Capt Rice, I handed over command of the Squadron to Flt Lt Mackenzie and was attached to the staff of 224 Group.
>
> "I went to HQ in January 1942. No radar was left by then. We depended on observers on the ground reporting in. We were relaying the reports telling the squadrons where the Japanese aeroplanes were. I might say there was little doubt about that – they were usually overhead."

Sections of 243 Squadron Buffaloes were scrambled on 8 January, when Japanese bombers were reported to be attacking Kluang, as Plt Off Snowy Bonham (WP-E) noted:

> "Patrol Kluang-Batu Pahat. Took off as Yellow leader with White Section to intercept enemy aircraft. We proceeded to Batu Pahat but no sign of enemy aircraft."

Amongst the pilots was Sgt Weber:

> "We bustered up there after enemy bombers and I ran out of petrol in the left tank in under 30 minutes, after which my chief concern was how much I had in my right tank – especially as we patrolled for, it seemed, an endlessly long time. However, we arrived back and somewhat to my chagrin I found there was still 20 gallons left. Then, of course, I had a strip torn off me for complaining but, indeed, of late I have developed 'a shortage of petrol complex' – and the sooner I get rid of it the better for all concerned.
>
> "In the very near future we are going to strike some very heavy daylight raids and here's hoping that we can cope. I am quite confident that at least I will prove up to the task as far as courage is concerned, anyway. The Japs are doing pretty well – they are coming down Malaya in great style – they now have 15 dromes that we built, for their use. Good show, Englishmen!"

Sgt Arthur was airborne during the day:

> "My plane was put u/s by Brian Baber this afternoon because of an oily windshield. As a result I flew Mr Bows's machine W8234 on a scramble with Veg Marra at 1800 hours. We were flying at 500 feet because of the rain and were supposed to be identifying three bogies approaching from the south. Owing to the poor visibility we couldn't see them as they turned in and landed at Sembawang [they were in fact Glenn Martins returning from the South China Sea operation]. When we told Ops we couldn't see them W/C Chignell replied 'Well you bloody well ought to!' That made Veg see red, and he rang up Chignell and told him of the flying conditions at Changi. The W/C then said he was sorry for using those unnecessary adjectives over the R/T."

The pilots of 21RAAF/453 Squadron were slightly more active, particularly that evening, as noted in their war diary:

> "The Shadow invited the boys down to the 'Island Club' tonight for a drink. We polished off first of all, the three famous bottles of sherry. These were acquired by the Squadron at a quiet little party at the airport on – just a sec while I look back – oh yes! Here we are, 20 November 1941. I see that the history of those bottles is not related by our diarist of that date. Only mention is the cryptic remark 'What happened to three bottles of wine that appeared from nowhere? Ask the boss!' Well now that the bottles are only bottles we will reveal their dirty past. Seems that Strangler, Tozzler and Wild

Bill were doing a recce down in the basement when they discovered the cellar. So 'down with capitalism! Up the workers!' And off went three bottles of the finest old imported sherry. These were conveyed by stealth to our table upstairs and eventually migrated by an underground route to the possession of the Shadow. He, with complete nonchalance, placed them on the table, autographed them, called the manager and instructed him to place them on ice. Which, believe it or not, said manager was only too pleased to do. So we brought them home and there and then decided that they would remain unopened until such time as we had a victory to celebrate. So we drank the three bottles of sherry tonight; drinking first of all to those who are no longer with the Squadron and then to ourselves and many more victories."

From Singapore, on the 9th, 21RAAF/453 Squadron despatched four Buffaloes led by Flt Lt Vanderfield northwards to Kluang, from where they were to carry out tactical reconnaissance sorties. All returned safely. Shortly before their return, Glenn Martins began taking off, their crews briefed to carry out a raid on shipping off Kuantan, but as the flight commander's aircraft was getting airborne it crashed into a stationary Hudson, its two 1,000-lb bombs exploding, killing two members of the crew and injuring the other two. 21RAAF/453 Squadron's diarist wrote:

"We had a spot of excitement this morning when a couple of thousand pounds of bombs went up. A NEI Glenn Martin crashed taking off and caught fire. Soon after its entire bomb load blew up and blew poor old Wop clean out of bed – or did he jump?"

The Australians' diarist continued:

"The Squadron, with Shadow leading, left for Kluang in the afternoon. The idea is to start early from there tomorrow morning and strafe the guts out of Kuantan which is reported to be a nesting place of the ME109s [sic]."

In fact, the two sentais of Ki-27s of the 12th Flying Battalion had just arrived at Kuantan, although it was obviously still believed by some that German aircraft were operating in Malaya. The operation against Kuantan did not materialise however, as revealed by the next two entries in the diary:

"Boys had to abandon the Kuantan show as the weather was foul. Shadow sighted a Ju88 [sic] and gave chase; but whatever you do, don't mention flaps to him! Van [AN185] struck a soft patch while taxiing at Kluang and stood his aircraft on its nose. So also did Congo but as he was doing about 50mph his aircraft [W8209] was considerably bent – in fact, it's a wipe off.

"Another attempt was made today to get to Kuantan but once again the weather was very bad. Greg had a small affair with a Wing Commander's car at Kluang, converting it from a saloon into a stripped sports model. His aircraft [W8219], however, is likely to recover [in fact, it was written-off.]"

All remained fairly quiet at Singapore in the meantime, the Buffaloes carrying out routine patrols while others continued to practice including Sgt Arthur, who recorded:

"This morning the CO took up a couple of sections of us for new type of attacks. Prof [Sgt Rankin] and I tossed to see who would go and I lost. They were just taking off when they were told to scramble. Veg Marra had to come back because of his oil temperature going up off the clock. Just as he landed, his prop spinner began to leak badly. The rest of the formation didn't see any bogies.

"Alan [Lawrence] and Babs [Baber] went over to Seletar to pick up a couple of new busses. They were met with the typical Seletar inefficiency. They were going to start up when they found there were no spark plugs in them. My kite is at present on a 30-hours.

The only thing of interest today was the shoot-up staged by Blondie and Fisken to give the gun posts some practice."

On a more personal level he wrote:

"The S/Ldr is having a blitz on those of us that don't shave in the morning. As I wasn't shaved I tried to keep out of his way when he was over at our hut. Just as I was getting out of his way he said 'Stay where you are Arthur.' I thought I was for it but he only wanted to see how tall I was to find out if he could use my chute.

"I haven't received any mail for a long time thank goodness. I like to receive letters but I don't feel in the mood to answer them. I wouldn't mind writing to Marie though. I started to write to Shortie's mother and Noeline [Vin Arthur's sister] today but gave it up. What would I give to be with somebody else tonight instead of spending it at this place. It is only the flying that stops me going crazy. I hate my days off because it means loitering around doing nothing and this is fatal over here."

243 Squadron received a new pilot during the afternoon, Sgt Ginger Baldwin of 27 Squadron finally getting his wish to transfer to fighters. He was given immediate instruction on one of the Buffaloes and, following several take-offs, circuits and landings, by which time it was sunset, he was considered suitable and consequently checked out. Sgt Russ Reynolds wrote glowingly of the new addition:

"The big read-headed Blenheim pilot is a born pilot, I believe. He took his kite up [towards the end of December] with no rear gunner or chute and succeeded in breaking up an enemy raid 'up country'. He got a Navy 0."

Added to his two victories on the first day of the war, the aggressive Baldwin apparently now had three victories to his credit while flying the Blenheim IF, a remarkable achievement by a remarkable man.

At this stage the Ki-43s of the 64th Sentai moved from Kota Bharu to Ipoh, while the Ki-21s of the 60th and 98th Sentais also moved forward to new bases. The arrival of Japanese aircraft at Ipoh had not passed unnoticed by Air HQ, and that night a dozen Vildebeest, each fitted with long-range fuel tanks, set out to attack the airfield. All but one of the biplanes located the airfield and released their bombs with some success – one Ki-43 and one Ki-27 were burned, and others damaged.

During the early morning of 10 January, radar operators at Singapore meticulously plotted the course of a single reconnaissance aircraft as it approached the Island, the Fighter Controller vectoring two patrolling Buffaloes of 243 Squadron to intercept. The twin-engined Ki-46 of the 81st Independent Chutai, flying from Kota Bharu, was initially sighted by Sgt Bert Wipiti, who succeeded in diving on to its tail, firing one long burst, gaining strikes on one engine and slowing it down. Joined by Sgt Charlie Kronk (WP-A), the two New Zealanders chased it down, firing all the way until it crashed in the jungle in southern Johore; the crew of two were killed. Both pilots were later interviewed by American correspondent George Weller of the *Chicago Daily News*, Wipiti simply stating:

"I slipped down from above and gave him a long burst in his motor." [87]

Kronk was more forthcoming:

"I came up from underneath and saw the big body of the plane with its great red circles on the wing right over my head. I thought, I cannot destroy a ship as beautiful as this. Then I pressed the tit and emptied everything I had into her. I kept firing until all my ammunition was gone. She was burning all the way to the ground, but the Japs seemed to think they could land her. But just as she reached the flattening point she seemed to burst into flame all over and an enormous sheet of flame shot up as she disappeared into the treetops." [88]

Vin Arthur, in his diary, wrote:

"Both chaps attacked it simultaneously, Wipiti aiming at the port motor and Kronk at the pilot. Both used up all their ammo. They fired at the plane all the way down from 9,000 feet to 0 feet. When it finally crashed into a hill in Johore the port engine was blazing furiously. When Wip and Charlie got back they both did victory rolls. I'm glad 243 got first blood and not 488."

That evening, having enjoyed a beer with others celebrating the victory, Sgt Russ Reynolds wrote in his diary:

"Greenslade, Newman, Kronk, Wipiti and self are sitting under the light in the big room discussing the day's activities. S/L Howell, F/L Garden & Bonham have just gone. The CO brought in a bottle of whisky from Far East HQ as a present for the victors. We brought some beer over from the Mess, so we all had a drink to celebrate. It's the best thing that could have happened, for we shall now go through them like a pack of cards, when they come down. S/L Howell, Kronk and Wipiti are going out to the crash with a truck tomorrow to get a 'rising sun', and a bit of wing to nail up over the dispersal hut. I am getting Bert to take my camera to take some photos."

Reynolds himself had been involved in an operation earlier during the day:

"Went on a flip to Kluang. We had to 'stand by' (strapped in, gloves on etc) in our planes at 11.30am. Scrambled at 11.45 and were away just over the hour. We went up there at 'gate'. Wipiti and self didn't, for it's tough on your motor. We kept the others well in sight though. 'Evict' [Control] informed us that there were five 'bandits' circling Malacca, so we went to Kluang. Couldn't see much damage – only a few scorched patches where aircraft had been burnt out. Bonham went above us for top cover, for the last time they raided here they brought 109s [sic] down with auxiliary tanks, which they jettisoned. They wrote off a Blenheim and a Wirraway. There was cumulus all over the place. We kept in touch with 'Evict' so we got all the developments – which were nil! The jungle looked very fresh and green but nevertheless still equally uninviting. Used 35 gals of gas which wasn't bad."

Next day Sgts Wipiti and Kronk accompanied Sqn Ldr Howell and the Station Engineer Officer to inspect the remains of the crashed aircraft. The two dead crewmen were found and a part of the fin of the Ki-46 was cut away and taken back to Kallang as a souvenir. Of this occasion, Vin Arthur wrote:

"Today the paper had a good write up for Wip and Charlie. They later went out and had a look at the Jap kite they shot down. The crew of two didn't have parachutes. The plane was bashed to bits and both the chaps badly burnt. One had his head facing backwards and bubbles oozing out of his ears. A couple of erks were asked to bury them but they left them there and later pleaded they had no shovels. Actually they were disturbed by the gruesomeness of the scene. The Air Force weren't the first to arrive there because the newsreel camera chaps had got there first and taken their photos."

Meanwhile, Sgt Eddie Kuhn (W8150/NF-I) narrowly missed opening the score for 488 Squadron later during the day when he sighted a single-engined aircraft and gave chase. As he closed the range, the Japanese machine – possibly a JNAF reconnaissance C5M – dived into cloud and escaped. Sgt Perce Killick also encountered a K-46 during this period:

"I was up on a training flight, although we were always fully armed when we were training, and I intercepted a twin-engined photo-reconnaissance plane coming out of a cloud. I got in behind him and wasn't fired on at all. That made me think it was a reconnaissance aircraft. He was over the centre of the island, on his own, at about 9,000 feet – other reasons why I felt it was on reconnaissance. I veered in from the right hand side and came in behind him. We were trained in short bursts. I think I got two attacks in. There was a bit of smoke that came out of him but he limped away into the cloud."

453 Squadron was also active during the morning. Three aircraft accompanied a section from 21RAAF Squadron to patrol over Kallang, while Sqn Ldr Harper led Sgts Clare and Board to Kuantan, but they were unable to carry out a planned strafe due to adverse weather conditions.

The Japanese thrust southwards was proving unstoppable and during the night troops entered Kuala Lumpur and Port Swettenham. An RAF officer and two-dozen airmen had remained to try to deny the enemy immediate use of the two airfields by attempting to crater the runways, achieving only limited success. Meanwhile, fuel tanks were opened and telephone lines cut. A small party of SOE men then arrived and set booby-traps, but all were forced to beat a hasty retreat when Japanese troops were reported on the outskirts of the town. It was estimated that it would take the Japanese about three months to clear the airfields at Kuala Lumpur and Port Swettenham and render them operational. However, after a number of casualties had occurred amongst the occupying troops, Australian prisoners were used to defuse the booby-traps and other obstructions – inevitably resulting in further casualties – and consequently Kuala Lumpur airfield was in use within three days.

CHAPTER VII

THE JANUARY BLITZ

12-19 January 1942

"The only thing about the Air Force which commands my respect and loyalty is the magnificent valour of the lads with whom I am directly associated . . ."

Sgt Rex Weber 243 Squadron

12 January

With bad weather having curtailed most operations on the 11th, action over Singapore was resumed in all its fury on the first day of the new week. The stage was set for the start of a fierce and sustained blitz. With the 12th Flying Battalion and its two sentais of Ki-27s having recently moved southwards to Kuantan, nearly all JAAF units were currently in northern and central Malaya. Early in the morning therefore, no fewer than 72 of the Battalion's fighters appeared over Singapore on a fighter sweep. As the formation approached, eight Buffaloes of A Flight led by Flt Lt Mackenzie were sent off by 488 Squadron, followed 20 minutes later by six more from B Flight led by Flt Lt Hutcheson. A trio of Dutch Brewsters also scrambled.

2-V1G-V's three Brewsters, which had been joined by a lone 488 Squadron aircraft flown by Sgt Jack Meharry were the first to be intercepted – by six fighters reported as Navy 0s – but managed to escape damage by flying into cloud, Ensign Swarts (B-3103) then claiming damage to one of five bombers he engaged, reporting that smoke appeared from its engines following his attack. Within minutes, 488 Squadron's A Flight was bounced by 27 fighters from 3,000 feet above and belatedly attempted to take evasive action by flying into the sun as these dived to attack. Mackenzie (W8183) recalled:

"We were ordered to climb out from Kallang and gaining height over the Causeway, we must have been over Johore, when low and behold, without any warning they hit us – bang! We'd only been warned that there were enemy aircraft approaching, but no exact position. I just happened to look up and saw them coming – coming straight down on us. We were in a hopeless position . . . I yelled to the boys, 'Break and fly into the sun!' I remember this damned little thing with a fixed undercarriage, turning like a top, and thought hell, I'm not going to get mixed up with those – not if I could help it. A few of us got hits as we scattered. Terry Honan was knocked down and another of the boys baled out, and we never fired a shot! I swung round and saw Terry in his parachute, then they hit me. I got a bullet between my legs, which hit the compass." [89]

Sgt Terry Honan's W8200 was hit in the engine almost immediately, which caught fire, and he baled out at 12,000 feet with a bullet in his left arm; he landed safely in a rubber plantation some 15 miles from Johore. Moments later Sgt Rod MacMillan's W8186/NF-X was also hit and fell out of control, with most of its tail unit shot away; he too managed to bale out and came down in the same plantation as Honan. He later reported:

"There was a group of Japanese aircraft sort of playing around and doing aerobatics at about 15,000 feet. We had been climbing up and were higher than them. When we turned towards them we were badly jumped by higher up aircraft in the sun. I don't think Mackenzie saw them and I didn't see them until I was on the receiving end. They (the lower group) were the bait and enticing us in. I was just lining up a bead on one of these Jap aircraft when I received an ungodly belt from behind. I think it virtually knocked me out and when I came to, the plane was spinning out of control. I tried to get it under control but had no success so I had to assume the tail was virtually blown off, and so I baled out. I think I was below 10,000 feet. I was scared that I might be shot at but nothing like that happened. I landed in a rubber plantation with the parachute all tangled up in the bananas of a rubber tree. I couldn't get it down so just left it there. My back was hurting – bad bruising. It wasn't more than that and I wandered out to see if I could find some civilisation, and came across Terry Honan, the other chap who had baled out. His plane had caught fire and he got out in a hurry, too. We must have been within 200-300 yards of one another when we landed. The Aussie Army picked us up and we got a ride with the GOC. He tossed us into his jeep and took us to Singapore."

Sgt Perce Killick's aircraft did not come under direct attack, but he saw Honan's aircraft in trouble:

"Terry Honan got shot through the left arm, between his elbow and his shoulder. I went down to protect Terry because they were notorious for shooting you in your parachutes. I just rolled over and dived to go down after him. His plane was on fire but he baled out OK. I covered him until he was about 100 feet off the deck, and then I started climbing up again but by that time it was pretty much all over. Rod MacMillan was my room-mate. He was hit behind in the armour plating, at the back of his seat, and was as black as the ace of spades from his collar down to his backside for about a week."

Meanwhile, Sgt Jim MacIntosh (W8171) tangled with a Ki-27, as noted in his logbook:

"Engaged two large enemy fighter formations – 125 Navy 0s and Army 98s [sic]. They attacked us from above. We were at 9,000 feet and they came over at 14,000 feet. We were eight and four of us were shot down. Two baled out and two force-landed. I forced Army 98 into jungle."

Apparently his claim was not confirmed. The remaining Buffaloes also came under attack, Plt Off Jack McAneny force-landing his damaged machine (W8150) at Sembawang, a bullet having pierced his petrol tank, whilst Plt Off Snow White landed W8191/NF-D at Kallang with damage to his propeller and fuselage, although he believed his adversary had also been damaged. In this disastrous first action for the New Zealand squadron, Plt Off Bunt Pettit's aircraft (W8141) was also hit, as he recalled:

"We'd been told to orbit base and we were swinging round. There was a lot of activity going on and some considerable excitement. In point of fact the Dutch squadron had engaged Jap fighters. They were about the same height as we were about half to three-quarters of a mile away on our port side. We were so busy watching them milling round that we very carelessly didn't notice a bunch of Japs getting up behind us, and we were attacked. As soon as the rattling started on the back of the armour plating I realised that they weren't playing about, and there was some serious business going on. We assumed they were Zeros but I'm not sure. They came in from behind us and I just jammed on left rudder to keep the plane in a skid and hopefully dodge, and throw their aim off. I looked round behind and this thing flashed over the top of me – they'd obviously come down in a dive. Strangely enough I thought it was an aircraft with a long glass cover over the cockpit, but I think it must have been a momentary impression rather than an educated view. I managed to get in several small bursts but these were made at too long a range and as a consequence were completely ineffective. I felt something go into my arm but it wasn't seriously inconveniencing me. The Squadron split and I reported that I had a slight arm wound and was ordered to carry on orbiting base, which I did. I gained a little height and was again attacked by several aircraft, but broke loose, and scrambled back again, by which time the sky was relatively clear. It's amazing how quickly it empties in action. I was eventually called back to base and landed. The so-called bullet was a splinter from a bullet or from the armour casing that it had struck."

When B Flight eventually arrived on the scene, Flt Lt Hutcheson and Sgt Perce Killick were the only two to make contact with the raiders. Hutcheson encountered two fighters which he identified as Navy 0s, although he managed to get away unscathed whilst the two Ki-27s attacked by Killick easily evaded him with their outstanding manoeuvrability. Sgt Eddie Kuhn later admitted:

"In this first engagement I was so confused that I simply fired at anything that appeared in front of me. I happened to mention this after landing to a horrified IO, who said 'But you could be firing on our own planes!' I replied, 'That's correct, but it's the truth!'"

The 11th Sentai pilots claimed ten of their opponents shot down during this combat, against actual losses of two Buffaloes shot down and five damaged. Close behind the Ki-27s came a formation of 30 bombers from the 7th Flying Battalion, escorted by 42 Ki-43s from the 59th and 64th Sentais. Whilst taking off from Sungei Patani one of the 59th Sentai aircraft had collided with three others; all four were lost, with two pilots killed and the other two injured.

Over Singapore the Ki-43 pilots reported a lack of defending fighters, subsequently the only victory claimed was a single Blenheim shot down by the 59th Sentai. There is no record of any such loss, although this might refer to the Blenheim that failed to return from the night attack against Sungei Patani. 243 Squadron was scrambled too late, Sgt Arthur noting:

"At 0630 we took off for Kallang and patrolled there for approximately three-quarters of an hour, to make sure no Japs stayed around. Marra and I acted as top cover. If there were any fighters about, we had to tackle them and let the rest look after the bombers. We then went to Butterworth and circled around another town before returning. A batch of 100 fighters and bombers must have followed us back because they started to raid Tengah just as we landed. Luckily all bombs fell wide. Most of them landed in rubber plantations around the drome. We quickly refuelled and took off after the Japs but didn't intercept them. When we landed we had done three hours in the air without any breakfast. In A Flight, Wipiti contacted the Japs and a 97 fighter sprayed his tailplane and petrol tanks with bullets. Luckily the self-sealing tanks worked for a change."

Nine Buffaloes led by Sqn Ldr Harper had also been scrambled by 21RAAF/453 Squadron from Sembawang, but these failed to intercept. After being directed to three sectors by a harassed controller, the Australians gave chase to one formation of 27 bombers which were leaving the target. However, the Buffaloes were seen by the Japanese crews and the bombers went into shallow dives with throttles wide open, and left their pursuers in their wake. Flt Lt Wells, the Adjutant, wrote:

"Our aircraft on many occasions attempted interception but were unable to gain the necessary height or speed to engage the enemy, or when they did engage them, they were greatly outnumbered, outmanoeuvred and out-gunned by the superior enemy aircraft types, particularly the Navy 0."

One of the Australian pilots summed up the situation less eloquently, when he commented:

"Bombers outpacing fighters – you've got to f**king well laugh!"

Following the Buffaloes' return, the pilots were told to await further orders in the alert hut, not particularly advisable, as Flt Lt Kinninmont explained:

"The alert hut was a large room at one end of our double-storied brick Station Headquarters building. Fifty yards across the road was the edge of the aerodrome, and down to the left were four huge iron hangars. Straight out from the alert hut our fighters were lined up ready to go. Other Buffaloes were dispersed in built-up earthen pens around the edge of the field, back in the rubber. Hangars and workshops and all vital sections were roughly inside this headquarters area. Thus the pilots spent most of their time in the centre of the choicest target on the station; which fact left them quite unconcerned." [90]

Later in the day, 21RAAF/453 Squadron made their last attempt at a strike on Kuantan, only to find the target covered by cloud right down to the ground. During the return flight the Buffaloes flown by Flg Off Dainty Wallace and Sgt Grant Harrison collided while weaving. The latter's propeller was knocked off and, as he was too low to bale out, he force-landed W8202 amongst trees just off the Mersing[91], as he later recalled:

"On the way back, as we were passing Mersing, we flew very low and ran into turbulence. It was getting towards midday and the turbulence at that time was very severe. We were flying very fast, with the throttle full forward. We were following our CO, and the Buffaloes were spread out in a wide V formation. Because of its large radial engine, vision forward and below the Buffalo was very limited, and I was forced to concentrate on the aircraft in front of me. A Buffalo behind me, flown by F/O Dainty Wallace, flew too close to me from behind and slightly above – and the next thing I knew he had knocked my canopy off and had hit and bent my airscrew. Fortunately, I still had a bit of airspeed, about 280mph, and I gained as much height as I could. I just pulled up. I lowered my flaps by working pumps by hand. I went through my crash-landing procedures. Switched off the ignition, tightened my safety harness and crash-landed in the trees." [92]

Harrison was unhurt and set out for the coast. On the second night he found himself in a mangrove swamp and had to sleep in a fishing hut; during the night the tide rose and three crocodiles appeared and kept him company! Following their departure next morning, he once more set out for the coast and, after a six-day trek, was found by an Australian Army patrol.

Meanwhile, closely escorted by Flg Off Barrie Hood, Wallace struggled to keep his damaged AN171 airborne but when they reached the sea near Tengora, he was forced to ditch, injuring himself in the process. However he succeeded in reaching the shore and, after struggling through dense jungle for two days, came across a river. He built himself a raft and floated down river until he too was found by an Australian Army patrol. Although the patrol was only two miles from its base at Jemaluang, it took five days to penetrate the jungle. Wallace was eventually flown back to Singapore in a MVAF Moth sent to collect him.

Later, at 1400, there was another scramble when 70 of the 12th Flying Battalion's

Ki-27s returned, this time engaging aircraft of 243 Squadron and three Brewsters of 2-V1G-V. Leading A Flight of 243 Squadron, Flt Lt Garden (W8139/WP-B) attacked nine Ki-27s head-on in misty cloud, claiming one destroyed as it closed on him; he reported seeing the pilot's face as the Japanese aircraft passed below so close that its radio aerial dented the starboard wing of his Buffalo. He then claimed a second shot down and a third probably destroyed before being attacked, as he recalled:

"There were three of them in formation on my tail and I could not out-turn them. Meanwhile they were hammering my mainplanes and fuselage with their machine-guns. I was dying for an excuse to bale out, until I remembered the advice of Flt Lt Tim Vigors, which was to the effect that when you think all is lost and death and destruction are imminent, just shut your eyes, work the rudder left and right, open the throttle to maximum and 'pudding basin' the control column. I did just that and when I opened my eyes there was not an aircraft in the sky to be seen, but my aircraft had suffered considerable damage and was flying extremely badly and vibrating severely. I turned for home. As the aircraft came to a halt at the end of the runway, it slowly collapsed around me."

A section from B Flight also engaged the fighters, Flg Off Blondie Holder claiming two and Sgt Geoff Fisken (W8147/WP-O) one. Of his second – and almost last – victory, Fisken recalled:

"We were about a thousand feet above them and we came out of a cloud and there were about 20 Japs below us. One turned towards me and I went down and we both kept firing at one another. I recall seeing his cannon shells coming at me. Luckily I pulled up and he went downwards, otherwise we would have both died. He blew up underneath me. The next thing, my plane went into what seemed like an uncontrollable, inverted spin, reacting to the exploding Jap plane. Unable to correct it, I decided to get out, but I couldn't disconnect my oxygen mask. The problem was apparently a result of a modification I had made to my helmet, which was made from a very soft snakeskin, bought from the 'Reptile Store' in Singapore. The oxygen mask wouldn't button on to this helmet, which opened from the back and was then tightened up after you put it on. I had got around the problem by sewing the helmet onto the oxygen mask. The mask was connected to a stainless steel oxygen tube by a bayonet-type junction. A stray bullet had gone right into this arrangement stopping it from loosening. 'It'll break,' I thought as I clambered out.

"But it didn't and I was left hanging from the side of the plane, swinging by my head and my hands, as it continued its spin towards oblivion. So I got back into my spinning plane. I had begun to see scenes from my life, my childhood on the family farm back in Gisborne, flashing before my eyes. I remember little else happening as my plane spun on its four-mile journey towards the ground. Somehow it managed to come out of the spin and I was able to pull it back to an even keel and return to base. This was the one occasion in the war when I had the experience of seeing my life playing before me. I must have been pretty close to checking out. Don't ask me how I did it, but I must have done all of the right things."

On landing back at Kallang, Fisken taxied his damaged machine up to the dispersal area:

"When I stopped the plane, I asked the mechanic for a pair of pliers but still couldn't undo the oxygen pin – it was bent – and later found that several bullets had done the damage. It was only when I took off the helmet – it had never entered my head to take the helmet off – that it sunk in I would have been free! Chiefy [Flt Sgt Mothersdale] came along as I was calling myself all the bloody fools in the world! I remember standing on the runway, hearing the Engineer Officer saying, 'What are you doing just standing there?' 'I've just undone the bloody strap!' I replied. He was a little confused until I explained. The kill of a Japanese Army 97 fighter was confirmed by an independent observer, as was the spin and my recovery. Our squadron had lost another pilot that day, though."

George Mothersdale recalled Fisken's return:

"W8147 was the last to taxi in. As Fisken climbed down from the cockpit I asked 'How did it go Fisk – any joy?' and then I could see that he was concerned about something, and we – the groundcrew and myself – were somewhat shaken by his reply. He said 'Not sure – I went out of control so I tried to bale out and couldn't. I got one leg over the side and was stuck, so I tried to get back in again and couldn't – I was stuck with one leg in and one leg out!' We looked at each other and I then asked how he managed to get back in the aircraft, to which he replied: 'I managed to get hold of the stick, and then got my hand on the throttle and had another go. When I heaved the stick about I managed to get it back under control, so I got back in and flew it back home!' And that accounted for his eyes looking somewhat bloodshot."

Sgt Reg 'Slim' Newman (W8137/WP-C), a 22-year-old from Taranaki, was not so fortunate and died from his wounds following a force-landing at Kallang. Another Buffalo (W8187/WP-R) returned badly damaged, although Sgt Ginger Baldwin was not hurt. This may have been the occasion recalled by Plt Off Marra:

"Baldwin was a quick-tempered fellow, but really a good guy. He was like a lot of the blokes, you couldn't keep him down. I didn't see it but Baldwin got in front of a squadron of Jap bombers and, during a head-on attack, he pushed the tit and nothing happened. Somehow or other he managed to get around and do it again – and for the second time nothing happened."

Another pair of Buffaloes flown by Plt Off Bonham (WP-F) and Sgt Greenslade (WP-A) was also jumped but both pilots managed to evade by diving into cloud. Bonham then pursued a formation of 27 bombers:

"Chased enemy aircraft 50 miles. Attacked alone 27 Type 96 Mitsubishi bombers. One probable, another damaged. Confirmed at later date. Force-landed at Seletar owing to rear gunners hitting petrol tank and hydraulics etc."

Sgt Arthur wrote:

"Ops wouldn't let Veg and I go after the Japs but made us fly over the drome. Mowbray Garden flew the S/Ldr's kite [W8193/WP-V] and got it well and truly shot up. Mowbray claims to have got two certs and one probable. Actually only one Jap has been seen to crash . . . Fisk and Blondie claim to have shot down one and two respectively. Newman tried to dogfight them and got a couple of shots in his stomach, one across his forehead and one through his tail. He made a good forced landing but died while trying to doctor himself up with the first aid outfit."

The three Dutch pilots also reported engaging nine Ki-27s at 13,000 feet, Lt August Deibel (B-3110) claiming two shot down, but was then shot down himself and baled out slightly wounded in the head. The commanding officer, Kapt Jacob van Helsdingen (B-396), claimed one as did Sgt Gerardus Bruggink; the latter force-landed with a damaged engine. It would seem to have been a very successful action for the Buffaloes, with eleven Ki-27s claimed shot down; however, although Japanese losses are not known they almost certainly did not match the claims made against them.

A little later, sections of Buffaloes from 243 Squadron were again scrambled, following which Fisken (W8147/WP-O), in his second action of the day, reported:

"Big raid on Singapore – 125 Jap bombers and 45 fighters. Two bullet holes in plane after scrap with 18 Navy 0s."

He later commented:

"By comparison, the Zero and the Buffalo were miles apart – the Zero could out-pace, out-climb and out-manoeuvre the Buffalo but could not out-dive it. To go into a Zero on even terms or at a slight disadvantage was literally committing suicide, and after a few early lessons when in that position, you turned over on your back and dived for the deck. In one of our first encounters I put my undercarriage and flaps fully down – I remember thinking I'd hit a brick wall but I did manage to turn inside the Zero and give him a few seconds' burst. I didn't wait to see the result as there were plenty of Japs around."

Plt Off Edgar Pevreal and his No.2, Sgt Rex Weber, came across a lone fighter, but the former's guns refused to fire. Weber was only able to fire a few shots before the fighter – identified as a Type 0 – turned inside him, so he wisely dived for home; he wrote:

"I have been up twice and in the last flip I should have shot down a Type 0 if I could have thought straight, but I got excited and Pev's guns all stopped – so I was left alone to deal with him, and after a few haphazard shots he started to show me just how well his plane could turn. If I had tons of guts I would have stayed about but Rex A. had heard too much of the turning capabilities of the Type 0. Personally, I should be surprised if my friendly Jap had trouble getting home. I am glad to say that I had no great fear. However, I have no intention of rushing anything and my motto will be caution and hope."

Plt Off Noel Sharp (W8138/NF-O), attached from 488 Squadron, claimed another fighter probably destroyed, and it is believed that Sgt Russ Reynolds submitted claims for two probables also, but Sgt Noel Rankin – a native of Invercargill and one of the older pilots at 28-years of age – was shot down in W8234 and killed; his parachute (but not his body) was later recovered from the sea. Marra remembered:

"Oliver and Rankin were great mates. Rankin was shot down one stinking wet day. We had had a pretty busy time too and Oliver thought he might have been paddling round in his Mae West. At that stage we didn't have dinghys, just the Mae West, and they were the type you blew up manually. They weren't the bottle-operated type. So Oliver asked the CO if two or three of us could go off late afternoon when things had quietened down and there were unlikely to be any more raids, and have a look around. Well, we searched round in this awful weather where we thought Rankin would probably be, but we couldn't find him. It was blowing a gale, the water was all dirty and I don't know whether, even if he had been there, we could have found him. A pilot in a Mae West that he'd had for six months or so, which was no longer bright yellow, would have been difficult to spot. This upset Oliver and I think he dreamt about it. A couple of days later he decided he would get some of those bastards but he never came back either."

On his second sortie of the day, Max Greenslade (WP-A) was more successful than earlier:

"Separated in cloud from leader. Dived on nine Navy 0s, and straight on to base. One damaged. Part of tailplane flew into air. Navy 0 [last seen] losing height."

Kallang's Station Commander, Wg Cdr Chignell, accompanied 243 Squadron on one scramble in the Station HQ's Buffalo, as recalled by Flt Sgt Mothersdale:

"I saw Wg Cdr Chignell scrambling with some of A Flight's pilots. As he passed me I wished him good shooting. Later, I was at dispersal when some of A Flight's aircraft taxied in. As he passed me I enquired if he'd had any luck and he gave me a grim smile and said, 'No place up there for an old timer!'"

Chignell was 36-years-old. He had flown the odd Hurricane sortie during the Battle of Britain while stationed at Biggin Hill but it is not known if he had participated in combat.

A number of Buffaloes from 488 Squadron were also scrambled, but could not gain sufficient altitude to engage the raiders. One of these, W8135 flown by Sgt Vern Meaclem, suffered an oil pipe fracture, and crash-landed in a swamp near Seletar, the aircraft being a complete write-off although without injury to the pilot. Of the day's losses, LAC Max Boyd of 488 Squadron reflected:

"All our kites in action and we lost five of them. All the pilots parachuted to safety. We started the day well but finished badly. We observe the whole range of pre-take-off human emotions as we help strap the pilot into the cockpit. Four straps, one over each leg, and one over each shoulder, all to a central post, then the locking pin has to be inserted. Sometimes the pilot's hands shake so much in the excitement that we fit the pin although he is supposed to do that himself for security confidence. When he takes off the last contact he has with this earth is with his flight rigger and flight mechanic. When and if he returns we welcome him. Pilots often entrust their wallets to them with instructions on what to do in the event of non-return. The plane, pilot, rigger and mechanic are the sharp end of fighter warfare, and at the point of take-off are all equal as men. Seldom do officers pull rank at this action-packed time. The Sgt Pilots become as one of us. We feel the loss of a pilot very badly as we have come to know them so well."

The bad weather during the day had also frustrated the JNAF's first attempt at a daylight raid on Singapore, 81 bombers from the three Borneo-based kokutais being forced to turn back. Thus, at the end of this first traumatic day of the blitz, a total of 54 sorties had been flown by the defenders, during which three Buffaloes had been shot down, three had crash-landed due to combat damage, and at least four more damaged; a further three were lost in accidents. At the end of the day Weber confided to his diary:

"Today has been the big day as far as the Singapore Fighter Command is concerned – the Japs have been sending fighters over here all day and our lads have been doing their best, but as I have known well all the time – thanks to the inability of lots of people to organise, train and run a fighter force – it was just a great big shambles. Poor old Slim Newman was shot down and also Prof Rankin."

Of this period, Jim MacIntosh remembered:

"On the occasion that Rankin went missing we were informed, I think it was the following day, that his aircraft had been found crashed on one of the Dutch islands, south of Singapore and his ripped parachute nearby."

Vin Arthur did not share in the success of 243 Squadron:

"I had two scrambles today and didn't see a single Jap. The last time my kite got a bad oil leak. As I flew through the air the oil would smoke on the exhaust pipe and I would leave a trail of black smoke behind me."

488 Squadron's Plt Off Bunt Pettit was off flying for a few days following his wound, but was not idle:

"I was appointed liaison officer with the Dutch squadron. There was nothing very much I did or could do for them – they seemed to be fairly well self contained. If they wanted supplies of any description, or if there was something I could do for them, they'd ask. Their English was certainly a lot better than my Dutch. It was interesting to be with them and, on occasions, help them a little. I can't remember any specific thing except discussing with them the relative performance of their aircraft and ours. Our Buffaloes had 1100 horses, while they had 1200 hp motor, and they had an electrically controlled pitch, as opposed to ours, which was hydraulic. Their aircraft were slightly better than ours. They were permanent Dutch air force and I think they knew a lot more about Buffaloes than we did, and they were more likely to shoot down a Jap than we were, because, first they had a superior aircraft, and, secondly they were more experienced. I only worked with them during their time on the ground on Kallang and I think it was just some formality to give them some link with British HQ. It was a nominal title rather than anything of any much use."

Earlier during the day, 243 Squadron had received its second Buffalo night fighter – W8231, promptly named 'Black Magic' – as Flt Sgt George Mothersdale remembered:

"Modifying the two Buffaloes for night operations was an improvised job. These two aircraft taxied in A Flight's dispersal at Kallang on the morning of the 12th, one at 0700 and the other at 0900. They stood at the end of A Flight's aircraft line all day and were taxied away next morning. I did not see them again at Kallang. They apparently went to Tengah. Apart from the modified exhaust manifolds and matt-black finish, they looked like standard Buffaloes. It is highly probable that a flight was formed with the two aircraft in the night interceptor rôle, and that a flight commander to specialise in this rôle was appointed. I do not know the tactics employed but the enemy aircraft were aluminium surface-finished – that's how they looked from the ground – and they made easy sightings in any degree of moonlight; they reflected glints and in a searchlight beam the complete aircraft shone and reflected the light. They flew at night in a Vee formation, a consolidated target for attacking aircraft."

While night sorties were undertaken mainly by Sqn Ldr Howell and Flt Lt Garden, Plt Off Terry Marra also participated:

"I started doing quite a lot of night work at this stage. They came up with a wonderful scheme. The exhausts of the Buffalo were big round things and at night there was a sheet of flame pouring back. You were visible for miles, with these two sheets of flame. They modified one Buffalo and instead of having one exhaust we had five or six small ones coming out all round the cowl, with a sort of V fishtail. It made a different noise. I got the first one that was modified."

13 January

It was on this morning that the second reinforcement convoy, codenamed DM1, carrying 51 crated Hurricanes and 24 pilots, made its approach towards Keppel Harbour. Air HQ anticipated a heavy Japanese reaction and all units were told to expect to defend the convoy should it come under attack. Sgt Don Clow of 488 Squadron recalled the briefing:

"We had been especially briefed to make sure that if we were sent off, then we were to intercept. The CO couldn't tell us what was on the convoy, but went so far as to say that it didn't matter if all the Buffaloes were shot down in the process – the convoy had better get through. So we guessed it was the Hurricanes coming – we had heard rumour of it. We had been alerted to expect to go off earlier in the morning than we did, but it was raining quite heavily. Then, as the rain cleared, we were scrambled. We went down south of the island. As we climbed up we finally saw the enemy aircraft – roughly 50 of them – bombers."

The JNAF had again attempted to carry out a raid on Singapore, 81 bombers once more taking off from Borneo early in the morning, but again bad weather interfered, and only a single chutai of Kanoya Ku G4Ms was able to bomb their primary target – Keppel Harbour – the attack commencing at about 0930. Others attacked alternative targets, and the 30 G3Ms of the Mihoro Ku were intercepted by eight Buffaloes of 488 Squadron, which attacked from behind and below. Flt Lt Hutcheson's aircraft (W8148) was at once hit by fire from the rear gunners and dived away to force-land at Tengah, as recalled by Sgt Peter Ballard of 4AACU:

"He made an emergency landing at Tengah after combat and was confronted by Grp Capt Watts[93], who ordered him off the airfield immediately, because his aircraft there would be likely to encourage further air attacks on Tengah. John was not impressed at all!"

Plt Off Wally Greenhalgh (W8168/NF-T) – with only two of his guns firing – attacked one bomber and saw smoke issue from one of its engines:

"The only partial success I had was that I probably got a Jap bomber. We had eight aircraft in the air, because at that stage we were struggling to get any more than eight or ten aircraft up. I was flying No.2 to Johnny Hutcheson and we got behind and above these Navy Type 96 bombers. I managed to get in a couple of decent bursts into them from behind and then we were driven off. There were a few Zeros on our tails and the last I saw was one [bomber] disappearing with smoke coming out of one engine. But whether it crashed or got home I wouldn't know."

Plt Off Jack Oakden (W8185/NF-V) was shot down by the rear gunners, who gained direct hits on his fuel tank; Plt Off Marra of 243 Squadron recalled:

"Oakie got shot up when he was out over the drink. So he thinks 'this will be a piece of cake, I've done this before' [see Chapter I]. In he comes, levels out, hits the water – and is 20 fathoms down before he could do anything! But he got out of that one, too. Some fishermen picked him up and brought him back."

Sgt Bunny De Maus' aircraft was hit before he could even get within range, although he was able to land safely. Sgt Clow (W8235) was another victim of the gunners:

"We were too low and too far behind, without the rate of climb that was needed, and they were on their bombing run. We were just coming up in a straight line towards the convoy so we simply turned in from where we were and flew in behind the bombers. There was a Dutch pilot and Johnny Oakden alongside and, while I lost sight of the Dutchman, I saw Oakie firing. I selected one aircraft and had a go at it. The starboard motor was smoking a lot, and he was going down in a slow turn to the right, but I got hit several times by return fire. They actually holed the petrol tanks and fuel was running into my cockpit. I stayed a while and then decided to bale out and I went into the sea. I had a bit of trouble as there was a breeze blowing and I got tangled up in the water. I got towed around for a while and of course I didn't have a dinghy – just the alternative mouth-inflated Mae West. I swam to an island – just a heap of rocks.

"I didn't know how long I would be there and noticed there was another one just a bit further away so I swam there, but it was the same. Of course I was thinking about water – before too long I would need a drink – so there was another island, quite a long way away, and about half way across I could see a heap of rock stretching about 50 feet or so up into the air. I could see rough water and waves breaking, so I guessed there would be rocks there. It was a long swim, but I had hung onto my Smith & Wesson revolver. I fired three or four shots, which created enough noise to cause a dog to bark on the middle of the island. Somebody came and picked me up in a canoe, and I spent the night with them on the island. I was picked up by a Dutch rescue party the following morning who took me to Sambau where our rescue launch picked me up."

The bombers' gunners underestimated their success on this occasion, claiming only one of three attacking fighters shot down. Recorded the 488 Squadron diarist:

"Today, although we did not meet up with the fighters, because we did not attack from above, we were badly shot up by rear gunfire. The Japanese bomber formations of 27 packed aircraft throw out such an accurate and heavy rear-gun barrage that they are very difficult to attack. Some way must be found to break up these mass formations and attack bombers independently. No doubt there was a fighter escort in the near vicinity, but it did not pick up our fighters owing to cloudy conditions and also because we attacked from below. In the last two days, 488 Squadron has lost seven aircraft, had many others damaged, with no casualties to the enemy. No blame can be attached to the pilots, who have done their best with Buffaloes. Until we fly as wings of 36 aircraft we will be unable to inflict heavy damage to the enemy."

These were not 488 Squadron's only losses however, for even as the air battle was taking place, Sgt Eddie Kuhn, who was air testing AN187, had to bale out into the sea when the engine seized and caught fire:

"I radioed base and gave a positional report. The Buffalo was now in a dive and still on fire so I exited. It exploded when it struck the ground, creating a large circle of fire, which I was afraid I might drift down into. I pulled the shrouds and came down in the sea away from the danger. I was in the drink for four hours and out of sight of land until a Chinese fisherman in a sampan rescued me. I gave him all the money I had and allowed him to retrieve and keep the chute, which was in demand because it was made from silk. In return the fisherman gave me some 'Craven A' cigarettes, which were glorious. Eventually an Army launch appeared, onto which I was transferred and taken back to Singapore."

The efforts and losses of the New Zealanders were not all in vain however, and none of the ships they helped defend was damaged. The convoy eventually arrived safely at Keppel Harbour under escort by 14 Buffaloes of 21RAAF/453 Squadron led by Sqn Ldr Harper. The unloading began without delay. The Squadron diarist for the day, Sgt Jim Austin, wrote:

"Another convoy patrol this morning. Mick couldn't go as he was waiting down at the docks all ready to get things organised. Shortly after this patrol landed, the Japs came over. A big storm was working in from the east and the whole island was practically blacked out. Still the Japs managed to let off some bombs – some of the brass hats at Air HQ (tis rumoured) are now in need of a little polishing. Van, Greg, Alf and Keith went up to do a patrol to look for dive-bombers, but the rain came on in earnest and soon the drome became u/s."

Later in the day one section of light bombers also raided Singapore, escorted by the two Ki-43 sentais. The Japanese pilots reported engaging six Buffaloes, four of which they claimed shot down. 243 Squadron had scrambled after the incoming raid in very heavy rain with thick cloud, which caused their formation to become scattered. The leader, Flt Lt Garden (W8242/WP-K), broke cloud to find himself alone:

"Dead ahead I saw some single-engined Japanese aircraft which had not observed me, and were larking on the tops of the clouds amongst themselves practicing mock attacks on each other. I stalked these and when I got close to them I chose one particular victim; at that moment he saw me and we went into a tight turn but I was able to hold him, and with a long burst I crippled him. He dived to the ground."

The Army later reported that the fighter had crash-landed in Johore and that the pilot then shot himself in the head. Of this incident, war correspondent Ian Morrison recorded:

"The Japanese aerial personnel who were taken prisoner suggested that they are the élite in the enemy's armed forces, as is the case with Germany and also, to a large extent, with ourselves. It is not true that the Japanese fly without parachutes. Nor is it true that in the big bombing formations only the commander's plane is equipped with all the proper navigational instruments. But it is true that one Japanese fighter pilot, who crashed in Johore, climbed out of his plane, and, after holding back a group of curious Malays, pulled a pistol out of its holster, put it to his head, and shot himself. The flyers are perhaps the most fanatical of any section of the Japanese forces." [94]

Other sections of Buffaloes also ran into raiders, Plt Off Marra (W8231) and Sgt Arthur (W8140) being set upon by eight Ki-43s whilst attempting to attack a bomber formation, as the latter graphically recalled:

"Today, Veg and I had our first encounter with the Japs. At approx 1100, two of A Flight and two B Flight sections scrambled led by F/L Garden. He didn't climb fast enough so Veg and I out-climbed him. Somehow we then lost the rest of the formation. We were stooging around at 25,000 feet waiting for something to come, when my oil temperature suddenly went up and the engine missed badly. I thought it had run out of petrol so changed tanks. However, the engine continued to cut whenever a load was placed on it. All the while dense black smoke was issuing from the exhaust. I then thought it was time to pancake so I signalled Veg and down we came. He had to come down because his R/T was u/s. I then took off [again] with Veg, flying Black Magic W8231. Around Changi we saw 27 Jap bombers heading for Kallang at about 20,000 feet, so immediately climbed furiously through the clouds. Again I had trouble with the oil temperature rising. When at 16,000 feet, Veg spotted 35 bombers. We immediately flew parallel to them, climbing up to their altitude of approx 20,000 feet."

Suddenly eight Ki-43s came hurtling out of the sun:

"Veg saw them first and yelled 'Bandits, 6 o'clock! Look out!' We both immediately pulled around and I went into a spin. I left her in the spin until I reached a layer of clouds about 1,000 feet below. Veg, when he pulled round, started to do a half roll when a Jap overshot him. He let rip a short burst at the Jap after righting himself and then dived into the clouds. As he went into the clouds another Jap overshot him. Veg had about six bullet holes in his kite, one being through his perspex, not six inches from his head. After I got in the cloud I tried to pull up out of the cloud behind the Japs, but three of them were waiting for me so I scrammed. I tried this three times and each time found three Japs waiting for me. As the Type 0s can easily outmanoeuvre a Buff, I knew it was useless to dogfight them. After the last attack my engine began to spew oil, which smoked furiously on the exhaust pipe, giving the impression the kite was on fire. I then returned to the drome and made a hurried landing. Coming in, the engine cut twice due to a petrol pump failing. In the middle of the drome, leaning on one undercarriage leg, was the kite of a 488 Flight Commander.

"When the Japs were shooting at me they should have got me. Veg saved my life by warning me in time. It was a strange feeling during the flight – actually it was a kind of feelingless. Kronk tried to dogfight some today and got his plane badly shot up."

Marra gave an account of his fortunate escape from injury:

"Suddenly we were engaged by eight Type 0s. It had always been a concern of mine whether you would hear a bloke behind you firing during a scrap – hear the fire above the noise above your own motor. Well, I found out that you could hear it all right. There was a bit of a skirmish. The first guy had a go, as did the second, as they went past. I thought I might get a bang at the second in a circle we were doing. The first Jap in the meantime had pulled up again while I was giving his partner all I could. I couldn't see any strikes though. The next thing I knew was that a bullet came through the canopy and my radio mast, which sat out in front, just disappeared. It sounded to me like a 16-inch shell but it was probably only a .30 bullet. So I knew it was time to get out and I did a hike. I must have been leaning forward, thank goodness, because it went between my head and the armour plate. The entry hole lined up with the exit hole and the bullet could only have gone between my head and the armour plate. It must have been fired from the beam. There were four bullet holes in my aircraft, obviously from the Navy 0s behind."

Plt Off Noel Sharp (W8138/NF-O) claimed one fighter shot down, while Plt Off Pevreal (W8184/WP-G) and Sgt Kronk (W8139/WP-B) jointly claimed a probable; Pevreal recalled:

"There were two of us [Kronk was his No.2]. There was supposed to be a fighter sweep over Singapore. It was fairly cloudy and we flew around for quite a long time, and we didn't see them until way up above us were about 50 Zeros [sic], heading back home. Needless to say, we let them go. They looked to be about 10,000 feet above us and two of us weren't going to do too much harm to them. It looked like suicide to me. We did finally get onto one – he must have had engine trouble for he was streaming smoke. We managed to get up close to him . . . we fired at him and he disappeared into the oil smoke clouds. Whether we hit him or not, I don't know, but he was still going fast and trailing smoke."

Wellington-born Sgt Russ Reynolds (W8238), another 19-year-old, failed to return from this sortie, as recalled by Sqn Ldr Howell, who had taken off at the head of six Buffaloes:

"We took off to engage a very large number of bombers and fighters. The Flight separated after being attacked by the escorting fighters, and Sgt Reynolds was believed to have taken cover in a cloud. His Flight Commander had a dogfight with six Navy 0s before he could take cover, and did not see anyone from his Flight again until he landed. Sgt Reynolds did not return and neither he nor his aircraft were seen again. He was an extremely popular young lad, nicknamed 'Smiler'."

Reynolds'aircraft was reported by others as having been shot down into the sea south of Singapore at midday, causing Weber to confide to his diary:

"A bad day – no organisation, no leadership, no aircraft. Morale as low as it could be. Poor old Russ Reynolds missing. A game lad who did not relish dying anymore than I do but who had sufficient guts to carry on with the job. I wonder if I will be alive tomorrow."

Sgt Jim MacIntosh was also involved:

"I was one of two pilots of 488 flying with 243 Squadron when we intercepted 15 bombers over Malaya. We were successful enough in that interception for the Jap bombers to drop all their bombs in the jungle. The two squadrons had to combine because we were so short of aircraft and on this occasion someone else and I went over to 243, with our Buffaloes and flew with them. From memory there were six of us. We converged on the bombers – they obviously had no fighter support – well up Johore state and we did various attacks. I remember doing a dive attack – and coming up underneath firing. All 15 bombers dropped their bombs, and turned away north. They didn't get over Singapore."

CBS broadcaster Cecil Brown was among those painfully aware of the Buffaloes' limitations and wrote:

"The Brewster Buffaloes are proving ineffective, the main trouble being that they cannot get up high enough or fast enough. One Brewster fighter pilot told me that his 'ship' cannot operate above 17,000 feet. The Jap Zeros, and of course their bombers, stay up above that altitude, and we don't have a chance to hit them. Besides, we are so slow in getting up in the air that the Japs drop their bombs before we can do anything about it. The big advantage of the Brewster is that it's a strong crate, and when you crash you have a chance to walk away alive." [95]

In his diary, Vin Arthur commented on the day's activities:

"The bombers dropped their dirt on the residential area around here, the house the officers of our Flight are staying in having a bomb land on the lawn. It blew the guts out of the house. Blondie's car, which was quite handy, was perforated. A bomb landed beside a lorry outside the house and blew it to smithereens. When we got there the lorry was burnt out and half the burnt corpse of the driver was lying in a drain of dirty water. A bomb also landed pretty near our house and wrecked two houses in the vicinity."

14 January

Bad weather again saved Singapore on the 14th, 51 JNAF bombers being turned back once more before reaching their target. 243 and 488 Squadrons had been scrambled to meet this force, as Arthur later recorded:

"At approx 1100, all the planes on the station were ordered off. 243 was supposed to fly behind 488 but B Flight out-climbed the rest. We climbed up to 27,000 feet without any difficulty and waited for the Japs. However, they turned back so we pancaked. If the Japs had come over we could have shot them down like flies. If only Veg and I were at 27,000 feet yesterday. I was very pleased to get W8178 back. She climbed like a son of a gun and I had no trouble with the oil temperature. Veg and I just soared ahead of the others."

A Buffalo, probably from 453 Squadron, falling victim to a Ki-27 over northern Malaya sometime in December 1941.

Pilots of 243 Squadron

Top left: Sqn Ldr Frank Howell DFC.

Top right: Flt Lt Tim Vigors DFC – posted to 453 Squadron.

Bottom left: Flt Lt John Mansel-Lewis – killed in a flying accident 4 April 1941.

Bottom right: Flt Lt Mowbray Garden.

ilots of 243 Squadron

p left: Flt Lt Ron Bows.

p right: Flg Off Blondie Holder.

Bottom left: Sgt Geoff Fisken RNZAF.

Bottom right: Plt Off Ron Shield RNZAF – killed in a ground collision with Sgt Shorty Elliott.

Pilots of 243 Squadron

Top left: Sgt Shorty Elliott RNZAF.
Top right: Plt Off Jim Cranstone RNZAF.

Bottom left: Plt Off Edgar Pevreal RNZAF.
Bottom right: Plt Off Terry Marra RNZAF.

Pilots of 243 Squadron

Top left: Plt Off Gordon Bonham RNZAF.

Top right: Sgt Rex Weber RNZAF.

Bottom left: Sgt Slim Newman RNZAF – killed in action 12 January 1942.

Bottom right: Sgt Max Greenslade RNZAF.

Pilots of 243 Squadron

Top left: Sgt John Oliver RNZAF – killed in action 15 January 1942.

Top right: Sgt Russ Reynolds RNZAF – killed in action 13 January 1942.

Bottom left: Sgt Prof Rankin RNZAF – killed in action 12 January 1942.

Bottom right: Sgt Charlie Kronk RNZAF.

Pilots of 21RAAF and 453 Squadrons

Top left: Sqn Ldr Bill Allshorn RAAF, CO of 21RAAF Squadron.

Top right: 21RAAF, (back row, left to right): Flg Offs Barry Hood and Bob Kirkman; (front row, left to right): Flg Offs Dick McKenny, Geoff Sheppard and Flt Lt Max White.

Middle left: Sqn Ldr William Harper RAF, CO of 453 Squadron, in the cockpit of his Buffalo with victory markings from his previous service in the UK.

Middle right: Flt Lt Doug Vanderfield RAAF (later in the war).

Bottom left: Plt Off Tom Livesey of 453 Squadron.

Pilots of 21RAAF and 453 Squadrons

Top left: Flt Lt Congo Kinninmont RAAF, 21 RAAF Squadron and later acting CO 453 Squadron.

Top right: Plt Off Bob Drury of 453 Squadron died from his injuries following combat on 22 December 1941.

Bottom: A Flight 453 Squadron, (front, left to right): Sgt Bill Collyer, Sgt Jim Austin, Sgt Alf Clare and Sgt Mac Read (killed in action 22 December 1941); (back, left to right): Sgt Keith Gorringe, Sgt Bill Halliday, Sgt Ross Leys, Sqn Ldr WJ Harper RAF, Flt Lt Doug Vanderfield, Sgt Harry Griffiths, Sgt George Scrimgeour, and Plt Off Geoff Angus.

p: Deadly opponent of the Buffaloes – a Ki-43 Oscar the 64th Sentai.

ttom: The tail of Lt Tadao Takayama's 64th Sentai -43, which crashed on 22 December 1941 following combat with 453 Squadron. Although Japanese reports indicate that the wings of the aircraft collapsed as it pulled out of a dive, it can be seen that it had undoubtedly also been hit by large-calibre bullets.

Buffaloes of 453 Squadron

Left: TD-N (W815[...]
Sgt Ron Oelrich
flying over Keppe[l]
Harbour; note lack
of sky blue band
around fuselage.
Plt Off David
Brown was killed
in this aircraft on
13 December 194[1]

Right: TD-G (W8231).
Sgt Harry Griffiths in the
cockpit of 'Shirley'; converted
to night fighter and renamed
'Black Magic'.

Left: W8157 with
Australian guard and
local children.

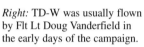

Right: TD-W was usually flown
by Flt Lt Doug Vanderfield in
the early days of the campaign.

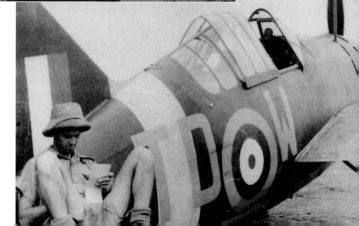

The New Zealanders

Top: Left to right: Plt Off Butch Hesketh (died of wounds 15 January 1942), Plt Off Jack Godsiff (injured in crash 4 January 1942) and Sgt Eddie Kuhn.

Middle left: Sgt Charlie Wareham flew many photo-reconnaissance sorties and was awarded the DFM.

Middle right: NF-T (W8168) of 488 Squadron under repair.

Bottom: Sgt Jim MacIntosh.

Top left: WP-C (W8137) shot down on 12 January 1942. Sgt Slim Newman was killed.

Top right: W8223 in which Plt Off Jack Godsiff crashed on 4 January 1942.

Middle right: Remains of a 488 Squadron Buffalo, believed to have been W8153 in which Flt Lt John Hutcheson crashed on 14 November 1941.

Bottom right: The wreck of W8197 following Sgt Harry Griffiths' crash on 18 September 1941.

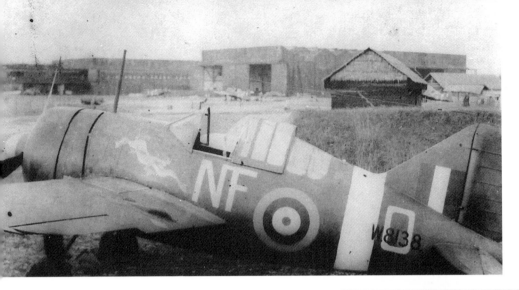

488 Squadron

Top: NF-O (W8138) was the personal aircraft of Plt Off Noel Sharp, who later flew with 243 Squadron.

Middle left: NF-U (W8198) was destroyed by bomb splinters at Kallang on 22 January 1942.

Middle right: Noel Sharp with his aircraft.

Bottom left: Sgt Jack Burton with NF-J (W8148).

488 Squadron

Top: Plt Offs Tony Cox and Jack Godsiff in doorway; (standing, left to right): Plt Off Noel Sharp, Sgt Deryck Charters, Sgt Jack Burton, Plt Off Frank Johnstone, Sgt Alex Craig, Sgt Don Clow, Sgt Rod MacMillan, Plt Off Len Farr, Sgt Perce Killick, Plt Off Wally Greenhalgh, Sgt Jim MacIntosh, Flt Lt John Hutcheson, Flt Lt Jack Mackenzie, and Sqn Ldr Wilf Clouston; (squatting, left to right): Sgt Jack McAneny, Plt Off Harry Pettit, Sgt Vern Meaclem, Sgt Bunny De Maus, Sgt Terry Honan, Plt Off Peter Gifford; (crouching, left to right): Sgt Eddie Kuhn (behind Pettit) and Sgt Greening (behind Gifford).

Middle left: John Hutcheson RNZAF.

Middle right: Jack Mackenzie DFC RAF.

Bottom right: NF-X (W8186), from which Sgt Rod MacMillan baled out when shot down on 12 January 1942.

488 Squadron

Top left: W8168 before receiving its code letter; note the visible '8' of the serial number.

Top right: Sgt Terry Honan posing with well-worn aircraft.

Left: Plt Offs Pete Gifford and Butch Hesketh neatly attired; note Gifford's large pistol.

Above: Sgt Jack McAneny. He was killed in action 19 January 1942.

Top left: Sqn Ldr Frank Howell flanked by the victors, Sgt Bert Wipiti (left) and Sgt Charlie Kronk.

Top right: Souvenir being salvaged from 243 Squadron's first kill – the remains of a Ki-46 of the 81st Sentai shot down over Johore on 10 January 1942.

Middle left: Trophy on display at dispersal.

Middle right: Charlie Kronk being congratulated by Flt Lt Mowbray Garden.

Bottom: Kronk being congratulated by ground personnel.

Top: Group of 243 Squadron B Flight pilots with F/Sgt George Mothersdale (far right); (rear, left to right): Sgt John [Ol]iver, Flt Lt Bertie Bows RAF, Plt Off Jim Cranstone, [Sg]t Prof Rankin, Sgt Geoff Fisken; (middle row, left to right): [Sg]t Vin Arthur, Flg Off Blondie Holder RAF, Plt Off Terry [M]arra; (seated): Sgt Alan Lawrence and Sgt Brian Baber.

[M]iddle: Photograph taken by Army photographer of force-[lan]ded Ki27 on Johore Racecourse circa 15 January 1942, and given to Sgt Jim MacIntosh in POW camp.

Bottom: Last Buffalo from Singapore – painting depicts Plt Off Tom Watson, a Canadian pilot from 232 Squadron, flying an abandoned Buffalo from Singapore to Palembang in Java, accompanied by three Hurricanes, 10 February 1942.

Dutch Brewster Pilots

Top: B-398 of 2-VIG-V.

Middle left: Lt August Deibel of 2-VIG-V with B-3110.

Middle right: Kapt Andrias van Rest of 1-VIG-V.

Bottom left: Kapt Pieter Tideman of 3-VIG-V.

Bottom right: Kapt Jacob van Helsdingen of 2-VIG-V.

Top: WP-W (AN196), possibly captured at Kota Bharu, December 1941.

Middle: Buffalo graveyard – probably Sembawang – showing the remains of six aircraft.

Bottom: Buffalo K – probably at Sembawang.

Top: GA-D (AN194) of 21 RAAF Squadron, captured in northern Malaya, December 1941.

Middle: Captured Dutch Brewsters and RAAF Buffaloes.

Bottom left: Dutch Brewster B-3114 clearly shows the 'Java Rhinoceros' emblem of 2-VIG-V.

Bottom right: At least eight Buffaloes fell into Japanese hands; some were repaired and tested by the Japanese, including this one resplendent in Japanese markings, one of four transported to Japan for evaluation.

Apparently a small number of escorting A6Ms proceeded to Singapore as escort for a Ki-46, these meeting sections of patrolling Buffaloes of both 243 and 488 Squadrons. Sgt Perce Killick of the latter section intercepted the reconnaissance aircraft that was deemed to have been probably destroyed:

"I picked up this bomber [*sic*] and had one run at him. I would say it was about 18,000-19,000 feet. One of his props had stopped – the left hand side. I don't know whether it was me, or whether it had already been stopped by someone else, but during my attack I noticed that one of his motors was out. I came in from the right hand side and got one burst at him before I caught a flash in my rear vision mirror, which was a fighter coming in. Maybe it was a sun flash on his windscreen or something but he never fired on me. He didn't get close enough. The bomber dived straight ahead into some very thick cloud and I also dived away into it in the other direction."

The 243 Squadron section were also engaged by the A6Ms, as Sgt Fisken (W8147/WP-O) noted:

"One Navy Type 0 probable – definitely damaged. Confirmed later. 18 bullets (in own aircraft)."

Fisken later recalled:

"I had made two modifications to my Buffalo to substantially increase its killing power. I'd noticed that bullets that had hit my own plane were spread out all over, without having caused significant harm. So I obtained permission to modify my guns so that they would fire in a narrower arc. It wasn't generally recommended but the result was a much greater concentration of firepower.

"The second modification was in the type of ammunition used and this was adopted by all of us. At first we were only allowed to use solid machine-gun ammunition – the old British idea that you had to be a gentleman and all that. It wasn't for us, and we soon began using a combination of armour-piercing, incendiary, tracer and ordinary solid bullets. The incendiaries were particularly effective; once you saw smoke starting to appear from your target, it was almost certainly a sign of success. The last 200 rounds were all tracer, to let you know when your guns' ammunition was used up. We weren't supposed to use more than eight seconds of firing in one burst, partly because a plane can only carry a small amount of ammo, and secondly because the performance of the guns deteriorates after they get hot."

Somewhat later, a number of 11th Sentai Ki-27s swept over the island. The Japanese pilots reported no engagements but did, however, report seeing an aircraft carrier in harbour, obviously misidentifying a newly arrived merchant vessel in the poor weather conditions that prevailed.

The bad weather did not prevent Flg Off Daryl Sproule and Sgt Henry Parsons of 21RAAF/453 Squadron from carrying out a tactical reconnaissance over Kuantan during the early morning. They observed some 30 fighters – identified as Navy 0s – on the ground, and a few in the air. Low clouds provided excellent cover and both aircraft returned without being intercepted. Sqn Ldr Harper's popularity with his men was not improving:

"After the war with Japan had commenced, work had been started to make dispersals for aircraft and ground organisations in the rubber, away from the airfield. This made it difficult to keep an eye on the troops during raids, and the Engineer Officer of 453 Squadron reported that he was finding difficulty in locating men to work on the aircraft. I found that some men were going off their billets and into the woods and were not being stopped. I therefore let Flt Lt Kinninmont lead the flying and commenced to organise the men again in No.453.

"Parades with roll-calls were organised throughout the day and I instructed Flt Lt Wells [Squadron Adjutant] to arrange a system whereby certain reliable NCOs were given approximately 15 men and they were responsible that their men be kept at work. This did not prove entirely satisfactory, as some of the NCOs were as lackadaisical as some of the men. Great difficulty had been experienced throughout in trying to develop a sense of responsibility and importance of position in the Officers and NCOs. There were no Warrant Officers and only two Flight Sergeants in the whole Squadron, one of whom – Flight Sergeant Discipline – was extremely weak, and the remaining Sergeants and Corporals had risen from amongst the men with rather mushroom-like speed; too many of them were not satisfactory from the disciplinary aspect.

"I had occasion to speak severely to Flt Lt Wells who would not support me in making the men get to reasonably near the shelter trenches in an air raid. He contended that they should be allowed to go to trenches some distance away, if they liked. This gave a bad lead to the NCOs and, owing to the shortage of other officers, I had to go around to the dispersal points myself to ensure my orders were being obeyed. It was not practicable to obtain an exchange for Flt Lt Wells at this stage, owing to the difficulty of obtaining an Adjutant who could take over immediately."

That evening Vin Arthur completed his diary entry for the day:

"Prof's machine was found today. The engine was 12 feet into the deck. His parachute cover was about four yards away from the kite. We haven't found anything of Prof yet. I hope he turns up. Somehow I feel he is still alive. Reynolds hasn't been found yet but the 488 chap who was lost yesterday was found OK on one of the Dutch islands."

On a high note, he added:

"Hurricanes are being assembled at Seletar. I hope I get one. I am glad the Hurrybirds are almost ready because the Buffs can't cope with these Jap kites."

Aircraft of the MVAF's Detached Flight at Kahang continued to carry out daily reconnaissance sorties at the behest of the Army. Until now they had escaped attention from marauding Japanese fighters but, on the 14th, a Moth Major was shot down by two Japanese aircraft and the pilot wounded. The two-man crew was soon rescued by an Australian Army patrol. American correspondent George Weller of the *Chicago Daily News* recounted comments made by ground personnel with whom he mixed:

"In the slit trenches of Singapore Island, where the smeary mechanics whose gifted tinkering alone kept these ancient crates aloft used to exchange gags while bombers throbbed overhead. They called the MVAF's Puss Moths 'Malaya's secret weapon' and the Vildebeest 'Singapore's secret weapon'. 'The Puss Moths,' they used to say, 'can only hop from twig to twig, but the Vildebeest can fly all the way from one branch to the next.'" 96

Weller's copy was not very flattering about the Buffalo, either:

"The Buffalo was a plane built to defend an aircraft carrier and to make attacks upon enemy destroyers and cruisers at sea . . . it could dive like a stone, dropping 15,000 feet without ever fluttering a wing. The Buffalo, well named, was built heavy and solid, to be slammed down on the rising and falling back of an aircraft carrier on a bucking sea. A Buffalo could jump off a deck like an up-tossed clay pigeon. But its top fighting speed was less than 190 miles per hour, whereas the Japanese Zero could go 320. The Buffalo had no cannon. It took off fast, but climbed very slowly, taking as much as fifteen minutes to reach the 18,000 or 20,000 feet floor of the Japanese high-level bombers, and floundering around there unable to find enough air for its heavy weight in the thin atmosphere. At low levels it had a fighting chance against the Zero, but at 20,000 feet the Zero could fly round the Buffalo like a hummingbird around a puffing pelican." [97]

15 January

At first light two Buffaloes from 21RAAF/453 Squadron flown by Flg Offs Geoff Sheppard and Barrie Hood set out from Sembawang to carry out a recce of Gemas and Seremban. At Segamat they came across a large number of transports accompanied by many troops riding bicycles, and these were duly strafed. As they departed, bodies were seen littering the road, trucks were left on fire and a staff car disabled.

The erroneous report of the sighting of an aircraft carrier in Keppel Harbour the previous day by 11th Sentai pilots brought out the Navy bombers again, but when the 27 G4Ms of the Kanoya Ku, escorted by three A6Ms, arrived over Singapore at 0945, no shipping was seen. Rather than return with their bomb load intact, Tengah was targeted instead and the Sergeants' living quarters, Ops Room and SHQ area sustained damage. This raid was followed by a five-minute strafing attack by the A6Ms, during which a dummy Blenheim and aircraft of 4AACU were targeted. On the return flight some of the G4Ms bombed an airfield in southern Johore, but little damage resulted.

Meanwhile, from their Malayan airfields, two sections of eight bombers raided Tengah and Sembawang. The Buffaloes were up in strength to meet the raiders, all units scrambling aircraft. As the opposing fighters engaged in numerous dogfights, units of the 7th Flying Battalion bombed Seletar and Singapore City, under escort from 64th Sentai Ki-43s. The latter strafed Seletar where they claimed one aircraft in flames and six others damaged. One Ki-43 was hit and force-landed near Kelong on return. Actual damage inflicted during the attack on Seletar amounted to two Sharks of 4AACU suffering bullet holes.

Covering Ki-43s of the 59th Sentai claimed six intercepting Buffaloes shot down. Patrolling 1st Sentai Ki-27s claimed a further seven Buffaloes shot down from a force of 13 encountered over Singapore. At least two Ki-44s of the 47th Independent Chutai accompanied the raiders, Capt Yasuhiko Kuroe intercepting a Buffalo; he later wrote:

"We were ordered [to fly over Singapore] for the first mission . . . I pursued the Buffalo which flew over Tengah airfield . . . after five bursts it fell to the ground."

Following his initial attack on the Buffalo, Kuroe was joined by Capt Susumu Jimbo in the other Ki-44. They were jointly credited with the victory, almost certainly the aircraft (W8183) flown by Plt Off Butch Hesketh of 488 Squadron, which crash-landed on a narrow strip of land by the oil tanks alongside Alexandra Hospital. Hesketh, a 26-year-old from Auckland, had been mortally wounded and was dead by the time ground personnel reached the wrecked machine. Sgt Arthur wrote:

"I had the morning off today, or at least half of it. At 0930 there was the usual station scramble. Mowbray Garden led 243 and mucked about doing circuits instead of going flat out for height. Our chaps were pounced upon by Jap fighters as soon as they came out of the cloud layer at 16,000 feet. After short bursts our chaps had to take cover. Johnnie Oliver was with Mr Bows when 12 Jap fighters pounced on them. Bertie got away but Oliver [W8178/WP-Y] is missing. I'm sorry to lose my kite but it's nothing like the loss of a pilot.

"Butch Hesketh, ex-243 B Flight, but on loan to 488 was killed today. He was seen to fly over Alexandra Hospital before he crashed. Wipiti was shot through the arm by a fighter and Kronk [WP-M] just escaped by the skin of his teeth. Both turned into the Japs on a spiral dive when they were attacked. Marra [W8143] who was with them pulled straight up on the chap that was attacking him, and let him have it. As the Jap went spinning down, Veg thinks he shot him [Air HQ in fact awarded him a victory when the Army reported finding a crashed Ki-27 in the area of combat]. We are going to have a terrible time holding our own till the Hurricanes are ready. Things are serious when chaps like Butch get shot down. When the raid withdrew, I bolted across to the drome to see if I could take off, but Ops wouldn't give me permission."

Sgt MacIntosh added:

"We were also given a report at the time that Oliver went missing that he had crash-landed in Johore settlement and he was actually alive when they took him from the aeroplane. How accurate it was I wouldn't know."

Of the action, Plt Off Marra related:

"I was with Wipiti and Kronk, who were in A Flight, and they must have had two serviceable aircraft, and we, in B Flight, had one. We took off and were climbing up and could see the bombers. But suddenly a whole lot of little Army 97s descended on us. There were just the three of us, and they came along and all tipped over just as one would on the edge of a precipice. They were a very small aircraft, had fixed undercarts, and didn't have very much armament – which was a good thing. They were a good 2,000 feet above us. Wipiti and Kronk were great cobbers. I had never flown with them on anything like this. They took off to get down into a bit of cloud. My natural instinct was to go my own way so I picked out the Jap that I decided was going to have a go at me, which is very difficult to do. My idea had been to let your opposition commit himself to his attack, before you started to counter it. I found that if you countered it before he committed himself, you warned him, and it was a much tougher fight. They were coming down with me just going under them and at the very last moment, I stood the old girl on her tail, and went up through them. I was too quick – from full deflection to no deflection – they couldn't catch me.

"When I was able I looked down to see where Wipiti and Kronk were. There were about four 97s chasing them and one was firing. Kronk was flying No.2 and I could see a Jap behind firing at him, although I was unable to decide whether he was hitting him or not. Anyway, the aircraft after Wipiti and Kronk were all going down so I turned over after them as fast as I could. I then observed two 97s pull up to regain height and, as soon as I saw this, I knew I had to do the same. But they outclimbed me – went past as though I was standing still. After a bit of a dogfight, during which we went round and round, we all broke off.

"Afterwards the Army reported that there was one Army 97 down behind the lines, and following a discussion with Wipiti and Kronk, it was decided it must have been mine. It must have been one of those I got a poke at. Evidently I had only damaged him at the time but he hadn't been able to get home. He'd come down a bit later on."

Most of the returning Buffaloes were damaged although all were able to land safely at Kallang. Two Ki-27s were claimed shot down, one jointly by Sgts Jim MacIntosh (W8171), Don Clow (W8235) and Jack Meharry, this apparently coming down on the Johore Racecourse, while Sgt Eddie Kuhn reported attacking another, which he saw roll over and go down vertically, apparently out of control; he recalled:

"I came out of a layer of cloud and saw two enemy aircraft, one of which I attacked head-on. It went down into cloud and although I never saw it crash, it landed alongside an Army base and was duly confirmed."

He was then attacked by the other Ki-27 and his aircraft was badly damaged. This may have been the occasion when Plt Off Noel Sharp came to his aid:

"Noel was incredible – after I had scrambled and tangled with the Japs, Noel took off in an unarmed Buffalo and joined in."

The Dutch unit lost one of the three Brewsters it scrambled, which Kapt van Helsdingen led into the air, when Ensign Swarts was shot down and killed in B-3103. The K-27 claimed by Sgts Clow, Meharry and MacIntosh may have been the subject of a later discussion, as the latter recalled:

"I was given a photo when I was a PoW in Changi by a chap who was an Army photographer, of a Japanese fighter – a 97 fixed undercart job. When he heard that I was one of the Singapore pilots he showed me the photo. This aircraft had gone down, through low cloud and glided down with propeller stopped and force-landed on the Johore race-cum-golf course. The photographer took a photo of it and they took the Jap pilot PoW. I would say that nobody knew who had shot that aircraft down because it had one bullet hole in the right hand side. It had gone through the right hand side of the engine cowling, and had shattered the crankcase, where the two magnetos sit on the rear of the radial engine. Of course once the magnetos were out it just came down in a dead-stick landing. I did hear of reports later on, while a PoW, of Japanese aircraft coming down up the east coast of the jungle, not being able to get back to base. Nobody would know who got them."

From Sembawang six of 21RAAF/453 Squadron's Buffaloes had also scrambled, the sections led by Flt Lts Vanderfield (TD-O) and Kinninmont, but three were forced to return, the others climbing to 20,000 feet to patrol. They spotted a formation of 21 Ki-48s some 4,000 feet below them and were able to make just one diving pass, Vanderfield and Kinninmont each claiming one shot down. A third was credited as probably destroyed to Plt Off Leigh Bowes. Kinninmont later recalled:

"We whistled down and closed in. I picked off one of them and gave him a packet at zero range. Smoke poured from his port engine and I pulled out to watch him go down. Whether he did crash or not I couldn't tell as I then had a crack at one of the others. I must have hit him because oil from his engine suddenly began spurting out like a gusher, covering my aircraft to such an extent that I couldn't see a thing. I hung on to him and tried to manoeuvre into a favourable position."

Kinninmont's aircraft (W8157) was damaged by return fire and he force-landed back at base. 243 Squadron was meanwhile despatching sections on scrambles and patrols throughout the morning. Flt Lt Garden (W8242/WP-K) and Sgt Weber (W8139/WP-B) ran into a number of fighters escorting bombers, both pilots attacking one of the former in turn, as remembered by Weber:

"Mowbray attacked a Type 0 and I followed with a fair burst but very poor sight. Then dived away in one hell of a hurry, but poked my head out of cloud later to find myself in the midst of Type 0s, with one in a very good position to shoot down. I fired a very long burst and thought I had succeeded when he turned over and disappeared in the clouds with Rex A. following hard on his heels. I then came home."

The fighter attacked by Garden and Weber may well have been an A6M of the 22nd Air Flotilla, PO1/c Hiroshi Suyama of this unit failing to return from a sortie over

Singapore. Sgt Greenslade (W8164/WP-J), at least, managed to reach the bombers, carrying out an attack on one from below and claiming some damage before his own aircraft was hit.

Over Malaya during the early afternoon, a dozen more of 21RAAF/453 Squadron's Buffaloes accompanied a mixed bomber force of six RAAF Hudsons, three Blenheims and six Glenn Martins to attack a small convoy of ships, which had been sighted off Port Dickson by two Buffalo pilots earlier in the morning. The convoy could not be located and most aircraft returned to Sembawang with their bomb loads intact. However, some of the Hudsons attacked barges on the Linggi river, the crews claiming to have sunk two and damaged three others. With the day's raids over, 243 Squadron received a visit from its former A Flight commander, Flt Lt Tim Vigors, as noted by Vin Arthur:

> "He is terribly thin and white after his experience. His hands are red and tremble continually. His fingernails, at least those that weren't burnt off, are black and charred. From now on I wear my gloves in the air."

Rex Weber added:

> "It was great to see this gallant gentleman alive and rapidly regaining his health. Although still in a dreadful mess he is very cheerful and is living for the day when he gets another go with the Japs. He came out to this God forsaken country and for nine months tried to teach us how to shoot down Japs, then the little blighters shot him down first time – so he considers that he has a long account to settle with them. And, if he has only got a Tiger Moth, he is going up after them. Well, good luck Tim, and may you get many of them and may you return to your horses and country you love so well."

16 January

The JNAF returned to attack Singapore during the morning, 24 Genzan Ku G3Ms raiding Seletar without interception, although four bombers were hit by AA fire. According to Japanese records, a dozen escorting A6Ms from the 22nd Air Flotilla allegedly claimed a total of ten Buffaloes shot down from amongst an estimated 20 engaged over Tengah although, in fact, no Buffaloes were lost on this date.

A section of Dutch Buffaloes was scrambled, Sgt Bruggink reporting attacking a bomber formation but without apparent result. 488 Squadron was also ordered off on the approach of the bombers, but without adequate warning they failed to gain sufficient height to carry out an attack. However, Buffaloes of 243 Squadron encountered some of the escort, Sgt Charlie Kronk (WP-A) engaging six Type 0s and claiming one probably destroyed. Flt Lt Bows and Plt Off Cranstone (W8221), flying as a section, were chased and fired at by an estimated twelve Type 0s using cannons. However, neither was hit and both returned safely to Kallang. Meanwhile, Sqn Ldr Howell led two sections in an attempt to climb above the incoming raid. Sgt Arthur wrote in his diary:

> "I flew W8231 'Black Magic'. She behaved terribly with the engine running very ragged. As usual, she spewed oil all over the windscreen and on the exhaust pipes so that I left a thick curtain of smoke behind me. We flew in tight formation through very dense cloud to 13,000 feet and waited for the Japs. As my engine was duff, I kept getting left behind. The Japs made a bit of a raid low down but no damage was caused. When I landed I had five gallons of gas left. We had been lost over the Dutch Islands for a long time. When we came out of the clouds the S/Ldr said, 'If anybody knows

where we are, lead us home.' Nobody did, so we stayed lost for a good while till by good luck we found Singapore."

Rex Weber added:

"We spent 80 minutes stooging about in filthy weather. Then the CO said that we had better go down to find our position, and when we sighted sea and land, he asked if any of us knew where we were. But everyone remained very silent, very silent indeed. A little later he gave me the thumbs up sign and, with an amusing gesture, pretended to wipe the perspiration from his brow. Later, we were again flying in cloud and slush, when Control told us to go to some point, but of course it was a sheer impossibility to find any particular point in such conditions. This fact was made clear to Control, who came back with 'Can't you do something about it, Squadron Leader?' The CO, much to my amusement and inner satisfaction, came back with 'Come up and do something about it yourself.' We were brassed off and I was glad to pancake. Cloud flying is very tiring."

The JNAF also despatched two C5M reconnaissance aircraft to Singapore, one crew to check on Tengah – where 21 small aircraft were counted – the other to search for a battleship reported by a G3M crew, supposedly near the west coast of the island. The latter machine was intercepted by four Buffaloes, again led by Sqn Ldr Howell (W8193/WP-V), who spotted the aircraft – which he believed to be an 'Army 97' fighter – over the south tip of Johore; he reported:

"We had a pretty good idea where he was and as we broke through the clouds there he was, just in front of us. We moved up into position behind him, then I let him have one good burst. The enemy immediately went straight down, bursting into flames as he went, and before he crashed one wing came off altogether. I don't think he ever knew what hit him." [98]

Howell's No.2, Sgt Max Greenslade (WP-J), added:

"I pumped more lead into recco plane after [the] Squadron Leader. Army 97 in flames."

Of the brief action Flt Lt Mowbray Garden, leading the other section, recalled:

"Sqn Ldr Howell was the complete professional. He positioned himself beautifully, and with his No.2, attacked this aircraft from astern and shot it down. Immediately he fired, its starboard wing fell off, and the aircraft plunged to the ground. The Flight armourer told me that Sqn Ldr Howell had expended only ten rounds of ammunition in the destruction of this aircraft."

All who witnessed the action were impressed with Howell's swift execution, including Sgt Weber:

"We went up with the 'Old Man' who proceeded to lead the formation in a manner which made each member feel as much at home as if he was lolling back in an armchair before a blazing log. The R/T was very good and led us right to a single bandit. Then the CO showed us how to think quickly, correctly and strategically. Without the enemy sighting us, we all four proceeded to close up on his tail, and the CO opened up with a deadly blast from about 50 yards – the enemy aircraft almost immediately went down in flames."

Howell was later presented with a bottle of champagne by a local restaurateur, who announced that a similar gift awaited every pilot or gunner who so disposed of an enemy aircraft. Shortly after this however, Howell entered hospital for a few days, suffering from a severe attack of dysentery. In his absence the B Flight commander, Flt Lt Ron Bows, assumed temporary command of 243 Squadron.

Air reconnaissance had shown a heavy concentration of Japanese vehicles on the main Gemas-Tampin road following an ambush by Australian infantry. As a consequence, six Glenn Martins and a dozen Buffaloes of 21RAAF/453 Squadron, the latter led by Sqn Ldr Harper, were at once sent off. En route to the target area Flg Off Geoff Sheppard encountered a single-engined reconnaissance aircraft, but had time only to knock some pieces off it before being compelled to return to escorting the Dutch bombers. Sgt Clare, diarist for the day, wrote:

"Much fun and games by the boys today. The Shadow, Van, Mick, Congo, Keith, Strangler and Wop strafed hell out of Nippon at Gemas. Much damage was done, some of the highlights of the trip being the tank the CO set on fire and old Wop killing a Jap with a single tracer."

Although five of the Buffaloes were hit by ground fire, all returned safely. Sgt Halliday, alias Wop, who flew W8205, gave his account of the action:

"As I saw one Japanese brass hat dashing for cover outside what looked like a Japanese HQ, I tried to part his hair for him. It should have been easy as his hair was standing on end!"

Flt Lt Kinninmont added:

"I should think there were about 1,000 vehicles of all types in one lot we attacked. We sneaked up and dived almost into the middle of them. You should have seen them scatter. They could not get off the road quickly enough. Our CO got a beauty on a tank which immediately caught fire and I saw several other transports burning – and tracers were spattering the trucks. The fighters returned to base with scarcely a round of ammunition left amongst them."

The Glenn Martins were fired upon by 'friendly' AA fire as they flew across Southern Johore, with several suffering minor damage. Nonetheless, they bombed the marshalling yards at Gemas and the Gemas-Tampin road, where more than a dozen fires were reported amongst the motor transport.

Another six Buffaloes from 488 Squadron later escorted Blenheims to the same target, but their attack did not achieve as much success as had the earlier raid. Nonetheless, it was believed that many Japanese troops had been killed and considerable quantities of transport and light armoured vehicles destroyed during these attacks. Lt General Gordon Bennett, commander of the Australian Division, recorded that prior to this attack the Japanese had been "careless and weak in road discipline". Next day however, apart from charred remains, not a vehicle remained to be seen on the road.

Four more Buffaloes of 21RAAF/453 Squadron carried out an attack on Muar during the afternoon, as noted by Clare:

"Blitzed two barges, two sampans and two launches: much slaughter was done and an enjoyable time was had by all."

Six Hudsons were also despatched to attack barges on the Muar, where new landings were now taking place; all returned safely. Meanwhile, two Buffaloes of 243 Squadron departed Kallang to carry out a reconnaissance of Mersing, where a landing was reported; the task was not accomplished, as Sgt Weber explained:

"It was a terrible flight through cloud, storms and bumps. Later B Flight sent off two far more experienced pilots to do the trip, but Fisken lost Holder in the clouds and they both soon returned."

At the end of the day Sgt Arthur updated his diary:

"Veg Marra had his victory confirmed last night. That is three confirmed in our Flight. We haven't seen any Hurricanes yet – I hope they hurry up. We have been having unusually bad weather lately, a thing we are to be very thankful for."

17 January

The battle over Singapore now intensified, although the day began with further offensive operations by the RAF against the landings, which were taking place on the Johore west coast, between Muar and Batu Pahat. Early in the morning six Buffaloes from 21RAAF/453 Squadron escorted nine Vildebeest to the Muar to attack barges, spending 45 minutes over the target area, bombing and strafing. The Australians had nothing but admiration for the crews of the biplanes, as expressed by Sgt Keith Gorringe in the unit's diary:

"Today we hand it to the 'Pigs' (as the Vildebeest were affectionately known) and those who fly them. The super-speed specials stayed on the target for 45 agonizing minutes. Not satisfied with laying eggs, they went down and gunned the Japs with all they had. Hats off chaps!"

Flt Lt Grace and Sgt Clare took the opportunity to join in the attack, strafing shipping and a schooner before returning to their charges. During the return flight along the west coast, the Buffalo pilots noticed three Japanese fighters identified as two Navy 96s (probably Ki-27s) and one Navy 0, which were attempting to intercept the rear section of the returning bombers. In a swift action, all three were claimed probably shot down, Clare (probably AN180) being credited with one Navy 96 and the Navy 0, shared with Flt Lt Vanderfield (TD-O), while the second Navy 96 was shared by Vanderfield and Flt Lt Grace. It seems possible that the Navy 0 was actually a Ki-43 of the 64th Sentai flown by Lt Rokuzo Kato, who had been engaged with others in an attack on Pakan Baroe airfield, just across the Strait from Muar.

Half an hour after the return of 21RAAF/453 Squadron from its escort duties over Johore, Sembawang was raided by two-dozen G3Ms of the Mihoro Ku. Until this raid, the RAAF base had escaped the bombers. Japanese propaganda – broadcast over the airwaves from Penang radio station – described this immunity to the high regard in which they held Australians, and on one occasion promised that "when paratroops were dropped on Singapore Island, only geisha girls would be dropped at Sembawang!" On this occasion Sembawang received a severe blitzing, resulting in three Buffaloes being destroyed and five others badly damaged, about which Sgt Gorringe, the diarist on this occasion, commented:

"The wily Nippon sent over his promised messengers to the Australians. Three of the best, or worst, went as burnt offerings. Penang radio has been talking about silly little Buffaloes . . ."

453 Squadron's LAC Basil Young was one who had a narrow escape, as noted in his diary:

"Working on AN173. About 0930 the baptism commenced. Twenty-three bombers came directly overhead and let go a packet – upwards of 100 heavy bombs struck the hangar and orderly room area where a large number of men, including myself, were sheltering. Miraculously, only two casualties (minor). Nearest [bomb] about 12-15 yards. AN173 and AN215 set alight and tanks exploded – cartridges exploded everywhere. My shirt with wallet, pay book, pen and pencil and about 12 bucks burnt. Respirator, cape and mug rendered u/s. One hell of an experience but everybody came up smiling. A very close call."

Flt Lt Wells wrote:

"Casualties in the Squadron consisted of several minor wounds by shrapnel. Morale of the Squadron on this occasion was most commendable. All ranks were on the job before the enemy aircraft were out of sight, endeavouring to salvage what aircraft and equipment it was possible to salvage, and rendering assistance to individuals wherever it was needed."

Three RAAF Hudsons were also destroyed and three more badly damaged; additionally, 453 Squadron's Tiger Moth was destroyed. The Operations Room was amongst the buildings hit, as recalled by Plt Off John Coom, one of a recent batch of RNZAF pilots to reach Singapore, who had been posted to the Station:

"I was in the Operations Room and we heard a stick of bombs getting closer and closer across the drome. The Operations Room was supposed to be bomb proof with a blast wall and double concrete roof with sand in between. Just as well, as we got a direct hit right in the top corner of the double roof. As I dived under the operations table I remember a Flight Lieutenant trying to take cover in a lot of maps hanging in a corner! Afterwards the air was so thick with dust it was hard to see anything. Outside was a shambles with aircraft burning and ammunition exploding and whizzing all over the place. My little Tiger Moth was in a hangar with a Hudson, which was almost completely burned, and the Tiger Moth had all its fabric burnt off, leaving a perfect skeleton in the middle of a yellow pool on the floor."

Although a number of airfield buildings had been badly hit and the water main damaged, disrupting services for some time, casualties amongst the personnel were very light due to the airfield's excellent slit trench provision, and the men were out dealing with fires and unexploded bombs almost before the attack had ended. Indeed, Sgt Ray Wheatley RAAF dashed into a burning hangar and, in spite of the explosion of considerable quantities of ammunition and fuel stores, succeeded in organising the removal of three Dutch Brewsters. In one aircraft he found a wounded pilot, Ensign Frits Pelder of 2-VlG-V, who had been hurt by an exploding bullet, and Wheatley helped him to safety, thereby probably saving his life; for this action and other deeds he was awarded the George Medal.

On the approach of the raiders three of the Dutch Brewsters had immediately been sent off, while 243 Squadron scrambled all available Buffaloes after this formation, Flg Off Holder (W8193/WP-V) and Sgt Fisken (W8147/WP-O) getting right amongst one section of G3Ms, as the latter recollected:

"That was a big day and we had a lovely time. We came out of a cloud and we were about 4,000 feet above them – Navy 96 bombers – in a straggled vic formation. There was only Blondie Holder and I, and I thought thank God we've got height to get some speed up. We dived down and went straight through them, firing all the way and then came up underneath them again. On each occasion I set fire to one going down and hit another one in the belly coming up. Because we had built up sufficient speed – I suppose we were doing 500mph by the time we were at the bottom of our dive – we were able to pull back again, and could get right up underneath their bellies before we started to slow down. We claimed three bombers – two definitely went into the jungle before they outdistanced us but several others were leaving a trail of smoke."

Fisken was apparently credited with one destroyed and two shared with Holder, plus two probables. Sgt Kronk (W8242/WP-K) reported attacking 40 Army 97 bombers but did not make any claims. Gunners in the bombers claimed to have shot down one of three attacking fighters. Rex Weber wrote:

"One of the remaining Dutchmen was killed and the other two were badly shot about. Fisken and Holder got right into a formation of bombers and got three certainties – or very probables – and others damaged; the rest of us did very little."

One of the damaged Brewsters may have been the aircraft an Australian Hudson pilot, Flt Lt Herb Plenty, witnessed crash-land at Sembawang:

"Someone noticed the first such casualty, one of ours, about to crash-land on Sembawang. He called: 'There's a Brewster coming in. Shot up. Looks as if it's on fire, too, by the smoke trailing behind it.' We watched the fighter approach steeply over the trees and land carelessly on its belly, without the undercarriage lowered. The pilot wasted no time in evacuating his cockpit, emerging quickly in a sprint through the smoke and dust enveloping his machine. He had run less than 30 yards when the Brewster exploded in a fierce mantle of flame and billowing black smoke pumping skywards and drifting across the airfield.

"Next, in the sweep of quickly changing events, attention soon became diverted from the burning wreck: 'There goes a flamer!' Its over-revving engine, out of control, whipped the air with a whining crescendo as the stricken, burning plane dived vertically, leaving a long black ribbon of smoke tracing the terminal plunge. 'Impossible to see if it was Japanese or a f**king Brewster.' Curly followed with what he hoped was a humorous observation: 'Probably was a Brewster, since the Zeros have something like a fourfold chance of shooting those down as the Brewsters have of downing Zeros.'" [99]

It would seem that the Australians had witnessed the fate of Dutch pilot Sgt Andrias Voorbij, whose aircraft (B-3105) crashed in the sea near Biliton Island, some miles south of Singapore. Plenty continued:

"A minute later, two more aircraft were shot down. One of those was a Brewster, from which the pilot's escape was signalled by the blossoming of a white parachute canopy at a height of about 6,000 feet. At this stage, the battle had lasted some ten minutes, the initial engagements having been at 15,000 feet. Now the core of the mêlée swirled around about 8,000 feet. After a further five or six minutes of combat, during which ferocity did not abate, the Japanese had used most of their combat fuel-reserves, leaving them just sufficient for their return trip. The aerial jousts were over as suddenly as they had started. Chattering machine-guns ceased and engines no longer howled under high power. The Japanese fighters began joining their leader in a slow climb northward, arranging themselves in an orderly formation.

"But two Japanese pilots, in a parting gesture of hate, dived towards the descending parachute and poured long bursts of gunfire at the Brewster pilot swinging helplessly in the canopy rigging. A concerted and immediate growl of rage rose from most of us, conveying our feelings that the Japanese pilots had just perpetrated an act amounting to unfair tactics, treachery, and an outrageous course of conduct. Previously, among British and German pilots, an unwritten code of honour – chivalry, if you like – assumed that pilots descending by parachute should not be shot at by opposing aircraft. The Japanese served notice that they held no such gentlemanly opinions." [100]

Pilots of 488 Squadron had also been scrambled, Plt Off Gifford (W8173) claiming damage to a Ki-27 but was hit by another, returning with seven bullet holes in his aircraft. Sgt Jack Burton recorded in his diary that it was not only the enemy they had to deal with:

> "On arriving at the dispersal hut this morning all machines were ordered into the air. We only had seven and some of those were u/s. However, up they went. P/O Sharp and self took two new aircraft that had just arrived. My aircraft had no oxygen, no wireless and no guns – and Sharp's had no guns! We were ordered to the Dutch islands but decided to join the formation. During the climb an oil leak in one of the pipes sprayed oil all over the cockpit and myself. At 19,500 feet I could not stand it without oxygen any longer and, as my aircraft was beginning to play up, I had to break off and go home. P/O Johnstone, who was with us up to 15,000 feet, disappeared and he turned up late in the day having baled out over the Dutch islands after his motor cut out on him."

Plt Off Frank Johnstone, who had baled out of W8195, parachuted onto one of the islands, from where he swam to a sampan and was later picked up by an RAF ASR launch. It was the third complete engine failure suffered by the New Zealanders in a week, all caused through lack of oil after full-throttle climbs. One of these Buffaloes was probably that on which LAC Max Boyd had been working:

> "This morning we looked up and saw nine planes not quite heading in our direction. I took little notice and went on fitting an oxygen bottle to the aircraft on which I was working. To do this it is necessary on a Buffalo to climb through the side hatch in the fuselage to reach a point behind the seat. To get into the fuselage the wireless mechanic has first to remove the wireless chassis by releasing four mounting points, and then the rigger climbs in.
>
> "The air raid siren went. I still took no heed except to speed up considerably. Then from behind the clouds came another 63 planes – bombers! Two waves of 27 and one of nine. It was a terrifying sight. The wireless was quickly replaced with no thought given to me being inside and the pilot was already being strapped in for immediate take-off. I banged and yelled and never have I seen such action. The wireless was removed. I was almost dragged out and the wireless was replaced. All this seemed to happen while time stood still, no panic just urgency. The pilot then gunned the motor and we all rushed madly for the foxholes and dived into the nearest we could find."

Sgt Arthur also reported on the morning's events in his diary:

> "At approx 0930 a whole lot of us went up after a few Japs, then we all came down to refuel. That is, most of them did. My engine went duff and the oil temperature went up off the clock. As I had 103° – and the engine seizes after four minutes at 104° – I decided it was time Vin Arthur came back. I landed with the oil temperature still off the clock. The NCO on the ground said it was only the gauge u/s so I immediately went off again with Fisk. This time, I ignored the oil temperature even though it went right off the clock and the band got caught up on the petrol pressure gauge below it. Suddenly, black smoke poured back from the engine cowling and oil came back all over the fuselage and engine. I returned again and by this time the ground staff were convinced it wasn't the gauge that was at fault.
>
> "As I was landing, so were the rest of the chaps. Veg had to come back early because of engine trouble. While we were refuelling, the Japs sent lots of unescorted bombers over, approx 60 planes in all. I saw a stick of bombs land right in the city and some more on Kallang. Actually very few bombs were dropped. Just before the raid our first Hurricane was flying about. Apparently we blew the guts out of the fighter base

yesterday and so the Japs sent over a decoy raid to get our fighters out of gas for when the main body came over. Veg and I couldn't chase the bombers because both our machines were u/s. Fisken and Blondie gave chase with Bertie. Bertie was led off in the wrong direction by Mowbray, but Blondie and Fisk contacted the bombers and pursued them to Mersing, possibly shooting down five."

While the attack on Sembawang was underway, eight escorting A6Ms strafed Tengah, where the pilots claimed damage to eight bombers. In fact three dummy Blenheims were destroyed and three Blenheim IVs were badly damaged, as were two 4AACU Sharks and one Swordfish, while other aircraft including several Buffaloes were impaired to a lesser extent. The AA defences claimed hits on three of the fighters as they swept across the airfield at low level.

Meanwhile, Singapore City had suffered an early attack by a dozen Ki-21s from the 98th Sentai, followed mid-morning by 27 Ki-48s from the 75th and 90th Sentais, which bombed Tengah airfield under the cover of 59th Sentai Ki-43s. The Ki-48 flown by the commanding officer of the 90th Sentai was hit in the starboard engine by AA fire, and the pilot was obliged to force-land at Kuala Lumpur an hour later. On the ground at Tengah 11 aircraft were claimed destroyed by the raiders. Still the torment and devastation was not over. Within the hour, at 1110, 60th Sentai Ki-21s bombed the GHQ, while escorting Ki-43s from the 64th Sentai's 2nd Chutai gave cover. At the same time, Lt Masabumi Kunii and Sgt Maj Shokichi Omori swept down to strafe the flying boat anchorage at Seletar. Here the Japanese pilots mistook the Catalinas for Sunderlands, and between them claimed four in flames and one damaged. Four were indeed hit, one of which sank in flames. Only three Catalinas now remained serviceable, although persevering servicing crews had one of the damaged machines back in flying condition next day. Also based at Seletar was the Walrus amphibian from the sunken *Prince of Wales* whose crew had been made available to the Catalina unit; the Walrus' pilot, Lt Clem Bateman, recalled:

"A Squadron Leader [Frank Howell of 243 Squadron], who had taken passage to Singapore in *Prince of Wales*, sought me out at Seletar and asked if I could do search and rescue for the RAF fighters – I said I would willingly do this but he should get the blessing of the Naval staff, who would almost certainly agree, but I heard no more of this, probably because I was put out of action by being too close to a bomb."

At the current rate of attrition, the Buffaloes could not be expected to last more than a few days, as Sgt Burton of 488 Squadron noted:

"At the completion [of the day's activities], only two of our Squadron's aircraft were fit for flying. As a result of having more pilots than machines, P/O Sharp and myself have been transferred over to 243 Squadron as they have lost seven pilots. I have been attached to B Flight and expect to be right in the fireworks tomorrow."

Plt Off Peter Gifford also transferred temporarily to 243 Squadron. The number of defending fighters available was further depleted during the day when the surviving five Brewster B-339s of 2-V1G-V withdrew to Palembang in Sumatra, flying on to Java next day. Here the survivors of various Dutch Brewster units were to be reformed, Kapt van Helsdingen being assigned to command a unit of eight such aircraft at Semplak (see Chapter X). Help for the fatigued Buffalo pilots was to hand however. With 21 Hurricanes now assembled and currently being air-tested, 232 (Provisional) Squadron was almost ready to join the action; divided into three flights, two were to operate from Seletar and the other from Kallang. Great things were expected of the Hurricanes.

The services of one of the Hurricanes was immediately lost when it narrowly missed colliding with a large coal truck, which had suddenly appeared on the airfield as it was landing. The aircraft caught the ground with the wingtip and ground-looped, the port undercarriage leg buckling under the strain. Flt Lt Kinninmont was among those delighted to see the Hurricanes:

"At the sight of those planes, morale skyrocketted 100 per cent, and the sun shone again and the birds sang. That evening at all the nightspots the gay topic of conversation was 'Hurricanes'. The miracle had happened. The Hurricanes were here and their world was saved. 'Boy! More stengahs – long, with ice!'" [101]

Sgt Weber of 243 Squadron wrote in his diary:

"We had a great thrill when we saw our first Hurricane overhead. And today to see the Squadron in the air was a sight for sore eyes. They are indeed sleek looking creatures – streamlined, speed personified. Well, if the gen is anything like pukka . . . it seems likely that we will get them. Oh Boy! Let's hope that we are alive and fit to fly them."

Correspondent Cecil Brown agreed:

"This afternoon six Hurricanes flew back and forth over Singapore. It was a sort of pep show for the people. They look good, and that means that now they have been assembled they will crack back at the Japs." [102]

Sgt Arthur added:

"Quite a few Hurricanes were flying today. I'd give my right arm for one. Today Bertie [Flt Lt Bows] passed out during flying due to lack of oxygen. After a short dive, he recovered. When Cranstone was coming in, one undercarriage failed to lock and he landed more or less OK without damaging a wing tip. Today a 488 chap is missing. Now one Flight in 488 has no planes."

Of his minor prang, Plt Off Jim Cranstone remembered:

"I remember getting to where the Jap bombers were – the usual 27 – and we were chasing them. I seem to remember getting hit – my canopy blew out and the shock of it coming off and the air blast temporarily stunned me and I lost control of the old Buffalo. I went into a spin from 23,000 feet right down, completely out of control. I thought that this was it, and I gave up and the damn thing came out of the spin of its own accord. I think the starboard undercarriage might have been twisted – whether it was because of the excessive airstream on the downward flight or from a few shots in my aircraft [W8221], I don't know. Anyway, as I landed I was conscious that there were signals coming from the control tower and a bit of panic on, but I didn't interpret things very accurately. The Buffalo's wheels opened outwards towards the wingtips, and locked into place at an angle – not vertically. Because the starboard wheel was twisted outward, the friction created by the tyre on the ground stretched it out against its hinges so I came to a standstill with the starboard wheel vertical, standing on its own, and the left wheel down."

On returning from an afternoon sortie in W8147/WP-O, Plt Off Snowy Bonham encountered a lone fighter which he identified as a Zero:

"While returning to base after 'mince up' with enemy aircraft, met lone Zero. Had squirt and attacks. Guns jammed when bullets hit cable near instument panel. Set upon by two more Zeros attacking from rear, using cannon. Returned to base."

One serious consequence of the first major raid on Sembawang was that the local labour force departed almost to a man, hence vital aerodrome repair work, as well as cooking and cleaning, had to be undertaken by Service personnel at the expense of more important work. Those not involved in aircraft maintenance and other essential work were now employed in filling-in bomb craters in an effort to keep the aerodrome serviceable for operations – a difficult task with the limited means available. At Sembawang there were just six trucks, one small hand roller and a few ramming poles at the disposal of the airfield-repair workforce. Following the raid, Grp Capt McCauley, the Station Commander, wrote:

"I ordered that all RAAF aircraft, the Buffaloes and the bombers not on operations, were to become airborne. I was not going to lose any more aircraft through strafing attacks. I extended the revetments already built by the RAF around our airfields to protect our fighters from strafing attacks. I complained strongly to RAF Headquarters that, whenever we were attacked by the Japanese, my fighters were ordered off and were never able to reach the attacking formations. The Japanese attack force came in at 25,000 feet over the centre of Singapore and our fighters, having to climb up to them, were at a great disadvantage. But we were able eventually to fight the Japanese on their own terms.

"I asked RAF Fighter Command if I could put up a RAAF fighter squadron to fly cover over Singapore at 25,000 feet and wait for the Japanese attack force. Up until this time therefore, the rôle of the RAAF fighter squadrons had been more or less symbolic because they really could not get into a position to attack the Japanese formations. I decided to send them into combat with more than half a chance of surviving."

On a lighter note, correspondent Ian Morrison added:

"Excellent fish were to be had in Singapore in peacetime, but the fishing was done almost entirely by Japanese fishermen. During the months before the outbreak of war many of these men left Malaya with the assistance of the Japanese authorities. Later doubtless they played an important part as guides to the Japanese forces. Those who remained were interned on the outbreak of hostilities. The result was that there were few fishermen left. The Japanese, however, continued to provide the island with fish. Whenever they bombed the big air base at Seletar or the civil port at Kallang several of their bombs were certain to fall into the sea. Hundreds of fish would be blown to the surface and later collected, chiefly by Chinese, who sold them in the markets at high prices." [103]

18 January

At dawn three Blenheims, with an escort provided by four Buffaloes of 21RAAF/453 Squadron led by Flt Lt Kirkman, departed Sembawang to bomb the railhead at Gemas. Following a low-level attack, the Blenheims flew down the west coast of Johore to observe if any landings were being carried out, while the Buffaloes strafed motor transport on the Gemas road. Whilst engaged in strafing, Flg Off Daryl Sproule reported meeting a Ki-27, which he claimed shot down. When over the sea at 1,500 feet, just south of Muar, the Blenheims fell foul of four 59th Sentai Ki-43s, led by Maj Hirobuni Muta, which were patrolling over the Muar landings. Two of the bombers were hit, one of which evaded the attackers, although the pilot had to crash-land at Tengah on return, while the other was relentlessly pursued and shot down into the sea; the crew survived.

While the Australian Buffaloes were away, Japanese raiders were back over Singapore, as witnessed by Cecil Brown:

"We had two air raids this morning. During the first one, about ten, I was out at the house and about thirty Jap bombers came over, spreading out in a V formation. There was a great deal of ack-ack. In the second raid I was at the hotel downtown, or rather in my favourite ditch out in front. I couldn't see any aircraft, but five or six bombs fell downtown. They came down uncomfortably close today.

"I don't care much for bombings, especially when you feel so unprotected. When the bombers are overhead you just wish you had a gun or a pistol or something with which to defend yourself. You become very sensitive to sounds and noises. A motorcar starting off in second gear sounds like the beginning of a siren. A fan overhead sounds like the low drone of the Jap bombers with their pulsating beat. A car back-firing is like a shot from an aircraft cannon. The sound of car treads on asphalt highways seems like the start of the screaming dive of a Japanese bomber. Even the whistle of the wind in the trees sounds like the downward rush of bombs, and a truck bumping along a highway sounds like a stick of bombs crashing in the distance.

"Some people prefer to be out in a trench where they can see where the raiders are. They feel too cramped and the period of nervous tension is too long when they are inside waiting for the bombs to come. Personally, I prefer to follow the bombers in their flight and to watch them make the run over their target. You can spot the bombs coming down and determine fairly well if they are going to get you or not. Indoors you know the raiders are overhead and you have an hour or two waiting to get killed. If you can see the bombs coming down you know in a minute whether they are going to get you or miss you. I prefer a minute of abject fear to an hour of apprehension.

"One Asiatic I know is all set to do some refined looting. His weapon during an air raid is going to be a pair of pliers. His intention is to rush about, yanking out the teeth of Chinese air-raid victims. It should be a profitable business since the Chinese put wealth into their gold teeth." [104]

Despite the usual height disadvantage, the first raid of the day proved to be far from an unmitigated disaster for the defenders. On the approach of 26 G4Ms of the Kanoya Ku, escorted by 11 A6Ms and accompanied by two reconnaissance C5Ms from the 22nd Air Flotilla's Fighter Group, Flt Lt John Hutcheson led off a composite formation of Buffaloes from 243 and 488 Squadrons. These clawed for altitude to allow them to attack the bombers, passing some fighters in cloud as they went. On clearing the cloud layer they saw more aircraft ahead, but the Japanese fighters – estimated as nine strong – were now below them, so they dived to attack head-on. The diarist recorded:

"A fairly hectic day all round. The first scramble was at 1000 hrs. F/Lt Hutcheson was leading the two squadrons. At 11,000 feet enemy bombers were sighted at 20,000 feet over the Naval Base. They were shadowed whilst the Buffs sought to gain height. At 18,000 feet nine Type 0s set the ball rolling by attacking and an interesting time was had by all. P/O Sharp [W8138/NF-O], flying for No. 243 Squadron, bagged a flamer and lost most of his rudder. Sgt Killick bagged a flamer but retained his rudder. F/Lt Hutcheson, Sgt Meaclem and Sgt MacIntosh collected a probable each. No aircraft were lost by the 'home team'"

Of the action, Hutcheson noted in his logbook:

"Patrol base at 18,000 feet. Attacked by Type 0s. Shot large pieces off port wingroot of Type 0. Probable. Later confirmed."

Perce Killick's victim apparently crashed in Johore:

"There were bombers with their fighter escort. We had a dogfight and one Jap seemed to get isolated and broke away and I went after him. It was a Zero. I chased him down to low altitude – about 2,000 feet – shooting at him from side on and behind. He was a flamer – flames were leaping out – and he never had a chance to bale out. I didn't actually see him hit the deck, as I was veering away at that time, but he crashed virtually into an AIF camp. It was opposite the river going into Johore. The Aussies got his body out, and his personal effects, and they phoned the Squadron to ask which pilot had shot a plane down over there. They fished me out and said if I was to come over I could collect his personal effects. I didn't go until about three or four days later and they gave me everything except his sword. I don't remember the name of the pilot but he was a Major. I got back to the drome with all his gear – his wristlet watch, paybook, photos of his family and a ring – and wrote a letter to his wife. I bundled everything up, made it into a parcel and I mailed it off to her." [105]

Although no Buffalo was lost, Sgt Meaclem's aircraft returned displaying the scars of battle. This would be the only occasion during the whole campaign when the Singapore Buffalo pilots were to find themselves in such an advantageous position. Apart from the 488 Squadron claims, Sgt Charlie Kronk (W8242/WP-K) of 243 Squadron was awarded a probable:

"Attacked from above by Type 0s. Broken up. Later attacked six. Petrol poured out. Not confirmed."

Kronk was flying No.2 to Plt Off Snowy Bonham (WP-J), who noted:

"Sgt Kronk and self intercepted three enemy bombers flying north, pursued by what looked like six Buffs. No.2 went high – attacked fighters which turned out to be Navy 0s. Broke off attacks on bombers owing to Navy 0 jumping on my tail."

Only Plt Off Edgar Pevreal (W8154) succeeded in penetrating the fighter screen and reported gaining strikes on one of the bombers, which was credited to him as probably destroyed:

"I remember hitting one. I was closing pretty fast and it was just a momentary burst and I remember seeing something fly up, when someone yelled over the R/T 'Fighters!' They [the bombers] were being escorted by 97s, which nobody saw until we were in close to the bombers. I broke off pretty quick."

Plt Off Sharp's aircraft (W8138/NF-O) was badly damaged, most of the rudder being shot away, but he was able to land safely. Plt Off Veg Marra (W8143), who believed his opponent was a Messerschmitt 109, recollected:

"I had two other aircraft with me and we were endeavouring to gain height to intercept some bombers. Bandit fighters appeared ahead of us, but as we were about to climb into cloud we pressed on. Conditions were very cloudy – in layers with 2,000 feet between. On clearing the layer, Sgt Arthur called up to say there were 12 bandits at 6 o'clock above and attacking. As luck would have it, the first bandits we had seen appeared just below us at 11 o'clock. This was the only occasion in the whole campaign that I found myself above enemy fighters, even though we had more enemy planes above us. We made a head-on attack on those below us before the top cover arrived.
    "He opened fire first but I was diving and he was climbing and I could see his tracer was going underneath me. I wasn't a bit worried about that. As soon as I reckoned I was in range I pushed the button, and I hit him in front of the cockpit and could see his panels start to fly. He went underneath me and I never saw him again. We didn't have camera guns, and I knew full well that the other guys would be looking behind because

they were protecting their own skin. The Japs upstairs came screaming down on me. The other two, Arthur and Baldwin, just disappeared. We didn't have far to go to get back into the cloud and that's where they probably went. That was our defence. You would whip into the cloud, fly around for a bit and then come out, and see what was going on. That's what I did, too – I hopped into the cloud. The Japs stuck around with me for quite a while. I popped out about four times, and each time I came out a couple of them would come down at me, so I would duck back in again. Everywhere one looked there was an enemy aircraft. I think there were so many of them that they were getting in one another's way, or chasing one another. From this action I was credited with a probable."

Of the incident, Flt Sgt Mothersdale remembered:

"Terry Marra climbed down from the cockpit and I could see that he was elated, he could hardly contain it. When I asked how he had fared, he said 'I think I got a Messerschmitt!' As the pilots were grouping together to walk to the dispersal hut, I heard him ask 'Did you see that fighter I got – did you think it was a Messerschmitt?' I distinctly heard one of the pilots say 'Yes – I think it was a Messerschmitt – it looked like one.'"

Sgt Vin Arthur, who was heavily involved in the action, also believed Messerschmitts were present, as his diary reveals:

"At approx 0930, two B Flight sections took off. We didn't see anything so we pancaked. About ten minutes after we landed, we all had to go up again. Veg, Ginger Baldwin, a chap from 27 Squadron, and I took off with Blondie's section. We lost Blondie and so continued on by ourselves. We saw several supposed Hurricanes but these were ME109s [sic]. One even came down and had a look at Ginger but we didn't recognise it. I saw it coming and yelled out to Ginger to duck, but he didn't hear. The suspense of waiting and watching a chap meet his death is not the kind of thing I can stomach. Suddenly five ME109s came out of the clouds about 100 feet below us. Ginger and Veg dived down on them. I didn't dive down on them but turned up at two Type 0s that were diving on us. I couldn't get an attack in, so half-rolled away into a layer of clouds below.

"All the way down I was waiting for the bullets to come screaming into me, but none came. By Jove! It takes guts to turn into a plane that is firing at you. As I climbed up through the clouds again for another go, a Type 0 with an auxiliary petrol tank slung under the fuselage shot under me and climbed in front of me. I got behind him and fired furiously. I don't know whether I hit him – I jolly well should have done. As I emerged through the clouds another Type 0 dived down on me. I waited until he was coming at me then lifted my nose and fired a long burst at him. As nothing else was kicking about, I returned. While I was half-rolling down after trying to attack the Japs first, I saw a lot of tracers around the plane. Suddenly the cockpit seemed to explode and the plane spiralled down with blue smoke trailing out behind. I last saw the plane as it disappeared through a layer of cloud at 2,000 feet. It undoubtedly crashed. I am quite expecting to hear my Jap was seen to crash. Ginger reckons he got one also."

It is not possible to provide any explanation as to why some Buffalo pilots continued to report engagements with Messerschmitts, when there were none in service with the Japanese air forces; nor were there any Japanese in-line-engined fighters at this stage of the war. Another of the pilots engaged in this action was Sgt Jim MacIntosh (W8198/NF-U), whose admiration for the Buffalo was increasing with every flight:

"On this occasion I proved conclusively that the Buffalo was equal to the Zero in manoeuvrability. In the initial attack, they came in from the north at about two o'clock on us and a Zero, for some reason, turned right around in front of me. It was incredible. I didn't even have to aim my aircraft and instinctively pressed my guntit. He flew right through my fire, rolled away and went down, appearing to me to be upside down. He was still inverted in a 45° dive when he disappeared into cloud layer at about 5,000 feet. He may have got out after but it was a pretty stupid way to go down from 12,000 feet to 5,000 feet upside down at 45°. He must have fired at some other Buffalo and swung round in front of me, without realising that I was there. I definitely hit him because little silvery slivers came back as he rolled over. After the mix-up, we went down to the top of this everlasting cloud layer that used to lay over Malaya. Another Buffalo joined up with me and I did a head-on attack against a vic of three Zeros, and passed underneath them.

"There again I got what I consider to be quite an effective burst into the leader because what appeared to be most of his engine cowling peeled off and fluttered back. The Buffalo was very sensitive – just a little flick of the control – and I ducked down below the fire of the Zero. As I passed underneath I observed a fourth Zero up top of me at about the two o'clock angle and I had to turn towards him. He was approaching in a right hand turn. So I flicked over again into a sharp left hand turn, which meant this time I was turning with the torque of my Buffalo. I was round and was levelling off to take aim at him before he was three-quarters through his manoeuvre. But he didn't complete his turn. As soon as he saw that I was round and firing on him, he just dived into this layer of cloud beneath me.

"So I proved twice in the course of this combat that the Buffalo was equal to the manoeuvrability of the Zero. I mentioned in my claim that I thought I had got two but Squadron Leader Clouston said I couldn't claim them. However I received a congratulatory note from HQ, awarding two probables out of that lot."

MacIntosh's No.1 on this occasion – Plt Off Jack Oakden in W8174 – did not enjoy such a successful sortie, as noted in his logbook:

"Chased out of the sky by superior numbers of fighters. Navy 0s and Army 97s. Neck saved by smoke from burning oil tanks."

The 22nd Air Flotilla did, in fact, lose two of its aircraft during this engagement, including that flown by PO2/c Yoshihiro Sakuraba, who was killed; five Buffaloes were claimed shot down in return, a further being claimed probably destroyed. It would seem reasonable to assume that more than one Japanese pilot made a claim against a Buffalo on observing black smoke issuing from its engine, an effect of oil spewing out onto its exhausts rather than battle damage – a frequent problem experienced by the Buffalo pilots.

Two hours later another raid approached, this time from the north. The Ki-21s from the 7th Flying Battalion escaped interception on this occasion, while a strong force of escorting fighters hunted down the Buffaloes as they again struggled upwards. The 3rd Chutai of the 64th Sentai reported attacking ten Buffaloes over the city and claimed all shot down, two of them by Lt Masabumi Kunii. Meanwhile, Ki-27s of the 12th Flying Battalion fought with five Buffaloes in the same area, but without result, although accompanying Ki-44s from the 47th Independent Chutai claimed one of these shot down. Buffaloes from 243 and 488 Squadrons were again involved, as recorded in the war diary:

"At 1145 the 'home team' again took the air. This time the 'visitors' had the advantage of height and made very effective use of it. However quick anticipation made it possible for the 'home' players to reach cloud sanctuary in safety. A little later two of No.243

Sqdn were rather thoughtless and brought many Type 0s down through the cloud. This resulted in great activity by all concerned. Sgt Kuhn carried F/Lt Hutcheson's gratitude by removing an unfriendly Jap from his tail and he later removed a further Jap from the census returns. F/Lt Hutcheson was shot up by two Jap fighters and made a crash landing on a Dutch island. One Jap continued to fire at him right up to the time he crashed. Rather unfriendly. P/O Cox is missing as a result of this last action. Tony did not see a great deal of action but he was very keen and a very good No.2."

Hutcheson's aircraft (W8177) was badly hit just at the moment when Control called to ask his position. "Upside down!" was his calm response, before falling away, hotly pursued by his two attackers, to crash-land on the shore of a little island west of Samboe; he was subsequently returned to Singapore by a launch of the ASR Service, as noted by the Squadron diarist:

"All members of the Squadron are very grateful to the Air/Sea Rescue Service for the fine way in which they have retrieved our pilots. They are always on the job, keep a sharp look-out, and have saved many lives of men from squadrons stationed on the island."

Plt Off Tony Cox's aircraft (W8141) was seen to crash into the Phillips Straits, and the 22-year-old New Zealander was killed. Five of 243 Squadron's six aircraft returned damaged. One of these was flown by Sgt Kronk (W8242/WP-K), whose tail wheel was shot off; another by Plt Off Marra (W8143), while Plt Off Sharp (possibly W8201) made his second emergency landing of the day, this time using trim tabs only; his aircraft being deemed irreparable. Marra reported:

"It must have been about 2 o'clock. There were 18 Type 0s flying around the aerodrome. We called up Ops, who said we had better go: Well the whole squadron took off – there were 12 of us and it was crazy because there were no bombers – no harm was going to come to Singapore if we just let those guys fly around. Anyway up we went and the Japs maintained their altitude until we were about 2,000 feet below them and then they started to peel off and come down, one at a time. A Buffalo would go down, chased by a Type 0, followed by another Buffalo and so on. Before long everyone's going down which was stupid because the Type 0s were going to outspeed us. I was trying to look after the guy's tail ahead of me when suddenly I could hear guns screaming behind me, so I lay back on the stick to gain some height but I blacked out.

"When I regained vision I was back where I came from, and looked around but could see nobody. Then suddenly all hell broke loose. There was a big bang in the back, bits and pieces flew off including my radio mast – things were really happening. I just stuck the nose down, heading towards the harbour in Singapore, hoping the old girl would keep me going. When all the fighting behind me stopped I leveled out. I'd collected a big hole out in the wing, and while British aircraft had cables controlling surfaces, these Buffaloes had aluminuim rods. The cannon shell I'd taken in the wing had cut the rod to an aileron, which was flapping up and down in the breeze. I was worried that I might lose a wing and I wasn't getting too much control with the rudder either. The motor was coughing and spluttering and I thought I had better find out quickly whether I ought to bale out or not. I throttled the old girl back and I found that at 120mph I lost control. We normally landed the Buffalo at about 60, but I decided that 120mph was worth a go. So I approached the circuit at Kallang. Although the aerodrome was round, it had a bit of an extension and I made up my mind that I was going to have to use it. I could land even though it wasn't going to be quite into the breeze.

"Just as I am coming around, another aircraft appeared and used the extension ahead of me. This was Bonham – he had one bullet in the aircraft, which had also gone clean through his knee. So I had to complete another circuit and hope that the old girl's motor kept going. I fired my blister gun to let them know I was in some strife and they cleared things fairly quickly and I was able to get down all right. The wheels came down and she certainly used all the runway up. In fact I almost landed in the wire on the other side. When I finally got out and looked the aircraft over, if I had seen it before I tried to land it, I would have jumped out and used the parachute. It was a wonder it flew at all. That was the end of that aircraft – she never flew again. They used her for bits to keep others flying."

Plt Off Bonham had attempted to mix it with his attackers, but had his knee shattered by a bullet. In great pain and fainting from loss of blood, he nonetheless managed to land his badly shot-up aircraft (W8164/WP-J) back at Kallang. Sgt Weber, who was not flying on this occasion, wrote:

"Bonham had his R/T on 'send' and when he was wounded let it be known to all the world in very choice language. Still, it was an excellent show to get his kite down safely under such circumstances, and no one can say that the lad has not got stacks of stomach."

Flt Lt Bows agreed that Bonham had made a splendid attempt to bring back his damaged aircraft and promptly recommended him for a DFC; the subsequent citation read:

'P/O Bonham took off with other members of No.243 Squadron to intercept some enemy fighters. In the ensuing dogfight in which the enemy had the initial advantage of height and superior numbers, P/O Bonham fought courageously and pressed home his attacks. During the engagement his knee was shattered by a .5 bullet. Although seriously injured and in great pain, he managed to fly his aircraft back to base and carry out a successful forced-landing, before fainting from loss of blood. In this he showed great courage and determination and saved a very much needed aircraft.'

That evening Weber approached Flt Lt Garden:

"I suggested to Garden that we went up with full tanks and stooge up to 24,000 feet some 15 minutes before the raid usually comes over. We would then not waste a ton of petrol bustering up there, and would be certain to be over the top of the enemy – always an advantage. But then, of course, a Sergeant Pilot has no right to make suggestions to an officer and a gentleman! It's a pity there are not a few more Englishman like our CO."

Vin Arthur's diary again provides his version of events:

"About 1400, I had a scramble with A Flight. Just as I was coming in to land the cover came off the top of the left mainplane, making the stalling speed about 110mph. I came in very fast and made a fair landing. I pulled the emergency release gear because I thought the selector box had seized up. The second time Veg went up with Blondie he was badly shot up. His ailerons were shot away, one completely and one partially, his rudder and tail plane were extensively damaged and a cannon shot went into his engine. It fair made Veg jump. I believe a Type 0 shot Veg. He wasn't injured and made a lovely job landing his kite. Veg's idea of fighting is best. He ignores the Japs till they are really close. Then he lifts up his nose and lets them have it. That idea of his has shot down two Japs for him. I have done a lot of shooting but so far I haven't had my Japs confirmed."

While the raiders continued to bomb Singapore, a small RAAF formation endeavoured to strike back. At 1120, two Buffaloes of 21RAAF/453 Squadron departed Sembawang to escort three RAAF Hudsons to the Muar area, where Japanese barges had been reported. Maj Muta's Ki-43s were still on patrol and correctly identified the raiders as three Lockheeds and two Buffaloes. Flt Lt Herb Plenty, one of the Hudson pilots, recalled:

"I flew No.2 and became separated during a steep turn near the river mouth; as the Zeros dived to attack . . . I did not have enough power to hold formation on the outside of the turn. I could see no future in straggling behind the other two as every Zero would have pot-shotted me, so I dived for the trees 1,000 feet below . . . I flew at treetop height and full power, for Singapore. One of the first victims was a Buffalo [AN174 flown by Sgt Norm Chapman, who was killed], which spun down in flames half-mile ahead of me. As I flew over the burning wreck, I remember wondering how much longer before I met the same fate. However, I flew through the hills with three Zeros attacking for about 20 miles before they turned back. Not a single bullet hole was found in the Hudson." [106]

The pilot of the remaining Buffalo (AN170), Sgt Henry Parsons, followed pursuit of the Ki-43s chasing Plenty's aircraft and succeeded in deterring one from the attack, claiming it possibly destroyed. One of the Hudsons, badly damaged during the attack, crashed on returning to Singapore with the loss of all the crew. Elsewhere off the east coast, a patrolling Catalina clashed with a Kanoya Ku G4M, the flying boat sustaining slight damage, while the Japanese bomber departed leaving a trail of smoke from an obviously impaired engine. The Catalina pilot radioed for assistance, and on receiving the signal of distress, Air HQ ordered a flight of Buffaloes to go to its assistance, and it was duly escorted back to Seletar.

That evening, when Sgt Arthur was writing-up his diary, he noted:

"I had a look at a Hurricane today. By Jove! She is a hot number and I am going to do my best to get on them. The bombers that came over set fire to two oil tanks near the Naval Base. Black smoke has been pouring out of the fire all the afternoon and now at night there is a vivid red glow in the sky."

19 January

Singapore was to receive a brief respite as action concentrated over the Muar area, where the situation was now serious for the defenders. The Buffaloes of 21RAAF/453 Squadron were very active during the day. Two, flown by Flt Lt Kinninmont (W8157) and Plt Off Livesey, went off at first light, initially to escort two Albacores, which were to attack Gemas, followed by a reconnaissance south of Malacca. A two-seater reconnaissance machine was encountered en route and was claimed shot down by Kinninmont. 488 Squadron also despatched two Buffaloes on an offensive sortie to Mersing, during which Flt Lt Mackenzie – who had just returned to the Squadron following a spell in sick quarters with a bad attack of boils – and Sgt Meharry sighted two Japanese aircraft, which immediately made for cloud cover. Despite a search, they could not be contacted.

At 0645 another flight of eight RAAF Buffaloes departed Sembawang to escort three Glenn Martins to carry out an attack on Muar, where the ground battle was going badly for the defenders. The Buffaloes were also to provide cover for five Wirraways of Y Squadron from Kluang, now to be thrown into the battle in the rôle of ground-attack bombers. Their task was to destroy three petrol dumps that had been left by retreating forces. River traffic, as well as motor transport on the Muar-Gemas road, was also to be targeted. Each Wirraway was armed with twenty 40-lb anti-personnel bombs. As the Wirraways, led by Flt Lt Park Thompson, approached the target area, three Japanese single-engined aircraft were spotted by the escorting Buffalo pilots. The intruders were tentatively identified as 'Navy 96s', one of which was claimed shot down by Flt Lt Bob Kirkman, while the other two fled, pursued by the Buffaloes. The 'fighters' were, in fact, a trio of Ki-51 single-engined light bombers of the 27th Sentai, the crews of which reported sighting four 'Blenheims' (apparently the Glenn Martins) and six Buffaloes. One of the Ki-51s was immediately shot down, and was obviously Kirkman's victim. Flt Lt Vanderfield and Sgt Gorringe pursued the remaining pair, each claiming a victory, one of which was reported to have been a dive-bomber, the other another 'Navy 96'; a second Ki-51 was indeed lost in this action. Five Ki-43s of the 59th Sentai swiftly came to the aid of the luckless 27th Sentai crews, shooting down 23-year-old South Australian Sgt Henry Parsons, who was killed when his aircraft (AN170) crashed near Batu Pahat. Only the previous evening Parsons had told a friend that he was going to shoot down a Japanese aircraft to make up for the loss of his close buddy, 26-year-old Victorian Sgt Norm Chapman, killed the day before. Meanwhile, Sgts O'Mara, Board and Ross Keys carried out a ground strafe:

"Tearing about with reckless abandon they sprayed everything in sight. Matt is now more convinced than ever that he won't go to Heaven as he had some very fine sport shooting up a church."

The Wirraways meantime attacked a launch towing two troop-filled barges crossing the river, the pilots initially using their forward-firing guns, their gunners their twin-Vickers as they climbed away; bombs were also aimed at the craft although none were apparently sunk. Not one of the vulnerable Wirraways escaped damage from ground fire during these attacks, but only one was shot down; the crew survived a crash-landing and were soon rescued by British troops and returned to Kluang in the afternoon. Following the return of the surviving Wirraways to Kluang there was an air raid. Although little damage was inflicted, it was decided that the Flight should evacuate to Kahang airfield as a safety measure.

Near Batu Pahat, as the Buffaloes returned to Singapore, about six aircraft – again thought to be Navy 0s – were observed attacking a ground target. Flt Lt Kirkman got in several bursts at one, confident that he had probably caused it to crash, before continuing back to Sembawang. The Glenn Martins however, having bombed a suspected Japanese Army HQ from 6,000 feet, departed the area devoid of fighter escort and were intercepted by the Ki-43s almost immediately, and all three were shot down.

243 Squadron belatedly scrambled two sections of Buffaloes as news of the Glenn Martins' plight reached Air HQ, but they arrived too late to help. Sgt Arthur returned to report that from a distance he had seen Japanese fighters attack one of the bombers, which went down in a near vertical dive, the fighters following. One of these then turned into the bomber and raked it with fire, hitting the long 'greenhouse' cockpit and fuselage, the doomed aircraft crashing in a mass of flames.

At 1340, five Buffaloes of 21RAAF/453 Squadron led by Sqn Ldr Harper took off from Sembawang for an offensive sweep over Muar. They were joined by more Buffaloes from 488 Squadron, the New Zealanders detailed to fly top cover. On approaching the target area, a formation of 'Navy 0s' was sighted below and while preparing to attack these, a further 40 [sic] were reported at higher level. These dived on to the Buffaloes and shot down two 488 Squadron machines. Plt Off Jack

McAneny (W8171) was killed, while Sgt Deryck Charters managed to bale out of his
stricken AN189. McAneny, from Auckland, was just 19-years-old; Charters was
captured by Japanese troops and later died whilst in captivity. Plt Off Wally
Greenhalgh recalled:

"We were part of a composite squadron with about six aircraft from 453 Squadron and
four of our own (488 Squadron). A Squadron Leader [Harper] was leading us. We went
up the west coast of the peninsula about 100 miles north of Singapore. The object was
to strafe ground forces that were supposed to be advancing down that road. We made
one sweep over this particular road and didn't see anything and came back to have
another look and were down at about a thousand feet, maybe 2,000 feet, when a
squadron of Zeros jumped us. We were led into this dirty great bank of cloud that was
hovering round there. I was a couple of wingspans away from Jack McAneny when we
went in and when I came out I didn't see any of our guys again. A Zero flashed past in
front of me as I came out of the cloud and I gave him a burst and then I started to look
around for somebody to team up with. I got down to ground level and after stooging
around there for a couple of minutes, I decided it wasn't a very healthy place to be and
tootled off home. I think I was the last to see Jack alive. Deryck Charters was also shot
down and taken prisoner after that particular flight. Len Farr had much the same
experience as myself and he came back about a minute after I had landed."

Only Flt Lt Kinninmont (W8157) was able to counter the attack positively, shooting
down a Navy 0 for his second victory of the day, while Sgt Halliday reported that he
"was chased home by half the Jap Air Force." The attackers were once again Maj
Muta's Ki-43s, which caught the Buffaloes at low level over Batu Pahat, claiming four
shot down for the loss of one of their own aircraft. Although the Australian formation
escaped damage in this attack, the incident caused Harper to send a memo to Air HQ:

"With reference to the fighter sweep carried out this afternoon, it is necessary in order
to ensure that the squadrons are not surprised from above, that some section should act
as top cover through the whole operation. It was requested through the medium of
Station Operations that 488 Squadron be advised to act as top cover, 2,000 feet above,
when possible. The top cover squadron however either flew level or below the main
formation, and owing to the difference in R/T wavelength between [my] aircraft
[Harper was flying a 21RAAF Squadron machine] and 453 and 488 Squadrons, [I] was
unable to detail a top cover, and having only five of my own aircraft was unable to
allocate any for the task of top cover. Some top cover was then provided by one section
of 453, the leader of the section seeing the need for someone to do this. This was
however insufficient and the squadrons were jumped from above by enemy fighters
when attempting to attack further aircraft below them."

Buffaloes of 243 Squadron were scrambled when news of the action was received at
Singapore. Rex Weber wrote:

"I had one squadron scramble and we stooged about the skies at 20,000 feet for an hour
and a half. There have been no raids over the island today. I am dead tired and so are
the rest of the boys."

In his diary, Sgt Jack Burton added:

"Contrary to expectations we did not get a raid today. What is in store for us during the
next few days is the question we are all asking, for the break today suggests that the
Japs are preparing for something big in the way of an attack. The oil tanks, which were
bombed yesterday, still continue to burn and when nightfall came a bright red glow lit

up the sky, indicating much damage has already been done and still is being done by this huge fire.

"The total number of serviceable aircraft on Kallang today is: 488 A and B Flights, six machines; 243 A Flight, four machines and B Flight two, while there is a total of eight temporarily u/s. The future does not look bright. We learnt today that the new Hurricane pilots have had only about eight hours flying in the above machines so we cannot expect much help from them yet. Out of 52 Hurricanes which are on the island only 18 are to be assembled and the balance held for reserve and spare parts. How in the name of goodness can we hope for success with such organisation. The Dutch squadron has already returned to Java, as they are disgusted with affairs over here, and we cannot blame them. At the present moment the whole island is dependant on less than 20 fighters. If the Japs only knew this they would let hell loose on us and we could not do much. Those of you who may in time come to read this diary will have some idea of the 'strongly fortified Singapore' of which we heard so much away back in 1938."

At about the same time as this action was being fought, two further 488 Squadron aircraft had been sent to reconnoitre Kuala Lumpur aerodrome and town, now about 100 miles inside Japanese-held territory. Taking advantage of cloud cover, Flt Lt Mackenzie and Sgt Jack Meharry reached Rawang, 15 miles north of Kuala Lumpur, apparently unobserved, then turned south and passed over the town at 5,000 feet, continuing on to the aerodrome. Mackenzie recalled:

"Jack Meharry and I flew a deep penetration sortie up to Kuala Lumpur. Our orders were not to attack, just to come back and report what was on the airfield there. It was purely a reconnaissance mission. In fact we flew some miles north of the base and then came out at Rawang, then flew back down the main road, straight to the airfield. When over the airfield, and flying at about 1,000 feet, we probably looked like Japanese Zeros and in fact there was one Zero going into land. We flew a couple of circuits while counting and noting the dispositions of the aircraft. Then we headed straight back into the hills because if we'd got mixed up with that lot we wouldn't have had a hope. There were some fighters practicing aerobatics just over to our right as we went over. Just as we completed our second circuit the ground gunners realised what we were and opened up on us. I was very tempted to have a go at the Zero going in to land – we were only a few hundred yards from him, but that wasn't what we'd been sent up for." [107]

Both returned safely, their reports of "masses of Japanese fighters" at Kuala Lumpur prompting Air HQ to order immediate strikes. That night nine Vildebeest were sent to carry out an attack but these were only able to inflict slight damage to one transport aircraft.

Despite the setbacks there was still an air of optimism, for the Hurricanes were ready to go into action on the morrow. Sgt Arthur of 243 Squadron wrote:

"We tried to bolster up the courage of the Hurricane boys today, with the result that they suggested they look after the bombers and we take on the fighters – maybe!"

On learning the news that the Hurricanes were ready and would obviously attract swarms of Japanese fighters, Sgt Weber confided to his diary:

"Tomorrow will be a big day and here's hoping I live through it. Just in case – all my love dear folks."

CHAPTER VIII

BUFFALO SWANSONG

20-31 January 1942

"Today, the powers that be showed their gratitude to 453 Squadron by presenting us
with all the Buffaloes left on the island . . . the boys were enormously cheered up by
this news!"

Comment in 453 Squadron's war diary

20 January

This day was to see the heaviest raid yet on Singapore, a force of about 80 bombers
approaching during mid-morning. The crews of the Ki-21s of the 12th and 60th
Sentais had been briefed to raid Seletar, while 26 Mihoro Ku G3Ms were to attack
Sembawang and 18 G3Ms of the Genzan Ku had Singapore City and the harbour as
their target. 64th Sentai's Ki-43s provided cover for the Ki-21s, whilst 18 A6Ms
escorted the Navy bombers, and two C5Ms accompanied the force to observe results.
Despite the magnitude of the attacking force, there was a hint of optimism on this
morning, as at Seletar the Hurricanes were ready to go into action and great things
were expected of them.

A dozen Hurricanes scrambled to meet the raiders and, as they dived to attack the
bombers, they were jumped by Ki-43s. The Hurricane leader (the CO) was shot down
almost immediately and was killed but his victor was promptly shot down by another
Hurricane. Meanwhile, the other flight engaged the bombers and claimed eight shot
down and three probables, while two of the escort were also shot down – but at a cost.
Two more Hurricanes fell to the Ki-43s with one pilot killed and the other severely
burned. The 64th Sentai claimed five Hurricanes in all, for the loss of three of its own.
At Kallang a hangar was destroyed and with it two of the MVAF's aircraft, with a
further three damaged, as were a number of Hurricanes parked on the other side of the
airfield.

Sembawang also received a share of the bombs, as noted in 453 Squadron's diary:

". . . we were peacefully enjoying the morning sunshine when a faint drone of
unsynchronised motors was heard approaching Sembawang. Funk holes were
immediately in great demand and sure enough shortly afterwards the air was filled with
a great whistling, followed by the most terrifying succession of bangs, booms, bongs,
and other assorted noises. When the chaos and shouting had died down and the smoke
had cleared away, it was obvious to even the meanest intelligence that once more Tojo
had dropped million dollar bills, champagne and geisha girls on his beloved Aussies –
blast him! Not much damage was done and once more, after the boys had had the usual
'nervous one', they soon recovered their good spirits."

A mixed formation of Buffaloes from 243 and 488 Squadrons were also scrambled,
but these were ordered off too late and failed to intercept the raid. They couldn't
gain sufficient height to reach the bombers. One of those who scrambled was Vin
Arthur:

"This morning we went out on a scramble. All the kites on the station took off including
two out of the six Hurricanes. The Buffs did not intercept the bombers. I had a bad oil
leak from the propeller again. I have had a gut full of oil leaks now. It proves these kites

can't take a long, stiff climb. When I pulled out of the formation, I was lost. I stooged around for a long while, utterly lost. At last I saw the smoke from the fire at the Naval Base and made my way home. Later, Bowsie, Blondie, Fisken and Cranstone went up after some bombers. Bowsie contacted them but didn't shoot any down."

Plt Off Peter Gifford, flying his first sortie with 243 Squadron, reported that he dived on 40-plus fighters but in doing so "rippled the leading edge and wrenched the ailerons" thereby rendering W8173 unserviceable. Better success was achieved later however by Buffaloes from these two units against bombers of the 3rd Flying Battalion attacking Batu Pahat, where the destruction of five Buffaloes on the ground was claimed by the Japanese crews, as well as a bridge at Yong Peng. The Buffaloes were almost certainly dummies or badly damaged aircraft that had been abandoned. Six Ki-48s forming part of this force fell foul of four Buffaloes of 243 Squadron led by Flt Lt Garden – on his third scramble of the day – and two from 488 Squadron, the latter flown by Plt Offs Oakden and Gifford. Sgt Arthur was again involved:

"This afternoon I went off with three of A Flight and two of 488 Squadron to look after Japs that were dive-bombing and machine-gunning the front line. When we got up there we met two formations of Jap 97 bombers, three planes in each formation. I did about five attacks with Mowbray, and then left him. I made gallons of petrol pour out of the left engine of the centre plane. I then left that formation and attacked the other formation. During my last attack on this formation I damaged the port engine of the left plane. As gallons of petrol poured out of both planes, I presumed I punctured the petrol tanks. I was met by quite heavy fire from the rear gunners. I think they were using explosive cannon shells. One cut my aerial. As I lost the rest of the formation, and as I had no R/T contact with base, I returned home."

In addition to the two bombers damaged by Arthur, Sgt Kronk (W8184/WP-G) was credited with one confirmed, as was Plt Off Sharp (W8162) whose own aircraft was hit by return fire, while another was claimed badly damaged by Flt Lt Garden. Rex Weber commented:

"It is evident that our shooting is very wild or otherwise their bombers take a devil of a lot of punishment."

Plt Off Gifford (W8181/WP-P) added:

"Trip past Muar to attack enemy dive-bombing aircraft. Six Buffs attacked six 97s and knocked hell out of them – cannot understand why enemy aircraft did not fall apart. Return to Kluang hugging the cloud with P/O Oakden."

Jack Oakden's (W8168/NF-T) only comment was:

"Intercepted and put wind up six Army 97 bombers. Got shot up slightly by return fire. Guns jammed."

Vin Arthur echoed the thoughts of his colleagues when he wrote in his diary at the end of the day:

"I hope we meet some more of those bombers unescorted like we did today. Today, four oil tanks at the Naval Base and the aerodrome at Seletar were hit by bombs. I believe Orchid Road was badly hit by bombs. The Japs were obviously aiming for Fort Canning, Air HQ, and the residence of General Wavell."

21 January

At first light six Buffaloes from 243 Squadron were led by Flt Lt Garden on a sweep over the Batu Pahat-Parit Sulong area, where two gunboats and several barges were seen and attacked on the river. Sgt Fisken recalled:

"Blondie Holder and I got into some barges on the Muar river. There were about six barges with Jap troops and machine-guns mounted on them. We got down to about 10 to 12 feet above the water and machine-gunned them. We blew lots of them overboard and we were pleased to do it, too. I can remember my tracers hitting a machine-gunner on the back of the barge, and he floated about 20 yards away from where he was struck. We weren't popular for thinking it was a hell of a good job. You might say it was callousness but I had heard some terrible stories of what the Japs did to pilots who baled out."

Later, while patrolling over the area at 22,000 feet, the other section of Buffaloes was bounced by an equal number of Ki-43s, Garden having a large hole blown in his port wing. In a confused dogfight, Sgt Wipiti (W8147/WP-O) was able to shoot down one of the fighters, both wings being seen to fall off as it went down in flames. Sgt Kronk (W8242/WP-K) claimed another as probably destroyed; the 64th reported the loss of one of its Ki-43s. While 243 Squadron had found some action, eight Buffaloes of 488 Squadron led by Flt Lt Mackenzie carried out an uneventful patrol over the Muar area, all returning safely.

The JNAF was again over the island in force, 25 G3Ms from the Mihoro Ku, 27 G4Ms from the Kanoya Ku, together with nine escorting A6Ms, undertaking the raid. A single C5M accompanied the raiders. Ki-21s and Ki-48s of the JAAF's 7th Flying Battalion also raided in strength, escorted by Ki-43s from the 64th Sentai. The Mihoro bombers struck at Keppel Harbour, claiming one merchant ship sunk and one damaged, but were then attacked by fighters identified by the crews as 'Spitfires', gunners claiming one of these shot down. Three Hurricanes had scrambled from Seletar, the leader claiming to have shot down one of the bombers, which then exploded and brought down the aircraft on either side. Three more Hurricanes from Kallang were engaged by Ki-43s, losing one of its aircraft although the pilot survived with injuries, his crash-landed aircraft having been located by a MVAF Moth. Another Hurricane from Kallang, which took off on its own, also failed to return.

Meanwhile, with Kallang also under attack, both 488 and 243 Squadrons scrambled all available aircraft to intercept the bombers raiding the harbour. Geoff Fisken remembered:

"My groundcrew were strapping me into my plane as the bombs were dropping on the drome a few hundred yards away – luckily I made it while they dived for their slit trench.

"We tried to save our planes by sprinting to them, quickly jumping in and taking off, if there was time. There was little warning of attacks but I was able to get in my Buffalo and get it off the ground several times. Mechanics and riggers got the planes started as soon as the air raid siren went off. We were sometimes even taking off when the bombs were dropping."

By the time the 243 Squadron Buffaloes were airborne and had gained sufficient height, the bombers were on their way home. Led by Flt Lt Bows, they finally caught up with the G4Ms of the Mihoro Ku. Bows ordered a head-on attack, a manoeuvre that did not please Sgt Weber:

"Our leader acted like an inexperienced 'erk' and led us round in front of the enemy where we had no chance to attack. About this time we were set upon by a single Type 0, which came from above. I followed him down but held my fire and did my best to get on his tail without him noticing but he absolutely out-climbed me, leaving me well behind. Nevertheless, as I followed him up he took me into a good position to attack the main formation. Now, that attack was one of the biggest moments of my life, and I carried it out pretty well. But once again I couldn't get my sights decently aligned. On my break away I skidded right up into the 27 huge bombers and bullets were flying in all directions. My petrol started to stream out and as my position was many miles off the east coast, I headed for home. Yet again I had attacked without great result. The remarkable feature to me was my almost entire absence of fear. It is great that in the air one hardly knows the meaning of real fear, yet if bombs land in the vicinity when on the ground, one is actually terrified."

As a result of attacks by other pilots, Sgt Ginger Baldwin claimed one bomber shot down but was badly shot up and landed at Sembawang, Flt Lt Bows confirming his victory. Plt Off Jim Cranstone (W8187/WP-R) gained strikes on another:

"We had a bit of a mix up over southern Malaya and I got separated and I don't know whether I was out of ammunition or whether it was gun stoppage, but I know I couldn't do anything about it. Next thing there was this Zero flying beside me – and of course the moment I spotted him my heart dropped into my flying boots, and I took evasive action. But every time I thought I was okay, he ranged up alongside and gave me the fingers and then he just took off."

Presumably the Japanese pilot was also out of ammunition. Geoff Fisken (W8147/WP-O) reported strikes on another bomber before he attacked a Navy 0 near Bakri, just east of Muar, claiming this as probably destroyed. The latter claim was later upgraded to a confirmed victory, Fisken's fifth success in little more than a week. One reason he succeeded was due to the tactics he applied, as he later recalled:

"The only thing to do was to get as much height as possible above any Japs before making an attack – preferably two or three thousand feet – when you could make the initial attack and have enough speed created in the dive to get around for a second go, even if it meant putting your feet on the dash board and blacking out slightly. This did not always work as the Jap planes outnumbered us by 10-20 to one, but when it did we got victories. When it did not we got out and lived for another go next day."

The section in which Plt Off Marra was flying failed to catch the bombers:

"It was a very wet day, and Ops called us up and sent us off. If I remember correctly Pevreal was leading this one. The cloud was in layers, and we climbed up to about 21,000 feet and we couldn't see anybody. So we called Ops who told us they were about somewhere, although they weren't sure where, and that we had better come back. We began descending through this cloud and we came into one of these clear layers and, blow me, we are nearly on top of a whole lot of Jap bombers. They opened their bomb bays and released their bombs quickly and turned tail. I thought it would be a formality, but we weren't able to catch them. They were in a shallow dive and so were we, but we just simply couldn't catch up. They were in a big V formation, about 27 of them, and I got right at the back of the V, so that if anybody overheated or started to slow up, I would be the first guy to meet him. Finally we decided we couldn't catch them and it was called off. After returning home we were all in the dispersal hut and were all laughing at the fright we must have given these Japs despite how little damage we had done to them."

With the defending fighters thus engaged, Kanoya Ku bombers raided Tengah practically unhindered, claiming 13 bombers destroyed on the ground. Losses included two RAF Hudsons and two Blenheims destroyed, plus two Hudsons and a Blenheim damaged. Vin Arthur watched the raid from a vantage point, as he noted:

> "I saw the bombing wonderfully. About six sticks of bombs were dropped, each lot nearer the drome. We saw rows of houses, ships, etc, go sky high. Three large fires were started, one burning all afternoon. From the look of the smoke, I would say it was petrol. I believe the town is pretty badly shattered in some parts. We distinctly heard the bombs whistling before they exploded."

Singapore City had indeed been hit hard. During the course of these raids, at least 383 civilians lost their lives, with over 700 injured; there were now an estimated 150 funerals a day, although many Chinese and Malays in downtown Singapore simply disappeared without trace under the ruins of demolished buildings. Sgt Weber visited the city shortly after the raid, and saw victims of the raid being collected for burial:

> "The wardens were loading corpses on the back of an old lorry as though they were mutton from an abattoir."

With the raids over, two Albacores were despatched from Seletar during mid-afternoon to attack small boats reported near Batu Pahat, while six Buffaloes of 21RAAF/453 Squadron provided cover. No enemy aircraft were sighted on this occasion. Flt Lt Kinninmont was again involved, as noted by the Squadron diarist:

> "Now it was unfortunate that Congo [Kinninmont] and Greg [Board] happened to form a section as both of these have gotten themselves a reputation of being 'hairy goats' in the air. And when two hairy goats get together, well someone's got to lose some hair. And so it came to pass. Greg tried to attract Congo's attention by gently tickling his under surface (or belly) with his wing tip – which proceeding improved neither Greg's wing tip nor Congo's belly. However, both got out of it unhurt."

Sgt Board added:

> "There was nothing I could do, my wing went into his fuselage and broke the tip off. I went back with a bit of my wing missing and the others went on. A part of my wing was still in the belly [of Kinninmont's aircraft] when he came back." [108]

Four Buffaloes, two each from 243 and 488 Squadrons, patrolled off Singapore during the afternoon, only to be intercepted by four Hurricanes although identification was made before guns were fired. Before flying ended for the day, Flt Lt Mackenzie and Sgt Kuhn of 488 Squadron carried out a recce of the main Endau-Mersing road, returning without incident. Of this period, Sqn Ldr Harper wrote:

> "The rôle of the two Squadrons was changed several times from that of Army support to pure fighter interceptor; however we were somehow never on our fighter rôle when the Japanese were bombing the island, which was done fairly regularly. The main task of the Squadron on most days seemed to be to send two aircraft out each morning to do a recce for the Army. I was several times approached by the pilots, who spoke in a manner showing they had little confidence in the RAF's ability to run its affairs, and

they were openly in favour of moving nearer to Australia, so they could come under Australian control and put up a better fight. While there may have been considerable wisdom in what the Australians said, my orders were to get on with the job. It may show the extent to which the dislike of the Royal Air Force was prevalent when I say that it was necessary for the Station Commander, Grp Capt McCauley, to assemble his officers before him and instruct them to cease drawing comparisons between the two Services."

The Australian pilots at Sembawang were, at least, trying to make the best of a worsening situation – and never seemed to lose their sense of fun and enjoyment:

"During these days we are living down in our bungalow in the bushes. Here, at nights, we're wont to regale ourselves with many assorted and peculiar drinks and large quantities of canned geezil. For instance, it is a common sight to see Ocker, Barrel Bum, Matt and Strangler gurling brandy-sherry cocktails and eating salmon and prawns."

That evening, on a more somber note, Sgt Vin Arthur made what was to be the final entry in his diary:

"We had ten serviceable Buffs in 243 and 488 today. Ten Buffs and a handful of Hurricanes against the hordes of fighters and bombers the Japs send over. Now the people of Singapore wonder why we can't keep the Jap planes off the island. Some of the British heads ought to have their necks rung for this. I hope in the interests of the RAF, the Japs bomb Air HQ."

22 January

Singapore was again visited by the JNAF, 25 Genzan Ku G3Ms and 27 Kanoya Ku G4Ms, with nine A6Ms and two C5Ms from the Fighter Group, appearing overhead during the late morning. The G3Ms attacked Kallang just as four Buffaloes of 488 Squadron were taxiing for take-off, led by Flt Lt Mackenzie. Three got off, but W8191/NF-D was hit by shrapnel. Plt Off Farr managed to get airborne but could not maintain control because of damage to the aircraft or his own injuries. The Buffalo crashed, as LAC Max Boyd recalled:

"Another was just taking off when shrapnel hit the pilot. He still took off but the plane dipped, wiping off the undercarriage, and ploughed through a house and petrol dump building. They found the pilot still in his seat which had been pushed right back to the tail of the plane. He was badly injured but still alive."

Twenty-five-year-old Plt Off Len Farr from Auckland died in hospital three days later. Two airmen forming part of Sgt Eddie Kuhn's groundcrew – AC1 Archie Service and LAC Ivan Anderson – were killed instantly at their posts, after starting up Kuhn's aircraft. Jack Mackenzie recalled:

"We were told to scramble. Eddie Kuhn, Don Clow, Len Farr and myself rushed out, hopped into our Buffaloes, got going, opened up and headed out for take-off. All four aircraft were facing towards the airfield and I'll never forget that one. As we gained speed, so the bombs came down, hundreds of little anti-personnel ones which seemed to race us across the airfield. I remember the bombs going across and past me on my right wing. They got Len Farr – he was blown into a petrol dump by the bomb blasts when we took off. The other three of us were buffeted but we managed to stay airborne. It is a frightening thing when the airfield blows up almost in front of you." [109]

Sgt Charlie Kronk (W8242/WP-K) also took off in the only immediately available 243 Squadron Buffalo, his groundcrew braving the attack to get him off. Two more 488 Squadron Buffaloes, W8198/NF-U and W8174, were damaged beyond repair when red-hot bomb splinters set them on fire. The Station HQ building was also destroyed, five airmen led by Sgt Ivan Yanovich of 488 Squadron distinguishing themselves when they put out a fire in the armament-filling room despite exploding ammunition. Sgt Rex Weber, sheltering in a trench, witnessed the whole affair, and recorded in his diary:

"To my mind they [the groundcrews] are the heroic boys because it is bad enough – terrifying, in fact – to be in a decent sort of shelter where you are really very safe, but to be out in the open with the exceeding likelihood of bombs landing in the close vicinity, and then do your job, is deserving of very high praise . . . Today our boys went off with quite a fair squadron formation made up from both squadrons of eight aircraft, and stayed up for nearly an hour. Then they were told to pancake, and by the time they had refuelled, the main bomber formation was bombing Kallang, while the Hurricanes were just pancaking according to their orders, received when they were at 23,000 feet with sufficient petrol for another hour and a quarter. The bombers came over in perfect formation, and it was evident from the moment they were sighted that it was their run on Kallang.

"I judged the drift correctly and turned away from the trenches on the perimeter of the drome, towards those nearer the road, then ran back again from there when I found all those holes full of men or half full of water. However, once again I decided that the main trench system was too near the line of drift and stumbled – by this time feeling the effect of too many cigarettes – back towards the roadside, and found a decent hole empty of men. Just in time as the bombs started to drop and I for a time watched them glint in the sun but when they began to explode I crouched well down in the pit – not actually very afraid, but at the same time jolly thankful when the tremendous noise ceased. The bombing was very good and destroyed two 488 planes on the ground, another when it was taking off, and the pilot received fairly serious injuries, and knocked buildings about, besides a few holes in the drome."

This was possibly the occasion when Sgts Baber and Lawrence of 243 Squadron narrowly escaped injury. They were engaged in ferrying damaged Buffaloes from Kallang to Sembawang, where there were repair facilities; Baber recalled:

"If Alan [Lawrence] flew the plane I would go and pick him up by car or if I flew the plane he would come and pick me up. The flight commander said that it was up to us to make up our own minds whether we should fly an aircraft or not, because they were obviously damaged, but we could never say no. But we managed the job without any troubles.

"I had flown an aircraft across [to Sembawang] and Alan came to pick me up. As we left this aerodrome, driving off down the road, sirens were going, indicating a raid was imminent. We could hear the drone of many aircraft above us and I looked out, and there were three lots of 27 – quite a big raid. I could see one aircraft drop out and I said to Alan I think he is after us. Alan put his foot on the accelerator and I said for God's sake stop, which he did. We jumped out of the car into a ditch and a bomb landed just up ahead of us. I could see it all happening – this aircraft purposely being instructed to drop out and have a go at us."

Meanwhile eight Hurricanes, which had just landed at Kallang, were led off again by Sqn Ldr Brooker, who had taken command of the unit following the death of the CO.

More Hurricanes from Seletar joined the battle. They claimed several bombers shot down but lost five aircraft to the escorting A6Ms, three of the pilots being killed. Flt Lt Kinninmont commented:

> "The RAF boys flying them [the Hurricanes] began to mix it with the Zeros which we knew was practically impossible. The Zero was just about the nippiest, most highly manoeuvrable fighter in the world. They buzzed around the Hurricanes like vicious bees. The RAF Hurricane pilots fought gallantly and courageously against overwhelming odds and during their brief period of operation in Malaya they scored several brilliant victories and shot down many Japs. But they too 'took the knock.'" [110]

The Buffaloes meanwhile engaged the Japanese raiding force, two of which – identified as Navy 96 bombers – Sgt Bert Wipiti claimed shot down for his third and fourth victories. The escorting A6M pilots exacted swift revenge, shooting down two of the Buffaloes into the sea with the loss of both pilots: Sgt Ginger Baldwin – the aggressive former Blenheim pilot with five victories to his credit and an inspiration to others – was killed when his aircraft (W8187/WP-R) was seen to fall into the Johore Strait; his body was not recovered. The second loss was Sgt Vin Arthur, the young diarist from Taranaki, whom fate had destined was not to return to his beloved Marie back home in New Zealand. His Buffalo – Geoff Fisken's faithful W8147/WP-O – was shot down north-east of the Horburgh Light, south of Pulau Tidman. The sea swallowed him and his aircraft. One of the Hurricane pilots involved in this action, Plt Off Jerry Parker, later recalled:

> ". . . about four Buffaloes were coming in from above and astern of the bombers so that they would meet them at about the same time as we would attack from the side. I thought that this was pretty silly of the Buffs as they would be far easier targets for the rear-facing Jap gunners, who could bring every gun to bear on them, but on the other hand they would be diverting much and perhaps all of the defensive fire from us."

Following the first attack on the bombers, the Hurricane pilots manoeuvred to carry out individual attacks. The same Hurricane pilot reported:

> ". . . there was a violent thump on my armour-plate and a clang in my ears like a gong. A quick incredulous glance in my rear-view mirror showed me a Buffalo – there was no mistaking the stubby wings extending through the mid-section of the barrel-like fuselage – with his guns flashing directly behind me. I had no doubt he was aiming at me and not at the bombers, and I smartly dived away . . ."

When, on returning to Seletar, an inspection of the Hurricane revealed a bullet of Japanese manufacture, it was suggested that perhaps the Japanese were using captured Buffaloes fitted with Japanese armament! Clearly, it had been attacked by an A6M. The A6M pilots of the 22nd Air Flotilla had had a field day, claiming no less than eight Hurricanes, which they incorrectly identified as Spitfires, and two Buffaloes, to raise the unit's score to 40, plus a further 30 destroyed on the ground during strafing attacks in operations over Singapore. The cost had been almost negligible, just five A6Ms, two C5Ms and two bombers shot down, plus two further bombers force-landed due to battle damage.

On the mainland, Japanese troops were now filtering through the British positions in the Muar-Batu Pahat area. 45th Brigade called for an airdrop of food and morphine, and for an attack to be made on the other side of the Parit Sulong bridge. In response, two MVAF Moths managed to drop a small amount of food and medical supplies, while in the way of an air strike all that could be offered were two Albacores and a Shark from 4AACU. Buffaloes from 243 Squadron were promised as escort but at the last moment these had been required for air defence. However, all three biplanes carried out their mission with creditable success, and returned safely to Singapore.

That evening, Rex Weber added wry comment in his diary on the day's events:

"If I had the ability to write I could write a good story on today's doings and misdoings on the part of our higher ups, but unfortunately after the happenings of the last few days my mind is less coherent than ever. If it wasn't for the fact that it seems quite impossible, I would say that certain key men in control of Singapore Air Defence are Fifth Columnists. However, owing to the aforementioned impossibility, all I can say is that they are grossly, criminally incompetent. Maybe, and maybe not, all the men who receive promotion due to length of service, and not competency, have been sent here. It certainly seems that, once an officer in the Air Force, you are set for promotion to very high rank so long as you remain in the Service.

"The number of wing commanders and their like who knock around this island doing mere office boy jobs is incredible, and what's more, that's all they are capable of doing. Many of them haven't got the guts of the average coolie, let alone taking their places as leaders. No doubt this has been the dumping ground of all the incompetents that ever disgraced the British nation. I wonder if all the British campaigns have been conducted in such a disgraceful fashion. It seems evident that the solution to our fighter problems is to send them up with full petrol tanks, about 9.15am, to the highest possible altitude, which is about 25,000-27,000 feet, and keep them there until the main bomber formations come over. Then let them attack these perfect formations and immediately return to base.

"We have had practically all our jolly fine old aircraft shot up, and some fine chaps and pilots lost, simply because when the main formations come over we were just taking off. I am sorry to say that both Vin Arthur and Ging Baldwin are missing, presumed killed."

Obviously morale among some of the fighter pilots had almost reached rock bottom.

23 January

Early in the morning five Buffaloes – two from 488 Squadron and three from 243 Squadron – took off led by Flt Lt Mackenzie, with orders to patrol over a bridge between Batu Pahat and Kluang, to enable retreating troops and transport to get across with minimal interference. Mackenzie wrote:

"The Japs came down on us while we were flying very low over the bridge. They had a go, then flew off. Once again we found ourselves in a hopeless position. We'd been flying around for quite a while as a composite flight from 488 and 243 Squadrons – for we ourselves had by that time virtually no aircraft left. We had to patrol low in order to protect the bridge because the Japanese had good little dive-bombers which would have taken out the bridge in no time had we been much higher. As it was we were down to around 1,000 feet when they simply fell on us. Our tactics really were all wrong, for one shouldn't hang around the same spot, low down, and only about 100 miles from an enemy fighter base. It was just too easy for them. But our orders were to stay until troops were across or until we reached our endurance time." [111]

The Ki-27s picked off the Buffalo (W8184/WP-G) flown by Sgt Max Greenslade of

243 Squadron; again Rex Weber recorded events:

"Old Maxie had about as exciting an experience as one could want. They – six of them – were sent over the front line to guard a bridge. Of course, to a mere Sergeant, it is quite evident that a formation of six Buffs could do little but get shot down once the enemy got word back that six British planes were waiting to be shot down, and that's exactly what happened. Twenty-seven Jap fighters came over and attacked them – F/L Mackenzie, who was leading, very wisely dived into the early morning sun, but poor old Maxie got separated and before he knew where he was had lead pumped into the plane from all directions . . ."

Greenslade managed to put up a fight before he was shot down:

"18 Army 97s level and nine below. Got into dogfight. Had a crack at three – two damaged. Plane caught fire so baled out. Shot at on way down."

Flt Sgt Mothersdale takes up the story, Greenslade having told him:

"I was real worried then about being too low to bale out – I didn't think I had 600 feet. I tipped the crate on its side and went out. The trees were coming up at a hell of a rate and when I could see the chute opening it seemed so slow I didn't think it would make it . . ."

His parachute opened just in time to let him down gently into a rubber plantation. He managed to pull most of the parachute through the branches and used it to get down to the ground. Weber continued the account:

"His next problem – which end of our jungle equipment needle pointed north; that was decided by the sun and the direction of the enemy bombing of our Army positions. After about an hour's walk in no-mans land, during which time he only saw what we now surmise were Japs, two in number, he stopped an Aussie motor cyclist, and by much hitch-hiking he was back at Kallang for lunch, which is not bad work seeing that the front line is at Batu Pahat, over 100 miles away. He spent the rest of the day trying to reassure himself that he was alive, and telling us just how marvellous a sensation it is sitting down, or standing up, when falling through space, before the chute opens . . . I am amazed about myself – even though I had written the little chap off when he didn't return, I was not very upset – yet I have known Max well, and felt ever increasingly friendly towards him for a long time now, and my chief reaction was that I would revenge him by every means in my power. As I see it we all feel the same – war does make one callous."

Sgt Jim MacIntosh (W8171) was also on this sortie:

"We covered this bridge, while the army did their so-called strategic retreat. We had stayed there for about ten minutes, over our allotted time, when Japanese aircraft converged on us. I roughly estimated about 27 aircraft – dive-bombers escorted by Zeros. Mackenzie rightly gave us the order to dive, because we had been there long enough to have depleted our fuel and anyway we had already completed our task. To engage those numbers was pretty pointless. I don't know what happened to Max Greenslade – he must have misunderstood the order, or didn't hear it – but he was shot down. We others dived from 14,000 feet down to jungle level out towards the coast. I know I went straight down, and I found that the Buffalo coming out of what was a terminal velocity dive, was beautiful. The response of bringing that Buffalo out of that dive was just all you could wish for.

"Singapore, we estimated was well over a 90-mile trip back, and those Zeros did everything in the book to try and head us off. They were on the left and right hand sides and behind us and they did everything to catch us but not one of them got within firing range. For 90-odd miles we proved that the Buffalo, given a fair chance, could not be caught by a Zero. Mind you it was a funny aircraft in that, if you could give it a little boost, in a dive, and get it up to speed, it would hang on to it. If you were at full throttle and you played around with your variable pitch gear, you could hang on to your speed. The Buffalo wouldn't pull itself up in straight and level flight nearly as well as if you could give it a little boost of speed. Once there though it would carry on and keep that speed up remarkably well. The more I flew the Buffalo the more confidence I got in it."

At Singapore, air defence was left to the Hurricanes, which were soon in action to challenge the morning raid by 27 Ki-21s escorted by 64th Sentai Ki-43s. One bomber and one fighter were claimed shot down for the loss of one Hurricane, from which the pilot baled out. Seletar was the main target for this raid, where a Hudson, a Swordfish and a Walrus were destroyed, and seven other aircraft damaged. Two more Hurricanes were lost during the afternoon, one being shot down and the other running out of fuel following combat. Both pilots survived.

By the end of the day 243 and 488 Squadrons could muster only two serviceable aircraft between them. The latter unit was now advised that it was to be re-equipped with Hurricanes, its two remaining Buffaloes being handed to 243 Squadron, together with the pilots for them. Nine Hurricanes were allocated to the New Zealand unit. Four were collected at once, the remainder over the next two days.

With Japanese forces advancing rapidly down the east coast of Malaya, air reconnaissance was vital. Flt Lt Phillips, who had completed about 50 sorties over the mainland, was tour-expired and subsequently rested. On more than one occasion he had returned with battle damage to his aircraft, inflicted by intercepting fighters, but had always completed his tasks, weather permitting. The announcement of a well-earned DFC was imminent. Sgt Charlie Wareham was still with the unit, having logged more than 30 sorties. He would shortly receive an equally well-earned DFM. To replace Phillips, Flt Lt N.F.V. Henkel, a former flying instructor at Kuala Lumpur, was posted to the unit. On a visit to Seletar, where the PR Buffaloes were based, Sqn Ldr Donald Pearson, the former CFI of the Wirraway OTU at Kluang, approached Sqn Ldr Lewis of 4PRU with a request to join his unit:

"Squadron Leader Lewis I knew quite well, so I phoned him up and said I was interested, and he said. 'Oh well I don't think so at the moment but I'll let you know. In any case you're Acting Squadron Leader and we haven't a space for a Squadron Leader – you'd have to drop back to your flight lieutenancy'. I said I didn't mind that provided I was getting back to operational flying. A few days after that, he got in touch with me again, ordering me to report to Singapore immediately as Henkel had done a terrible thing: he'd raised the undercarriage of his aeroplane while on the ground which made him rather unpopular with the unit – and with the AOC! They accepted my reversion to Flight Lieutenant and I was flying operationally again on Brewster Buffaloes."

In the meantime, however, Sqn Ldr Lewis undertook a number of sorties himself, as noted by Plt Off James McEwan, an Intelligence Officer at Seletar:

"During these critical days as January was drawing to its close, the man entrusted with the task of surveying this coast and keeping track of Japanese activities was the Commanding Officer of the photo-reconnaissance unit. Lewis, a Squadron Leader, was a very big man, hewed like Hercules, with broad shoulders and very powerful, sun-tanned legs, which his shorts revealed. For his sole use had been assigned the best aircraft that was available, but it is an indication of the poverty of British resources at the time that this turned out to be a Buffalo. Stripped of every dispensable article of equipment, it had been tuned up in an effort to add a few knots to its modest speed, and equip it more adequately for its vital rôle.

"Lewis carried out his sorties usually in the early morning, this being, in this freakish climate, the time when visibility tended to be at its best. His flight path followed the east coast, its purpose simply to look out for, and report, any signs of enemy activity on the neighbouring seas, but especially in the Mersing/Endau sector. It was obviously a very lonely mission, and just as clearly a dangerous one, to which fact several scars on his aircraft bore graphic testimony. What had saved Lewis from something even worse was his outstanding skills as a pilot.

"By Friday, 23 January, the fate of the whole Mersing/Muar line hung precariously in the balance. If the enemy was to make his predicted descent on Mersing or Endau, he could not find a time more favourable to his purpose. Everything depended on the eyes and the camera of that lonely pilot in the morning skies. But during these fateful days, the climate was to furnish a decisive illustration of its fickleness. From south of Mersing even as far north as Kuantan, the whole coast was enveloped in a veil, murky beyond penetration. On his return from a sortie, neither Lewis nor his camera had anything to report. Whatever activities the Japanese might be pursuing in its concealment were beyond our ken." [112]

The activities the Japanese were pursuing were to become all too evident in the next couple of days.

That evening, Cecil Brown of *CBS* left Singapore aboard a USN PBY departing for Java. His licence to broadcast from Singapore had been revoked by the British authorities because they considered he did not adhere to the local rules, which did not permit the truth about what was really happening in Malaya and at Singapore to be divulged to the world. Another correspondent, Ron Matthews of the *Daily Herald*, was also admonished for writing: "It would be incorrect to say the Japanese have air superiority; they have air monopoly." It was apparent that even at this late stage of the conflict the British authorities were still being pig-headed. Although Brown had witnessed this short-sighted attitude at first hand, he was magnanimous in his praise for the ordinary British soldier and British people in general. But of the British Command at Singapore, he was scathing:

"Singapore showed that in critical circumstances red tape, traditional ways of doing things and observing hard and fast rules of textbooks rather well guarantee defeat. Singapore showed that to fight a 1942 war it requires daring commanders, men with agile minds, men who are not even content to imitate the enemy but have the capacity to outsmart him. One lesson of Singapore is the need of commanders who are not burdened by a defensive mentality. The cry of most officers in Singapore . . . was attack, attack and attack again. And that is the answer right now too. The Japanese took the initiative and have held it since. Singapore furnished proof that this war must be fought 24 hours a day and seven days a week. The Japs fight 24 hours a day; they are not observing week-ends.

"This is a ruthless war, without rules. What I've seen of it bears no resemblance either to football or cricket. In the operations to date it's apparent that either gangsters must fight like gentlemen or the gentlemen like gangsters. There isn't much chance of the Axis changing. The Japanese machine-gun pilots coming down by parachute. The Japs take the attitude, too, that a hospital ship carries wounded who, when they recover, will return to fight them. Sinking hospital ships isn't humane, but the Japanese military view is: anything goes. Singapore is evidence, too, that wishful thinking won't keep the Japanese away. If it would, the Japs would never have swarmed from Thailand into Malaya.

"Singapore showed that this is total war, and that every man, woman and child is part of the war machine. If, at Singapore, the military authorities had recognized that unavoidable fact, the morale of the people and resistance to the enemy might have been better sustained. Concealing a reasonable picture from those people who must later fight – as the people of Singapore were called upon to fight – had disastrous effects. After more than a week of fighting at the start of the war, the people were first informed that the Japanese were already seventy-five miles inside Malaya. They were shocked and frightened by this tardy news. They viewed all subsequent announcements with suspicion, and from then on, fantastic rumours of the approach of the enemy were spread. That is one of the greatest lessons of Singapore – that suppression of a reasonable account of the progress of the war provides every facility to the Fifth Columnists to destroy confidence." [113]

24 January

During the morning five Hurricanes and six Buffaloes were ordered off from Singapore to intercept enemy aircraft reported attacking troops in the Ayer Hitam area. By the time they arrived no aircraft were to be seen by the Hurricane pilots, although the Buffaloes from 243 Squadron encountered a number of twin-engined bombers over the Kluang-Gemas area, Plt Off Pevreal (WP-M) claiming two damaged, while Sgt Kronk (WP-L) reported gaining strikes on another.

A new supply convoy reached Singapore with further equipment and reinforcements. Included amongst personnel were a number of RAAF and RNZAF pilots, all of whom were inexperienced, while many had not completed the training programme. It was expected, even at this late stage, that training would continue at Singapore. 21RAAF/453 Squadron received almost two dozen of the new pilots but, as virtually all serviceable aircraft were required for operations, little training could be given. Nonetheless, time was found to convert a handful of the would-be fighter pilots to the Buffalo, although none were allowed to fly on operations apart from the odd convoy patrol. After an aircraft was damaged by one of the newcomers, the *ad hoc* conversion course effectively ended. Some of the pilots were transferred to other units.

Despite the arrival of the latest convoy the situation by land and air remained desperate. With the radar stations on the mainland no longer operational, control of the fighters at Singapore was becoming more and more difficult, as Sqn Ldr Clouston explained:

"The fighter defence of Singapore depended firstly on the radar warning system and, secondly, the scratch and rather inaccurate Observer Corps. The radar station at Mersing [243 AMES] provided us with approximately 30 minutes warning of an impending raid. As the Buffaloes took almost this time to reach a height of 25,000 feet, the average height of Japanese raids, it was vital that this station be kept operating as long as humanly possible. However, that was not to be and, on Army instructions, the station was dismantled and evacuated weeks before it was necessary. It was later set up on Singapore Island but its efficient range was not as great as Mersing.

"From the moment of the closing down of the Mersing station, the fighters defending Singapore were operating at great tactical disadvantage. The maximum warning we received of a raid was, at the most, 20 minutes and this naturally resulted in the patrols being always below the attacking Japanese aircraft. This one fact alone contributed much to the weakening of the defence. It says much for the quality of the pilots in the squadrons that there was no weakening of morale as a result of the tactical disadvantage in which they were forced to fight."

25 January

Atrocious weather conditions allowed Singapore respite from the daily bombing raids. Three Hurricanes were airborne in the morning to carry out patrols over the island in case any sneak raiders approached undetected, but two failed to return, victims of the weather. Both disappeared in the worsening conditions with visibility down to 300 feet. Both, it was assumed, had crashed into the sea.

Later in the morning, with an improvement in conditions, a dozen Buffaloes were scraped together to carry out a sweep over the Kluang-Gemas-Batu Pahat area. Sgt Rex Weber of 243 Squadron was involved, the entries in his diary containing increasing criticism of the leadership, both at squadron level and higher:

"This afternoon six aircraft from our Squadron and six from the Aussie squadron went up into the enemy country past Batu Pahat to ground strafe transport, etc., but our leader, in his wisdom, took us up the coast sufficiently near to give plenty of warning to any road transport, and when we came down the road we only saw one solitary truck, which we all attacked. Evidently there were concentrations in the vicinity and I am told that a ton of stuff [AA fire] was shoved up at the following aircraft. Personally my strafing was little and wild, because I saw only houses, possibly inhabited by Malayans, to shoot at. Altogether, it was to my mind a very weak effort."

Another involved in the strafing attack was Sgt MacIntosh:

"It was a late afternoon trip and we flew up the coast of Sumatra, right on the deck out to sea so as to come in above all this reported motor transport at Batu Pahat. We crossed the coast and flew down this particular road, and we came upon a Japanese motor convoy – about eight troop-carrying trucks parked alongside a road. We strafed them quite effectively and received a considerable amount of return fire from them – machine-guns and probably what looked like a Bofors-type gun. Tracer was coming up at us as we dived in there. I think we inflicted quite considerable damage on them because, when we circled round, the trucks were smoking and partly on fire."

Nothing was seen of the Japanese air force during the sweep, but a later patrol intercepted 27 Army 97 bombers at 15,000 feet over Johore. Plt Off Gifford (W8221) noted:

"I was the last to give up the chase. Made use of cloud to get between 100-150 yards and deliver four attacks. P/O Cranstone reported that I damaged one, but I did not see it myself and so did not claim. The bombers dived gradually and levelled out about 100 feet above thick flat cloudtop. I overtook them in the cloud. 14 bullet holes in kite."

Another member of the patrol, Sgt Greenslade (WP-H), reported that he had damaged his victim to such a degree that he thought it was unlikely to reach its base, and claimed it as probably destroyed.

Further up the east coast, the latest Japanese strike was imminent: a planned landing at Endau, situated on the estuary of the Sungei Endau, a few miles north of Mersing. Ki-27s of the 11th Sentai from Kota Bharu, together with others of the 1st Sentai from Kuantan, provided patrols during the day over a convoy of two transports,

Kanbera Maru and the larger *Kansai Maru*, which carried supplies to support the thrust of the Japanese Army down the east coast. As they headed southwards, they were joined by a cruiser, two destroyers, five minesweepers and three submarine chasers. To cover the operation from further afield were two more cruisers and two destroyers, while the aircraft carrier *Ryujo* stood by further out, escorted by a single destroyer.

The force had been sighted by patrolling Hudsons, which had reported the threat to Air HQ. Overnight, a plan of attack was hurriedly devised, but any strike force that could be assembled would be pitifully weak.

That evening, Rex Weber again confided his private thoughts to his diary:

> "My word, the Asiatics in this city are reacting much as they were expected to behave – after dark in particular Singapore becomes a city without services of any kind and much the same applies during the day. The Malays are displaying the greatest cowardice, while generally speaking the Chinese are reacting fairly well – of course the Indian (an air raid interrupted this last sentence) soldiers remain quite unconcerned.
>
> Our Squadron, and our Flight in particular, have to use up the remainder of the Buffs, while thanks mainly to inter-Imperial reasons, the two Aussie fighter squadrons are to be equipped with the Hurricane, also 488, so I think the best thing we can do each day is to stooge down over the Dutch islands, and every now and then write off, in some very safe way, one of our old Buffs.
>
> The things that are being said these days about our higher-up officers are not possibly to be confused with compliments. It seems that they are yellow, besides stupid and beastly. Certainly from what I have seen, all that eyewash about the old school tie clique leading their men through the fires of Hades has not shown up about this neck of the woods – all they do is lead their men to the nearest funk hole, and there they wait until the aforementioned men lead the way out; in fact, they usually remain a little longer – no doubt because of their indispensability and value. The only thing about the Air Force which commands my respect and loyalty is the magnificent valour of the lads with whom I am directly associated – every day they face an almost inevitable death as though it is all just a grand game – never would you suspect that any of them had all the joy of life before them, back in God's own country."

Rex Weber and his conscience would be in even greater torment in the next few hours.

26 January – the sacrifice at Endau

From the Singapore Strait, a motorable road ran as far north-east as Endau, also serving Mersing located on the coast a few miles to the south – and the airfields at Kluang and Kahang in Central Johore. The British, established on the line of the Mersing, were hoping to hold a line Mersing-Kluang-Batu Pahat. Japanese forces first made contact with the Mersing defences on the 22nd.

It was obvious to the British Command that an early Japanese attempt could be expected to land supplies here to prepare the forces in the area for their part in the final push on Singapore, and to bring in supplies to allow the Kahang and Kluang airfields to be put into use as soon as they were captured. It was also believed that troops were about to be landed at Endau for the purpose of engaging the Australians down the coast at Mersing; this was not to be the case, however, since the main force of Australians had by now withdrawn in accordance with III Corps orders. The rearguard defenders at Mersing had already been assaulted and overwhelmed.

While most RAF activity was directed towards western Johore, where severe fighting around Batu Pahat was underway, some of the Hudsons still remaining in Singapore had kept a regular watch on the approaches to Endau. At 0745, two RAAF Hudson crews spotted a convoy some miles north-east of Endau, heading southwards, just before both Hudsons came under attack by three Ki-27s from 12th Flying Battalion. Following a short engagement they escaped into cloud and returned to base. Next on the scene was a PR Buffalo in the hands of Sqn Ldr Lewis. By then the landings at Endau were imminent. Intelligence Officer Plt Off McEwan, at Seletar, later wrote:

> "When, at 9.30am, [Sqn Ldr] Lewis entered the Ops Room at Seletar it was clear from his face that the period of waiting and uncertainty was at an end. The Japs, he reported, were at Endau! Over the small port, weather conditions for his purpose had been well-nigh perfect; and he was confident he had got some good photographs. A little north of the town he had located an enemy force which he estimated to consist of two cruisers, twelve destroyers, and two transports. They were making for the estuary, and clearly were intending to land troops there. Shortly before 8.00am he had sent off a sighting signal to the Air HQ, giving them the details." [114]

The only striking force available on Singapore were 21 obsolete Vildebeest and three Albacores, plus nine RAAF Hudsons. The two RAF squadrons were thus ordered to prepare as many aircraft as possible for an attack, but most had been operating against motor transport in southern Johore during the night. Seven of the Vildebeest had later carried out a second mission to Batu Pahat. The crews were tired; the aircraft had to be prepared, refuelled and rearmed. It was clear that no early attack could be made. This was unfortunate because a torpedo attack on the vessels at sea might have achieved some success – at least against the all-important transports. However it was likely that the ships would be anchored in the shallow waters of the estuary by the time an attack could be made, and the aircraft were therefore each armed instead with three 500-lb armour-piercing bombs. Meanwhile, 225 Bomber Group in Sumatra was ordered to despatch all available bombers, and ABDA Command was contacted with a request that USAAC B-17s from Java should also be sent to Sumatra, but in the event these arrived too late to join in the attacks.

The first attack was to be made by Hudsons and a dozen Vildebeest. It had been intended that 4AACU's lone Shark accompany the strike force but, perhaps fortunately for Sgt Tubby Saul and his gunner, it developed an engine defect. The aircraft began taking off at 1350. Flt Lt Garden of 243 Squadron was ordered at the last moment to muster all his available A Flight Buffaloes and to rendezvous with the Vildebeest over an island north-east of Singapore; meanwhile, Flt Lt Bertie Bows was to take B Flight to a point south of Endau to cover the return of the strike force. Their orders were to "escort them to where they are going and bring them back." Garden was given no indication of the destination or target:

> "I had five serviceable aircraft and formed with them two sections, one of myself with Sgt Weber as my No.2, and the other section of three led by Sgt Wipiti."

He accordingly led off his flight and found the Vildebeest flying at 1,000 feet in close formation. Garden commented:

> "I met the Vildebeest as arranged and escorted them up the coast of Malaya. Owing to their low speed of 90mph, this made them rather difficult to escort as we had to use a lot of petrol going backwards and forwards and around them to use up our excess speed. At one point the Vildebeest reversed course through 180°, which gave me the

impression they had been recalled, but after approximately two minutes they altered course through 180° again. Flying at 1,000 feet, we were just below cloud."

Sgt Weber, Garden's No.2, added:

"We stooged along in this company at about 1,500 feet, knowing full well that those gallant boys were going to almost certain death. My one thought was 'what courage.'"

A little way behind and somewhat higher came the nine RAAF Hudsons escorted by six Buffaloes of 21RAAF/453 Squadron and nine Hurricanes of 232 Squadron, the latter led by Sqn Ldr Brooker. The British formation approached the area at about 1500 hours. The weather was overcast, with cloud up to 4,000 feet, but the sky was then reasonably clear up to about 12,000 feet, above which was more cloud. The strike force flew up the Endau estuary through a bank of cloud, emerging from this to see the black hulks of the two Japanese transports lying a couple of miles offshore. Landing craft carrying elements of the 96th Airfield Battalion and its signals unit, were making their way to the shore, the craft also loaded with drums of aviation fuel, bombs and stores. As the biplanes approached, flashes from the decks of the covering warships showed that the gunners had spotted them, but they managed to hold their formation until the defending fighters descended on them – nine Ki-27s of 11th Sentai's 2nd Chutai and ten Ki-27s of 1st Sentai, together with a lone Ki-44 of the 47th Independent Fighter Chutai, flown by the Commanding Officer, Capt Kuroe. Garden's report continued:

"Arriving at the Endau estuary the weather was suddenly clear and apart from a hump of cumulus at 1,500 feet there was no cloud cover at all. Above us were many Jap fighters. I stuck to the Vildebeest until they broke up to bomb, and climbed up, turning to port, to meet the fighters. At this point the flak began making a mess of the Vildebeest, which were going up in flames right, left and centre. Quite soon the air was full of broken and crashing Vildebeest and parachutes.

"Meanwhile, what seemed to me to be an enormous force of fighters was descending on us from the sun in one long line-astern formation. I told Sgt Wipiti on the R/T to proceed immediately with his section and engage another separate formation of fighters slightly to the south, whilst I coped with the formation of about twelve, which had taken an interest in Sgt Weber and myself. What Sgt Weber did, I don't know, but I saw the formation swing to attack me in line astern. I tightened my turn and kept the leader of the Jap formation in view as he was closing in on me. I knew I couldn't out-turn him, so didn't try. I waited until he got close enough to fire and when he opened up – I saw his gun ports blazing – I pulled up sharply and jinked at the last moment and he went below me. I rolled over on my back and shot him down from upside down. I set him on fire and he crashed. However I made the mistake of watching the results of my handiwork that split second too long and I was hammered by the next one, which blew a large hole in the right hand side of my aircraft and wrecked all the electric switches which operated the guns and gun sight, and other controls as well."

Owing to the damage inflicted on his aircraft, Garden could not get the Buffalo to fly above 500 feet, although he was able to return safely to Kallang, where he found that one bullet had gone through the carburettor; he continued:

"I cannot remember what happened to Sgt Wipiti, but he got something. I returned to the Ops Room in person and was advised to detail two pilots from my Flight for strafing duties over the beaches – I advised P/O Pevreal [WP-M] and Sgt Kronk [W8242/WP-K] to do this. They both arrived back safely."

Plt Offs Wally Greenhalgh (W8181) and Jim Cranstone (W8226) provided top cover to the two strafing Buffaloes, the latter reporting an engagement with a Type 0, which he believed crashed in Johore. This was later confirmed as destroyed, presumably by the Army. All the Buffaloes returned safely to Kallang, although several also carried the scars of battle damage. Rex Weber later wrote in his diary:

"The formation of twelve biplanes was very, very good but the next thing I saw when we entered the battle area, was a general scatter of Vildebeest being constantly harried by Japs. Mowbray led me out of a cloud right into the midst of six fighter 97s in the immediate vicinity, with myriads of enemy fighter aircraft all about. I didn't know which way to turn – I had one fighter blazing away on my tail, one to the side, and one coming down on me from directly above. Actually, I have no idea what I did. For one moment I tried to attack, but decided I had better find cover, and soon I was scooting for clouds, which seemed miles away. Just about this time my motor cut and I had visions of being a prisoner of war. Imagine my joy when she picked up, but at the same time I was feeling a coward for keeping in cover and deserting the Vildebeest. However, when I got back I found I had indeed been lucky – my plane was riddled and the cause of the engine trouble was a bullet in the carburettor system. I was amazed to find all our chaps back safely – actually I wouldn't have been at all surprised if I had been the only survivor. How the slow old Vildebeest got home is more than I can say, because when I saw them last, the 97s were shooting them to hell. From all reports I gather that this sacrifice of brave men was all in vain – the damage sustained by the enemy shipping was negligible."

The six 21RAAF/453 Squadron Buffaloes were soon involved in hectic combats, during which three were damaged, including that flown by Flg Off Geoff Sheppard, who claimed one fighter shot down, as he recalled:

"Earlier in the campaign a few of us had noticed that the Japanese, whenever they attacked, carried out a stall-turn and came down on us as they were always above. We thought it could be a good idea to attack any individual while at the top of a stall turn. In my case I probably carried out the silliest manoeuvre by a pilot who lived to tell the tale.

"Six Japanese fighters went into orbit above me and one of them started a stall turn to come down on me. They would have been probably 2,000 and possibly 3,000 feet above us. I had put my nose down slightly, got a speed of 350mph on the clock and I attacked in a vertical climb and he blew up on fire only feet from me. Obviously this put me in a silly position with the other five aircraft, as I was out of speed and, indeed, between the climb and the recoil action of my guns. The aircraft stalled and I went into a violent spin, which probably saved me. I spun for something like 8,000 feet, with hard left rudder and two hands on the stick, to get the aircraft out of the spin. Finally I did get out of the spin close to the ground, and dived for a cloud with the remaining Japanese on my tail. Even though I was side-slipping I was shot through the canopy, wings and petrol tank, but I got away. I had 126 holes in my aircraft when I landed back at Sembawang."

Two more Ki-27s were claimed shot down in the mêlée, one by the Buffalo leader, Flt Lt Grace, who also claimed a second damaged, the other by Sgt Ross Leys. Although they did not see their victims actually crash, their claims were apparently 'confirmed' by virtue of their impressions of the flying attitude of the Japanese aircraft when last seen! Flg Off Barrie Hood's Buffalo was targeted for attack by one determined Japanese pilot, a burst of fire hitting his seat and port fuel tank:

"Everything went all right until we were within a mile of the target. Looking up to starboard I spotted a whole herd of fighters just starting to peel off and heading in our direction. My No.1 turned to port and I had to turn to starboard to meet three Zeros [possibly the Ki-44s] who were having a race to see who could get the kill first. I just couldn't get the first Zero in my sights, but he evidently had me lined up all right. Avoiding his fire I looked around and saw another one on my tail about 150 yards away who opened up just as I turned around.

"A cannon burst hit my seat and my port tank and petrol ran everywhere. The port tank was badly hit but the motor was ticking over nicely, so I decided that discretion was the better part of valour and dived towards a thick cloud. I was in a bad way and with my full tank emptying fast I decided to head for home. With petrol fumes in my eyes, I didn't like my chances of making it, but kept in cloud cover as much as I could and throttled back. The final approach to landing was the worst when I began to lose the last 100 feet. I didn't see the ground when I touched down but made a safe landing and apart from a pair of very sore eyes I was OK." [115]

Of the action, the Squadron's diarist wrote in the customary light-hearted style:

"We took part in one of the biggest shows of recent weeks. For some days Tojo had been working a large convoy down towards Endau, so it was decided to do this convoy over. Accordingly nine Hudsons were despatched and No.453 escorted them. Someone told Tojo the show was on and he had 100 fighters waiting up there. However, the show was on and the convoy was well bombed. All the Buffs got home safely but two of the Hudsons failed to return. On this show, too, we lost some of our old friends, the 'Flying Pigs.' Of 12 of them that went up only one returned. This squadron had done a magnificent job in Malaya flying aircraft with a top speed of about 85 miles per hour."

By this time the Hurricanes had also become involved in a series of dogfights, the sky appearing to the pilots to be full of Japanese fighters and burning Vildebeest. All the Hurricane pilots returned safely, claiming six Ki-27s shot down. But the cost to the strike force had been very heavy: five Vildebeest failed to return, although some of the crew members survived and managed to make their way back to Singapore on foot or by sea. One Vildebeest navigator, lucky to have survived the onslaught, later complained about the lack of protection from the Buffaloes:

". . . Buffaloes, instead of escorting our aircraft, were strafing the barges plying between the transports and the shore."

This criticism was presumably aimed in the direction of Plt Off Pevreal and Sgt Kronk, but they had been ordered to strafe the landing craft.

The 11th Sentai claimed five Buffaloes, two Hurricanes, two biplanes and two Hudsons shot down, while pilots of the 1st Sentai reported shooting down six biplanes. The only loss recorded was that of Lt Mizotani of the latter unit, who managed to bale out safely. Other Ki-27s were undoubtedly damaged but apparently all returned safely to base.

Back at Singapore a second strike was prepared with all haste. Nine Vildebeest and three Albacores were to participate; each aircraft was armed with six 250-lb bombs. All serviceable fighters were ordered to escort the strike force and seven of the original nine Hurricanes set off, together with the only four Buffaloes that could be made serviceable, including three flown by 488 Squadron's Sgts Don Clow, Rod MacMillan and Bunny De Maus. The fighters had been delayed, the biplane bombers having taken off without them and were therefore devoid of escort when they reached

Endau, where ten 1st Sentai Ki-27s and two 47th Chutai Ki-44s immediately attacked. With no fighter protection or cloud cover, the attacking force was doomed. Five more Vildebeest were shot down, as were two of the Albacores. When the Hurricanes finally arrived one was also shot down, from which the pilot baled out; he eventually got back to Singapore. In return, four Ki-27s were claimed. The Buffaloes suffered no losses nor made any claims. MacMillan remembered:

> "Just before we got to the place we struck a cloud layer, a hundred to a couple of hundred feet thick. We had been flying up there under the cloud cover, weaving about, because the Vildebeest were very slow. Without any warning we were led up into the cloud cover. So the whole group got completely disconnected. I came out of the top of the cloud and there didn't seem to be any aircraft there, so I went back down through it and decided all I could do was to go out to the meeting point. There I found a couple of Hudsons and I simply came back in formation with them."

Again the Japanese pilots overclaimed, reporting successes over 14 biplanes and one Hurricane, to bring their total for the two actions to a round 30. The two Ki-44 pilots, Capts Kuroe and Jimbo, each claimed a victory. No further losses were recorded.

The operation had been a total disaster. Not only had the landings not been stopped, the two transports suffered only minor damage. The sacrifice had been heavy. Of the 38 missing crew members, eight survivors would eventually make their way back to Singapore; two others survived to be taken prisoner. In the aircraft that did return, ten of which had suffered damage of varying degrees, were a further six wounded crewmen. Even the soldiers defending Singapore, who used to joke with typical British humour that the Vildebeest was Singapore's secret weapon – "Puss Moths can only hop from twig to twig, but the Vildebeest can fly all the way from one branch to the next" – were saddened and shocked by the losses. Endau was just one more disastrous operation in a whole series of tragedies for the British and Commonwealth forces. DFMs were awarded to two surviving crewmen, and two posthumous Mention in Despatches for the squadron commanders, both of whom were killed. Had such gallantry occurred nearer home, undoubtedly a Victoria Cross or two would have been awarded[116].

Later that afternoon, with the RAF licking its wounds and lamenting its losses, Sgt Fisken managed to scrounge a flight in one of the Hurricanes (BG722), which he flew for some 20 minutes.

January 27
At dawn, two Moths of the MVAF set out from Singapore to reconnoitre the Senggarang area as no news had been received of the 6/15th Indian Brigade. When near Senggarang one of the biplanes suffered a couple of bullet holes through one wing – fired by unseen troops – although no serious damage was inflicted. The other aircraft went on towards Batu Pahat airstrip. The reconnaissance proved successful as shortly after, almost 3,000 of the missing men were successfully located – cut off west of Rengit and these were rescued over the next four days from the swampy coastland south of Batu Pahat by two gunboats. Sgts Wipiti and Kronk (W8242/WP-K) had earlier carried out a two-hour recce in the area but had failed to sight the missing men; both returned safely. Another recce flight was undertaken by Buffaloes led by Plt Off Gifford (W8143):

> "I led B Flight 243 on recco to report on enemy shipping which had been bombed on previous day, as enemy were effecting a landing at Endau. Went up to 22,000 feet in

almost no cloud. Dived down through cloud over Endau. Circled round and flew back along the roads at 500 feet. Chased bandit (Hudson) 15 miles out to sea."

The harassed RAF was given no respite. Early in the morning three Hurricanes took off in an attempt to intercept a reconnaissance aircraft. They were not successful but one Hurricane failed to return. At 1000 the Hurricane crashed at great speed into a small rubber plantation in Johore and exploded. Somewhat later in the morning, two Buffaloes of 243 Squadron were up on patrol when two dozen G4Ms from the Kanoya Ku, escorted by 19 A6Ms and accompanied by two C5Ms, attacked Kallang, the Japanese crews claiming five aircraft burned on the ground. The Buffalo pilots, Plt Off Pevreal and Sgt Greenslade were set upon by the escort, the latter's aircraft (WP-H) being badly shot up although he was able to land safely.

488 Squadron's Hurricanes were all being refuelled as the bombs started falling and eight pilots, who were sheltering in a sand-bagged gun emplacement, were buried when a bomb exploded close by. They were dragged out shocked but uninjured; however the Hurricanes had been less lucky. Two were completely destroyed, three badly damaged and three slightly damaged. Almost all of 243 Squadron's remaining Buffaloes were destroyed or damaged, and two Blenheims were burnt out. Hangars, buildings and three petrol tankers were also set on fire. Geoff Fisken was amongst those sheltering and witnessed the destruction of a nearby Buffalo:

"I was relegated to the slit trench brigade – it was eerie listening to the bombs coming down. The Buffalo must have been hit by a 'daisy-picker' – a [fragmentation] bomb with a long spike on the nose, which detonated when it touched, usually a few feet off the ground. A lot of the troops received bad leg wounds from them."

Sqn Ldr Mackenzie had also witnessed the damage fragmentation bombs could inflict:

"I remember an occasion when our Engineering Officer and I dashed along the road, which was between our airfield and dispersal, during a bomb attack. There was a lorry load of women being taken to their factories and, when they saw the aeroplane, they all jumped out to run for some deep ditches. The fragmentation bombs hit just when the women got out and one or two of them were cut to shreds. It was a horrible sight." [117]

Fisken continued:

"After this raid there was a petrol tanker, which had just been filled, parked quite close to our dispersal hut. The tanker had been hit in the motor and from the middle of the tanker there was a stream of petrol, under pressure, with a flame on the top – about 40 feet high just like an oil well burning. About 60 fellows gathered around and pushed it about 200 yards away, where it eventually burnt out and exploded; those fellows on the ground never seemed to show any fear though I'm sure they were just as scared as everyone else. Groundcrew worked hard to get everything repaired but as the Japs moved further down Malaya it was a battle against time, as well as against the Japs."

Forty minutes later, whilst personnel were attempting to salvage aircraft and stores, a second wave of bombers approached. Most bombs fell near 243 Squadron's dispersal, destroying two more Buffaloes and two Hurricanes. Sgt Weber recorded:

"We were bombed well and truly on two occasions. 'Hell, look at them!' was the first warning I had in each case – and then I did look, knowing full well that 27 heavy bombers were making a perfect run up on our exact position. Without much hesitation Bert and I made tracks for a decent hole and soon the bombs were whistling down in our very close vicinity. First lot, Bert's and my old morale was in very good order and we joked to keep up the courage of the other boys. Next lot, I crouched very low all on my lonesome except for Garden, who was more scared than Rex A., and I was definitely unhappy, yes miserable, in fact. I wonder if that is a triumph of understatement. They landed very close indeed and four huge craters were all within a chain to a chain and a half away from our shelter.

"The explosions were terrific but by far and away the worst part is when you hear them, as it seems, hundreds whistling down, and you feel certain that a direct hit is certain. Then you console yourself with the thought that anyway you will not know anything about it. The damage was pretty bad, about six kites, three oil bowsers and huge holes all about the drome, but the demoralizing effect was by far the most detrimental part – the troops were all down in the mouth."

Meanwhile the two Buffaloes in the air attempted to harry the raiders, but were engaged by escorting fighters, Plt Offs Marra and Cranstone claiming one damaged between them, as the former recalled:

"They sent two of us off, Cranstone and I, to get after these bombers – 54 or something, and goodness knows how many fighters. Of course nobody knew that. Off we went. We could see it was a lovely fine day- a bit of cloud below us – but where we were a nice fine day. We were climbing up towards the bombers and along came one Type 0. I think he mistook us for Japanese aircraft because he tried to come in and formate on us. Well we soon enlightened him we were foes, not friends. As soon as he recognised the big roundels on our side, he woke up and started to pull away. I got a squirt at him and Cranstone reckoned that I hit him good and hard.

"As our base had had it that day we landed back at Sembawang. We went to the Operations Room, and were told to leave our aircraft there as Kallang was unserviceable and road transport would be provided to take us back. We went back to Kallang with a truckload of ammunition, and a couple of hundred guys and we all ended up at Tengah. We had to organise two feeds a day for our crowd, until a boat arrived to get us to Sumatra. We helped in the Operations Room but generally we had to be back on Tengah to see that everyone was fed and stayed put. We had a roll-call every morning and night, so that when we got the go ahead to leave everybody was there. We had a car by this time – you could just go and help yourself as the civilians were parking them in big lots on the playing fields at Singapore, so we were mobile."

Those at Sembawang were not happy with their lot, either, as recorded by the Australian duty diarist:

"Now, after having been bombed, battered and bewildered we are subjected to further annoyances, namely the presence of Jap shells. The AIF has evacuated the mainland and the Japs have set up their artillery there. Sembawang is an easy target and is under constant observation. Shells whistle over onto the drome and among the buildings. We do not like it!"

Following this attack, what remained of 243 and 488 Squadrons' aircraft were handed to 453 Squadron, together with seven pilots including Sgt Fisken, as the latter noted:

"By the end of the month our officers and some of our pilots had been evacuated. As Malaya caved in, 243 Squadron was disbanded. I next moved to 453 Squadron at Sembawang in Singapore with three other Kiwis – Rex Weber, Charlie Kronk and Bert Wipiti. We kept our own planes, which were becoming an increasingly scarce resource.

Out of the four original squadrons, there was now just one."

Plt Off Frank Johnstone, Sgts Bunny De Maus and Jack Burton were the three pilots attached from 488 Squadron. Sgt Weber was none too keen about the move:

"Then, to make matters worse, the AOC decided to disband 243 Squadron and the Sergeant Pilots have now been attached to 453 Squadron. After all, we had done a pretty fair job and to lose our entity entirely, beside all the associations of this place, has come as a very severe blow. Besides, we had all been building our hopes on receiving Hurricanes, and I truly think that we would have wrought havoc amongst the Japs."

Plt Off Pevreal was among those who was informed he was to join the new Hurricane squadron due to arrive from Java:

"I went to Tengah and there wasn't a soul in sight. There were dead bodies or bits of bodies all over the place. It was rather horrifying and I knew we had lost the war then. We finally located some ground staff who said everybody was in the underground ops room. Three of us stuck together from that time – Terry Marra, Jim Cranstone and I. There were no aircraft. Three days later we were posted to 232 Squadron at Seletar. There were no aircraft there either. We went into the Mess and managed to get a beer and something to eat."

On learning that 453 Squadron was to remain as the last Buffalo unit on the island, its current diarist responded to the news with the usual hint of sarcasm:

"And today the powers that be showed their gratitude to the squadron by presenting us with all the Buffaloes left on the island. Now this was a truly magnificent gesture, especially as these Buffs were in first class condition and fully operationally serviceable – that is apart from the fact that the motors were quite *passé* and the kites were full of bullet holes. Anyway the boys were enormously cheered up by this news. Also we had added to our ranks some Sergeant Pilots from 488 and 243 Squadrons. And our own reinforcements consist of nine Australian Sergeant Pilots; unfortunately they were not operational and we were apparently expected to train them all in one Buff, on a bomb-torn aerodrome. So now do you wonder why 453 is getting properly brassed off?

"From this time on we went back to being a sort of fighter squadron-cum-recce squadron. We were maintaining usually two kites on readiness, which bored off into the blue when the air-raid sirens went. Tojo was however most inconsiderate as he always kept his bombers at 26,000 feet and his fighters two or three thousand feet above them; and Buffaloes just wallow around like pigs in mud at that height – if they can get there. The recces were divided into two groups, the milk patrol down south, and the meat run up north."

One of those posted to 453 Squadron was Sgt Jack Burton of 488 Squadron, who wrote in his diary:

"This morning, P/O Frank Johnstone, Sgt De Maus and self received orders to pack our gear as we had been posted to the RAAF squadron at Sembawang. This was indeed a sad blow, as none of us liked the idea of saying farewell to the rest of the boys. However as the squadron has now only seven Buffaloes left, there was an overflow of pilots, and as three were to be shifted a ballot resulted in us going along with six others from 243 Squadron, which has now been disbanded. We shifted late in the afternoon, and our first impressions of our new drome were not pleasant, as wrecked buildings and aircraft and hundreds of bomb craters were evidence of the importance of this large aerodrome.

We were met by our new CO, Sqn Ldr Harper, who took us to meet some of his pilots. A very cordial welcome was given us and we were made to feel right at home. We learnt that out of nearly 40 aircraft only two were serviceable and, as there are now 36 pilots, the prospects of flying are slight for a few days at least."

At the same time, 21RAAF and 453 Squadron were reconstituted as separate units, the former with no aircraft. The AOC sent an appropriate signal to Air Ministry, outlining his intentions:

"On arrival 48 [Operation] 'Opponent' Hurricanes, am rearming 488 and 243 Squadrons with Hurricanes [the latter did not happen], making with 232 Squadron three Hurricane squadrons. All remaining Buffaloes with sufficient Buffalo pilots are being concentrated in 453 Squadron. No aircraft available now or near future for 21RAAF Squadron. All squadrons have been much depleted in action and since 21RAAF Squadron was originally on Wirraways, it has numerous air observers and newly arrived pilots trained on Wirraways only, who cannot be employed or trained on fighters here. No object in 21RAAF Squadron remaining Singapore without aircraft and am therefore shipping it at once to Australia to rearm, as it can do so better there than here."

Next day 21RAAF personnel, apart from a few of the more experienced pilots, embarked for Australia, via Sumatra and Java. They boarded the SS *Takliwa* and set sail for Palembang, arriving in the early hours of 1 February 8.[118] Of this period, Sqn Ldr Harper wrote:

"Towards the end of January, the two Australian GR squadrons [Hudson] located at Sembawang – plus 21RAAF Squadron – retreated from Singapore to Sumatra. The Station was placed under RAF control with Grp Capt Whistondale as Station Commander. This officer was eccentric and often spent time with his hobby of stamp collecting with the airmen, when the Station organization was in urgent need of attention.
    "At the same time as this change, all the remaining Buffalo aircraft in Singapore from the other squadrons were given to me along with an assortment of pilots. A Fighter Ops dispersal organisation had been set up, and we were now fully under the control of Kallang Fighter Ops. The aircraft we had been sent however, had already been well used by other units and they required considerable checking and servicing in every case, except one, before we would operate them. As the aircraft were made reasonably serviceable they were tested, and it was found that a large proportion of the Cyclone engines were suffering from a serious lack of power. Spare engines were not available and the number of aircraft, therefore, available for operational work never exceeded six, though there were several more flyable.
    "The enemy had a constant fighter patrol five miles north of the aerodrome, and the Controllers at Fighter Group refused to send pilots up. This was a form of stalemate. No policy was given for some while to the Squadron, and they stayed at readiness with no hope of flying. In fact, before one raid they were told by Fighter Control to clear off the aerodrome, as there was a raid coming. I was, at this stage, unable to tell the Flights what was required of them except to carry on and make the aircraft serviceable. These matters were not well received, and the Flight commanders had, understandably, no enthusiasm in the running of their Flights."

Further tension was created when he asked the AOC to intervene:

"Furthermore, with the departure of all the RAF personnel, except one or two officers of the Headquarters Staff, and those, of course, of 453 Squadron, no RAF troops had been brought in, and out of a Squadron of 150 men we were forced to provide 50 for manning the Station. Some of the men worked extremely well and creditably, although we were so short handed, but others were not so good and we often had difficulty in finding them. I had, in fact, on one occasion, to ask the AOC to assist me by talking to the troops."

Members of 453 Squadron were already disillusioned and, to compound matters, an investigation was carried out by the Service Police for supposed deserters (a spin-off from the problems with some of the RAAF personnel in Malaya). The situation was further exacerbated when pep talks by the AOC, the Station Commander and then by Air Vice-Marshal Maltby, suggested Australians, amongst other disparaging remarks, were 'yellow'. The Squadron diarist commented:

"On top of all we've had to put up with, we have been put under suspicion of desertion or something – the Squadron was visited by the Air Force Police who proceeded to check up on us and probe into our activities. They must have been horribly disappointed as they failed to unearth any criminals. We would very much like to find out who was responsible for ordering this police investigation. Then having failed to make criminals of us, the AOC came out and put up a very black show, which further endeared the RAF to us. In plain blunt language he called us 'yellow'; this because our boys took cover when the shells came over. Now, why should a white-livered, broken-down, half-witted old brass hat be allowed to call a squadron, which has fought since the first day of war, a lot of cowards?

"He was backed up in his statements by the Station Commander [Grp Capt Whistondale], a gentleman who, when he himself got into a bit of shell fire, proved that he was the last one to accuse anyone else of having the wind up[119]. Later still we had a visit from an Air Vice-Marshal who wasted an hour and a half of our precious time with a whole lot of sanctimonious poppycock. 'We will continue to operate our aircraft from Sembawang', says he. And thus history is being made. For the first time in any war aircraft are to be operated from an aerodrome between two lots of artillery. What stamina! What bravery! What bloody foolishness!! Not forgetting, of course, the proper modulation of the voice!!"

28 January
Early morning saw the safe arrival of another convoy in Keppel Harbour. This, together with the two preceding arrivals, had between them brought the rest of the 18th Division. Hurricanes and Buffaloes patrolled overhead to provide protection, but on this occasion the Japanese bombers were conspicuous by their absence. However, at 1000, the usual 27 bombers attacked Kallang, but the men managed to get away in lorries before bombs were dropped. This time they missed the aerodrome but destroyed an aircraft dispersed near maintenance and the remainder falling mostly on civilian property. Both Flt Lt Mackenzie and Sgt Clow suffered ear trouble as the result of bomb blasts. Mackenzie recalled:

"I got buried by a bomb and lost my hearing. I was stone deaf for several days and it was the only time I flew an aeroplane where I couldn't even hear the engine!" [120]

Later, four Mihoro Ku G3Ms found another convoy, en route from Australia, heading northwards in the Banka Strait. The Japanese crews reported six transports and five destroyers, which they bombed without result.

January 29

Attacks on Singapore continued unabated, 26 Genzan Ku G3Ms – with 18 escorting A6Ms and a C5M – attacking Seletar during the morning. JAAF units also raided Sembawang. 64th Sentai Ki-43s provided an escort to the island, but only Sgt Maj Shokichi Omori, who had been delayed taking off and arrived alone, met some unescorted bombers and accompanied them to the target. On return, he reported seeing five Hurricanes and Buffaloes above and, when these dived to the attack, he claimed two shot down with ease, driving the others off.

Two of the bombers were hit and damaged, one force-landing at Kuala Lumpur on return. A section of Hurricanes and a pair of Buffaloes were involved in the interception, the Hurricanes claiming one bomber shot down and one probable, while Sgt Keith Gorringe also claimed a bomber probably destroyed but was then attacked by a fighter. With his undercarriage damaged Gorringe was obliged to crash-land on returning to Sembawang. Meanwhile, Flt Lt Kinninmont, in command of the Buffalo Flight, pursued the departing bombers, believing that he damaged one before they outpaced his aircraft. It would seem that Gorringe was a victim of the tenacious Omori, the other being a Hurricane, which crashed on return.

Eight of the Mihoro Ku bombers returned to attack the latest Singapore-bound convoy, which was carrying several thousand troops including at least 2,000 Australians, claiming to have left one transport on fire. The escorting destroyer claimed hits on three of the bombers, while the convoy in fact steamed on unscathed and reached the island safely.

At this stage a dozen more Hurricanes – which had flown from the deck of the aircraft carrier HMS *Indomitable* to Java – arrived at Singapore from Palembang, guided by two Blenheims. They landed at Seletar, moving to Tengah next day. Watching their arrival were some of the pilots of 243 Squadron who had been sent to Seletar, expecting to be posted to the new Hurricane unit, which, in the event, did not happen. In fact, Flt Lt Mowbray Garden had been appointed Flight Commander, only to be advised that the Flight he was to take over no longer existed. Plt Off Marra recalled:

> "We reached the drome about 15 minutes before about 50 Japanese bombers. Suddenly we could hear a raid coming in. We scrambled out of the Mess to some slit trenches that were located under some trees on the golf links, which were just across the road [Flt Lt Garden jumped into a trench, only to find it already occupied by a corpse!] I'd heard that if the bombers got directly over you, and you hadn't heard a bomb coming, once they started to drop them they'd go past you – the trajectory would see to that. There was a bit of noise going on, but I hadn't heard any bombs. The aerodrome was some distance away and I thought that they were going to land on the aerodrome. Suddenly 'crump!' and one landed alongside me. 'Crump, crump, crump', the ground was starting to rock and there was an almighty great crash close to me, branches of trees, mud and dirt. After everything had passed us I leapt up from the top of the trench and asked if anybody was hurt. There were a few guys looking a bit shaken but nobody was injured. We decided to get out to the aerodrome to do what we could. The hangars were burning, the bulldozer had been hit, there were trucks on fire and the Officers' Mess was burning – it was in a shambles. Anyway we got some shovels working. We knew the Hurricanes were coming so everybody was trying to fill in craters and finally we repaired it sufficiently to be used.
>
> "By this time there was one guy flying round the circuit in a Hurricane and he was wearing a Bombay Bowler. He made a copybook approach and landing. The RAF used

to issue ferry pilots a sun helmet – a real Livingstone job, known as a Bombay Bowler, converted to fly in and equipped with earphones, microphones, etc. One can imagine how these looked in the cockpit of a fighter plane! The Hurricane taxied up to us and stopped. The pilot slid the canopy back and in a very English voice, enquired: 'I say, what is going on around here?' The trouble was that they hadn't come prepared to fight a war. They'd all come with twelve .303s in them, and every gun was full of bees wax. So we volunteered to clean them, so they could take part in what's going on."

The new arrivals were shortly to be treated to the realities of the situation – to their cost. Other new arrivals during the morning included an Empire flying boat that alighted at Singapore, conveying Air Commodores S.F. Vincent DFC AFC and H.J.F. Hunter MC, who had been sent to form new fighter and bomber groups, respectively. They were in for a surprise, as Vincent recalled:

"Feeling rather like relieving heroes come to save the situation, I rang up AVM Pulford, the AOC, to let him know we had arrived, to be flattened by the news that he didn't even know we were coming . . . However, it was decided to send Hunter away at once to Sumatra to try to organise the few bombers remaining, while I should stay to endeavour to get the few fighters reorganised and functioning." [121]

With most of Singapore's airfields now coming under shellfire, a reappraisal of the position was made and some change in dispositions would follow. To make room for the new arrivals, others were moved around, as Sgt Burton noted:

"Late in the afternoon all Sergeant Pilots shifted to new quarters and here it was that, for the first time in my life, I have had to 'rough it'. Situated in amongst the rubber trees, seventeen of us were given sleeping quarters in an old hut, built from tree trunks and thatch leaves. This had previously been the quarters of a bomber squadron and they left it in a disgustingly dirty manner. Dirt and filth was everywhere and had to be cleaned up first. There is no lighting except a couple of kerosene lamps, while there is only one facility for washing and then, at times, there is no water running. Ants roam the floor in their thousands and get into everything you possess. There is little ventilation and the place has a dirty, musty smell. Conditions are certainly not all that one would wish for. However, as a result of the quarters at the drome being useless, we have had to make the most of everything.

"As you lay in bed at night, continued artillery fire from the front line at Johore can be heard and it certainly brings home the real horrors of war. The Japs are within 30 miles of Singapore and still making progress. However, compared with the hardships some poor chaps have had to endure, ours is small, so I must not complain but accept what has come my way, and make the most of it. The Australian boys all seem decent chaps, but are rough in speech and living conditions – are always bright and cheerful. Boy! Oh boy! These lads certainly like their beer and I think they must spend all their money on same."

Rex Weber was still making despondent entries in his diary:

"Yesterday I did not write up my impressions of that day as I was in the depths of demoralization. Things sure have been happening during the past few hours. It would almost seem that the gutless wonders who have been running this show are now preparing to leave Singapore to its fate."

30 January

Twenty-seven bombers, with fighter escort, raided various targets, including the docks, during the morning. A number of Hurricanes managed to intercept and several claims were made. Sgt Fisken of 243 Squadron accompanied the patrol in Hurricane BE728, but made no contact with the raiders. Throughout the day, G3Ms from the Mihoro Ku hunted for the convoy, but either failed to locate it or bombed without effect.

In bad weather, three Buffaloes patrolled off Singapore in an attempt to provide some protection for the convoy. Sgt Matt O'Mara became separated from the other two, Sgts Board and Scrimgeour, and subsequently lost. Out of fuel, he belly-landed his aircraft (believed to have been AN205) in a swamp on Bintan Island, several miles south of Singapore, the impact rendering him unconscious. The Buffalo had in fact come down within a few hundred yards of where a Hurricane pilot, who had crash-landed nine days earlier, was being cared for by local natives. The same natives lifted O'Mara from the wreck of his aircraft and carried him to the hut where the seriously injured Hurricane pilot was being looked after. On recovering his senses, O'Mara put a call through to Singapore, advising of his whereabouts. On learning of his safety, the Squadron diarist wrote:

> "While searching the skies Matt had wandered from the straight and narrow and had force-landed on an island some 50 miles south of Singapore. We know not what he did down there nor how he got back but, tis said, he was being well cared for by a Winker – did he have a nice little fraulein handy, Matt?"

Air/Sea Rescue Pinnace *No.53*, skippered by Sgt W.A. Bullock, was sent to convey both pilots back to Singapore. While they waited on the beach, three A6Ms flew low over the island, obviously attracted by the crash-landed Buffalo, but did not open fire.

Air HQ was still desperate to learn what was happening on the mainland, which meant that the PRU Buffaloes were still being heavily employed. By this time Flt Lt Donald Pearson was getting into his stride:

> "While photographing Kuantan airfield, two Jap fighters took off and attempted an intercept. However, I spotted them taking off and headed north to Kota Bharu. I returned well out over the China Sea."

Meanwhile, Flt Lt Garden was ordered to take 100 key men to Java, where he was to reform 243 Squadron with USAAC P-40s, which were on their way by sea transport. The Dutch, who were to air ferry these personnel, misunderstood the order and they were flown instead to Palembang. When the party eventually reached Batavia, they were informed that the expected P-40s had been lost at sea[122]. Garden commented:

> "There was nothing now to fly, and any sort of organisation was somewhat chaotic. Ultimately, I was instructed to board a freighter at Tjilatjap on the south coast and, with a number of airmen in my charge, eventually did so."

31 January

Further violent action erupted in the skies over Singapore on the last day of the month, when the siege proper of the island officially began following the blowing up, at 0800, of a section of the Johore Causeway. Although a 30-yard-wide breach was thought sufficient to stop the invaders, it was in fact easily crossed at low tide. Sgt Jack Burton wrote:

> "All day long loud explosions indicated that further 'scorched earth' policies were being adopted and volumes of smoke could be seen in Johore and in the vicinity of the Naval Base. The remaining serviceable Buffaloes, numbering four, now took to the air during the raids but only two were serviceable at the end of the day. Charlie Kronk

made a crash-landing on Tengah aerodrome and received a severe shaking but miraculously escaped injury. I called on the boys of 488 Squadron and learned that they were also packing, ready to evacuate. Kallang, like the rest of the aerodromes, is now almost deserted and wreckage of burnt-out planes and buildings tell a sad story of the result of the Jap bombings. During the night artillery fire across the causeway indicated we were up on the front line."

Hurricanes were scrambled on the approach of the Japanese raiders, which were again escorted by Ki-43s from the 64th Sentai, whose pilots reported meeting 15 Hurricanes. They claimed no fewer than eight shot down for the loss of one Ki-43. One bomber and one fighter were claimed for the loss of one Hurricane and its pilot, plus three more that crash-landed.

Later, during the afternoon, two sections of Buffaloes were ordered to patrol south of Singapore, there to rendezvous with three Hurricanes. On running low on fuel, one section returned early – and were pursued by the Hurricanes who thought they were enemy fighters. One opened fire on Sgt Charlie Kronk's aircraft, as he noted:

"Led two sections. Ran out of petrol. Control would not allow me to land. Shot-up by Hurricane. Crash-landed at Tengah."

Kronk managed to put the Buffalo (W8226) down between two tree stumps, and it was not badly damaged. Flt Sgt Mothersdale witnessed its arrival:

"At about 1530, a Buffalo, with propeller static, was seen pulling out of a dive near Tengah, which brought it over the airfield. The pilot levelled out to land, on or alongside the runway, but it was obvious to watchers that he would overshoot. The aircraft was still at some 30 feet and at speed with undercarriage and binding flaps retracted, as it passed by: from where we stood it looked undamaged. We watched in apprehensive silence as it continued on beyond the runway, beyond the airfield, and into the airfield extension with its lines of solid tree stumps; still airborne, some 300 yards away, it passed out of sight behind the trees, and the stillness of the afternoon prevailed."

One of the Hurricane pilots also witnessed his return:

"A Buffalo came gliding out of the distance, its engine dead. When about 300 feet up, the pilot apparently saw that he couldn't make the drome. He turned and disappeared behind a wood nearby, and the crash truck and ambulance went off in that direction. Later we learned that the pilot had cracked but wasn't seriously hurt. His engine had been damaged in combat and he'd glided all the way back, trying to make the aerodrome, and falling only a few hundred yards short."

Mothersdale continued:

"Men hastily detailed were setting off on foot to give help – we were without transport – when the airfield ambulance followed by a truck with airmen aboard passed at speed on the road nearby, heading for the scene. Fifteen minutes later the ambulance came back and swung in to our site. The pilot, khaki-shirted Sgt Charlie Kronk[123], smiling his customary good-natured smile when he recognised us, was in the cab with the driver. We were glad to see him, obviously unhurt and purposeful, his spirits unruffled."

It was now decided to maintain only the surviving Buffaloes (believed to have included W8138/NF-O, W8163/GA-P, W8173/NF, W8237 and AN209) and a force of about eight Hurricanes on Singapore, which were to operate from Tengah. 488

Squadron was ordered to fly its remaining airworthy Hurricanes to Palembang, since heavily cratered Kallang was now practically untenable. There was obvious unrest in the camp, Rex Weber writing:

"We discussed, in all seriousness, plans for our own private evacuation per means of some small auxiliary. However now we have joined 453 Squadron we may, in fact, almost certainly will, evacuate to Sumatra, to be re-equipped with Kittyhawks [P-40s]. Maybe we may see Sydney before long – at least much sooner than we could ever have suspected . . . we are almost right in the firing line. All the dromes on the island are scenes of utter desolation and destruction. The Naval Base has been blown off the face of the earth. Oh! What futility. I am going down town now for a feed – here's hoping."

With these revised arrangements, Air Commodore Vincent and his 226 (Fighter) Group Headquarters were therefore sent to Palembang (where the airfield was known as P1), while all surplus personnel from the defunct 243 Squadron followed 21RAAF Squadron in being evacuated from the area. With them went Grp Capt McCauley from Sembawang, who now took over command of the secret jungle airfield known as Palembang 2 (P2), some 50 miles south-west of P1.

CHAPTER IX

THE END FOR SINGAPORE

1-15 February 1942

"The Battle of Malaya has come to an end, and the Battle of Singapore has started
. . ."124

General Percival, 1 February 1942

Apart from the few Buffaloes and Hurricanes remaining at Singapore – the new
arrivals having returned to Palembang – the only other aircraft there were four
Swordfish and the few surviving Sharks of 4AACU, which were to spot for the coastal
guns, and a handful of Moths of the MVAF. When the Army had finished withdrawing
onto the island they took over operational control of these aircraft. The *Straits Times*
carried General Percival's proclamation to the people of Singapore:

"The Battle of Malaya has come to an end, and the Battle of Singapore has started.
For nearly two months, our troops have fought an enemy on the mainland who has
held the advantage of great air superiority and considerable freedom of movement
by sea. Our task has been both to impose losses on the enemy and to gain time to
enable the forces of the Allies to be concentrated for this struggle in the Far East. Today,
we stand beleaguered in our island fortress. In carrying out this task we want the help
of every man and woman in the fortress. There is work for all to do. Any enemy who
sets foot in the fortress must be dealt with immediately. The enemy within our gates
must be ruthlessly weeded out. There must be no more loose talk and rumour-
mongering. Our duty is clear. With firm resolve and fixed determination we shall win
through." 125

While these changes were occurring in the British camp, the JAAF also had its units
on the move, as it prepared for the final assault. By the end of January the units of the
3rd Flying Division were based at Sungei Patani, Aeru Tawaru (south of Sungei
Patani), Ipoh, Kuala Lumpur, Kuantan and Kluang. The strength of this force totalled
about 169 aircraft, comprising 30 Ki-21s, 20 Ki-48s, 20 single-engined bombers
(Ki-30s and Ki-51s), 80 fighters (Ki-27s and Ki-43s) and 19 reconnaissance aircraft
(Ki-15s and Ki-46s)126.

The Japanese were back before midday on 1 February, 60th Sentai Ki-21s,
escorted by 64th Sentai Ki-43s, attacking Sembawang. War correspondent Kenneth
Attiwill wrote:

"That day the docks of Singapore were ablaze. From ten o'clock in the morning until
four in the afternoon formations of Japanese aircraft had been pattern-bombing the
three-mile-long commercial waterfront with high explosive and incendiaries. The Jap
twin-engined bombers, based on the captured British airfields in Malaya, came in
waves of 27 in perfect V formation at a height of 20,000 feet. Waspish Navy Zero
fighters circled and weaved in escort; occasionally one looped, and flashed a reflection
of the bright tropical sunshine. There was little to stop them. On the bomb-blasted
airfields of Singapore, fighter opposition had dwindled to 20 serviceable Hurricanes
and six Brewster Buffaloes; and each time they rose to attack one or more was shot
down. Puffs of anti-aircraft shell burst followed each formation of raiders, but the Japs
seldom broke their tidy pack.

"Government notices in the newspapers and pep talks over the radio, urging workers to carry on in spite of air raids, could not compete with a Japanese voice on the air from Penang calling: 'Hello Singapore! How do you like our bombing? You saw what happened yesterday? That is a trifle to what is in store for you. Singapore will soon be a heap of ruins with not a living thing in sight. Today we are coming to bomb the docks.'" [127]

The Ki-43s engaged six Buffaloes, led by Flt Lt Kinninmont, as the remnants of 453 Squadron strove to continue the fight. Plt Off Frank Johnstone (W8205) noted:

"Our six Buffaloes were the only aircraft airborne. Wipiti could not get above 11,000 feet. Enemy aircraft at 27,000 feet. One Buffalo shot down."

One Buffalo was indeed shot down, Sgt Geoff Seagoe baling out with nothing worse than a bullet-grazed heel. Kinninmont claimed damage to one Ki-43, and another fighter – which was thought to be a Messerschmitt 109 – was shot down by Sgt Fisken (W8237), who remembered:

"I shot down what appeared to be a differently camouflaged fighter. He burst into flames but had, meanwhile, shot out both of my Buffalo's elevators. I was then engaged by two Zeros, one of which I claimed probably destroyed, but sustained a bullet wound in the elbow. A piece of cannon shell bounced off the back of my armour plating, hit the side of the plane and went into my hip. I don't remember feeling any pain. I guess adrenalin had prevented me from noticing. This made my plane a little harder to fly, but I landed safely. When I got back and jumped out on the wing my leg was sore. My rigger pointed to my leg and fainted. My flying suit was soaked with blood. I asked a mechanic for pliers but couldn't pull the piece of shrapnel out of my hip, so they had to take me over to the hospital tent. The doctor cut it out and shoved a handful of sulphonamide onto the wound and strapped it up with a big plaster, which later got very itchy. When the doctor cut the plaster off we found several large Malayan ants under it. There were 22 bullet and shrapnel holes in my aircraft."

He added that the first aircraft he claimed was reported to have crashed by soldiers of the Argyle and Sutherland Highlanders on their return from the mainland.

That night the ground personnel of 243 Squadron were withdrawn from Tengah and moved by road transport to Keppel Harbour, where they embarked in SS *Wang Po*. However, detachments from both A and B Flights remained at Tengah to continue to service Hurricanes; these detachments were airlifted two days later in RAAF Hudsons to P1, where they continued to service the Hurricanes. Meanwhile, the *Wang Po* sailed at 0730 and arrived at Palembang the following afternoon.

Following dawn reconnaissances on 2 February, Japanese bombers again targeted Seletar, Singapore City and the harbour, while Ki-43s patrolled overhead in strength. For the handful of defending fighters it was a day of respite and repair, and for the pilots a day of enforced rest from flying and fighting. Sgt Jack Burton wrote:

"The CO of the Station gathered us together and informed us we were definitely not leaving Singapore and that we would defend the island to the last. It seems almost suicidal. However, the boys of Tobruk could take it so why can't we, was his opinion. The position as we all saw it was almost hopeless, for we can raise, at the extreme outside, only six serviceable Buffalo aircraft, and they last about one or two flights and usually go u/s. The remainder of the Buffs, after being stripped, will be destroyed as they cannot be made fit for operational flying.

"Six Hurricane aircraft and pilots came over to join us today, so together we have a total of ten aircraft to defend Singapore and if we are lucky should have 12 in a day or two. However, with Jap patrols above the aerodrome all day it is suicide to take off, so at the moment we are in a desperate position. News received yesterday was to the effect that Sgt Chas Wareham has been awarded the DFM, and this news was most gratifying to the 243 boys and myself. Charlie spent the day with us today after having delivered his aircraft over to the Station from where he is now operating. Sembawang is now the sole remaining aerodrome of Singapore and from here, we – the 'lone' squadron – hope to hold out until the return of other and stronger reinforcements."

His colleague, Rex Weber, wrote:

"Enemy aircraft overhead – in fact they are now established overhead – they are maintaining a standing patrol. We are still at a moment's notice ready for evacuation, but still the Buffs are being sent up. Where we are going to goodness only knows, but I am afraid that I will not get back to see my darling girl just yet awhile. More than likely we will go down to Sumatra to be re-equipped. All the flying I have done since coming here was a test flight yesterday. This city is now completely disrupted and disorganized. The Asiatics have little stomach for aerial bombardment."

With darkness, four Swordfish of 4AACU set out for their first and last operational mission from Singapore, their task to bomb Kluang airfield. All four returned safely.

There occurred only one interception on 3 February over Singapore, where large palls of black smoke now stretched across the sky from the burning oil tanks at the Naval Base. Japanese bombers escorted by Ki-43s were over the island and attacked targets at will, one or two bombs striking the former P&O liner-cum-troopship SS *Talthybius*, berthed in the harbour. Fires broke out and the vessel was abandoned. On the ground, work continued to raise unserviceable aircraft to a level of repair, which would allow them at least to be flown to Palembang. At Tengah, three Hurricanes were almost ready, although the working party would need to toil well into the early hours of the following morning to complete the task. At Kallang meanwhile, many 488 Squadron groundcrews – still awaiting the order to evacuate – were engaged in repairs to the airfield, while others managed to make sufficient repairs to two of the Buffaloes, left behind by 243 Squadron, to allow Plt Offs Peter Gifford (W8173) and Bunt Pettit (W8138) to fly them over to Sembawang before the end of the day.

Early on the morning of 4 February, four Buffaloes took off from Sembawang to carry out a reconnaissance along the mid-Johore road, which was now heavily defended by AA guns. Sgt Fisken, despite his wounds, volunteered to undertake the actual reconnaissance, while Flt Lt Kinninmont, Sgts Weber and Kronk were to act as top cover. In the early morning half light Kinninmont and Kronk became separated from the other two and, when unable to find them again, turned for home. En route they encountered two Ki-43s and, following a brief engagement, claimed both severely damaged. Meanwhile, the other pair continued the reconnaissance, Fisken flying right up to the area of Kluang airfield, much to Weber's consternation. The latter's fears were justified as, just as they turned for home, his Buffalo was attacked from behind by a 59th Sentai Ki-43; he wrote:

"Next thing I knew, just after we had turned with our tails to the rising sun, was that it had sprayed a vast load of lead into my cockpit, and to a lesser degree, my upper arm. I thank God for the armour plating – it had undoubtedly saved my life. That Jap had a sitting shot at me – he came up underneath to whatever range suited his purpose. What a magnificent sense of relief to find after the smoke, oil and glass had cleared away, that the engine was still running smoothly. I at once took violent evasive action and went down to warn Fisken, who was stooging along, unconcernedly. Then imagine my dismay when I found my wireless u/s and the Jap drawing up on Fisken's tail.

"Knowing that always one would have a nasty feeling inside somewhere if he was shot down, and although my sight and plane were u/s, and my eyes blinded with oil, I am happy at heart to be able to write that I did the right thing. I turned towards the enemy, who immediately left Fisken and came at me. Did my plane get thrown about – Oh Boy! – and continued to do so until it was fairly certain that he had left us some 20 miles from where we were first attacked. On arriving back over base, to add to my misfortunes, I found the undercarriage was inoperative. I always wondered if I would remember the correct emergency procedure and I had no difficulty in getting the crate down. But then my troubles had only just begun – I had to land the crate with my windscreen blocked, my eyes almost blind and flaps up, on a drome which had only a narrow strip free from bomb craters."

He got down safely, and added to his diary:

"Without a doubt, my perfect landing is my greatest flying triumph and I will here put it on record that if I am alive in 50 years hence, which I agree will be a remarkable achievement under the present circumstances, but which I have great faith that I will be, I will still be reminiscencing. It is amazing to me that I showed no great fear – yes, I was scared, but not worth mentioning, only that it was pretty hard doing the right thing at the right time. Really, I gave myself no chance at all of getting away scot-free out of the adventure."

Fisken also landed safely, his aircraft (W8143) having suffered negligible damage:

"Rex Weber stayed up at about 15,000 feet, top cover for me. I was fired upon a lot, but I think I was too low for their gunners as I was barely above the level of the planes dispersed on the airfield. Rex probably saved my life. He was attacked by a Zero and wounded in the arm. His R/T then failed and he dived to warn me visually. There was a Jap behind me and Rex came down right over me to warn me – I saw the Jap and was waiting for him to fire – watching him through my rear-view mirror all the time. Whether it was because he was out of ammunition of whether he was leaving it for the gunners on the ground, I don't know, but he just disappeared. I hurt my knee when landing. My flying days at Singapore were over. Others had been less lucky."

During the afternoon, Flt Lt Kinninmont and Sgt Ross Leys were briefed to carry out a reconnaissance of the area north of the town of Johore. Kinninmont took off successfully but Ross Leys' aircraft was damaged by shellfire, which prevented him from following. Nonetheless, Kinninmont carried out the task alone and returned safely. By this time, the advancing Japanese – now just across the Johore Strait – had inflated an observation balloon from the Sultan's Palace at Johore, as Fisken recalled:

"The Japs were now watching our airfield from an observation balloon they had put up above a tower at the Sultan's Palace just across the Johore Straits. We never got permission to shoot it down, in case it offended the Sultan."

Ships of Convoy BM12 – loaded with troops and equipment – were now rapidly approaching Singapore and were being harassed on the way by Ki-48s of the 3rd Flying Battalion. At 1115 on 5 February, the largest of the vessels, the liner-cum-troopship *Empress of Asia*, was attacked off the Sultan Shoal lighthouse about nine miles from Keppel Harbour, and was severely damaged, fires breaking out. She was loaded with the automatic weapons and heavy guns of the 18th Division and although these were destroyed, there was only small loss of life.

Shelling of Sembawang was so intense that the airfield had now become untenable, and at last Air HQ ordered all flyable aircraft to proceed to Tengah. Sqn Ldr Harper reported:

"At approximately ten o'clock on that day I had gone to the Mess to bathe and change, when the enemy commenced to shell the aerodrome and buildings from across the Johore Straits. As the shelling continued, and shells were bursting about 30 yards away, I circumnavigated the Mess and made my way to the Guard Room. I learned here from the Engineer Officer that instructions had come through to fly all aircraft off the aerodrome to Tengah, a few miles away, in order to avoid the shelling."

488 Squadron's personnel were still at Kallang, although during the morning Plt Off Gifford had taken a group of men to Sembawang to help get all the serviceable aircraft away. The unit's diarist noted that "Sembawang was most likely the closest operational aerodrome to any fighting front." A sentiment echoed by Sgt Weber, for he confided to his diary:

"Ridiculous though it may seem to we lesser individuals, our squadron is now situated in no-man's land, between two opposing armies, and, of course, well within artillery range – for that matter, rifle range."

Meanwhile, Sqn Ldr Harper sprang into action:

"A driver was sent round in a van to pick up the pilots from their dispersal. Meanwhile, along with the few pilots present, I flew an unserviceable Hurricane belonging to 232 Squadron to Tengah, as it would have been left on the airfield owing to a shortage of Hurricane pilots. Altogether, my pilots, under shellfire, flew ten aircraft off the aerodrome. Two aircraft were hit in taxiing and one pilot was hit and blown out of his aircraft by a salvo of three shells."

A shell landed two yards from Plt Off Frank Johnstone's Buffalo (W8157) just as he was about to start up and shrapnel passed through its fuselage, putting it out of action. Having escaped injury, Johnstone leapt out, dashed to another aircraft and took off amidst a shower of explosions. Despite the shellfire, five Buffaloes and two Hurricanes managed to get away but, as they approached Tengah, the Japanese opened fire on that airfield also. One of the newly arrived Australian pilots, Flg Off Pat Gleeson, was slightly wounded when a shell burst under his Buffalo as he came in to land; a second Buffalo was also damaged in this manner. Harper continued:

"Shortly after the first pilot landed at Tengah, that aerodrome, which was an equal distance from the enemy artillery to Sembawang, also came under fire, and the pilots had then to be asked to start their aircraft and fly them out to Kallang. It was difficult to keep the pilots and crews confident in the command when pilots are asked to fly out of one aerodrome being shelled into another an equal distance from the source of shelling."

As if the situation was not already developing into a bloody shambles, Harper then found himself facing the wrath of Grp Capt Rice:

"I was detained for the remainder of the day by Grp Capt Rice of the Fighter Group, who had ordered a Court of Inquiry to be held because our Squadron pilots were late during readiness that morning (he cancelled his decision later that evening). I was therefore away the whole day and had no opportunity to control the Squadron and ground troops, which were, in my absence, under the control of Flt Lt Wells, the Adjutant. I had no idea that any of the men had gone down the road towards Singapore town."

It transpired that half a dozen men of 453 Squadron had been found some distance from the aerodrome by Air Vice-Marshal Maltby. They had left their posts without permission; it was also the occasion when a number of RAAF officers had spoken disrespectfully to the Provost Marshal in front of the troops. Harper's report continued:

"I found out in Java that two of the men[128] who were concerned in the departure from the airfield to Singapore, were individuals who were mentally unbalanced and had been under observation by the Station Medical Officer for some time, and they most probably influenced the other four who were with them. With regard to the occasion concerning the Provost Marshal, I questioned my officers when I learned of this matter and they assured me they were not involved; there were other Australian officers belonging to Station Headquarters still on the Station, and I have every reason to believe that they were the ones concerned."

Meanwhile at Seletar, Sqn Ldr Lewis told Flt Lt Pearson:

"We've got our marching orders. In a couple of days we're going to fly the two aircraft out to Java. I shall be flying one and Wareham and you will have to toss up for who flies the other."

Sgt Wareham won the toss but Pearson, unhappy at the prospect of leaving by sea, searched the airfield for a means of escape:

"After I lost the toss, and had been told that I should have to travel by sea to Java, I found an unserviceable fighter Buffalo on Seletar airfield, which had been left by one of the Australian squadrons when they had been withdrawn. I managed to get a battery for it and ran the engine, which appeared to be OK. There was a hole in the oil tank about an inch or so from the top, two bullet holes in the airscrew, the flaps were u/s, and the brakes very weak. However, I had the aircraft refuelled and asked Sqn Ldr Lewis if I might make the attempt to fly out with him and Wareham, in the two serviceable PR aircraft, the following day. I suggested I flew as fighter escort."

As the shelling of Tengah intensified, orders came through to evacuate that airfield. Plt Off Gifford's 488 Squadron party again offered assistance, helping all flyable aircraft to get off to Kallang – even though this airfield was heavily pitted and cratered from recent bombing attacks – before moving there themselves.

Before taking off from Tengah the pilots had been briefed to patrol over the *Empress of Asia* before proceeding to Kallang. By now the troopship was burning steadily although rescue and salvage operations continued. The patrol was uneventful and, on reaching Kallang, two of the aircraft were damaged by taxiing into water-filled bomb craters, the whole surface of the airfield being under several inches of water following a torrential rainstorm. Shortly after these aircraft had landed at Kallang, a high level bombing attack was directed against the airfield, effectively rendering it unserviceable.

Meanwhile the rest of the Hurricanes had scrambled, but failed to find any hostile formations. On returning to Tengah they were again met by heavy shellfire, two shells exploding on either side of one aircraft as it levelled out to land, causing its pilot almost to lose control. While the Hurricane pilots were having lunch, a Buffalo came in to land just as a shell hit the ground beside it. The fighter turned over and caught fire, the pilot – Flg Off John Hastwell – being rescued by some of the Hurricane pilots. Hastwell, one of the new RAAF arrivals, was badly burned on the face and head, and was driven to a nearby Army hospital for treatment. One of the Hurricane pilots, Flg Off Art Donahue, witnessed the incident:

> "Through the windows of the Mess we saw a low thatched-roof wooden building on the far side of the drome catch fire and begin burning hotly. A Brewster Buffalo landed, and as it was taxiing to the edge of the field a shell crashed beside it, turning it upside-down and injuring the pilot. Someone took my car to drive him to the dressing station. When I got it back I had to clean blood off the seat and dashboard." [129]

Due to the shelling Kallang was now practically untenable and orders to evacuate to Palembang came through, with the exception of the operational Hurricanes, which were to remain. By evening most aircraft had got away. Sqn Ldr Harper commented:

> "Early in February we were instructed that the Squadron groundcrews were to stay at Singapore and fight – all aircraft which could fly were to go to Palembang. I instructed Flt Lt Kinninmont to take the aircraft and their pilots to Sumatra and I remained with the ground troops. There was some feeling among the men at this order. They maintained this was a case of misemployment of trained personnel, and again in supporting my superiors I made myself unpopular.
>
> "However, when the troops were reconciled to it, considerable effort was put into preparing the ground defences: machine-guns were taken from crashed aircraft and mounted on tripods made out of parts of crashed Blenheim airframes, and the men were armed and prepared in squads. Arrangements were also made for the men to be led by trained Army officers in the event of any hand-to-hand fighting."

Although Kinninmont obeyed his orders, he was not happy with the decision for the groundcrews to remain to fight alongside the defenders of Singapore in what was already a lost cause:

> "Squadron Leader Harper had a queer attitude towards the whole thing, and did not seem worried whether the Squadron left Singapore or not. I could not understand his attitude at all in the end, but he had the Squadron in sections ready to defend the aerodrome and more or less fight with the Army. I think his attitude was more or less the attitude of the British Command there – to fight to the end and die for Singapore; just stay there and be killed.
>
> "However, he looked after the troops very well, he was always trying to organise things and get decent food, and also arrange sleeping quarters. With the pilots he was always trying to get them a day off, and that sort of thing. He always briefed us properly before the job, right to the end. He treated the Squadron very well including men and pilots. Towards the end when it was hopeless and only a matter of a day or two, he did not seem concerned, whether the Squadron got away on a ship, and the chaps were prepared to stay, although they could not have done any good had they stayed, because they had few arms: about four or five Tommy-guns and few rifles. That was what annoyed the chaps, as they could see no good reason why they were staying there to be killed or taken prisoner."

Four Buffaloes, two Hudsons and 13 uncombatworthy Hurricanes had gone. The Buffaloes were flown to Palembang by new pilots Flg Offs Peter Ash, Max Bott, Colin Lindeman (AN209) and Pat Gleeson. Soon after they landed at Palembang an air raid destroyed one and damaged a second (AN209) on the ground. They were followed shortly thereafter by two more Buffaloes flown by Flt Lt Kinninmont and Sgt Clare, but the latter was forced to return with serious engine trouble. Once rectified, he also safely reached Palembang.

There remained at Kallang just a dozen or so Hurricanes and four or five Buffaloes, the latter being worked upon to get them ready to follow the others to Palembang. At this point the remaining detachments of 243 Squadron were airlifted to Palembang, Flt Lt Garden being mainly responsible for arranging evacuation of the men. They were carried out by one of the last Dutch flights to be made from Singapore. Garden's engine fitter, LAC Paddy Moulds, remembered:

> "One thing I do know is that he did not forget us because he was responsible for organising a Dutch Beechcraft to fly all 243 Squadron personnel from Tengah to Palembang."

Many of the groundcrews remaining at Singapore were now issued with rifles and Browning machine-guns, in anticipation of a paratroop attack on Kallang, which, in the event did not occur; the paratroops would soon land elsewhere, however. That evening Rex Weber wrote in his diary:

> "Dear Diary, my one remaining link with some sanity, and reason, there is much to be written. I could write of disorganisation, of chaos and inability, of the futility and hopelessness of the situation here, of remarkably foolish plans – plans and dispositions, which, for all my own professed dullness, are to me the essence of stupidity. As I sit here it seems impossible that we Britishers can ever hope to muddle through to victory.
>
> "We have our Lords and Peers expressing airy abstract speeches, if they are not something worse, hypercritical lies, while in the meantime little is done to bring about any improvement. The majority of men in command are not only inefficient, but so few of them are capable of any great personal sacrifice for a cause which is so just and important that no personal inconvenience is too great. I can only rely on the justness of the cause to bring us through safely, and pray that my own darling folk are not touched by destruction, disease and death, in the wake of war."

Buffalo activity had all but ended by 6 February, and pilots were ordered to get away from Singapore by whatever means possible, as Geoff Fisken recalled:

> "We only flew at dusk or really dark, until we were told to get out in a hurry. We blew our (unserviceable) planes and gas reservoirs (fuel tanks) with the help of a pickaxe and a Very pistol from one of the planes – a great sight, I remember, and got to the wharf as quickly as we could. Singapore was now caving in. The streets were full of people, both troops and civilians, including women who had been reluctant to leave their husbands alone. People were evacuating in droves, leaving their cars behind. People just gave you cars – you could have your pick. We had a big Lincoln for a while, and a front-wheel drive Citroen. The ones we didn't want got tipped off the wharf, so the Japs wouldn't be able to get them. We all took turns in driving it.
>
> "One night while driving down the street we had a low-level attack by two Zeros – everyone was out in a hurry, heading for the safety of the shops. We were all right apart from the fact that we couldn't find Max Greenslade, a dapper little fellow. Singapore, at that stage, had seven-foot wide open drains carrying sewerage, and what have you,

in them, with a little crossing bridge over them at odd intervals. After the strafing we heard plaintive cries from the drain – Max had missed the bridge in his hurry to safety and finished up to his neck in it! He was covered in filth and stank. He wanted us to take him back to the aerodrome to change his uniform but we put him instead into a taxi and sent him home."

Of the hasty evacuation, Plt Off Marra wrote:

"Then the word finally came we were to be sent to Batavia via Palembang, in Sumatra. We carted everyone down to the wharf and climbed aboard a little riverboat. We had to leave our truck of ammunition on the wharf but we'd been told to take as many parachutes as we could so everybody that could carry a parachute was carting one. The doctor got Snowy Bonham out of hospital. Bonham was under contraction and they had his leg and a brick hanging up. When we were getting out of Singapore old Doc Morgan said I'm going to get Bonham. Well the Japs were all round the hospital and how he got him out I don't know, but he got him out."

Flt Lt Bertie Bows had made plans for Sgts Baber and Lawrence to accompany him and others in a yacht he had requisitioned, but as Baber recalled:

"For our evacuation from Singapore, Bertie Bows had organised a big yacht, which we provisioned. That was the way we were going to escape but it never happened. We were ordered instead onto a small coastal steamer and we came out via it. But before that, while provisioning the yacht, there was an Australian civilian who we called Russ, and he was going to come with us. He was a great cobber of Bows, who said he'd take Russ on the yacht. So when we finally got the word to go on this small coastal steamer, Russ said 'what's going to happen to me?' At that stage, as a male civilian, he was unable to leave as women and children had taken up all the berths. So Alan and I decided to get him aboard, which we did. I gave him a shirt with Sergeant stripes and Alan gave him a cap and that sort of thing and we took him on this little steamer and he just mingled with the others on board. We went to Palembang, which was the oil base in Sumatra and we disembarked there. We were camped in a school and after a few days were ordered to get rid of this civilian. We were going to be put on charge and were given half an hour to get rid of him. So the last we saw of poor old Russ was in the middle of Palembang without any passport, food or local money, but I did hear after the war that he had got out somehow or other. I don't know how."

Plans originally intended for 488 Squadron were now changed. Instead of Sumatra, all pilots were ordered to proceed to Batavia at once, while the ground personnel were to remain with the Hurricane squadron. The New Zealand pilots withdrew to Keppel Harbour that evening where, together with the remaining pilots and groundcrews of 453 Squadron, they departed aboard a cruiser and a transport ship. Among these was Sgt Greg Board:

"[We] drove through streets splashed with bodies and stained with blood, through which scurried huge rats feasting on the shattered bodies. Knowing the danger of imminent bomber attack, the captain of the cruiser slid neatly against the dock, never stopping; [we] leaped onto the deck, and the warship kept right on moving. All about [us] ships burned brightly, and hundreds of corpses bobbed in the water . . ." [130]

Other Australian pilots were scattered around Singapore Island, including Sgt Bill Collyer, who was in hospital at Changi, where he had gone to have the plaster removed from his leg. He had become friendly with an RAAF Service Policeman, Sgt

Keith Bernito, who was discharged and sent back to Sembawang, but assured Collyer he would return for him if 'abandon ship' was ordered. True to his word, when 453 Squadron was ordered to the docks, he returned – having 'borrowed' Air Chief Marshal Brooke-Popham's car, complete with the C-in-C's pennant in situ. They set off to drive the 15 miles to Keppel Harbour, encountering many road blocks en route, Sgt Benito returning the guards' salutes as the road blocks were hastily cleared for the C-in-C's car!

Another of the injured pilots, Sgt Harry Griffiths, was convalescing at the Australian General Hospital at Sembawang when the Japanese attacked the Station. He narrowly avoided being hit by a sniper's bullet before being driven through Japanese lines in the back of a truck. Although stopped by a Japanese guard, one look under the blanket thrown over Griffiths and four others laying in the back of the truck somehow convinced the enemy soldier that they were dead – and he allowed the truck to continue. Griffiths eventually arrived at the docks and boarded the SS *Empire Star* about to leave for Batavia (see Appendix I). Also aboard this vessel were the groundcrews of 488 Squadron. 453 Squadron's diarist wrote:

> "The Squadron left Singapore. The pilots travelled on a cruiser, HMS *Danae*, while the ground staff travelled on the *City of Canterbury*; the former were high in their praises for the treatment they received at the hands of the Navy. They were well fed and hospitably welcomed on board. One attempted air raid was made on the convoy but it was repulsed by ack-ack fire and Hurricanes. Some of the lads were in town when the Squadron packed up and left and these literally 'missed the boat'. The movement of the Squadron was not carried out with any show of lethargy, only a couple of hours notice being given."

Four Australian Buffalo pilots – Sgts Halliday, Scrimgeour, Summerton and Austin – remained at Sembawang:

> "The pilots left on the island were Wop, Gentle George, Barrel Bum and Tozzler. Also there were two of our new pilots, Randall and Ruge[131]. Somewhere in Singapore was Matthew."

A detachment of 453 Squadron's groundcrew also remained at Sembawang, to undertake salvage and denial work and to treat casualties. They calmly and methodically destroyed communication facilities, wireless equipment, stores, petrol, bombs, records and those buildings that could be demolished in time. When Japanese troops reached the western edge of the airfield, the Australians just had time for Corporal A.L. Bartley to remove the tattered RAAF flag from the Station flagpole. They eventually reached the harbour and embarked on a small Norwegian ship bound for Java.

During the night Seletar was again heavily shelled by Japanese guns sighted along the Johore coast, and one (W8166) of 4PRU's two remaining Buffaloes was destroyed. It had been intended that these would be flown to Palembang at first light by Sqn Ldr Lewis and Sgt Wareham, while Flt Lt Pearson was to accompany them in the patched-up abandoned Buffalo he had found. Following the destruction of his aircraft, Wareham was left behind to find his own way to Java. Therefore, at dawn on 7 February, despite his aircraft lacking functioning flaps and full hydraulics, and having bullet holes through the airscrew and in the oil tank, Donald Pearson joined the aerial evacuation:

> "Lewis [in W8136] and I took off from a badly damaged Seletar airfield and set course for Palembang, which was to be our refuelling stop as we planned to do the trip to

Batavia in one day. The CO had borrowed my maps before take-off from Seletar, but I had memorized them very carefully the night before. On approaching land above cloud, the CO indicated that he was not sure of our position (we had no radio). As I had already spotted the Palembang river through the cloud gaps, I took the lead and immediately descended below cloud height and headed up river, to be met with scattered AA fire.

"We were soon recognised as friendly by the Dutch gunners and found the airfield without further trouble. We landed safely despite our problems, and refuelled immediately. I was delighted to find that I had lost very little oil. While refuelling was taking place, the CO asked me if I would care to spend the night and try to find our advance party; also, the weather forecast for Batavia was bad. However, since I had noticed there were two Group Captains and an Air Commodore sitting disconsolately on the steps of flying-control, I said. 'Sir, I've got a feeling that if we do, our aircraft won't be here in the morning. There are three senior officers there – they've all got wings and are all obviously itching to get out of here'. So we carried on, despite a very shaky formation take-off."

About 50 miles from Batavia they ran into very heavy monsoon rain, as forecast. However it was not too difficult to follow the coastline to Batavia. Pearson continued:

"Due to the poor visibility, and the fact that I could not trust the brakes, I decided to land well behind the CO. One of the disadvantages of a radial engine in a single-engined plane is the poor forward visibility on take-off and particularly on landing, except with tricycle undercarriage. I had lost sight of the lead aircraft on the approach but I knew he must be at least a runway length ahead. I landed shortly beyond the threshold, but I could still not see the other aircraft, even after I had slowed to taxi speed. On my right was a burnt-out B-17, a wrecked Blenheim on my left, and at the end of the runway another aircraft on its back with its wheels still turning and a very large man dressed in tropical whites running towards the wreck. The CO had overshot the end of the runway, run into soft mud, and turned over! I switched off and ran to the wreck where the giant Dutchman and I managed to retrieve dear old Lewis from the aircraft, which was already smoking but in the event did not catch fire. The rain continued and the medics whipped the CO off to hospital, where they put 25 stitches into him. He was in hospital for about a week and shortly afterwards he received orders to be evacuated to Australia."

Further aircraft, as they were rendered airworthy, flew out to Palembang during the day, including a Hurricane and a Buffalo (W8138/NF-O) flown by Sqn Ldr Brooker and Sgt Charlie Kronk respectively, which escorted a Hudson to the same destination – P2. The three aircraft were ordered to P1, arriving just as a raid was about to commence, which inflicted much damage and destruction among the aircraft assembled there, including Kronk's Buffalo, as noted in No.226 (Fighter) Group's History:

"The Japanese again raided P1 with bombers and low-flying fighters, and a large number of aircraft was destroyed on the ground. Once again the warning came late . . . Six Blenheims and three Hurricanes were totally burnt out and approximately eleven more Hurricanes damaged together with one Buffalo and one Hudson, which had just landed. In the air three Hurricanes were shot down – two pilots returning later. One probable Navy 0 was claimed with one or two damaged. In addition, one Blenheim which was just coming in to land at the time of the raid was shot down and the pilot killed."

Singapore's days were now clearly numbered. During an intensive air raid on 8 February, a Buffalo at Kallang was destroyed by fire as a result of the bombing; this was presumably an abandoned machine. 453 Squadron's diarist wrote:

"Things at Sembawang continued to deteriorate after the Squadron's departure, and the lads who remained had a very uncomfortable time. Shells and bombs were more numerous and the 'Grouper' [Grp Capt Whistondale] still had ideas of operating from the drome. One day he put a working party of about 30 men on the drome to fill in shell holes, but a few shells among these soon dampened their enthusiasm. So, with great purpose, the four operational pilots set about preparing their own evacuation of Singapore. Formations of Tojo's bombers constantly droned over the island; in fact so constantly that Ops Room gave up blowing the raid siren. Also the air was full of Jap fighter patrols.

"Midst this the worthy 'Grouper' had the bright idea that Wop should take off in broad daylight to go over Johore and shoot down an observation balloon. Fortunately Tojo hauled it down before Wop could take off, so yet another blunder was denied to the RAF. Wop, Barrel Bum and Gentle George departed from Kallang on Monday morning [9 February], followed an hour or so later by Tozzler, who had been round at the 'Seaview' drinking a quiet beer, when the OK to take off came through. All four landed safely at Palembang, u/s-ing three out of their four kites."

When the first three Buffaloes became airborne, they were instructed to intercept enemy bombers carrying out a raid on the island. However, the bombers were at a great height and the Buffaloes were unable to make contact. Of this episode, Sgt Halliday elaborated:

"Eventually we were told the time and got out of bed at 2am and went to the Wing Commander's quarters to start things moving, but after trying to awaken him we discovered he was in a state of intoxification and all we could get was 'Sorry chaps!' After seeing it was hopeless, I said 'Go back to sleep, you drunken bum.' We then got the aircraft up to the drome ourselves. As dawn was breaking, we left. However, I was the last off and the aircraft would not start on its own power. By this time a couple of bodies had appeared. I got one to crank the aircraft but, before it started, the Japs started to lob some mortar shells over and my bloke wanted to stop and run. However, I drew my .38 and persuaded him to keep going. As soon as it fired I took off, no warming up. On reaching the other side of the island an air raid was in progress, so I kept going to Sumatra."

Leaving Palembang next day, the four pilots landed safely at Batavia, where one Buffalo was damaged on landing. Other arrivals at Batavia on this date included two Buffaloes flown from Palembang by Flt Lt Kinninmont and Plt Off Leigh Bowes of 453 Squadron, together with Sgt Kronk of 243 Squadron in AN209, which had been patched up. Shortly after arrival at Batavia, they were strafed by Japanese fighters and all destroyed or damaged. Also at Batavia were Flt Lt Pearson and his party from 4PRU:

"After Lewis had departed, I was left with the job of getting all the personnel of 4PRU including Wareham, whose ship had been torpedoed, into one transit camp. At that stage they were scattered between many transit camps set up in and around Batavia. The only aircraft we now had left was one fighter Buffalo in a somewhat ropey condition. With me at this time was a very skilful corporal fitter and we had planned to fly the aircraft to Australia with Air HQ permission and the corporal cooped up in the fuselage. I pointed out to him that he might find it difficult to get out if we had to ditch.

He answered 'I'll risk that rather than be caught by the bleedin' Nips.' But, in due course, I was instructed to fly the aircraft to Bandoeng, to be handed over to the Dutch Air Force."

Some days later Flt Lt Pearson and his party of 300 airmen boarded the cargo steamer SS *Kota Gede*, which sailed for Colombo.

Meanwhile at Singapore, following the departure of the remaining PR Buffalo, it was left to a Swordfish crew of 4AACU to undertake a photographic sortie on the morning of the 9th, using a hand-held Leica 35mm camera. As the intrepid crew prepared to take off, the escort of Hurricanes arrived overhead – at about the same time as a formation of Japanese fighters appeared. The operation was immediately cancelled, much to the relief of the Swordfish crew.

Last Buffalo from Singapore

By the morning of 10 February, the authorities realised the end of resistance was nigh, and promptly ordered all the remaining flyable aircraft including the Hurricanes to leave for Palembang. Eight Hurricanes departed at first light, led by a Hudson. Due to the Herculean all-night efforts of groundcrews, working under constant shelling and bombing, five battered Hurricanes were made airworthy by the next morning. Two departed early in the morning, followed by two Tiger Moths and a Cadet of the MVAF, the remaining three Hurricanes taking off shortly thereafter – joined by a battered old Buffalo in the hands of one of the Hurricane pilots, Plt Off Tom Watson RCAF:

"There was a beat-up old Buffalo on the edge of the drome which had been there since we arrived. One of the groundcrew got it started for me. The three Hurricanes had taken off. I pointed the nose of the Buffalo south, pushed the throttle forward, and the thing took off. I had never been in a Buffalo before and had some trouble with the throttle controls, particularly as the pitch was controlled from the dashboard. Also it took me a bit of time to figure out how to raise the wheels. We were an odd looking lot, three Hurricanes and a Buffalo leaving a smoking Singapore behind us. We had no maps and I had no parachute.

"As the parachute was also your seat, I was sitting pretty low in the cockpit. I believe one of the Hurricanes did not make it, and I became separated from them. However, more by good luck than anything else, I found Palembang but it was socked in so I went on to P2 and landed there. Personally, I was rather pleased but the Commanding Officer did not share my pleasure and reprimanded me for flying an aeroplane on which I had not been officially checked out. My interest was to get to P1 where the Squadron was located and this presented a problem, as I did not know how to start the motor. However, an Australian pilot, Freddie Williams, got it going for me and I flew to P1. I was a bit concerned, as the radial-engined Buffalo could be taken for a Japanese plane, but there were no problems. The pilots in the Squadron were as glad to see me, as I was them. I put the Buffalo away at Palembang, in the trees alongside the aerodrome, and I suppose the Japanese took it when they captured the aerodrome."

That night, a number of Dutch Lodestars arrived at Sembawang, departing again at 0300 with evacuees including Plt Off John Coom:

"The take-off was like day as the Japanese had set some oil tanks alight over at Seletar, and they were like torches. There was also a tanker alight off Changi Point away to the east, and a vast pall of black smoke was over everything. To cap it all, a Zero came at us as we were climbing away, but we got into cloud."

Chaos was now descending on Singapore City, which was crowded with deserters who had begun robbing and looting. Others sought to force their way onto departing vessels and some groups of soldiers, mainly Australians, did succeed in escaping from Singapore, some reaching Palembang, some getting as far as Batavia (where they were placed under arrest), whilst others perished en route. With all the flyable aircraft gone, and with no hope of any more airlifts, Headquarters began ordering non-essential specialist personnel, including stranded aircrew, to leave. Among stranded air personnel forced to make their own arrangements to escape were a number of Buffalo pilots, including several wounded or otherwise disabled. One of these was Flt Lt Tim Vigors:

"I had spent five weeks in hospital and then, one day, the doctor suggested I leave as the Japs were only 20 miles up the road. I made my way to 'Raffles' hotel where I was sitting pondering on my next move when I met the Captain of a Qantas flying boat who was leaving next day for Australia, and he suggested I leave with him, which I did. The next day we just evaded the Japs and travelled to Java where we rested overnight. In the local hotel that night, we were approached by a General, who insisted he needed urgent transportation out. The result of which was that I suggested he take my place on the flight deck. The next morning they left Java but just one hour out they were shot down and all aboard were killed. It was certainly lucky for me that I switched. I managed to gain passage on a boat to India."

Another of the walking wounded was 243 Squadron's Sgt Aussie Powell, who was languishing in Alexandra Military Hospital, as recalled by a wounded Vildebeest air gunner, Sgt John Smith:

"A big Sergeant Pilot [Sgt Aussie Powell] came into my ward (he had only one eye as well!), introduced himself and suggested we do a bunk. I got all my belongings and off we went. At that stage I had my dog tags, Mae West and a pair of pyjama trousers! We got a mile into Singapore and got aboard a Chinese riverboat. We saw lots of wreckage and one night two destroyers belted past us; they couldn't have seen us. Another day a floatplane circled us a couple of times and then flew off. Four days later we sailed into Batavia."

Two more wounded Buffalo pilots, Sgts Geoff Fisken and Rex Weber, were told to leave by an Army officer. Together with Sgt Max Greenslade, they drove to the docks in a Daimler, which a wealthy resident had given them; Fisken recalled:

"We pushed it [the Daimler] into the water, then escaped on sampans along with a group of Australians. We were picked up by a medium-sized Indian Navy sloop [HMIS *Indus*], which took us to the North Australian coast."

With walking stick supporting his wounded leg and wounded arm in plaster, Fisken was fêted as 'the prodigal returning hero', which, of course, he was. Meanwhile, others were also making plans to leave, including Wg Cdr Gerald Bell, OC Kallang, who no longer had a Station to command:

"I remained to see the destruction of equipment and stores on the Station. This task was completed by the 11th . I then embarked with my Station Headquarters and Operations Room Staff on a freighter, which took us to Batavia." [132]

Meanwhile, off the eastern coast of Sumatra, hundreds of evacuees and escapees from Singapore, including women and children, were losing their lives. By the evening of 13 February, it was estimated that about 3,000 people had officially been ordered away from Singapore during the preceding few days, whilst as many as 5,000 more had departed by whatever means they could find – gunboats, motor launches, coasters, tugs, harbour launches, yachts, dinghies, tongkans (sailing barges) and sampans – many of these vessels not even seaworthy. Tokyo Radio warned:

"There will be no Dunkirk at Singapore. The British are not going to be allowed to get away with it this time. All ships leaving will be destroyed."

Japanese Naval aircraft – G3Ms and G4Ms from the Mihoro, Genzan and Kanoya Kokutais, together with F1M floatplanes and B5Ns from the carrier *Ryujo* – were now very active against the shipping leaving Singapore, though little effort was made to interfere with vessels carrying supplies towards the island; presumably it was considered these would be of immense use to the occupying forces.

The smaller vessels headed for Sumatra, the larger ones making for Batavia. Some made it, but many did not. Most of those who left Singapore in this period failed to reach freedom – many were shipwrecked amongst the numerous islands south of Singapore, where many died: some were rescued and others were captured. Exact figures will never be known but in excess of 70 steamships and smaller craft were believed to have been sunk, wrecked, abandoned, or beached, with civilian and service personnel losses estimated between 2,000 and 5,000. One that did reach Batavia was the *Empire Star*, which included ground staff of 488 Squadron and a handful of 4AACU, one of whom was Sgt Peter Ballard:

"When our small party from 4AACU boarded on the evening of 11 February we were given the option of joining hundreds of service personnel packed into the cargo holds like sardines, or of supplementing the ship's gunners at various machine-gun posts about the ship. We chose to supplement the ship's gunners. Our passage to Batavia was not a smooth one as we were subjected to both low and high level bombing attacks for the whole of the morning of 12th. We took some direct hits and suffered casualties [14 killed and 17 severely wounded] but fortunately were not disabled. I say fortunately because we had more than 2,000 people on board, and had we suffered the same fate as those ships which left a day or more later our casualties would have been heavy indeed."

One of the vessels lost on Friday the 13th was the old, 4,799-ton freighter SS *Derrymore*, which was loaded with ammunition and carried six Hurricanes in packing cases amongst her cargo. She had departed Keppel Harbour the previous evening and during the hours of daylight had escaped damage when attacked by bombers, but at 2020 she was hit by one of two torpedoes fired by the Japanese submarine *I-55*. Only nine of the 200 airmen embarked were lost, and the old vessel sank about 90 minutes later, taking the precious Hurricanes with her but allowing time for the majority of her passengers to take to life rafts. One party reached a small nearby island, from where they were rescued three days later by the Dutch minesweeper *Cheribon*. Among those who had been aboard was Sgt Matt O'Mara of 453 Squadron who, despite two broken ribs, managed to scramble onto a raft and was rescued after 19 hours at sea by the Australian minesweeper HMAS *Ballarat*. The minesweeper also picked up an injured Hurricane pilot and about 20 others from a small raft, half of whom had clung to its sides throughout the ordeal. Other survivors of the sinking, included Sgt Bert Wipiti of 243 Squadron and Sgt Charlie Wareham of 4PRU, the latter recalling:

"At 20 minutes past eight in the night we got torpedoed. My watch stopped at 20 past eight. I was on the deck when I saw the torpedo coming. It was a small ship and simply broke in half. There were a lot of people who could not swim and, of course, would not go into the water. We (Bert and I) organized some people to get hatch covers, which were fairly big pieces of timber, and began passing these into the water and tossing people off. This all happened within the space of about ten minutes. We were on the back end of the boat and, when the sea was up level with it, we just walked in.

"When it became daylight we could actually see, at various times, palm trees from our position in the water. Eventually, at 20 past one, an Australian destroyer did see us and picked us up. We were taken to Batavia to a school. I was suffering from sunburn and was sent to a camp up in the hills. I was there for two weeks. We were then told to go down to Batavia, where we met up with a lot of other personnel – Air Force, Army and Navy – and we were told to get on a train for Tjilatjap. When we got there, there were two ships tied up side by side. The one we got on went to Colombo, the other went back to New Zealand."

One of the many motor launches lost during the evacuation was RAF launch *ML310*, which carried amongst others Air Vice-Marshal Pulford and Rear-Admiral Spooner, Rear-Admiral, Malaya. Having first been attacked by a floatplane, the launch was then fired upon by a destroyer, forcing the skipper to head for nearby Tjebia Island. By the time a Japanese search party arrived towards the end of May, 17 had perished from starvation and malaria, including both senior officers.

During the afternoon of the 15th, one of the Air/Sea Rescue launches (*HSL 105*), which had departed Singapore with Air HQ staff on board including Grp Capt Rice (former OC 224 Fighter Group), Wg Cdr Robert Chignell (former OC Kallang) and Sqn Ldrs Wilf Clouston and Frank Howell, former commanders of 488 and 243 Squadrons respectively, was attacked seven times in the Banka Strait. A direct bomb hit after about 20 minutes severely damaged the craft, a splinter instantly killing the popular and respected Chignell; his body was put over the side. One other passenger was wounded and the craft caught fire. The crew and passengers were picked up by two small steamers, *Rentau* and *Renau*, but both were intercepted and captured at dawn, all aboard becoming prisoners. Sqn Ldr Clouston remembered:

"For a month we didn't know whether we were going to be shot or not, before we were all piled on to a very small ship and taken up the Palembang river to Palembang."

Grp Capt Rice died as a prisoner in 1943.

At 2000 on 15 February, resistance officially ended at Singapore, the British Empire suffering probably the worst and most humiliating defeat in its history.

* * *

For many thousands, the fall of Singapore meant three-and-a-half years of hard labour as slaves of the Japanese; many would not survive, but a lucky few thousand did manage to reach freedom. Among those making their way to Batavia were the ground personnel of 243 Squadron, as Flt Sgt Mothersdale recalled:

"The Squadron ground personnel were withdrawn from Palembang and moved by rail to Oosthaven, embarking for the six-hour crossing of Sunda Strait on the midnight departure ferry service to Merak. At Merak the personnel entrained for Batavia, and there moved into Laan Trivelli Barracks, a RAF Personnel Holding Unit. Flt Lt Bows, the CO, was appointed Camp Commandant at Laan Trivelli; the personnel strength of this PHU continually increased with the arrival of units withdrawn from Singapore and Sumatra and reinforcing units from the Middle East and UK. Air Vice-Marshal Maltby, who had been appointed AOC RAF Java, toured the unit and told Flt Lt Bows that his job was too big for a Flight Lieutenant and promoted him in the field to Squadron Leader.

At Laan Trivelli the Squadron, in common with many units not equipped with aircraft – and with unarmed personnel – provided working parties for unloading stores in the docks at Tanjong Priok for assembling a reinforcement of dismantled Hurricanes, which had arrived at Batavia from the UK. These Hurricanes were dispersed and assembled under trees in public parks and such places, and were air-tested and ferried forthwith from a military airfield and from Batavia Civil Airport.

On 21 February, the ground personnel of 243 Squadron were among a very large contingent of RAF [and RAAF] personnel, which embarked in SS *Orcades* at Tanjong Priok. The ship sailed at midnight and arrived at Colombo on the night of 27/28 February."

Among these were Sgts Baber and Lawrence:

"I think we must have been there [Palembang] for about ten days and then we got out on a train to a place called Oosthaven, then across to Batavia. There was a ferry from Sumatra across to Java, so we got out on that, then railed down to Batavia again. As we left Palembang the sky was full of parachutists – Japs. We saw them coming down. They were close all right. We were put on a train just leaving. We were then put in a big Dutch Army barracks and stayed there until we got on a ship [SS *Kedah*], which went across to Colombo. No one knew what was going on at all and an Australian squadron leader rounded us up. Bertie Bows and the RAF chaps and some of our NZ pilots left the ship at Colombo and we stayed on under the command of this Australian. His idea was that we would go back to Australia and form a squadron there and go up north. Everyone had their own idea about what to do – it was quite disorganised. I do remember an adjutant – F/O Tulloch – a great big Scotsman. He was domiciled in Singapore. His wife had left and gone to Australia. At Colombo he decided he would stay aboard and go with us to Australia. But just before the ship pulled out, the RAF had other ideas. A tender tied up alongside and a squad of armed marines came aboard and took poor, old Tulloch ashore, charging him with desertion! Lawrence and I came out together all the way to New Zealand."

The 2,000 surplus and unarmed RAF personnel from Java commenced disembarking at about 0600. The men assembled on the grass parade ground of Galle Face Barracks and were awaiting disposal instructions; Mothersdale continued:

"The Corporal i/c 243 Squadron Orderly Room came up to Nobby [Wt Off Nobby Aitken, Senior NCO A Flight] and myself and told us that the filing cabinet he had with him contained all the Squadron's files in it, including secret documents. He asked what he should do with it. He looked concerned – so did we when we learned its contents. We went to see the Wing Commander in charge, and he told Nobby to detail a guard to look after it, and he would arrange for its safe custody."

The eventual fate of the filing cabinet remains a mystery. Its contents do not appear to have survived. 243 Squadron no longer existed.

Others to reach Colombo included the Australians of 453 Squadron. After several frustrating days awaiting evacuation from Java, they also boarded the *Orcades*. The Squadron's war diary continued to be maintained in its own humorous and inimitable style:

"21 February: Towards noon of this day (Friday) from the good witch of the South came the dramatic word 'Pack!' You've seen a streak of lightning? Well, compared with the speed with which the lads jumped to it, a streak of lightning was as a Buffalo to a Navy 0. After much scrambling, shunting, whistle-blowing and bell-ringing, the Squadron eventually saw Buitenzorg disappearing (we hope) into the limbo of forgotten things. And so down to the docks where after a lot more scrambling etc, we were eventually delivered into the bowels of the *Orcades*; right down into the bowels with the temperature at about 120°F. Oh yes, mustn't forget the 'F'. This is very pukka and it also stands for Fahrenheit. Anyway to save anyone with tender susceptibilities, we'll say it was 'Fahrenheit' hot in our quarters. The boat sailed at 2300 for, so the sooksnipers tell us, Colombo. Colombo and what?

22 February: Spend a pleasant day on board getting organised. Expected to be well and truly bombed in the Sunda Straits but Tojo must have been feeling a little off colour and night came without incident. Financial difficulties are severe as we find that our dollars, guilders and other strange currency is regarded with great scepticism aboard the *Orcades*. We all feel sympathy with the famous 'poor little rich girl' of film fame – but as there's no grog to be had, things aren't quite so bad.

23 February: Water, water everywhere and not a drop of beer.

24 February: The Squadron is still at sea; Blue and Arthur are starting a collection of Dutch guilders. Anyone willing to contribute kindly go to their poker school in the Sergeants' Lounge.

25 February: Today marked the auspicious inauguration of the 453 'Sunshine Club'. Its aim is the abolition of cheer and hope; its motto the famous last words of Dreary O'Leary, the noted Irish pessimist: 'Ah! gloom, gloom, glorious gloom' and followed by three long drawn out moans and the shedding of many tears. Office bearers so far elected are Patron (Morbid Mick), President (Bad News Bill) and Secretary (Woeful Wally). Vacancies exist on the committee and anyone possessing a naturally unhappy outlook and a taste for misery may be elected on application to the Secretary.

26 February: Rumour hath it that we will dock tomorrow in the forenoon. The destination of the Squadron is still in dispute, but most of us are confident of seeing gum trees again very soon. In the early morning broadcast of the 'Sunshine Club', Bad News Bill announced that the two most likely destinations were Rangoon and the Khyber Pass. Two up and poker schools are flourishing and it now looks as though Blue and Arthur will be able to buy their own Duty Pilot's tower when they get home. Many cheers cads! Barrel is just 21 and never . . . well, perhaps we'll skip that.

27 February: Arrived in Colombo at 1130. The harbour is packed with transport all loaded with Aussie troops. Looks as though shore leave is definitely off the cards. The Shadow left the Squadron today to take over the command of 135 Squadron (Hurricanes) stationed in Colombo. With him went our old friend Gentle George. We had great hopes of getting George into a spot of 'Tooths Country Special'. 453 wishes these two the best of luck and good hunting. All the RAF disembarked today, with Strangler, Wally and others having good cause to remember this fact. If you want to hear some really first class Australian, just ask Strangler what he thinks of the pongos."

When the *Orcades* arrived at Colombo, Sqn Ldr Harper wanted 453 Squadron personnel to disembark with him. However, the Australians had been promised that they would be returned to Australia, so Flt Lt Vanderfield approached Wg Cdr Frank Wright with a request for the Squadron to remain on board. He agreed and overrode

Harper's authority. Harper was incensed and refused to say goodbye to his men. The diary continues:

"28 February: Congratulations to Curly – there were times when he doubted whether he would see this birthday, but he made it. Still lying in harbour doing a large spot of Sweet Fanny Adams.

1 March: So dawns the first day of a new month in the beautiful harbour of Colombo. Water under the bridge – Ceylon for good tea – many cheers, gentlemen, many cheers!

2 March: Despite the prophecy of all the 'Sunshine Club' that the ship had taken roots and would never sail, we departed from Colombo at 1500. After days of gazing at 'Ceylon for Good Tea' it will be great to see that familiar sign 'Woop Woop, a Good Rexona Town Welcomes You'. To pass the time on the ship it is suggested that a race meeting should be held. Races so far on the programme include:-

Race 1. The Ooloo Sprint
Race 2. The Rubber Tree Handicap
Race 3. The Tojo Trial
Race 4. The Funk Hole Flying
Race 5. The Nervous One Novice
Race 6. The Cockwash Cup (Restricted to Group Captains and above)

So rally round cads, nominations to be handed in to orderly room here – the sun comes over the yardarm on the day after the night of the full moon.

3-8 March: Sailing peacefully in the placid waters of the Indian Ocean. On Wednesday night we separated from the rest of the convoy and headed south-east. Nothing much has happened though we've seen some flying fish, dolphins and a hell of a lot of sea. Though we expected to reach Fremantle on Wednesday, it was announced yesterday that our first port of call would be Adelaide on Monday week! Without the usual amenities and perquisites, ocean travel is not really all it's cracked up to be. Our innards are being grossly insulted by the consumption of lime juice, the only beverage obtainable on the ship. I say lime juice but latterly the lime has been conspicuous in its absence. Nine o'clock each morn, sees the splendid physiques on 453 Squadron swing into action at PT – at least we see some of them. Congo made an attempt to glamorise the activities on the first morning but has not been an active participant since; can't take it, eh?

10 March: There is a great deal of speculation going on as to exactly what part of the Indian Ocean we are in at present. Our amateur experts with a wide variety of maps, instruments etc., have placed us at varying points within a circle of about 2,000 miles radius. The 'Sunshine Club' contends that 'Batavia is the spot' and that we're going there via the South Pole just to confuse Tojo. Actually the chill breezes do suggest that we must be somewhere near the land of the polar bear. Of course, most of the pukka gen comes by way of the fifth stoker to Dora, thence to the cabin boy who passes it on to the ship's cat etc. The latest is Adelaide either Friday or Saturday night. In case Dora is not a familiar character to readers, she/he/it (cross out words not required) is the ship's bicycle – a cute little piece of work. Who was the 'zoomer', the daring fighter pilot, who after showing 'tremendous' bravery in Malaya, was cruelly 'deserted' by his squadron, who then grabbed a Hurricane, took off, shot down the Jap Air Force, crashed, covered himself with glory then lost his dignity, sex appeal and hair down near the aft companionway on E deck?

11 March: Just a day and cold as f***! We've seen little of Doug, Mick, Curly and Tom lately; tis surmised they are confined to their beds due to some obscure alcohol deficiency disease. Or could it be that they are all concentrating on something? Van seems to be in good health; that's due the fact that he attends PT each morning. The average attendance is about two officers and two NCOs, so come on cads! Off the blots!"

The *Orcades* arrived at Adelaide on 14 March, and the RAAF personnel dispersed the following day. The Australians were still seething from the treatment metered out by the British High Command, as witnessed by the epilogue to the war diary:

"From the first day till practically the last, 453 Squadron battled day in, day out, against impossible odds, not only from the Japanese but from the incompetent, befuddled machinations and 'Higher' Command. Churchill has described Malaya as the biggest blunder in British military history since Ethelred the Unready. Yet, Malaya was at the same time one of the most glorious sagas of courage and tenacity in British history. We humbly remind Mr Churchill that never before have so few been called upon to stem such colossal masses of men and machinery, nor to face such impossible odds with practically their bare hands.

"And those responsible are not facing their mistakes. No! A Court of Inquiry is at present endeavouring to place the blame for everything upon the insignificant number of fighter pilots who were called upon to conquer a mighty war machine. They accuse us of low morale. Just a shade of difference from cowardice? As Australians who have never shirked a job no matter how tough, we cannot but help feeling utterly nauseated with the imbecilic, puny-minded, faint-hearted collection of weak-kneed, doddering, armchair fighters whose bravest deed was to reach for a telephone to order others into battle while they themselves grovelled, shivering and trembling under tables in reinforced concrete buildings.

"So much then for the epilogue to our diary. It is regrettable that so much bitterness has crept into its latter pages, but in truth these last pages give only a slight indication of our deeper feelings on return to Australia."

* * *

Two weeks after his arrival in Java, *CBS*'s Cecil Brown had made another no-holds-barred and impassioned broadcast to fellow Americans back home:

"The war goes on – inexorably. We fight beside the British who fought our war for two and a half years with incredible courage. They fought while they were short of planes, guns, tanks, rifles, submarines, military leadership, adaptability, dynamism – short of vision in denying truthful reporting of their cause to their comrades-in-arms in America – short of understanding that the native in the Empire could fight, too, for the ideal of freedom – short of everything except courage. They held off our Fascist enemies with pure naked courage. They are the kind of people who face machine-guns barehanded and fight off Stukas with rifles.

"This people's war for survival goes on. We Americans and we of the United Nations go on fighting and dying all over the world. It is a simple choice we are making. It is to fight and die as free men or to live as slaves. We fight formidable enemies who are strong, resourceful and cunning. The Fascists wage a total war, and they hold almost all the vantage points from which to fight it. We fight barbarians. They are not simply barbaric Nazis or barbaric Japanese militarists. We fight the German people and the Japanese people who seek not liberation for the world, but its total enslavement. There is not a single Fascist man, woman or even child who would reject the spoils of conquest or the vengeance of victory, if the Axis should win this war.

But we will win this war. We will win because we are going to be twice as smart as our enemies, we shall produce twice as speedily as they can and we shall murder them twice as fast as they murder us." [133]

It is tragic that there were few British commanders who showed the same analytical mind, determination and fighting spirit.

CHAPTER X

DUTCH BREWSTERS: THE FALL OF JAVA

"My view is that our drawback during the fighter actions was not an inferior aeroplane [the Brewster], but that we had too few of them . . ."

Kapt Pieter Tideman, CO 3-V1G-V

Following the fall of Singapore, Palembang quickly followed. Japanese paratroopers captured both P1 and P2 airfields during mid February, despite spirited resistance by RAF Hurricanes and Blenheims, aided by RAAF Hudsons. Pushed back to Java, the RAF Hurricanes continued to fight a losing battle, Dutch CW-21s, Curtiss Hawks and Brewster B-339s also trying their best to stem the Japanese advance – but, in vain[134]. On 22 February, six former Buffalo pilots of 488 Squadron joined a new Hurricane unit formed in Java, one being killed and the others being made PoW when Java fell in early March.

Dutch Brewster Operations
The Dutch Brewster squadrons in the East Indies were as ineffective against A6Ms and Ki-43s as had been the RAF Buffaloes, their casualties outstripping their claims. At the outbreak of war there were two operational Brewster squadrons: 1-V1G-V, commanded by Sumatran-born Kapt Andrias van Rest, was divided into four Flights (each of four aircraft), based at Singkawang in West Borneo, Samarinda II in East Borneo, Tarakan in north-east Borneo, and at Ambon on Amboina. 2-V1G-V was based at Buitenzorg in Java under Kapt Jacob van Helsdingen. On 15 December 1941, the latter unit moved to Singapore (see Chapter V). A third squadron, 3-V1G-V, a training unit, became operational when hostilities erupted. It comprised mainly pilots on conversion courses including a number of ex-airline pilots; the unit was commanded by Kapt Pieter Tideman:

"I commanded 3-V1G-V, operating Brewsters. This was a newly formed squadron and I was ordered to build it up with very young pilots just from primary flying school. I had the assistance of Lt Brunier[135], who had flown for some months with the RAF in England."

The Brewsters of 1-V1G-V's Singkawang Flight were the first to see action, on 19 December 1941, when three intercepted G3Ms of the Mihoro Ku raiding Pontianak flying boat anchorage in West Borneo. One G3M was hit and ditched in sea 20 miles south of Saigon during the return flight. One of the unit's pilots, Sgt W.E. Wessels, crash-landed and was killed. Then, on 28 December 1941, Brewsters of the Tarakan Flight engaged seven A6Ms of the 3rd Ku that attacked the airfield. The Dutch pilots claimed two Japanese Navy fighters shot down (one was in fact damaged) but lost three of their own. Lt J.N. Droog and Ensign G. Olsen were both killed when their aircraft crashed into the sea, while Ensign C.A. Vonck was rescued by a local fisherman after 12 hours in the sea; the fourth Brewster crash-landed. Thus, the Tarakan Flight ceased to exist.

By 15 January 1942, with Mendao and Tarakan secured, the Japanese next turned their attention to the neutralization of Amboina, where RAAF Hudsons were based. Eighteen A6Ms from the 3rd Ku arrived to meet two Brewsters of the Ambon Flight, the only two serviceable, which were promptly shot down. Lt F.E. Broers baled out into the sea from his blazing aircraft; he was rescued and admitted to hospital, and was later taken prisoner when the Japanese arrived. Meanwhile, Sgt W.J. Blans fought on alone, but when the port wing of his aircraft was blown off he baled out. He had been hit 17 times during the fight and fainted before he hit the water; he was picked up seven hours later, but was by then dead. One of the RAAF officers who witnessed the one-sided combat wrote:

> "The valiant pilots had taken off against the Japanese after sitting for hours beside the airstrip, strapped into the Brewsters. They had refused to leave their aircraft. The loss of the Dutch pilots saddened us indeed. We had profoundly admired their heroism even though it was futile."

The Brewsters of 2-V1G-V, which had recently withdrawn from Singapore, were ordered to Saraminda II airfield in East Borneo on 20 January, where they were joined by the similarly equipped Singkawang Flight from west of the island. Ens R.A. Rothcrans (B-3115) of the 2nd Squadron was lost to enemy action off Balikpapan on the 23rd, the 1st Squadron losing two more pilots next day when, during the afternoon, six A6Ms attacked the airfield. Led by Kapt van Rest (who had claimed a Japanese floatplane a few days earlier), the Brewsters intercepted and claimed two Zeros shot down, one by van Rest and the other by Lt Pieter Benjamins; one A6M ditched near a Japanese vessel and the wounded pilot was rescued. Two Brewsters were also shot down, both Ensign T.W. Kürz and Sgt T.J. de Waardt (B-3132) losing their lives. Most of the Brewsters were now withdrawn to Andir on Java, leaving just a flight of three at Samarinda II. Four days later two of these (B-3126 and B-3159) were destroyed on the ground by strafing A6Ms, the last remaining aircraft also being withdrawn to Andir.

By the beginning of February, 1-V1G-V at Andir possessed 15 Brewsters, while 2-V1G-V at Tjisaoek had eight aircraft and 3-V1G-V could muster a further 11 at Tjililitan. Two of the 3rd Squadron's pilots had recently been lost in bad weather accidents (Ensigns W.A.T. van Buuren and R.J.J. Hoogenhuizen) and a third (Sgt H.C. Voorn) was killed in a night training accident a few days later; a fourth aircraft was written off when Lt R.A. Sleeuw crashed on landing at Tjililitan. 1-V1G-V lost a pilot on 5 February when Sgt A. Berk crashed and was killed near Semplak.

On the morning of 9 February, Western Java suffered its first air attack, a bombing and strafing raid being made on the Batavia area by 27 bombers of the 22nd Air Flotilla, covered by 13 A6Ms and accompanied by a single C5M to observe results. Tjililitan airfield and Kemajoran Civil Airport were hit. At the former the alarm was given late and only four Brewsters of 3-V1G-IV were able to scramble and were immediately attacked by the escorting fighters. The Brewster of Sgt H. Huys was hit and set on fire just as it was gaining speed for take-off, but miraculously the pilot escaped without injury. His colleague Sgt J. Berk was not so fortunate and was killed when his aircraft was shot down, while Ensign C.H. Weijnschenk, the section leader, crash-landed his burning machine in a paddy field.

Meanwhile Lt J.A. Butner, a bomber pilot currently undergoing fighter pilot training with 3-V1G-IV, took off on his own. He immediately came under attack although he was able to land his badly damaged aircraft at Kemajoran. Only Sgt F.J. de Wilde returned safely to Tjililitan. B-3120 was among the Brewsters lost in this action. Four more of the unit's aircraft were destroyed on the ground and, following this attack, the two surviving Brewsters were flown to Tjisaoek to join forces with 2-V1G-V.

In the west, Java suffered its first attacks by the newly arrived JAAF units at Palembang, on 19 February. The first such raid was made on Buitenzorg by five Ki-48s of the 90th Sentai escorted by 19 Ki-43s of the 59th and 64th Sentais. Eight Brewsters of 1 and 2-V1G-V were scrambled over Semplak, the pilots reportedly meeting 35 Japanese aircraft. Two fighters, identified as Zeros, were claimed shot down, in all probability by Kapt Helsdingen and Sgt Bruggink. Sgts Jan Scheffer and P.C.'t Hart each fought a Ki-43, but both were shot down and baled out, while Ensign J. Kuijper and Sgt N.G. de Groot were also brought down and lost their lives. Lt August Deibel (B-398) fired twice at one fighter but, after a ten-minute dogfight, he was wounded by shell splinters, and force-landed on the airfield. On this occasion, the Japanese pilots identified their opponents as nine Curtiss Hawks and claimed seven "easily" shot down.

In the afternoon, at about 1640, a larger force of 28 Ki-43s from the 59th and 64th Sentais, together with nine Ki-48s, returned, this time to raid Bandoeng where a dozen Brewsters from Kapt Tideman's 3-V1G-V (now operating again as an independent unit) were up to engage the force, which they reported as a dozen bombers and 36 fighters. This time the Japanese – although engaging similar aircraft to those met during the morning – identified their adversaries as 20 P-43s. They again claimed seven shot down, plus three probables, one being credited to Maj Kato of the 64th. Tideman recalled:

"We could not reach the bombers properly – we did not shoot down any but got tangled up in huge dogfights with the Zeros [*sic*]. One of my best officers – Lt J.J. Tukker – was shot down and killed. A very good NCO, Sgt L. van Daalan [flying B-3122], was shot down but saved himself by parachute; he got severely burned on face and arms though. Also, Lt G.J. de Haas, an airline pilot (who was enlisted in my squadron, as were two other airline pilots, Lts Simons and André de la Porte[136]), saved himself by jumping after his machine-guns jammed.

"As for myself, I can only say that I had several severe dogfights. Although I must have hit quite a few Navy 0s, I did not see one of them go down to the deck because the Japs operated in groups of three: one taking up the fight, the second staying close behind him and the third taking a position higher on his tail. So, as soon as I got No.1 in my gunsight and opened up with my machine-guns, after a burst or two, I saw No.2 or No.3 coming in on me. So as not to get shot down myself, I had to turn my attention to the one behind. During the action I was hit badly several times (not personally) but was able to land normally. I remember the first hit I received came from a cannon shell hitting my right wing, where I could see a huge hole. I was shocked to death at first – later I got used to the sound of hitting bullets!"

The light bombers attacked the airfield, claiming five aircraft burned. It may have been during this raid that six Dutch fighters under repair – three Hawk 75As, two CW-21Bs and one Buffalo, an ex-453 Squadron machine – were destroyed by bombs.

Learning that the weather around Batavia was likely to be bad on the morning of the 21st, Maj Kato led the Ki-43s of the 59th and 64th Sentais, together with the 90th Sentai's bombers, towards Kalidjati. On approaching the target area, Kato left the 59th and 90th Sentais to head for the airfield, leading the 64th towards cloud-covered Bandoeng instead. Arriving there soon after midday, they spotted seven fighters identified as P-43s, which attacked from above but were evaded. Four more were then seen below and were 'bounced', and one was claimed probably shot down. Sgt J.P. Adam baled out after colliding with one of the unit's Ki-43s, which failed to return.

It seems very likely that their opponents were once more the Brewsters from 3-V1G-V; their commander, Kapt Tideman, recalled:

"Another attack came with 21 Zeros [*sic*]. We had nine Brewsters against them that day. Obviously their target was to strafe the airport at Andir. Again we managed to keep them busy in dogfights preventing them doing the strafing. This time I saw a Zero, which I had a good aim at, diving down steeply with smoke trailing behind. Again, I did not see the crash. Sgt Adam was so fanatic that he did not want to sidestep a head-on Jap. He collided, bringing down the Jap: he lost his own wing partially and jumped to safety with his parachute. After the action the Japanese retreated and I was able to form a patrol of three with Lts Simons [who had claimed one fighter shot down] and Benjamins. Cruising over the hills north of Bandoeng we waited for the all-clear signal to come from our ground station.

"Flying in formation, I was suddenly badly hit from behind and below. My Brewster was afire. However, as I was about to jump, the fire stopped and I was able to land normally. Afterwards, discussing how a thing like this ever could happen to us, Lt Simons told me, almost crying, that all of a sudden he had seen the Jap climbing up from below behind my tail. Grasping his mike to warn me, the thing had slipped out of his hand and he saw the Jap almost abreast, opening up on me at close quarters. Certainly I was lucky that time and my armour plate behind my seat took the beating, as we later discovered."

The RAF Hurricanes at Tjililitan were not engaged, but two were scrambled to investigate a reconnaissance aircraft reported in the area. One of the British pilots, Flt Lt Jerry Parker, reported:

"We had been warned of no other aircraft in the area but I saw half a dozen specks a very long way off in the distance, against some white cloud. It took me about a quarter of an hour of cruising and climbing to get into the right position against the sun and then the pair of us hurtled down against them, only to find they were Dutch Buffaloes. I was very pleased they had not seen us, but they joined up with us and we climbed back to 25,000 feet."

Three New Zealand pilots arrived at Semplak on 23 February, Plt Offs Edgar Pevreal, Terry Marra and Jim Cranstone, formerly of 243 Squadron, who had been posted to 2-V1G-V to assist the Dutch pilots, as Pevreal recalled:

"We were attached to the 2nd Squadron, which was somewhere in the middle of Java with Buffaloes. But, of course, when we arrived there they had an excess of pilots and only three aircraft, so we weren't welcomed. We were detached on the 24th and were posted to Bandoeng, and then to Tjilatjap. When we got there, there were two boats – we ended up in Bombay."

Another former 243 Squadron pilot, Sgt Jim MacIntosh, now flying with one of the Hurricane units, also arrived at Semplak where his aircraft was to have an immediate overhaul. While there he took the opportunity to fly one of the Dutch Brewsters, B-395, undertaking two two-hour sorties on the 26th. The first was an aerodrome defence patrol, and the second as top cover to a Dutch Brewster mission, commenting in his logbook: "Lone top cover. These Dutch kites are great. Twin-row Cylones."

On 27 February, five Brewsters of 1-V1G-V were sent to Blimbing airfield in Eastern Java to provide cover for Dutch warships searching for a Japanese invasion force approaching Java. At 1600, the Brewsters took off and covered the warships for two hours, although one failed to return (it is believed it landed elsewhere). Early next morning the four remaining Brewsters were scrambled on the approach of enemy aircraft, although none were encountered. Shortly after 1400, they were again scrambled and encountered A6Ms of the Tainan Ku. One Brewster was shot down from which Ensign Vonck baled out, the victim of PO1/c Saburo Sakai, who recalled:

> "I cut easily inside the Buffalo's turn, heeling over in a vertical bank and coming out of the turn 200 yards from the enemy plane . . . I jabbed impatiently on the button. Several bullets hit the Buffalo's engine and smoke burst back from the plane. The Brewster went into a series of repeated slow rolls until it disappeared into the cloud." [137]

Later in the afternoon the crew of a crash-landed RAF Vildebeest arrived at Madioen airfield, where they discovered on approaching the Dutch airfield commander, that there were two flyable aircraft on the airfield, which they could use to return to their base at Tjikampek, some 300 miles to the west. One of these was an abandoned Brewster, the other an American A-24 dive-bomber. The Vildebeest pilot decided to chance his arm in the American aircraft and, indeed, arrived safely back at his base. His crew returned by road. The Brewster was destroyed before the airfield was abandoned.

The initial landings on the beaches of north-western Java began soon after midnight on 1 March – a month which was to have tragic consequences for the defenders of the last bastion of the Netherlands East Indies. Dawn found the Allied air units under orders to counter-attack. The landings at Eretanwetan were the first to he reported and by 0200 RAF Hurricanes had been ordered to take off from Tjililitan at dawn, while the Brewsters at Andir were also made ready. At 0530 therefore, nine Brewsters set out for Eretanwetan, one flight led by Kapt van Helsdingen, the other by Kapt van Rest. The invasion fleet, when found, was estimated to comprise 11 transports in line astern, 50 yards apart and 200 yards from the shore, flanked by two destroyers, with a cruiser standing a mile out to sea.

Even as the Allied fighters were on their way, a Japanese bomber formation – estimated to be 50 strong – was heading for Bandoeng. The force comprised Ki-48s from the 27th Sentai escorted by 59th and 64th Sentai Ki-43s. Most of the bombers turned back due to bad weather, but the fighters of the 59th continued. They arrived soon after the Hurricanes had landed back at Andir, when an air raid warning was sounded and four CW-2lBs were scrambled, closely followed by the last three Brewsters of 3-V1G-V. One Curtiss fighter was shot down. 3-V1G-V's CO, Kapt Tideman, reported:

> "The odds were 3 to 1. We kept them busy until they had to retreat, for fuel shortage probably. When I thought they had all gone, I saw a single Jap proudly circling our base. So I attacked. Starting head-on, I got engaged in a real classic dogfight, with no other to interfere. It was a real pleasure and we both gave everything we had.
>
> "Although I gave him a few bursts, I did not down him and at times I could see him opening fire on me. He had the advantage of a better climbing performance but he was not able to use it to his advantage. Then I tried, after a long time, to force my hand. Because I had knowledge of the terrain, I dived into a ravine hoping he would follow, there to crash into the hills. It did not work! Straightening out in that dive, he followed me at first but steered clear and withdrew. By the time I could go after him again he was too far away, gaining [distance] on me: and that was that."

The Japanese pilots identified their opponents as Buffaloes only, claiming two shot down for the loss of one Ki-43, possibly claimed by Kapt Helsdingen. It would seem that one Brewster crash-landed on return. On the ground, 1-V1G-V was practically wiped out, six of its aircraft being damaged beyond repair, mainly by six strafing A6Ms of the 3rd Ku from Dempasar led by Lt Sadao Yamaguchi. 2-V1G-V also lost an aircraft on the ground during this attack. Flt Lt Jerry Parker, one of the half-dozen RAF Hurricane pilots who arrived at Bandoeng on 2 March, later wrote:

"We found more than a dozen Dutch Buffaloes on the aerodrome. Soon after our arrival an air-raid warning went and we saw a short skirmish between some Zeros and Buffaloes overhead. The Buffs left very smartly but one [probably the CW-21B, not a Buffalo] was shot down, the pilot taking to his parachute."

Another ex-RAAF Buffalo crash-landed next day, while one more was strafed and written off at Pameungpeuk on 3 March, a second receiving similar treatment at Kemajoren. Yet another ex-RAAF Buffalo was lost next day at Tjililitan. On the 6th, now operating from Andir and with Japanese fighters patrolling overhead, Parker, the Hurricane pilot, wrote:

"We were not at all anxious to take off, but soon we heard a rumour that we were required to decoy the Zeros to allow the Buffaloes, which, with extra fuel tanks, could cover most of the distance to Australia, to take off. I said they could stuff the Buffaloes."

Despite the protests, the Hurricanes duly took off and fortunately were not intercepted as they climbed away; Parker continued:

"I had seen no movement by the Buffaloes but was not at all worried by that . . . I went round the end of the hills to the west, hedge-hopped back to Andir and landed. We were told that 14 Buffaloes had left."

The remaining flyable Brewsters may have departed Andir but they certainly did not head for Australia. At dawn on 7 March, the last four serviceable Brewsters were led by Kapt Jacob van Helsdingen (whose 35th birthday it was) to attack Kalidjati. Flying in two widely-spaced pairs, the Dutch pilots (all of whom had fought with 2-V1G-V in Singapore) soon encountered Japanese fighters, six of these attacking van Helsdingen who was shot down and killed in B-396 over Lembang; Sgt Gerardus Bruggink, who was flying 600 feet lower, escaped into cloud and returned to Andir. The second pair saw only a single fighter at which Lt Gus Deibel[138] fired and saw strikes, before it escaped in cloud. Three more then appeared which Deibel engaged; two of these fell away under his fire but his own aircraft was hit and he too returned to Andir with his No.2, Sgt Jan Scheffer. They landed during a thunderstorm, Deibel's aircraft ground-looping, one of his wheels having sustained damage in the fight. It was the last operation for the Brewsters, which had fared no better than the Buffalo in combat with Japanese fighters. Next day, 8 March, the Dutch GHQ agreed to surrender and, as continued resistance would have been adjudged by the Japanese as banditry, the men were ordered to lay down their arms at 1430.

One small group of fighter pilots managed to avoid capture and escaped in a somewhat bizarre and daring fashion. Dutch Brewster pilot Ensign Frits Pelder, late of 2-V1G-V, who had been wounded at Singapore, and four RAF Hurricane pilots (two Australians, one Canadian and one New Zealander) all had one aim in common – to escape. Pelder was able to use his influence to persuade the commander of a Dutch Lockheed transport squadron to allow them to repair one of the unit's

Lockheed 212s – with a view to flying it to Ceylon. Following a search among the abandoned aircraft, L-201 was found to be the only one that had not had its undercarriage deliberately retracted. In an effort to immobilize it a tractor had been used to ram its tail section. The five men got to work, as one of the Australians recalled:

> "We found three Lockheeds which had been damaged by the Dutch. One had its tail missing, and another its nose. We took the tail off the second plane and fixed it on the first, patching it with ropes and pieces of bamboo. We completed the job with bits and pieces from the third plane, and filled the tanks with petrol drawn from the other two."

Forty-gallon wing fuel tanks were removed from an unserviceable fighter aircraft and were installed within the cabin. Extra cans of fuel were loaded into the aircraft and a rubber tube was run from the main tanks in the wings through hole in the side of the fuselage. This makeshift arrangement allowed fuel to be fed into the tanks in flight, via a hand-pump. With machine-guns fitted in dorsal turret and nose position, the escapers felt confident of their chances.

At 0900 on the 9th therefore, L-201 took off with Pelder at the controls and headed for Medan, 1,200 miles distant in Northern Sumatra, which they had been advised was still in Dutch hands. During the seven-hour flight, all five pilots took turns in flying the aircraft, which handled well and a safe landing was made. Following a day when the aircraft was thoroughly checked over and prepared for the next stage of the journey, L-201 departed Medan early the morning of the 11th, bound for Lho'nga, on the northern tip of Sumatra, the final refuelling stop. On arrival, willing hands hastily pushed the aircraft under cover as a Japanese reconnaissance aircraft circled above. The Lockheed's tanks were speedily topped up and Pelder took off just as nine bombers were reported heading for the airfield. As he pulled the aircraft out to sea, two bombers began their dives but the Lockheed was not attacked. By late afternoon, following an uneventful eight-hour flight during which each pilot again took a turn at the controls, Ceylon was sighted. Unable to find an airfield, a Hurricane was fortuitously seen cruising by and this was followed to Colombo, where a safe landing was made at Ratmalana airfield – they were the lucky ones.

At least eight Brewsters fell into Japanese hands, predominantly Dutch aircraft but including W8163/GA-P formerly of 21RAAF Squadron. One of the Dutch aircraft was B-395. Four of these aircraft were later shipped to Japan and evaluated by Japanese pilots at the Test Centre located at Tachikawa Army Air Force Base.

This was not the finale for the Buffalo, however, since the final consignment of five Brewster B-439s for the Dutch were never assembled. Although these had arrived at Tjilatjap shortly before the surrender, there had not been sufficient time too uncrate and assemble them. Consequently they were transhipped to Australia aboard the Dutch merchantman *Zandaam*, and would eventually see service with the RAAF. A further batch of 16 reached Australia directly from the United States; of this total of 21, a dozen were issued to 25RAAF Squadron for the defence of Perth.

* * *

Three months after the fall of Java the Americans found out for themselves just how outclassed the Buffalo was in combat against the A6M. During the course of the three-day Battle of Midway (4-6 June 1942), which witnessed the annihilation of Admiral Isoroku Yamamoto's Combined Fleet including the aircraft carriers *Akagi*, *Kaga*, *Hiryu* and *Soryu* – which effectively changed the course of history – the cost to the

US forces was not light. Among the USN and USMC fighters and torpedo-bombers lost were 17 out of 20 F2A-3 Buffaloes of VMF221, operating from Midway, that were shot down in combat with A6Ms on 4 June, with most of the pilots being killed. One of the few survivors wrote in his report:

> "The F2A-3 is <u>not</u> a combat aeroplane. The Japanese Zero can run rings around it . . . It is my belief that any commander that orders pilots out for combat in it should consider them lost before leaving the ground."

The poor showing of the F2A-3 at Midway led to it being withdrawn from US front-line service. Its successor, the F4F-4 Wildcat, did not fare much better.

AFTERMATH

On release from three-and-a-half years of imprisonment, various senior officers wrote reports in praise of the men under their command. Of the Buffalo PR Flight, Air Vice-Marshal Maltby, Assistant AOC Far East Command, wrote:

> "The PR Buffalo Flight, which had functioned almost daily with outstanding success under the command of Squadron Leader Lewis since the beginning of the campaign, finally lost all its aircraft by enemy air attacks on the 7th February [*sic*]. This Flight had carried out over 100 sorties, the majority of which had proceeded as far north as Singora. Aircraft were intercepted by Japanese fighters and hit on numerous occasions, although none was shot down. Throughout, no armour or guns were carried: the pilots had relied entirely upon evasion in order to fulfil their missions. The greatest credit is due to them for the valuable work they did."

The three main photo-reconnaissance pilots of 4PRU were decorated, Flt Lt Tony Phillips with the DFC, Sgt Charlie Wareham the DFM for 32 operational sorties, while Flt Lt Donald Pearson received a DFC later. Sqn Ldr Lewis, although he flew several important sorties, was not decorated. On one occasion it was alleged that, while it had taken him 50 minutes to fly from Singapore to Kuantan, he managed to make the return flight in 35 minutes after being chased back by Japanese fighters! Before the fall of Singapore, Grp Capt E.B. Rice, OC 224 (Fighter) Group had submitted his report of the fighting:

> "Throughout the whole of the war in Malaya the odds taken on by fighter pilots averaged 6 to 1 against. In the latter stages when mass raids were launched on the island, interception was carried out by as few as 12 aircraft, against odds as great as 182 aircraft, as happened on several occasions. During the concluding stages of operations here, when flights of 81 enemy bombers, made up in three flights of 27 aircraft each, escorted by a similar number of fighters, attacked the island, interception had to be attempted by no more than six sections of two aircraft each.
>
> "The Air Force claim to have brought down 183 planes between 9 December 1941 and 9 February 1942 [including those by Hurricanes], but have to admit the loss of over 100 per cent of its original number of aircraft. The excess of planes lost over those with which we commenced the campaign is explained by the arrival of reinforcements. I would emphasise that the figure of enemy aircraft destroyed by the Air Force, viz 183, is an absolutely minimum claim, inasmuch as it was impossible for fighter pilots fighting at heights of over 20,000 feet over jungle and sea to follow falling enemy aircraft. While the normal claims were submitted to the Air Ministry, in accordance with instructions, a number of claims fell into a special category by reason of the difficulty described above. These latter claims were logged, and were in the process of being investigated when evacuation was ordered, in the course of which these records were destroyed."

Fifty-one-year-old Grp Capt Rice did not survive his sojourn as a prisoner, and died on 5 September 1943. On his release from PoW camp, Sqn Ldr Frank Howell DFC[139] sent his report on 243 Squadron's performance to Air Ministry:

> "Up against superior aircraft, and outnumbered up to 6 to 1, they showed a spirit equal to, if not greater, than that of the pilots in the Battle of Britain. With practically no hope of rescue when shot down if they operated outside the island, they pursued the enemy

far up the coast and succeeded in probably shooting down well over 60 enemy aircraft. This figure cannot possibly be confirmed, as observers and communications were practically non-existent outside the island. But it is unlikely that these enemy aircraft, which were damaged, reached their bases up to 500 miles away.

"The groundcrews under P/O John David (Engineer Officer), P/O Phillips (Armament Officer) and P/O Fowler (Signals Officer) worked well, and did all in their power to keep the aircraft in the air, under very trying and exhausting conditions. The following four men were exceptionally good as regards to their work and their devotion to duty: F/Sgt Armstrong (armourer), Cpl Powell (rigger), AC1 Paddy Moulds (flight mechanic), AC1 Gray (flight rigger). As the majority of records were destroyed by bombing, I am unable to give a detailed report of the Squadron's activities. Great work was done by pilots and crews under difficulties."

He added:

"It is not understandable why RAF personnel were kept back in Singapore for over a week when there were no aircraft to operate. As those senior officers who were responsible for this are dead, and many of us miraculously alive after a very bitter experience, I will not add further to this."

The former CO of 488 Squadron, Sqn Ldr Wilf Clouston DFC, also survived captivity and similarly submitted his report following his return to the UK:

"The conduct of the young pilots of the Squadron, their bravery and unflinching optimism in extremely adverse conditions earned the respect of everyone. The technical staff supplied by the RNZAF were of a very high standard. They were the last Squadron personnel to be evacuated from Singapore and their courage and initiative during the period that Kallang was being severely bombed was to be highly commended. All the pilots of the reinforcing Hurricanes spoke highly of their ability and eagerness to help."

On a critical level, he wrote:

"The operation of the few fighter squadrons in Malaya was complicated by the divergence of opinion as to their rôle. There were three possible rôles in which they could have been employed, namely:

(i)   Defence of Singapore
(ii)   Army Co-operation
(iii) Protection of shipping

With the extremely limited forces at our disposal, the splitting of air squadrons into all three rôles was, in my opinion, disastrous. A very heavy wastage in pilots and aircraft was the direct result of trying to do both (i) and (ii) above simultaneously, resulting also in inefficient concentration of effort, and air superiority or even air parity being built up neither over Singapore Island nor over the front line. The third role, that of protection of shipping, was vital, and quite rightly aircraft were taken off all other duties to protect convoys.

"This was complicated however, by the determination of the Naval authorities to bring in their convoys during daylight hours, usually in the morning when a degree of interest could be guaranteed to be shown by the Japanese Air Force. This action of the Naval authorities was against the repeated warnings of Grp Capt Rice and the more experienced members of 224 (Fighter) Group. The maintenance of standing patrols over convoys from the time they crossed the Equator to their arrival in Singapore was at times almost impossible and greatly strained the resources of both aircraft and pilots. The fact that all convoys arrived safely, and the majority without incident, was purely a matter of luck and lack of foresight on the part of the Japanese; and in no way due to the fact that we did have a token force of fighters in the vicinity of the convoy."

He went on to say:

"The potential damage that might have been inflicted by this policy was so great as to appear now to have been definitely suicidal. In the case of the sinking of the *Prince of Wales* and *Repulse*, air support was not called for until after the attacks by the Japanese Air Force had commenced. Our fighters were despatched immediately but owing to the distance they had to travel from Singapore, the disaster was complete before their arrival.

"I would respectfully suggest that while some of the paragraphs in this report are outspoken, they are made after several years mature reflection and are tendered in the form of constructive criticism in the hope that such errors should not again occur."

Sqn Ldr William Harper, former CO of 453 Squadron, did not emerge from the campaign with very much credit, at least as far as the RAAF was concerned. A subsequent Court of Inquiry in Australia revealed that:

(a) He exhibited a lack of leadership and his conduct was unsatisfactory in that he was rarely available when required, and failed to show proper interest in the welfare of the officers and men of the Squadron.

(b) He was always a hard man to locate, as he was seldom at the base. At Kuala Lumpur on most occasions when the Japanese raided he was absent from the aerodrome.

(c) He failed lamentably to set the example expected of him by leading the Squadron into battle. He didn't fly at Ipoh, and he didn't fly at Kuala Lumpur. He flew for only ten hours in December. He was the only pilot in the Squadron not to see action with Japanese aircraft.

The Court also found 453 Squadron wanting on occasions, but this was due mainly to Harper's lack of leadership:

"That there was a deterioration in the morale of members of 453 Squadron which became evident after the Squadron had been in action at Kuala Lumpur; this deterioration in morale was due to a number of factors. (i) The members of the Squadron were dispirited owing to being beaten in action against the enemy, and the fact that they were obliged to use aircraft which were inferior both in performance and numbers to the enemy aircraft. (ii) The feeling that, notwithstanding this inferiority in aircraft, they were faced by a hopeless position in respect of being reinforced or re-equipped. (iii) The Commanding Officer's lack of understanding of his Squadron, which was accentuated by the fact that he did not fly with them when in action, except on two occasions; and also his stated opinion that he did not have much time for members of his unit or for Australians in general. (iv) The ineffective command exercised by Group Captain Whistondale, the Commanding Officer of the Station [Sembawang]. The evidence shows that this officer was most eccentric and allowed discipline to slacken. The accusation made by him against the members of the Squadron that they were 'yellow' was without foundation and totally undeserved.

"The Court further finds that Sqn Ldr Harper was temperamentally unsuited and insufficiently experienced to command an EATS squadron and that his lack of understanding and qualities of leadership were definite factors in the loss of morale of the Squadron."

In his defence, it was stated that his behaviour was possibly due to his highly nervous disposition, probably a result of his previous service in the UK.

As will have been noted, Sqn Ldr Harper did not lead his men into battle – probably his major fault as CO of 453 Squadron, particularly when commanding such inexperienced pilots – but some of the criticism aimed in his direction would seem to have been unjustified. He was apparently a good organiser, though perhaps in the circumstances prevailing that duty should have been left to the Squadron Adjutant, Flt Lt Wells. Clearly he gained the respect of his ground personnel, if not the pilots. He had got off to a bad start when he requested a number of better-trained replacement pilots, but, as noted, several of his pilots had no desire to be fighter pilots and had in fact been trained to fly multi-engined aircraft.

Undoubtedly it was an error of judgement by the Air Ministry to appoint an RAF officer to command an Australian unit when suitable RAAF officers, with combat experience, were available. Harper also possibly resented having been sent to Singapore in the first place. From the remarks made by several of his senior pilots, Harper – on a personal level – admitted that he was not overkeen on 'colonials' in general and Australians in particular. His lack of leadership and experience – and perhaps tact – in handling men became all the more apparent once a deterioration in relations with his officers had been allowed to develop. He also made it clear that he did not relish flying the Buffalo on operations, although he expected his pilots to do so. It should also be noted that all the experienced fighter squadron commanders were instructed by Air HQ to relinquish their respective commands in mid-January in order to perform controller duties in the Operations Room. [140]

*   *   *

Decorations for the Buffalo pilots were few and far between – Flt Lt Mowbray Garden of 243 Squadron received the DFC[141], as did Plt Off Noel Sharp of 488 and 243 Squadrons (who was lost flying a Hurricane in Java on 1 March 1942). Sgt Geoff Fisken, the top-scoring Buffalo pilot with five victories plus two shared, was commissioned on his return to New Zealand and was awarded the DFC, but not until September 1943 when he had completed his second tour. Flying P-40s with 15RNZAF Squadron in the Pacific, he was credited with a further five victories, making him the top-scoring Commonwealth pilot against the Japanese. Plt Off (later Sqn Ldr) Jim Cranstone received the DFC later in war, when on his second tour of duty, as did Plt Off Gordon Bonham, who was killed in action on 25 September 1944 after destroying five V1 flying bombs. Sgt Bert Wipiti, the young Maori, received the DFM for five victories (one shared). He was posted to India with his friend Sgt Charlie Kronk, the latter being killed in a flying accident on 28 May 1942 when his Hurricane crashed at Dum Dum. Meanwhile, due to his colour, Wipiti was given a hard time by the European whites in India. As a result he was transferred to the UK, where he trained on Spitfires but was killed in action on 3 October 1943, having increased his score by two shared victories. Flg Off Maurice Holder was not decorated however, and on his return to the UK was killed in a flying accident at 56 OTU on 27 August 1942. Neither was Sqn Ldr Ron Bows, a former Blenheim pilot, who returned to the UK and joined Bomber Command; he was killed in action on 20 February 1944.

Within 488 Squadron, Flt Lt John Hutcheson was awarded the DFC, while Sgt Don Clow was commissioned and received the DFC during his second tour. The Squadron's most successful pilot, Sgt Eddie Kuhn, was awarded the DFM. Flg Off C.W. Franks (Equipment Officer) received the MBE, Flt Sgt W.A. Chandler (Acting Engineer Officer) and Sgt John Rees (ground staff) the BEM. Of the performance of

488 Squadron's ground personnel, Sqn Ldr Mackenzie reported:

> "It was only through perseverance that the groundcrew kept the squadron flying. With their engineering skills and improvisation they performed marvels, under Flight Sergeant Andy Chandler. We had wonderful groundcrew. And old Cecil Franks our Equipment Officer – where he got his stuff from I don't know. I remember one time we were short of a truck, which was badly needed. Cecil appeared and here was a truck and there was also a Chinaman looking for his truck!"

Several pilots including Flt Lt Jack Oakden, Plt Off Harry Pettit, Grahame White, and Sgts Jim MacIntosh and Eddie Kuhn joined a Hurricane unit in the defence of Java in late February, and were all taken prisoner on the fall of Java; White died while a prisoner in November 1943. Of those who were evacuated, which included Sgt Perce Killick[142], Sgt Jack Burton was killed in action in the Solomons on 1 July 1943, while Sgt Jack Meharry was posted to the UK, commissioned and was killed in action on 5 August 1944. Sgt Bunny De Maus was also commissioned and was killed in a flying accident on 16 May 1944.

The Australians of 21RAAF/453 Squadron also received a share of decorations, although most were belated and were awarded during second tours. Flt Lts John Kinninmont, Mick Grace and Doug Vanderfield, and Daryl Sproule, each received DFCs, Kinninmont also being awarded the DSO in 1945 as Wing Leader of 78RAAF Wing. Sproule commanded 77RAAF Squadron in 1943, having achieved a further air combat victory, but was shot down and captured; he was executed by the Japanese on 16 August 1943. Sgt Mac Read, killed at Kuala Lumpur in December 1941, was recommended for the DFM but the award was not made due to his death. Sgt Eric Haines (armourer) received the BEM for his performance in Malaya. Sgt Jim Austin, one of the principal pilots responsible for the war diary, was killed in an accident in Australia on 25 September 1942 when he crashed while flying Buffalo A51-5 of 1PRU – a unit with which Harold Montefiore, John Hooper, Geoff Angus and Daryl Sproule also served in late 1942 – while Flg Off Dainty Wallace was later killed in action while flying a Beaufighter. Sgt Greg Board, the keen fighter, failed to get back on operations and was retained as an instructor, much to his chagrin. Postwar, he enjoyed exciting adventures as a 'pilot for hire', which included flying a Lodestar to the embryonic state of Israel during the 1948 Israeli War of Independence, thus violating the arms and aircraft embargo imposed by the United Nations[143].

* * *

The story of the Hurricane pilots involved in operations over Singapore and the Netherlands East Indies will be told in the next volume in this series – *Hurricanes over Singapore*.

APPENDIX I

THE TRIALS AND TRIBULATIONS
OF SGT HARRY GRIFFITHS 453 SQUADRON

On 3 January 1942, we were briefed to cover a convoy in the Sunda Straits approaching Singapore. I admired F/O Kinninmont (Congo) being the only pilot of 21RAAF Squadron to volunteer to stay and join us. So I elected to fly No.2 to him. As we left the briefing my flight commander, Doug Vanderfield, said I shouldn't have done that, as he will probably kill me! Our position was to weave in front of the Squadron and slightly higher to observe any enemy aircraft approaching our rear.

I did find Congo most difficult to fly formation with although I was never more than 20 to 30 feet away from him at any time. The weather was not good and we were flying above a heavy blanket of dense cloud and had not seen the convoy we were supposed to cover. Then, without warning, he dived into the dense cloud. I was unable to see him, as it was pitch dark and very turbulent. I couldn't understand why he didn't put his lights on. Finally I came out the bottom of the cloud base at about 2,000 feet, almost above the convoy, but no sign of Congo. I immediately climbed up through the murk and got to the top. I briefly saw an aircraft some distance away, and although I went after it, I could not sight it again or the rest of the Squadron.

Not having any idea where I was or what direction to fly, I decided to go back down to the convoy and take a direction from them. I completed a circuit of the entire convoy before setting a compass course similar to the leading ship. Having exceeded my endurance in time without sighting more than small islands, I endeavoured to look for any suitable place to put down. My main concern was to try to save the aircraft, as we were terribly short. Finally, after inspecting several of these islands I came across something more substantial. As I crossed the coast I saw a small jetty and what appeared to be a cleared open space for a reasonable landing. I prepared for a wheels-down landing and was making my final approach when, to my dismay, between 20 to 30 people ran out of the bush and congregated right where I had planned to touch down. Had I continued I would probably have killed most of them. I pulled away to port and avoided them.

The next thing I knew, I was drowning. My left arm was free and I was able to claw a channel to my mouth and got a wonderful gulp of fresh air. It was then I heard what sounded like crackling. My immediate thought was fire. I released my harness, parachute and other gear and started digging dog-fashion until I was free. The aircraft had flipped over and was upside down. I had apparently been drowning in my own blood. Fortunately, there was no fire, although I knew I was badly hurt and needed help. I saw a motorcar, which I tried to start, but had no luck. As I alighted I saw a large man, wearing a black fez on his head, looking at me from behind a tree. I beckoned to him and started to move towards him but he ran off and disappeared into the bush.

Next I saw what appeared to be a dwelling. When I got there I called out but got no reply so I went in. I came across a bucket of water and a badly chipped enamel basin, which I filled, and proceded to wash my face. I saw a piece of mirror on a wall, which revealed that my right eye was out of its socket and there was a deep gash across my right cheek, while my forehead looked like pulp. After washing my eye and replacing in its socket I went outside. After washing out the basin and throwing out the bloody water, I realised that I was still bleeding from the wounds as well as retching large quantities of blood. A short distance from the house was a lean-to with what looked like a carpenter's bench, which I laid on and then passed out. When I came to I observed several young men in uniform and wearing straw hats carrying what appeared to be small bore rifles. I quietly drew my revolver but before I had a chance to use it, I was grabbed from behind by an NCO, who took the weapon and then searched me, taking everything from my pockets.

At this stage I must have passed out again for the next thing I knew I was being placed in a bamboo hut near the jetty. After a while they returned and carried me on an improvised bamboo stretcher to the jetty and, as they lowered me into a craft which looked like a dugout or large canoe, the stretcher broke but they grabbed me before I had hardly hit the water and laid me in the bottom of the craft. The NCO was sitting in front of me. I tried to enquire who they were, mainly by sign language. I said that I was British. He caught on and said Japanese. I thought to myself why are they going to all this trouble? Many reasons flashed through my mind, some not very pleasant. I could hear a motor somewhere in the stern, which I imagined to be an outboard. I was not getting any of the breeze as we travelled and the sun was hurting my face. When darkness had fallen – I believe it was about midnight – I heard the motor slow down and soon stop. Several of them lifted me out of the craft and carried me to a grassy clearing. Then, by the aid of a hurricane lamp on a box, a youngish-looking boy started to repair the damage [to my face] approximately 12 hours after the crash. My feelings had returned to the extent that I couldn't take any more and asked for my revolver, which was denied, but he had finished his work or was resting when I observed two or three white men wearing long white garments. I could not understand what they were saying but they finally splashed me with water. I then guessed what they were about so tried to show them my metal disk, which didn't seem to mean anything to them.

It wasn't long before I was picked up and was on my way again. This time I was taken into a building and placed on a hard wooden bench. I heard a door being closed and a bolt being pulled; then silence except for the hum of hundreds of mosquitoes. As my eyes adjusted to the darkness, I could see a small aperture with bars high on one wall and knew I was in some sort of a prison. Morning came and the cursed mosquitoes eased up somewhat. Then I saw a small flap at the bottom of the door open and a metal dish was pushed in, also a mug, but there was no way I could get off the bench. I was still in pain and had no feeling in my feet and legs. Some hours later the plate and mug were withdrawn and others replaced them. I don't know how long this went on for as I kept wafting off. Finally, a big dark man accompanied by a smaller white man appeared in the cell. The dark man spoke excellent English and said he was the Head of the Police. He said the other person was the Resident Commissioner. I asked him who I was being looked after by and he said the Dutch, to my relief. I then realised the NCO had said Javanese and not Japanese. He spoke to the Resident Commissioner and then asked me if they could do anything for me. I asked for a message to be sent to Singapore advising where I was, and secondly, requested a mosquito net. He replied to get a message to Singapore would be very difficult, since a boy would have to go by canoe to some island where they had a pedal radio, and then a message would be sent to Batavia who would relay it to Singapore. This they apparently did. I was told there was only one mosquito net on the island and that was over the bed of the Resident Commissioner – he suggested that I be taken there [to his home]. It turned out to be a large spacious bungalow, with a wide, shaded verandah in the front. The policeman told me they were worried, as I had already eaten the last potato on the island! I told them I would eat whatever they ate. I said I liked rice.

Finally, I was able to leave the bed and sit on the verandah. I enquired the name of the island where I had crashed and was told it was Eron – or that was how it sounded [it was actually Oeroeng on Pulau Koenboer] and the island where I was housed was called Sam or Sim Bali, a most picturesque place with a white sandy beach although narrow with well-cut grass and coconut palms. There was a well-built, sturdy-looking jetty with a magnificent yacht attached, obviously for the Commissioner's use. I was taken to the policeman's house to meet his wife, who had baked a cake to celebrate my birthday – how they knew about it, I have no idea. Prior to this the Commissioner had taken me on a tour of inspection to view their fortifications, which I might add were somewhat primitive, mainly tall poles sharpened to a point at the top, embedded in what appeared to be playing fields; this was to cope with parachuters. As we arrived a sentry presented arms. The Commissioner sat stiffly in his seat and did nothing so I returned the salute, which seemed to please my escort. It was about this time that my police friend said to me that he thought it would be a nice gesture if he took me to the priests and thanked them for administering me with the last rights, to which I agreed, although they appeared a bit bewildered and just stared at me. Perhaps I wasn't supposed to still be around. It was then I thought about the person who had attended to my injuries and told my friend that I would particularly like to thank him. He told me he would do that on my behalf, adding that his medical experience was only two weeks at the hospital at Batavia, as a [first-aid] dresser. I realised the poor man must have been working with little, if any, equipment, for the bandages turned out to be strips of floral material, possibly pieces of sarong; and what I thought were stitches he was using, I think may have been metal clamps; there was certainly no anesthetic or even disinfectant.

All this may have been too much for me, for back at the policeman's house a table was set with a good-size cake covered with chocolate with white writing, which they held for me to read. Unfortunately, all I saw was a blur and couldn't distinguish a single word. They handed me a small glass containing an amber liquid, which I managed to place on the table before collapsing. When I woke I was back in bed being violently ill, which embarrassed me greatly but my police friend told me not to worry and that the houseboys would soon fix that up. About this time I was given a message, which said a naval vessel was being dispatched from Singapore to collect both the aircraft and myself and for me to prepare the aircraft for removal. In due course the vessel did arrive. I think it was the Captain who came to see me. He asked a few questions and departed. My further sickness turned out to be my first attack of malaria. I think it was only a day or so when the ship returned with the aircraft on board. I said a few hurried 'thank you's' and goodbyes, as they were anxious to get me on board and be underway. I was carried to the ship and placed in a small deck cabin, with a sailor positioned at the door for the entire trip. I was told they were in such a hurry to get me back that they went between the shore and a mine field, as it would have taken much longer to go out to sea and come in via the safe entrance.

Back at Singapore
Once at the wharf in Keppel Harbour I was lowered to a waiting ambulance and taken to Alexandra Hospital. The English ran their hospitals somewhat differently to the Australians. For instance, if you were able to get out of bed and it was the CO's inspection, you were required to stand rigidly at attention at the foot of the bed during the inspection. If unable to stand you were required to sit to attention. Failing this you were required to lie at attention. While in hospital I did receive a brief visit from S/Ldr Harper, accompanied by the Adjutant. He asked how I was and if I needed anything – and then left. As soon as I was well enough to leave my bed, I was packed off to a convalescent unit. It was a large square concrete building containing only steel beds, no mattress or palliasse, and was given two blankets which appeared none too clean; one blanket to be folded many times to cover the wire mesh. That night I was bitten by bugs, probably hiding in the blankets.

The following day we were lined up, given a heavy backpack plus a rifle, then headed off at the double. The next thing I knew I was lying on the grass on the side of the driveway. I saw a hut nearby with a sign CO. I barged in. The officer looked up and said 'I will never understand you bloody Australians'. However, I did manage to speak to Harper by phone, who in turn arranged for my release. On arriving back at Sembawang, I was put in a small room in the Station Hospital. It was not long before an orderly said he had to get me down to a slit trench. I tried to argue that I would stay put but finished up in a slit trench just outside the front entrance. Within minutes a formation of 27 heavy bombers dropped their load, most of which landed on the hangars and dispersal revetments but many overshot that area. After the raid I was taken back inside to view the room I had occupied. It was a blackened shell and the bed I had occupied was a twisted heap of metal. Apparently, the enemy wanted to dislodge us from Sembawang, for the raids increased considerably, whereupon they decided to put me back in hospital. This time it was the 2/13 AGH. Even that was hit by shellfire, killing a number of patients.

Escape from Singapore

Sometime later I realised I hadn't heard any of our aircraft. I spent the next two days endeavouring to speak to anyone at the aerodrome, finally speaking to Flt Lt Doc Alder [453 Squadron's MO], who seemed surprised and asked where I was. When I told him, he said he would come to see me. When he arrived he said he would take me to get some food. It was then I learned that the Squadron had departed for Batavia. Doc Alder was driving me back to the hospital when he suddenly did a violent U-turn and went back the way we had come. When I asked the reason, he said hadn't I seen the Japanese guards on the gate? I hadn't! I probably wasn't looking in that direction. We then proceeded back to the aerodrome area. We were actually in No Man's Land, for the artillery rounds were going in both directions. The enemy had captured Nee Soon village. Doc Alder rounded a curve in the road and an anti-tank gun opened up, the round going over us and lodging in an embankment. I was finally deposited in a house, which turned out to be a clearing station.

That evening I went out onto the porch to enable a better appraisal when a bullet, possibly from a sniper, missed the top of my head by an inch or two, bringing down a cloud of white plaster over me. I located the young doctor and told him that in my opinion we were surrounded. I said if it was up to me I would send all the serious cases by ambulance to hospital, and those who felt they could look after themselves to take the chance. Whereupon, after the ambulance had left, about six of us laid in the back of a utility, covered by a blanket, and we moved off. We had only gone a short distance when we were stopped. A Jap guard lifted a portion of blanket, shone a torch on us, then dropped the blanket. I remember thinking, what next? A grenade or a burst of machine-gun fire? But nothing happened and we started to move slowly forward, finally gaining speed, but then we came to a stop. The driver said that was the best he could do for us, so we climbed out and all seemed to head off in different directions. I realised we had stopped close to the Singapore Cricket Club and not far from the 'Adelphi Hotel', which I entered while I decided what I should do.

I was in a very large room at street level when a colonel came in. He asked me if I had any money. When I said a little, he asked would I have enough for a couple of drinks! I said I had and he replied it would probably be the last we would get for a while. As we approached the bar he asked me if my revolver was loaded. It was. He advised me to empty it, saying the Japs would probably shoot me with my own weapon when they arrived. We asked for two whiskies. The barman, a Chinese, said 'No, all finish'. The colonel called them a few choice names and then departed. I sat in a chair. All seemed hopeless and I waited for the finish. I was then startled to feel a hand on my shoulder and somebody saying 'Go to No.7 Go-down, there is a ship about to leave.' I had never heard of a No.7 Go-down and had no idea where to go but felt anything would be preferable to sitting there, brooding. I got out into the street and headed for the waterfront. I saw several men in khaki uniforms and pith helmets in the middle of the road, talking. I think they were civil defence. I asked them could they direct me to No.7 Go-down. They pointed down a street saying No.7 was the second building. When I arrived at the first building I went out on the wharf and, yes, there was a ship opposite the second building. It was then that that I saw a flash and a cloud of brown smoke, and thinking something may be coming my way, I ducked behind the building. When I got to the second building I headed for the gangway. I saw a chap in uniform dragging a kitbag. He was using a crutch and had blood oozing through the dressing on the end of a stump. He had apparently very recently lost a leg. I helped him to the gangway and got his kitbag on the platform and was about to get myself on, when someone above called out not to come aboard empty handed. There was a mountain of suitcases, packing cases, even sewing machines, on the wharf, so I grabbed a small white vanity case, the closest thing to me. I turned round only to see the gangway starting to move upwards but managed to grab hold of a chain and, with some help from the chap I had assisted, managed to sit beside him. When we got to deck level, he was taken off and probably taken to a medical section. I made my way forward, only to see crewmen holding the forward hawser across a bollard while another laid into it with an axe – there being nobody on the wharf to cast off. Maybe that was what they had in store for me. Anyhow we moved out into the outer harbour and dropped anchor. A rumour went around that we were in a minefield and were waiting for assistance.

The ship was the *Empire Star*, I believe it had accommodation for 24 persons, whereas there were over 2,000 on board including many civilians, men, women and children. The fires from Singapore were deflecting the light from a dense blanket of smoke from oil fires, which had been burning for days, and made it almost as bright as day. Some hours later we were again under way. Then, at about 1000 hours, three fighter-bombers appeared. We had been ordered to drop any firearms down the hold. The aircraft came in low, each dropping a bomb, killing many and starting a small fire which others were able to smother. The aircraft then started strafing the decks, causing havoc. Our firearms were quickly thrown up from the hold and everyone who was capable of using a rifle or machine-gun got in the act. I saw a crewman just in front of me with a machine-gun and a piece of rope, which he used to lash the weapon to a stay. As one of the aircraft approached he opened up, as did many of us. I saw him jerk forward and as he slowly slumped to the deck, it appeared that he was following the aircraft with the gun but he was dead. The three then flew off. As we watched them go we observed two big splashes. Some hours later a large load of bombs hit the water but not one struck the ship although a large wave came over the gunwale. Later I went below and the side of the ship looked more like a colander. We finally arrived at Batavia, where we hove to. We took up a collection for the ship and crew. I imagine everyone emptied their pockets in appreciation. We eventually docked and were taken to various locations. I finished up in a school playground. I heard that the Squadron was there, so tried to locate them.

I had a bad dose of 'dhobi itch', a parasite contracted through clothes being washed by the natives, and finally my crutch became red raw. I had to abandon the search, as I could no longer walk. I showed my problem to a medical orderly, who said he would try to get me something. Some time later he returned with a small bottle of neat iodine, which he administered. He went away returning with a doctor and an NCO. The doctor had one look at the problem, then said 'Sergeant, get this man on the ship'. I foolishly asked where the ship was going and he said 'What does it bloody well matter where the ship is going? You won't last long if you stay here.' I was taken down to the docks again and put aboard a smallish Dutch ship called the *Plancua* and put in a small cabin with two Scottish RAF lads. It stank. I started searching for the cause and, in a cabinet, I found a china pot with a large red rose on the side – which contained a large stool. I told the boys to open the porthole and I carefully threw it out. It landed right side up and bobbed up and down. A cheer went up and there was much laughter from the deck above. There was very little food or water. I was given a piece of French roll weighing about four ounces and told it would be my ration for the next four days. On the last evening of February, in the early hours of the morning, I realised we were under way. Then, about mid-morning, we steamed through an enormous amount of wreckage and I realised there must have been some sort of a naval battle. Later in the day we learnt the HMAS *Perth* had been lost by Japanese action. We eventually arrived at Colombo.

* * *

Sgt Harry Griffiths was soon returned to Australia, where he received his commission. Once fully recovered, he was posted to 2 OTU as a staff pilot before regaining his operational status. By the end of the war he was in command of 5 Squadron RAAF, flying Boomerangs from Bouganville in the Solomon Islands.

APPENDIX II

REFLECTIONS – GEOFF FISKEN DFC

The Buffalo
It was a real ladies plane – a beautiful plane to fly. Anybody could fly them. All the American planes were heavy – very heavy. We used to fly with our hoods open – it didn't worry us. There was no wind-blast when the hood was back in a Buffalo. It was a beautiful plane to fly in this fashion and it was always cooler. I think I was more fortunate than most because Vic Bargh and I tested every Buffalo that came off the assembly line at Seletar. We did hours and hours of it. That was the main thing, we built up more hours. We had about 150 hours in Buffaloes before the war started, so we knew what they would do and what they were like. I got a couple of trips in Hurricane Mk IIBs that 488 Squadron had in Singapore and I didn't think the Hurricane was as good as a Buffalo.

Lack of warning
The British always said that the Japs could never come in that way, from the north. They had all the guns pointing out to sea and, even after Kota Bharu fell, the hierarchy still considered it an impossibility for the Japs to come down through the jungle. Our major difficulty was trying to get some information. We very seldom got warning unless we were lucky enough to go up on a flight in the morning, and while in the air we might be told that the Japs were coming. But nine times out of ten, by the time we took off, they were over us. We never had any adequate warning when the Japs were coming. We had coast watchers in Malaya but we didn't seem to get the word quick enough, and we never had time to get the height.

Difficulties/Hazards
The jungle was dangerous. If a plane went in – and I often saw one crash when someone was shot down – you would circle it. Five minutes after, you wouldn't see where it had gone in because the rubber trees came up again. Most fellows preferred flying over the water as opposed to the jungle. In the area over which we operated it was mainly fine all the time. You'd have a huge downpour, but it was over and gone in an hour.

Japanese bombing
For their first effort they flew over Singapore at night. We were at the aerodrome that night. Everybody was standing out watching them – all the lights in Singapore were on – the whole city was alight. They just flew round and round, didn't drop a thing [*sic*], and then went home again. And everybody was saying 'Oh! we'll get those bastards'. We got a lot of bombing thereafter. Unless there was a direct hit, you were quite safe from them because Singapore was swamp and the bombs buried themselves at quite a depth. When they went off, the damage was largely contained and sometimes it didn't take long to fill the hole in. Mainly they bombed the dispersal huts and planes, but there were many dummy planes parked round the aerodrome as well, which were inadvertently targeted. The only time they did a lot of damage was when they dropped their daisy cutters – the bomb with big spike. The best result we would get from that was when they hit a coconut tree – they dropped all the coconuts!

Japanese pilots
They were very good when they first came out over Singapore – they were very, very good. Later on they would do some aerobatics – trying to coax you to come in. They would have another squadron up above them and if you didn't watch very closely that squadron got you as you were going in. If they could lure you away in ones and twos, they had you because numerically they had so many. They could certainly fly. But with

Buffaloes, if you had any height at all, you could get away from them by diving straight down, no trouble. We had the diving speed, and would hold together, whereas their planes wouldn't. We had armour plating on our Buffaloes and they had none at all. If you hit one of them they would often burst into flames. They were so very, very, light. The only really good chance we had was if we managed to come out of a cloud and they were a few hundred feet below us. We had a chance then, but apart from that, they had too many for us. The Zeros were the most difficult to combat by a long way.

Tactics

The only way we could get away was to dive as fast as we could. They wouldn't follow us down – they wouldn't follow you in a dive. There wasn't much combat at any time. Because they were so much lighter than us, and therefore more manoeuvrable, they had us beat. You would try and get as much height. Naturally the more height you had the better and safer you were. With a height advantage you could get up plenty of speed in a Buffalo, in a slight dive. The only way of getting a victory was to bash in and fire a three or four second burst and then get out of it. Otherwise there would be five or six more on your tail. Normally you had to go through their fighters to get to the bombers. They had great cover. There might have been masses of bombers but there would also be loads of fighters as well above, so the strategy was not to take any notice of the fighters – try to get through them as fast as you could. A fighter was no use to you, whereas if you knocked down a bomber, it was carrying a lot of explosives that could kill a lot of people and do a lot of damage to aerodromes, buildings etc. Normally you never worried about the fighters, unless one was sitting on your tail, of course, and then you had to get out of it. You had to be in the right position at the right time to get a plane, be it a deflection or tail shot or whatever. It was only a split second that you had and you had to take it. You would have committed suicide if you tried to dogfight with a Jap. It was an impossibility, so the only thing you could do – if you met them on even terms – was go for about a three or five second burst, and then get out of it because they wouldn't follow you down. If you didn't meet them on even terms – then you had to get out of it.

ROLL OF HONOUR

Buffalo Pilots Killed on Active Service or in Action
Singapore and Malaya

4/4/41	Flg Off J. Mansel-Lewis RAF*	243 Sqn	KoAS	*
8/10/41	Plt Off M. Irvine-Brown RAAF	453 Sqn	KoAS	W8208
13/12/41	Wg Cdr L.J. Neale RAF	OC Ipoh	KoAS	W8176
	Plt Off D.R.L. Brown RNZAF	453 Sqn	KoAS	W8158
	Sgt R.R. Oelrich RAAF	453 Sqn	KiA	W8225
14/12/41	Flt Lt A.M. White RAAF	21RAAF Sqn	KiA	AN201
18/12/41	Sgt A.G. Craig RNZAF	488 Sqn	KoAS	W8175
22/12/41	Sgt M.N. Read RAAF	453 Sqn	KiA	AN175
	Sgt E.A. Peterson RAAF	453 Sqn	KiA	W8207
	Plt Off R.W. Drury RAAF	453 Sqn	DoW	W8137
5/1/42	Plt Off R.S. Shield RNZAF	243 Sqn	KoAS	W8179
	Sgt P.L. Elliott RNZAF	243 Sqn	KoAS	W8199
12/1/42	Sgt R.J. Newman RNZAF	243 Sqn	DoW	W8189
	Sgt N.B. Rankin RNZAF	243 Sqn	KiA	W8234
13/1/42	Sgt A.R. Reynolds RNZAF	243 Sqn	KiA	W8238
15/1/42	Sgt J.B. Oliver RNZAF	243 Sqn	KiA	W8178
	Plt Off G.L. Hesketh RNZAF	488 Sqn	DoW	W8183
18/1/42	Plt Off E.W. Cox RNZAF	488 Sqn	KiA	W8141
	Sgt N.R. Chapman RAAF	21RAAF/453 Sqn	KiA	AN174
19/1/42	Plt Off K.J. McAneny RNZAF	488 Sqn	KiA	W8171
	Sgt H.W. Parsons RAAF	21RAAF/453 Sqn	KiA	AN170
22/1/42	Plt Off L.R. Farr RNZAF	488 Sqn	DoW	W8191
	Sgt M.J.F. Baldwin RAF	243 Sqn	KiA	W8187
	Sgt V. Arthur RNZAF	243 Sqn	KiA	W8147

* Killed as passenger in Blenheim that crashed
NB: Wg Cdr R.A. Chignell RAF (former OC RAF Kallang) was killed while attempting to escape from Singapore. Plt Off N.C. Sharp RNZAF, formerly with 488 Squadron, was posted missing while flying Hurricanes with 605 Squadron on 1/3/42, shortly before the fall of Java.

Buffalo Pilots who died while Prisoners of War

29/11/43	Flt Lt G.P. White RNZAF	488/605 Sqn	

(Died when PoW ship *Suez Maru* he was on was sunk by USN submarine *Bonefish* north-east of Kangean Island in the Java Sea.)

25/12/43	Wt Off C.D. Charters RNZAF	488 Sqn	

(Died from the effects of dysentry while PoW.)

NEI Brewster Pilots KoAS or KiA at Singapore/in East Indies

4/12/41	Sgt A.C. van Bers	2-V1G-V	KiFA	
19/12/41	Sgt W.E. Wessels	1-V1G-V	KiFA	
28/12/41	Lt J.N. Droog	1-V1G-V	KiA	
	Sgt G. Olsen	1-V1G-V	KiA	
15/1/42	Ens F. Swarts	2-V1G-V	KiA	B-3103
	Sgt W.J. Blans	1-V1G-V	DoW	
17/1/42	Ens W.A.T. van Buuren	3-V1G-V	KiFA	
	Ens R.J.J.W. Hoogenhuizen	3-V1G-V	KiFA	

20/1/42	Ens R.A. Rothcrans	2-VlG-V	KiA	B-3115
22/1/42	Sgt H.C. Voorn	3-VlG-V	KiFA	
24/1/42	Ens T.W. Kürz	2-VlG-V	KiA	
	Sgt T.J. de Waardt	2-VlG-V	KiA	B-3132
5/2/42	Sgt A. Berk	2-VlG-V	KiFA	
9/2/42	Sgt J. Berk	3-VlG-V	KiA	
19/2/42	Ens J. Kuijper	2-VlG-V	KiA	
	Sgt N.G. de Groot	2-VlG-V	KiA	
	Lt J.J. Tukker	3-VlG-V	KiA	
7/3/42	Kapt J.P. van Helsdingen	2-VlG-V	KiA	B-396

NEI Brewster Pilot who died while Prisoner of War
Sgt J. Scheffer   2-VlG-V

APPENDIX IV

KNOWN COMBAT CLAIMS AND CREDITS

Buffalo Pilots

Date	Pilot	Sqn	Claim	Serial
9/12/41	Flg Off H.V. Montefiore RAAF	21RAAF Sqn	Ki-27	W8236
13/12/41	Flt Lt R.D. Vanderfield RAAF	453 Sqn	2 Ki-48, Ki-51	AN185
	Sgt M.N. Read RAAF	453 Sqn	2 Ki-51	W8209
	Sgt V.A. Collyer RAAF }	453 Sqn	Ki-51	AN180
	Sgt M.N. Read RAAF	453 Sqn		W8209
	Flt Lt B.A. Grace RAAF	453 Sqn	Ki-27	W8159
	Sgt G.B. Fisken RNZAF	243 Sqn	Ki-48 probable	W8147
14/12/41	Sgt G.R. Board RAAF	453 Sqn	Ki-51	
15/12/41	Sgt G.R. Board RAAF }	453 Sqn	Ki-48	
	Sgt M.D. O'Mara RAAF	453 Sqn		
21/12/41	Sgt E.A. Peterson RAAF	453 Sqn	Ki-51, 2 Ki-51 probable	W8207
22/12/41	Sgt A.W.B. Clare RAAF	453 Sqn	Ki-51, Ki-51 probable, Ki-48 probable	
	Sgt M.N. Read RAAF	453 Sqn	Ki-43 (by collision)	AN175
	Sgt H.H. Griffiths RAAF	453 Sqn	2 Ki-27	W8231
	Sgt G.R. Board RAAF	453 Sqn	Ki-48	W8170
	Flt Lt R.D. Vanderfield RAAF	453 Sqn	Ki-27 probable, Ki-43 probable	AN210
	Sgt K. Gorringe RAAF	453 Sqn	Ki-27 probable	
	Sgt V.A. Collyer RAAF	453 Sqn	Ki-43 probable	AN180
	Sgt S.G. Scrimgeour RAAF	453 Sqn	Ki-27 probable	W8160
10/1/42	Sgt B.S. Wipiti RNZAF }	243 Sqn	Ki-46	
	Sgt C.T. Kronk RNZAF	243 Sqn		WP-A
12/1/42	Flt Lt M. Garden RAF	243 Sqn	2 Ki-27, Ki-27 probable	W8139
	Flg Off M.H. Holder RAF	243 Sqn	2 Ki-27	
	Sgt G.B. Fisken RNZAF	243 Sqn	Ki-27	W8147
	Plt Off N.C. Sharp RNZAF	243 Sqn	Ki-27 probable	W8138
	Plt Off G.L. Bonham RNZAF	243 Sqn	G3M, G3M probable	WP-F
	Sgt A.R. Reynolds RNZAF	243 Sqn	2 Ki-27 probable	W8238
	Sgt W.J.M. MacIntosh RNZAF	488 Sqn	Ki-27 probable	W8171
13/1/42	Flt Lt M. Garden RAF	243 Sqn	Ki-27	W8242
	Plt Off N.C. Sharp RNZAF	243 Sqn	Ki-27	W8138
	Plt Off E.A. Pevreal RNZAF }	243 Sqn	Ki-43 probable	W8184
	Sgt C.T. Kronk RNZAF	243 Sqn		W8139
	Plt Off W.J. Greenhalgh RNZAF	488 Sqn	G3M probable	W8168
14/1/42	Sgt G.B. Fisken RNZAF	243 Sqn	A6M probable (confirmed)	W8147
	Sgt P.E.E. Killick RNZAF	488 Sqn	Ki-46 probable	
15/1/42	Plt Off T.B. Marra RNZAF	243 Sqn	Ki-27	W8143
	Flt Lt M. Garden RAF }	243 Sqn	A6M probable (crashed)	W8242
	Sgt R.A. Weber RNZAF	243 Sqn		W8139
	Sgt E.E.G. Kuhn RNZAF	488 Sqn	Ki-27	

Date	Pilot	Squadron	Claim	Serial
	Sgt D.L. Clow RNZAF	488 Sqn		W8235
	Sgt W.J.N. MacIntosh RNZAF	488 Sqn	Ki-27	W8171
	Sgt H.J. Meharry RNZAF	488 Sqn		
	Flt Lt R.D. Vanderfield RAAF	21RAAF/453 Sqn	Ki-48	TD-O
	Flt Lt J.R. Kinninmont RAAF	21RAAF/453 Sqn	Ki-48	W8157
	Plt Off F. Leigh Bowes RAAF	21RAAF/453 Sqn	Ki-48 probable	
16/1/42	Sqn Ldr F.J. Howell RAF	243 Sqn	C5M	W8193
	Sgt C.T. Kronk RNZAF	243 Sqn	Ki-43 probable	WP-A
17/1/42	Flg Off M.H. Holder RAF	243 Sqn	Ki-48, Ki-48 probable	
	Sgt G.B. Fisken RNZAF	243 Sqn	Ki-48	W8147
	Flg Off M.H. Holder RAF	243 Sqn	2 Ki-48	
	Sgt G.B. Fisken RNZAF	243 Sqn		W8147
	Sgt A.W.B. Clare RAAF	21RAAF/453 Sqn	Ki-27	
	Flt Lt R.D. Vanderfield RAAF	21RAAF/453 Sqn	A6M	TD-O
	Sgt A.W.B. Clare RAAF	21RAAF/453 Sqn		
	Flt Lt R.D. Vanderfield RAAF	21RAAF/453 Sqn	Ki-27	TD-O
	Flt Lt B.A. Grace RAAF	21RAAF/453 Sqn		
18/1/42	Flg Off D.M. Sproule RAAF	21RAAF/453 Sqn	Ki-27	
	Sgt H.W. Parsons RAAF	21RAAF/453 Sqn	Ki-43 probable	
	Plt Off N.C. Sharp RNZAF	243 Sqn	A6M	W8138
	Sgt M.J.F. Baldwin RAF	243 Sqn	A6M	W8187
	Sgt V. Arthur RNZAF	243 Sqn	A6M probable	
	Sgt C.T. Kronk RNZAF	243 Sqn	A6M probable	W8242
	Plt Off T.B. Marra RNZAF	243 Sqn	'Messerschmitt 109' probable	W8143
	Plt Off E.A. Pevreal RNZAF	243 Sqn	Ki-48 probable	WP-E
	Sgt E.E.G. Kuhn RNZAF	488 Sqn	2 A6M	
	Sgt P.E.E. Killick RNZAF	488 Sqn	A6M	
	Flt Lt J.R. Hutcheson RNZAF	488 Sqn	A6M	W8177
	Sgt V.E. Meaclem RNZAF	488 Sqn	A6M probable	W8158
	Sgt W.J.N. MacIntosh RNZAF	488 Sqn	2 A6M probable	W8198
19/1/42	Flt Lt J.R. Kinninmont RAAF	21RAAF/453 Sqn	Ki-51, Ki-43	W8157
	Flt Lt J. Kirkman RAAF	21RAAF/453 Sqn	Ki-51, A6M probable	
	Flt Lt R.D. Vanderfield RAAF	21RAAF/453 Sqn	Ki-51	
	Sgt K. Gorringe RAAF	21RAAF/453 Sqn	Ki-51	
20/1/42	Sgt C.T. Kronk RNZAF	243 Sqn	Ki-48	W8184
	Plt Off N.C. Sharp RNZAF	243 Sqn	Ki-48	W8162
21/1/42	Sgt B.S. Wipiti RNZAF	243 Sqn	A6M	W8147
	Sgt M.J.F. Baldwin RAF	243 Sqn	G4M	
	Sgt G.B. Fisken RNZAF	243 Sqn	A6M	W8147
	Sgt C.T. Kronk RNZAF	243 Sqn	A6M probable	W8242
22/1/42	Sgt B.S. Wipiti RNZAF	243 Sqn	2 G3M	
25/1/42	Sgt M.A. Greenslade RNZAF	243 Sqn	G3M probable	WP-H
26/1/42	Flt Lt M. Garden RAF	243 Sqn	Ki-27	
	Sgt B.S. Wipiti RNZAF	243 Sqn	Ki-27	
	Plt Off J.M. Cranstone RNZAF	243 Sqn	A6M	W8226
	Flt Lt B.A. Grace RAAF	21RAAF/453 Sqn	Ki-27	
	Flg Off G.M. Sheppard RAAF	21RAAF/453 Sqn	Ki-27	
	Sgt K. Ross Leys RAAF	21RAAF/453 Sqn	Ki-27	
29/1/42	Sgt K. Gorringe RAAF	453 Sqn	G3M probable	
1/2/42	Sgt G.B. Fisken RNZAF	453 Sqn	'Messerschmitt 109' A6M probable	W8237

NB: In addition, during a photo-recce sortie in W8136 – probably on 9 December 1941 – Sgt

C.B. Wareham RNZAF of 4PRU believed that a pursuing Japanese fighter may have crashed while attempting to follow the Buffalo's evasive action. He was credited with a victory.

NEI Brewster Pilots

Date	Pilot	Unit	Aircraft	Serial
28/12/41	Unknown pilots	1-V1G-V	2 A6M	
12/1/42	Lt A.G. Deibel	2-V1G-V	2 Ki-27	B-3110
	Kapt J.P. van Helsdingen	2-V1G-V	Ki-27	B-396
	Sgt G.M. Bruggink	2-V1G-V	Ki-27	
1/42	Kapt A.A.M. van Rest	1-V1G-V	floatplane	
24/1/42	Kapt A.A.M. van Rest	1-V1G-V	A6M	
	Lt P. Benjamins	1-V1G-V	A6M	
19/2/42 ?	Kapt J.P. van Hesldingen	2-V1G-V	A6M	
?	Sgt G.M. Bruggink	2-V1G-V	A6M	
21/2/42	Lt H.H.J. Simons	3-V1G-V	Ki-43	
	Sgt J.P. Adam	3-V1G-V	Ki-43 (by collision)	
1/3/43 ?	Kapt J.P. van Helsdingen	2-V1G-V	Ki-43	
7/3/42	Lt A.G. Deibel	2-V1G-V	Ki-43	

According to Dutch sources, the following victories were credited:

Pilot	Unit	Claims
Kapt J.P. van Helsdingen	2-V1G-V	3 claims
Lt A.G. Deibel	2-V1G-V	3 claims
Sgt G.M. Bruggink	2-V1G-V	2 claims
Kapt A.M.M. van Rest	1-V1G-V	2 claims

APPENDIX V

BUFFALOES ISSUED TO RAF FAR EAST COMMAND

Singapore

There may be discrepancies

W8134 243 Sqn WP-M: written off after undercarriage failed on landing Kallang 16/8/41.

W8135 67 & 488 Sqns: engine seized, Sgt V.E. Meaclem RNZAF baled out unhurt 12/1/42.

W8136 67 & 243 Sqns; 4 PRU: fitted with single camera, crashed on landing Bandoeng 7/2/42, Sqn Ldr C.R.G. Lewis slightly injured.

W8137 243 Sqn WP-C: ground looped, damaged 5/11/41, Sgt R.A. Weber RNZAF unhurt; crash-landed after action 12/1/42, Sgt R.J. Newman RNZAF died of wounds.

W8138 67 & 488 Sqns NF-O: Plt Off N.C. Sharp's usual aircraft; damaged in combat 18/1/42, Plt Off N.C. Sharp RNZAF unhurt; flown to Palembang 7/2/42; destroyed in bombing raid 7/2/42.

W8139 243 Sqn WP-B; damaged in combat 12/1/42, Flt Lt M. Garden RAF unhurt; damaged in combat 13/1/42, Sgt C.T. Kronk RNZAF unhurt.

W8140 243 Sqn: used for gun-firing training, first to exceed 200 hours.

W8141 67 & 488 Sqns: damaged in combat 12/1/42, Plt Off H.S. Pettit RNZAF wounded; shot down 18/1/42, Plt Off E.W. Cox RNZAF KiA.

W8142 243 Sqn WP-N: to 453 Sqn 26/1/42.

W8143 67 Sqn RD-B: crashed on landing Kallang 13/8/41, Sgt C. McDonald RNZAF unhurt; repaired, to 243 Sqn converted to night fighter 'Black Bess'; damaged in combat 18/1/42, Plt Off T.B. Marra RNZAF unhurt.

W8144 67 Sqn RD-C: crashed attempting night landing 19/9/41, Sgt E.E. Pedersen RNZAF unhurt.

W8145 243 Sqn: badly damaged in combat 18/1/42.

W8146 67 Sqn RD-D: engine failure, wheels-up forced landing Kallang 21/6/41, Sgt C.V. Bargh RNZAF unhurt.

W8147 243 Sqn WP-O: Sgt G.B Fisken's usual aircraft; damaged in combat 12/1/42, Sgt G.B. Fisken RNZAF unhurt; damaged in combat 14/1/42, Sgt G.B. Fisken RNZAF unhurt; damaged in combat 17/1/42, Plt Off G.L. Bonham RNZAF unhurt; shot down 22/1/42, Sgt V. Arthur RNZAF killed.

W8148 67 & 488 Sqns NF-J: believe NF-J: force-landed after combat 13/1/42, Flt Lt J.R. Hutcheson RNZAF unhurt.

W8149 243 Sqn: skidded into irrigation ditch Kallang 8/4/41, Plt Off E.A. Pevreal RNZAF unhurt.

W8150 67 Sqn RD-E, 488 Sqn NF-I: crashed Sembawang after combat 12/1/42, Plt Off K.J. McAneny RNZAF unhurt.

W8151 453 Sqn: TD-C engine failed on take-off, crashed into dispersal 9/12/41 DBR, Sgt V.A. Collyer RAAF unhurt.

W8152 453 Sqn TD-F: shot down 13/12/41 Butterworth, Plt Off G.L. Angus RAAF wounded in leg.

W8153 67 & 488 Sqns: undercarriage failed, belly landed 3/6/41; to 488 Sqn, hit concrete parapet on landing 14/11/41 DBR, Flt Lt J.R. Hutcheson RNZAF unhurt.

W8154 243 Sqn: crashed in landing accident Kallang 14/11/41, Plt Off G.L. Bonham RNZAF unhurt.

W8155 243 Sqn: DBR in bombing raid 27/1/42.

W8156 67 & 243 Sqns: engine failed, force-landed 8/8/41; to 453 Sqn: returned to Singapore from Kuala Lumpur 23/12/41; destroyed in bombing raid 27/1/42.

W8157 453 Sqn: damaged in combat 15/1/42, Flt Lt J.R. Kinninmont RAAF unhurt; damaged by enemy shell while taxiing 5/2/42, Plt Off F.S. Johnstone RNZAF unhurt.

W8158 453 Sqn TD-N: crashed Sumatra 13/12/41, Plt Off D.R.L. Brown RNZAF killed.

W8159 453 Sqn.

W8160 453 Sqn: shot down 22/12/41, Sgt S.G. Scrimgeour RAAF baled out, burned.

W8161 67 Sqn: mid-air collision with Blenheim, crash-landed 23/9/41, Flg Off J.S. Wigglesworth RAF unhurt.

W8162 243 Sqn: stalled during slow approach with gun ports open 14/11/41; damaged in combat 20/1/42, Plt Off N.C. Sharp RNZAF unhurt.

W8163 21RAAF Sqn GA-P: returned to Singapore from Kuala Lumpur 23/12/41; to NEI 2/42, captured by Japanese at Andir.

W8164 243 Sqn: damaged in crash-landing 14/11/41 Plt Off G.L. Bonham RNZAF unhurt; damaged in combat 18/1/42, Plt Off G.L. Bonham RNZAF wounded.

W8165 21RAAF Sqn.

W8166 4 PRU: Fitted with three cameras, destroyed in shelling Kallang 6/2/42.

W8167 453 Sqn.

W8168 67 Sqn: crashed on landing 16/8/41, Flg Off J.F. Lambert RAF unhurt; repaired, to 488 Sqn NF-T; slightly damaged in combat 20/1/42, Plt Off F.W.J. Oakden RNZAF unhurt.

W8169 21RAAF Sqn.

W8l70 21RAAF Sqn: shot down 22/12/42, Sgt G.R. Board RAAF baled out unhurt.

W8171 488 Sqn: shot down 19/1/42, Plt Off K.J. McAneny RNZAF KiA.

W8172 Possibly 21RAAF Sqn.

W8173 67 & 488 Sqns: slightly damaged in combat 17/1/42, Plt Off P.D. Gifford RNZAF unhurt; rendered unserviceable following power dive 20/1/42, Plt Off P.D. Gifford RNZAF unhurt; possibly flown to Palembang 2/42.

W8174 488 Sqn: destroyed by bomb splinters Kallang 22/1/42.

W8l75 67 & 488 Sqns: crashed into tree 18/12/41, Sgt A.G. Craig RNZAF killed.

W8176 453 Sqn: crashed Sumatra 13/12/41, Wg Cdr L.J. Neale RAF killed.

W8177 67 & 488 Sqns: crashed after combat 18/1/42, Flt Lt J.R. Hutcheson RNZAF unhurt.

W8178 243 Sqn WP-Y/'Marie': Sgt V. Arthur's usual aircraft; shot down 15/1/42, Sgt J.B. Oliver RNZAF KiA.

W8179 243 Sqn: collided during take-off with W8199 5/1/42, Plt Off R.S. Shield RNZAF killed.

W8180 453 Sqn: force-landed Sumatra 13/12/41, Plt Off T.W. Livesey RAAF injured.

W8181 243 Sqn WP-P: undercarriage collapsed on landing 18/8/41, Sgt A.J. Lawrence RNZAF unhurt; to 488 Sqn then 453 Sqn; flown to Palembang 9/2/42.

W8182 243 Sqn: engine failed, ditched off Singapore 22/7/41, Plt Off F.W.J. Oakden RNZAF unhurt.

W8183 67 & 488 Sqns: shot down and crash-landed 15/1/42, Plt Off G.L. Hesketh RNZAF died of wounds.

W8184 243 Sqn WP-G: collided with Tiger Moth 7/11/41, Sgt A.R. Reynolds RNZAF unhurt; shot down 23/1/42, Sgt M.A. Greenslade RNZAF baled out.

W8185 67 Sqn & 488 Sqn NF-V: ditched after engagement with G3M 13/1/42, Plt Off F.W.J. Oakden RNZAF unhurt.

W8186 67 & 488 Sqns NF-X: shot down 12/1/42, Sgt R.W. MacMillan RNZAF baled out.

W8187 243 Sqn WP-R: damaged in combat 12/1/42, Sgt M.J.F. Baldwin RAF unhurt; shot down 22/1/42, Sgt M.J.F. Baldwin RAF KiA.

W8188 453 Sqn: undercarriage collapsed 12/9/41 DBR, Sgt A.W.B. Clare RAAF unhurt.

W8189 243 Sqn WP-Q: engine failed, overshot Kallang into sea 25/11/41.

W8190 67 Sqn RD-F: hit obstruction landing Seletar 8/9/41, Sgt E.E. Pedersen RNZAF unhurt.

W8191 67 Sqn RD-H & 488 Sqn NF-D: damaged in combat 12/1/42, Plt Off G.P. White RNZAF unhurt; hit by bomb shrapnel on take-off 25/1/42, Plt Off L.R. Farr RNZAF died of wounds.

W8192 453 Sqn: damaged in combat and force-landed 13/12/41, Sgt M.D. O'Mara RAAF unhurt.

W8193   67 & 243 Sqns WP-V: Sqn Ldr F.J. Howell's usual aircraft; damaged in combat 12/1/42, Flt Lt M. Garden unhurt.

W8194   243 Sqn: undershot Kallang, into canal 12/5/41, Sgt A.P. Saul RNZAF unhurt.

W8195   67 & 488 Sqns: engine failed 17/1/42, Plt Off F.S. Johnstone RNZAF baled out.

W8196   453 Sqn.

W8197   453 Sqn: engine failed, forced-landed 18/9/41 DBR, Sgt H.H. Griffiths RAAF unhurt.

W8198   67 Sqn & 488 Sqn NF-U: destroyed by bomb splinters Kallang 22/1/42.

W8199   243 Sqn WP-S: collided on landing with W8179 5/1/42, Sgt P.L. Elliott RNZAF killed.

W8200   67 & 488 Sqns: collided with Moth 30/12/41, Sgt W.R. De Maus RNZAF unhurt; shot down 12/1/42, Sgt T.W. Honan RNZAF baled out wounded.

W8201   243 Sqn: believed damaged in combat 18/1/42, Plt Off N.C. Sharp RNZAF unhurt.

W8202   453 Sqn: wheels-up landing Sembawang 27/8/41, Plt Off F. Leigh Bowes RAAF unhurt; to 21RAAF/453 Sqn collided with AN171 and force-landed, Sgt G.T. Harrison RAAF unhurt.

W8205   453 Sqn TD-H: possibly flown to Palembang 2/42.

W8206   21RAAF Sqn & 453 Sqns: shot down 21/12/41, Sgt K.R. Leys RAAF baled out.

W8207   453 Sqn: shot down 22/12/41, Sgt E.A. Peterson RAAF KiA.

W8208   453 Sqn: crashed attempting forced-landing 8/10/41, Plt Off M. Irvine-Brown RAAF killed.

W8209   453 Sqn TD-E: damaged in combat 13/12/41, Sgt M.N. Read RAAF unhurt; taxied into crater Kluang 8/1/42 written off.

W8210   453 Sqn: collided on ground with Dutch Martin 139, Sembawang 9/12/41, Sgt E.A. Peterson RAAF unhurt.

W8211   453 Sqn: damaged in combat 14/12/41, Sgt G.E.G. Seagoe RAAF wounded; damaged landing Ipoh 18/12/41, Sgt V.A. Collyer RAAF unhurt.

W8212   21RAAF Sqn.

W8214   21RAAF Sqn: caught fire 26/9/41, Fg Off R.H. Wallace RAAF baled out.

W8216   453 Sqn: crashed on take-off Ipoh 18/12/41, Sgt G.R. Board RAAF unhurt.

W8217   453 Sqn TD-B: hit unmarked bomb crater on landing at Ipoh 13/12/41 DBR, Plt Off F. Leigh Bowes RAAF unhurt.

W8219   21RAAF/453 Sqn: taxied into car Kluang 10/1/42 DBR, Sgt G.R. Board RAAF unhurt.

W8221   243 Sqn WP-X: damaged in combat and one-wheel landing 17/1/42, Plt Off J.M. Cranstone RNZAF unhurt; damaged in combat 25/1/42, Plt Off P.D. Gifford RNZAF unhurt; to 453 Sqn flown to Palembang 9/2/42.

W8222   21RAAF Sqn: damaged beyond repair Sungei Patani 8/12/41.

W8223   67 & 488 Sqn 'Pettit's Pride', Plt Off H.S. Pettit's usual aircraft; engine failed crash-landed 4/1/42, Plt Off J.C. Godsiff RNZAF injured.

W8224   21RAAF Sqn: shot down 9/12/41, Flg Off C.R. McKenny RAAF, baled out burned.

W8225   453 Sqn: shot down 13/12/41, Sgt R.R. Oelrich RAAF KiA.

W8226   453 Sqn: overshot landing 5/11/41, Sgt K. Gorringe RAAF unhurt; repaired, to 243 Sqn: attacked by Hurricane 31/1/42 crash-landed Tengah, Sgt C.T. Kronk RNZAF unhurt.

W8227   21RAAF Sqn.

W8230   151 MU: undercarriage collapsed 24/12/41 on test flight.

W8231   453 Sqn TD-G/'Shirley': Sgt H.H. Grifflths' usual aircraft, damaged in combat 22/12/41, Sgt Griffiths unhurt; to 243 Sqn, converted to night fighter 'Black Magic'; damaged in combat 13/1/42, Plt Off T.B. Marra RNZAF unhurt.

W8232   21RAAF Sqn: force-landed following combat 9/12/41, then destroyed on ground, Flt Lt F.H. Williams RAAF unhurt.

W8234   243 Sqn: Flt Lt R. Bow's usual aircraft; shot down 12/1/42, Sgt N.B. Rankin RNZAF KiA.

W8235   67 & 488 Sqns: damaged in combat 13/1/42, Sgt D.L. Clow RNZAF baled out.

W8236   21RAAF Sqn: shot down 9/12/41, Flg Off H.V. Montefiore RAAF baled out, unhurt.
W8237   453 Sqn: returned to Singapore from Kuala Lumpur 23/12/41; damaged in combat 1/2/42, Sgt G.B. Fisken RNZAF wounded; believed flown to Palembang 2/42.
W8238   243 Sqn: shot down 13/1/42, Sgt A.R. Reynolds RNZAF KiA.
W8242   243 Sqn WP-K: tailwheel shot off in combat, Sgt C.T. Kronk RNZAF unhurt; to 453 Sqn – flown to Palembang 9/2/42.
AN170   21RAAF/453 Sqn: shot down 19/1/42, Sgt H.W. Parsons RAAF KiA.
AN171   21RAAF/453 Sqn: collided with W8202 and ditched, Fg Off R.H. Wallace RAAF rescued.
AN172   21RAAF Sqn: overshot and overturned on landing Port Swettenham 15/12/41, Flt Lt J.R. Kinninmont RAAF unhurt.
AN173   21RAAF/453 Sqn: destroyed in bombing raid Sembawang 17/1/42.
AN174   21RAAF/453 Sqn: shot down 18/1/42, Sgt N.R. Chapman RAAF KiA.
AN175   21RAAF & 453 Sqns: collided with Ki-43 22/12/42, Sgt M.N. Read RAAF KiA.
AN176   1RAAF, 21RAAF/453 & 453 Sqns: flown to Palembang 9/2/42.
AN178   21RAAF/453 Sqn.
AN179   21RAAF Sqn.
AN180   21RAAF Sqn GA-B, 453 & 21RAAF/453 Sqns: returned to Singapore from Kuala Lumpur 23/12/41.
AN181   21RAAF Sqn.
AN183   21RAAF Sqn.
AN184   21RAAF & 453 Sqns crash-landed Kuala Lumpur 22/12/41, Plt Off T.W. Livesey RAAF wounded.
AN185   453 Sqn TD-V: Flt Lt R.D. Vanderfield's usual aircraft; damaged on landing 9/1/42, Flt Lt Vanderfield RAAF unhurt.
AN186   21RAAF Sqn.
AN187   243 & 488 Sqns: engine fire 13/1/42, Sgt E.E.G. Kuhn RNZAF baled out.
AN188   21RAAF Sqn: shot down and force-landed Penang 9/12/41, Flt Lt A.M. White RAAF unhurt.
AN189   21RAAF, 453 & 488 Sqns: damaged in combat 22/12/41, Sgt V.A. Collyer wounded; shot down 19/1/42, Sgt C.D. Charters RNZAF PoW.
AN194   21RAAF Sqn GA-D: captured by Japanese Northern Malaya 12/41.
AN195   21RAAF/453 & 453 Sqns.
AN196   243 Sqn WP-W: possibly captured by Japanese at Kota Bharu 12/41.
AN197   243 Sqn: crash-landed Pulau Bukum 3/1/42, Sgt C.F. Powell RAAF injured.
AN198   67 & 488 Sqns: crash-landed 24/11/41 DBR, Sgt E.E.G. Kuhn RNZAF unhurt.
AN199   67 Sqn & Kallang Station Flight: stalled making forced-landing 11/11/41 DBR, Plt Off E.W. Cox RNZAF unhurt.
AN201   21RAAF Sqn: shot down 14/12/41, Flt Lt A.M. White RAAF KiA.
AN203   21RAAF/453 & 453 Sqns.
AN204   453 Sqn: shot down and crash-landed 22/12/41, Plt Off R.W. Drury RAAF died of wounds.
AN205   21RAAF Sqn & 453 Sqn: believed force-landed Bintan Island 30/1/42, Sgt M.D. O'Mara RAAF rescued.
AN206   21RAAF, 453 & 21RAAF/453 Sqns: returned to Singapore from Kuala Lumpur 23/12/41.
AN207   21RAAF/453 & 453 Sqns.
AN208   21RAAF/453 & 453 Sqns.
AN209   21RAAF/453 & 453 Sqns: flown to Palembang 6/2/42; damaged in bombing raid 6/2/42; repaired and flown to Batavia 10/2/42; DBR in strafing attack.
AN210   453 Sqn TD-J: returned to Singapore from Kuala Lumpur 23/12/41.
AN211   21RAAF/453 Sqn: crashed in forced-landing on Pulau Koenboer 3/1/42, Sgt H.H. Griffiths RAAF injured.
AN212   21RAAF & 21RAAF/453 Sqns.
AN2I3   453 Sqn: shot down 13/12/41, Flt Lt T.A. Vigors RAF baled out injured.

AN215   453 & 21RAAF/453 Sqns: returned to Singapore from Kuala Lumpur 23/12/41;
         destroyed in bombing raid Sembawang 17/1/42.

Buffaloes issued to RAF Far East Command Burma

67 Squadron W8203, W8204, W8213, W8215, W8218 (probable), W8220, W8228, W8229, W8233, W8239, W8240, W8241 (PR aircraft), W8243/RD-B, W8244-W8250 (all previous seven ex-60 Sqn), AN168, AN169, AN182; AN190-AN193 (all previous seven ex-60 Sqn), AN200, AN202, AN214, AN216 and AN217.

CHAPTER FOOTNOTES

PREAMBLE
The Drift to War
1/2 See *Japan Must Fight Britain* by Lt Cdr Tota Ishimaru.
3 The Commonwealth Aircraft Corporation's Wirraway (an Australian aboriginal word meaning 'challenge') was based upon the North American NA-33 (known as the Harvard in the RAF). The first mass-produced indigenous Australian aircraft, the main reason for this design to be selected was that both airframe and engine were comparatively simple for Australia's embryonic aircraft industry to produce. The prototype first flew in March 1939 and proved disappointing as far as performance was concerned: top speed at 8,600 feet was 220mph, with a maximum climb rate of 1,950 feet per minute. Initially intended as a fighter-bomber, it was regarded as no more than an advanced trainer when it came into service with the RAAF.
4/5 See *The Burning Blue* by Paul Addison and Jeremy A. Crang.
6 See *The War in Malaya* by Lt General A.E. Percival.

CHAPTER I
Buffaloes are Good Enough for Singapore
7 See *The War in Malaya*.
8 Close inspection of the superb A6M had been possible when one was shot down by AA fire during a strafing attack on Taipingssu and Shuanglin airfields near Chengtu by the 12th Kokutai in May 1941. Details of its armament and tankage reached Singapore and were passed to Air Headquarters and the Air Ministry in London. Later, the British Air Attaché in Chungking forwarded estimated performance figures, which proved to be reasonably accurate. This data was also transmitted to Singapore and London, but lack of intelligence staff at Singapore resulted in the details being overlooked or discarded.
9 See *Wings over Burma* by J. Helsdon Thomas.
10 Flg Off John Mansel-Lewis had been credited with two victories during the Battle of Britain. Prior to that, in June 1940, he had participated in a disastrous attempt to ferry Hurricanes to Malta, during the course of which he ditched his aircraft in the Mediterranean in a vain effort to assist the crew of a Blenheim that had crashed into the sea, an unselfish performance that had gone unrecognised.
11 Just prior to the outbreak of war, the population of Malaya including Singapore was estimated to be in the region of five and a quarter million, of whom four and a half million were Chinese and Malays; Europeans totalled just over 28,000 and there were almost 8,000 Japanese resident in Malaya. In excess of half a million civilians lived on Singapore Island, of whom about 8,000 were Europeans, while 75 per cent were Chinese. With the influx of British and Commonwealth troops, Singapore soon became known to the majority, rather irreverently, as the place of "Chinks, drinks and stinks"; and to others as "a first-class place for second-rate people", a snide reference to the local European population.
12 Air Chief Marshal Sir Robert Brooke-Popham was a former Inspector General of the RAF and more recently Governor of Kenya.
13 Flying Hurricanes with 17 Squadron, Sqn Ldr Harper had been credited with one plus three shared victories during the 1940 fighting in defence of Britain, with probably two more claimed as damaged – hence the six victory markings shown on his aircraft.
14 See *Everything but the Flak* by Martin Caidin.
15 Sqn Ldr Wilf Clouston had been credited with 12 victories of which three were shared.
16 Flt Lt Jack Mackenzie, a grandson of former New Zealand Prime Minister Sir Thomas Mackenzie, was credited with six victories.
17 See *New Zealanders with the Royal Air Force* by Wg Cdr H.L. Thompson.
18/19 See *Malayan Postscript* by Ian Morrison.
20 See *The War in Malaya*.
21-27 See *Suez to Singapore* by Cecil Brown.
26 See *Retreat in the East* by O'Dowd Gallagher.
28 See *Singapore: The Japanese Version* by Masanobu Tsuji.

29/31 See *War Without Glory* by J.D. Balfe.

30 See *The Tattered Eagle* by Geoffrey Rex Collis.

32/33 See *Zero Fighter* by Martin Caidin.

34 See *The Zero Fighter* by M. Okumiya and J. Horikoshi.

35 Sqn Ldr Frank Howell had fought with 609 Squadron during the Battle of Britain and later commanded 118 Squadron and had about 10 victories to his credit.

CHAPTER II
Invasion

36 See *Singapore: The Japanese Version.*

37 See *War Illustrated.*

38 See *Singapore: The Inexcusable Betrayal* by George Chippington.

39/40/42 See *The Tattered Eagle.*

41 See *War Without Glory.*

43 See *War in Malaya.*

44-46 See *War Without Glory.* When Flg Off Barrie Hood and 21RAAF Squadron's Engineer Officer, Wt Off Fred Bernau, reached Penang by ferry two days later to inspect AN188, it was found to be extensively damaged and not repairable. Parts were salvaged and the remainder burnt.

47 See *Everything but the Flak.*

CHAPTER III
The Loss of the Capital Ships

48 See *Bloody Shambles Volume One* for more detail.

49 See *Aussie Air Stories II* by Fred Morton.

50 See *Everything but the Flak.*

51 See *Scramble to Victory* by Norman Franks.

52 See *The Zero Fighter.*

CHAPTER IV
Amok in Malaya – Buffaloes Overwhelmed

53 See *Shenton of Singapore* by Brian Montgomery.

54 See *Suez to Singapore.*

55 An entry in Fighter HQ Operations Diary for 12 December 1941 states: "Telecon with IO NORGROUP who was tasked to go to Penang and speak with a German pilot. No sign of him – appears that report was due to the confusion with Capt Heenan who speaks fluent German." Capt Patrick Heenan, of Irish stock, was Air Liaison Officer at Alor Star. He had been arrested on 10 December for spying on behalf of the Japanese. Taken to Singapore, he was evidently shot as a traitor on the eve of the capitulation (see also *Odd Man Out* by Peter Elphick and Michael Smith). In his book, *Singapore: The Pregnable Fortress*, Peter Elphick provides substance to the stories of German officers serving with the Japanese Army and German pilots flying with the Japanese Army Air Force. It is suggested that these officers were German nationals who had formerly served with the French Foreign Legion's 5th Regiment based in Indo-China.

56/57 See *The Tattered Eagle.*

58 See *War Without Glory.*

59 Based upon an article by Bob Piper in *RAAF News* April 1983.

60/61 See *Zero Fighter.*

62 The other 453 Squadron Buffaloes were flown by Plt Off Drury (W8156), Sgt Peterson (W8237), Sgt Gorringe (AN210), Sgt Clare (AN180) and Sgt Griffiths (W8157).

63 On 16 December, JAAF HQ announced that a total of 53 aircraft had been lost to all causes on operations (including accidents and bad weather), since the start of hostilities against Malaya. This total included 15 Ki-21s, 11 Ki-27s, ten Ki-43s, five Ki-48s, two Ki-46 twin-engined strategic reconnaissance aircraft, and ten various army co-operation, light bomber and tactical reconnaissance types. JAAF HQ also announced that during the period 10 to 14

December, the 12th Flying Battalion, comprising the 1st and 11th Sentais with Ki-27s, and the 81st Sentai with Ki-15s and Ki-46s, had made a number of airfield attacks in the Penang, Butterworth and Sungei Patani areas, claiming 28 aircraft on the ground, but losing three of its own, with one more badly damaged (included in the above totals).

64 The reference to 'Schmitt der Spy' presumably reflected the continuing rumours centred on Capt Heenan (see *Odd Man Out*).

65 See *Everything but the Flak*.

66-68 See *Aussie Air Stories II*.

69 Based upon an article by Bob Piper in *RAAF News* April 1983.

70 See *Tsubasa No Kessen* (*Wings of Bloody Combat*) by Yohei Hinoki.

71/72 See *Everything but the Flak*.

73 See *Aussie Air Stories II*.

74 Apparently Sgt Alf Clare (later Sqn Ldr) sent the pilot's personal effects back to Japan for delivery to his widow.

75 See *Singapore: The Pregnable Fortress*.

76 See *Glory in Chaos*.

CHAPTER V
All Quiet on the Singapore Front

77 See *Zero Fighter*.

78 See *War in Malaya*.

79 See *Everything but the Flak*.

80 See *Malayan Postscript*.

81 See *Scramble to Victory*.

82-85 See *Suez to Singapore*.

CHAPTER VI
Singapore – The Calm Before the Blitz

86 See *Suez to Singapore*.

87/88 See *Singapore is Silent* by George Weller.

CHAPTER VII
The January Blitz

89 See *Scramble to Victory*.

90 See *Royal Australian Air Force 1939-42*.

91 In 1962, the wreck of W8202 was discovered some 600 yards from the river bank, in dense jungle. Despite years of exposure, it was in a remarkably good state of preservation. The tail had been twisted and torn on impact, and the port wing, still attached to the fuselage, was buried in a swamp. The guns held 400 rounds of ammunition and the aircraft still had hydraulic pressure and a full oxygen tank. An RAF party from 390 MU, after inspecting the remains, took the guns and ammunition to Seletar.

92 See *Aussie Air Stories II*.

93 Grp Capt F.G. Watts, the Station Commander at Tengah, committed suicide by shooting himself in his office on the evening of 4 February 1942; he blamed himself for the failure of his men to prepare Hurricanes in time for a dawn sweep that morning.

94 See *Malayan Postscript*.

95 See *Suez to Singapore*.

96/97 See *Singapore is Silent*.

98 See *Epics of the Fighting RAF* by Leonard Gribble.

99/100 *See Singapore Slip* by Herbert Plenty DFC.

101 See *Royal Australian Air Force 1939-42*.

102/104 See *Suez to Singapore*.

103 See *Malayan Postscript*.

105 In 2000, Perce Killick received a phone call from the New Zealand Red Cross: "A woman said we have some visitors from Japan that want to meet you. I wasn't keen but my son said it

would do no harm to go. So I met this Red Cross woman who introduced me to two Japanese businessmen and their wives. They shook my hand politely, and then they said why they were there. Their father was the pilot I'd shot down in Singapore and their mother, who was too old now to come out to New Zealand, asked them to see and thank me for sending his personal belongings back. They couldn't understand how an enemy pilot would do that sort of thing."

106 See *Singapore Slip*.

107 See *Scramble to Victory*.

CHAPTER VIII
Buffalo Swansong

108 See *The Zero Fighter*.

110 See *Royal Australian Air Force 1939-42*.

109/111 See *Scramble to Victory*.

112/114 See *The Remorseless Road* by James McEwan.

113 See *Suez to Singapore*.

115 See *War Without Glory*.

116 See *Bloody Shambles Volume 2* for additional details of the tragic Endau operation.

117 See *Scramble to Victory*.

118 A few days after arriving at Palembang, personnel of 21RAAF Squadron left by road and train for Oosthaven, where they boarded the SS *Ban Goen* for the trip across Sunda Strait to Merak. Here they boarded a train for Batavia, arriving on 8 February. Eventually they found an old, small freighter, the SS *Giang Ann*, which was available to take the party, 450-strong, to Australia, and departed on 17 February and reached Fremantle on 4 March.

119 Grp Capt Whistondale was killed on 1 March 1942 when Kalidjati airfield in Java was overrun by the Japanese. He was last seen returning to his office, allegedly to retrieve his stamp collection. His car was ambushed and he and his passenger were killed.

120 See *Scramble to Victory*.

121 See *Flying Fever*; Air Commodore Vincent had shot down enemy aircraft in both World Wars.

122 The USS *Langley*, an old training carrier with 32 assembled P-40Es lashed to her deck, on her way to Java, was attacked and sunk by G4Ms from the Takao Ku on 27 February. A British freighter, the *Seawitch*, with a further 27 crated P-40Es, actually reached Tjilatjap, but arrived too late for the fighters to be assembled and operated. They were offloaded onto lighters and sunk in harbour to avoid them falling into enemy hands.

123 Flt Sgt Mothersdale, in his recollection of the incident, believed Sgt Charlie Wareham to have been the pilot, but in fact it was Sgt Kronk.

CHAPTER IX
The End for Singapore

124/125 See *War in Malaya*.

126 By the end of January, during operations over Malaya and Singapore, the JAAF had lost 32 Ki-27s and 23 Ki-43s; 60 per cent of these losses were due to enemy action, but a substantial proportion of them had been destroyed on the ground by bombing rather than in air combat.

127 See *The Singapore Story* by Kenneth Attiwill.

128 The two 'missing' airmen had in fact been invited to enjoy a cup of tea, presumably to calm their nerves, with Sgts Greg Board and Ross Leys of 453 Squadron whom they encountered during their time away from the airfield. The two pilots later drove them back.

129 See *Last Flight from Singapore* by A.G. Donahue.

130 See *Everything but the Flak*.

131 These were believed to have been Plt Off Norman Randall, who was later killed flying P-40s with 76 RAAF Squadron, and Sgt Arthur Ruge, killed in a flying accident at the RAAF's 2 OTU.

132 Wg Cdr Bell, former CO of 243 Squadron and OC RAF Kallang, was one of the many thousands trapped on Java when the island fell to the Japanese. Having attempted to reach the coast in the hope of finding some means of escape, he decided to make for the airfield that had

been designated by the Japanese as the concentration point for members of the Allied air forces. There, he and a colleague discovered a crated Tiger Moth in a hangar:

"We decided to erect this aircraft, fit extra fuel tanks and make an attempt to fly out. Our plan was to fly at low-level and head for the island of Sumba, some 800 miles to the east. Accordingly, we moved the aircraft bit by bit, during the night hours, to a shed in an outlying part of the airfield, where in the course of the next ten days or so, we put it all together. We were to take off at dawn, but during the previous night the Japanese Command summoned the SBO in camp and instructed him that should any of the aircraft be removed, a number of prisoners would be shot. With bitter disappointment therefore, we destroyed the Tiger Moth on which we had pinned so much hope."

At another camp, Boei Glodok, two Canadian Hurricane pilots and a Hudson pilot, who made an attempt to steal a Japanese twin-engined Ki-56 transport aircraft on the nearby airstrip, were captured, tortured and executed.
133 See *Suez to Singapore*.

CHAPTER X
Dutch Brewsters – The Fall of Java
134 See the next volume in this series – *Hurricanes over Singapore*.
135 Lt Jan Brunier had been awarded the Dutch War Cross in recognition of his service with the RAF's 92 Squadron, flying Spitfires on operations over Northern Europe. He had been credited with two victories. Before the fall of Java he helped form a Dutch Hurricane unit.
136 Lt André de la Porte escaped from Java and later served with 5PRU in Burma.
137 See *Samurai* by Saburo Sakai.
138 Lt August Deibel was killed in a flying accident on 12 June 1950, when his Meteor jet fighter crashed in the Netherlands.
139 Sqn Ldr Frank Howell, having endured the rigors of prison camp, was killed in a freak accident following his return to the United Kingdom. On 9 May 1948, whilst filming Vampires of his Squadron (54) taking off and landing at RAF Odiham, he was struck on the head by a wingtip of one as it came into land and killed outright.
140 Following a brief period in command of 135 Squadron at Ceylon, Sqn Ldr William Harper was posted to command a Kittyhawk squadron in the Middle East, and later still, the first Spitfire squadron to operate outside of Europe. Postwar, Harper emigrated to Rhodesia and began farming before turning to mining. In 1958, he was elected to the Southern Rhodesia Parliament and became President of the Dominion Party the following year. When the Rhodesian Front came to power in 1962 he became a Cabinet Minister and, in 1964, was appointed Minister for Internal Affairs. He resigned in 1968 and four years later was a founder member of the United Front Party.
141 On his return to the UK, Garden was posted to 56 OTU and then joined 181 Squadron in September 1942 but almost straight away was posted to 12 (P) AFU. He did not return to operations. Postwar, he returned to his prewar profession. Sadly, in the 1970s severe diabetes necessitated the amputation of both legs.
142 Sgt Perce Killick, who was safely evacuated, recalled: "In about September/October 1941 I had my fortune told by a beggar in the streets of Kluang. He had credentials from the King of Egypt of all places. He told me I would be back in New Zealand by the end of March – I arrived in Auckland on 31 March 1942. He told me I would marry a girl whose name would begin with B, and I married a girl named Beryl. He told me I would have a break in my life at 38 – we were divorced when I was 38. He said that I would marry again and live to a very old age, and although he did not name the girl, I married a second time and I am at the old age stage now. There were three of us there the night he told us our fortunes. He told Eddie Kuhn he wouldn't be home for at least three and a half years – and of course Eddie went to a prison camp. The third person he wouldn't tell his fortune. This was Tony Cox and he went missing on his first major operation."
143 See *Spitfires over Israel* by Brian Cull and Shlomo Aloni with David Nicolle.

SELECT BIBLIOGRAPHY & ACKNOWLEDGEMENTS

Bloody Shambles Volumes 1 & 2: Christopher Shores and Brian Cull with
   Yasuho Izawa
Burning Blue, The: Paul Addison & Jeremy A. Crang
Defeat to Victory: John Bennett
De Luchtstrijd om Indië: P.C. Boer
Epics of the Fighting RAF: Leonard Gribble
Everything but the Flak: Martin Caidin
Eyes for the Phoenix: Geoff Thomas
Fall of Singapore, The: Frank Owen
Flying Fever: Air Vice-Marshal S.F. Vincent
Glory in Chaos: E.R. (Bon) Hall
Japan Must Fight Britain: Lt Cdr Tota Ishimaru
Last Flight from Singapore: A.G. Donahue
Malayan Postscript: Ian Morrison
Mates and Mayhem: Lawrence Watt
New Zealanders with the Royal Air Force, Volume III:
   Wg Cdr H.L. Thompson RNZAF
Odd Man Out: Peter Elphick and Michael Smith.
Ragged, Rugged Warriors: Martin Caidin
Remorseless Road, The: James McEwan
Retreat in the East: O'Dowd Gallagher
Royal Australian Air Force, 1939-42: Douglas Gillison
Samurai: Saburo Sakai
Second World War, The: Volume III: W.S. Churchill
Scramble to Victory: Norman Franks
Singapore; The Inexcusable Betrayal: George Chippington
Singapore: The Japanese Version: Masanobu Tsuji
Singapore: The Pregnable Fortress: Peter Elphick
Singapore Slip: Herbert C. Plenty
Singapore is Silent: George Weller
Singapore Story, The: Kenneth Attiwill
Suez to Singapore: Cecil Brown
Tattered Eagle, The: Geoffrey Rex Collis
Their Last Tenko: James Home
Tsubasa No Kessen (Wings of Bloody Combat): Yohei Hinoki
War in Malaya, The: Lt General A.E. Percival
War Without Glory: J.D. Balfe
Wings over Burma: J. Helsdon Thomas
Zero Fighter, The: M. Okumiya and J. Horikoshi
Zero Fighter: Martin Caidin
Air-Britain Serial Registers W1000-W9999 and AA100-AZ999

Official Reports
History of No.226 (Fighter) Group
Grp Capt E.B. Rice RAF (Air 20/5578)
Grp Capt J.P.J. McCauley RAAF (ACT/A1196)
Sqn Ldr W.J. Harper RAF (Air 20/5578)

Wg Cdr F.N. Wright RAAF (Air 20/5578)
Sqn Ldr W.F. Allshorn RAAF (Air 20/5578)
Sqn Ldr F.J. Howell DFC RAF (Air 20/5578)
Sqn Ldr W.G. Clouston DFC RAF (Air 20/5578)
Squadron ORBs (Air 27 series)
HQ No.1 Training Group RAAF Court of Inquiry 30 March 1942 (File 72/1/352)

Periodicals/Newspapers *Aussie Air Stories II* by Fred Morton; various copies of
  RAAF News, War Illustrated, Flight

Diaries/Logbooks/Interviews/Select Correspondence
Diaries: Rex Weber RNZAF (deceased); Vin Arthur RNZAF (deceased) – copy
supplied by Mrs Joyce Richardson, a friend of Bert Wipiti; Jack Burton RNZAF
(deceased), Russ Reynolds RNZAF (deceased); Doug Vanderfield DFC RAAF, Max
Boyd RNZAF, Basil Young RAAF; Interviews by Paul Sortehaug with Charlie
Wareham DFM RNZAF (deceased); Rod MacMillan RNZAF, Edgar Pevreal RNZAF,
Jim Cranstone DFC RNZAF, Eddie Kuhn DFM RNZAF, Jim MacIntosh RNZAF,
Terry Marra RNZAF, Don Clow DFC RNZAF, Brian Baber RNZAF, Harry Pettit
RNZAF, Geoff Fisken DFC RNZAF, who also kindly provided the Foreword;
Logbooks: Charlie Kronk RNZAF (deceased); Mac Read RAAF (deceased); Gordon
Bonham RNZAF (deceased). Correspondence: Mowbray Garden DFC RAF
(deceased); Peter Ballard RNZAF; Geoff Sheppard RAAF (deceased); George
Mothersdale RAF (deceased); Wg Cdr George Darley DSO RAF, Wg Cdr Donald
Pearson DFC RAF, Harry Griffiths RAAF; Bill Collyer RAAF; Geoff Angus RAAF
(deceased); 453 Squadron war diary; 488 Squadron war diary.

ADDITIONAL ACKNOWLEDGEMENTS

The authors thank Christopher Shores and Yasuho Izawa, Brian Cull's co-authors on *Bloody Shambles*. Practical assistance has been received from Nathan Sortehaug (Paul's brother); Dennis Newton of New South Wales, Australia; American researcher/writers Ray Duke of Vacaville, California, and Arthur Nicholson of San Antonio, Texas; Sqn Ldr David Wilson RAAF and Mollie Angel, RAAF Historical Section, Canberra, Australia; Sqn Ldr Andy Thomas RAF, Sqn Ldr Andy Anderson RAF (Rt'd), Michael Robinson, author of *Best of the Few*, and Martin Goodman; as ever, Brian Cull's gratitude is extended to Jack Lee, gentleman and scholar. The authors also thank the various organisations and institutes for their co-operation including the staff of the Public Record Office at Kew, London; Air Historical Branch of the Ministry of Defence; the Australian War Memorial at Canberra, Australia; and the Bury St Edmunds Public Library.

Of course, the acknowledgements would not be complete without an expression of gratitude for the authors' long-suffering families: Brian Cull thanks his wife Val for her continuing support and encouragement in helping him to complete this book, his fifteenth for Grub Street, none of which would have come to fruition without her at his side and steering him through difficult times. Mark Haselden similarly thanks his wife Rae, the mother of his two very young sons, for her understanding while he was devoting much of his limited leisure time to research. Paul Sortehaug, in New Zealand, who has practically devoted his life to research and writing, mainly about New Zealand airmen in both World Wars, is grateful for the support of his family and in particular his nephew Nathan.

MAPS OF THEATRE

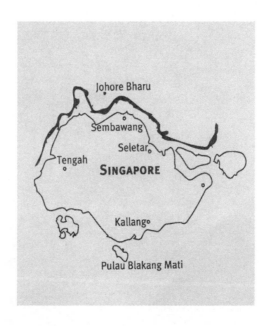

INDEX OF PERSONNEL

De Maus, Sgt W.L. RNZAF 488 Sqn 29, 100, 124, 172, 176, 217, 232
Drury, Plt Off R.W. RAAF 453 Sqn 37, 38, 77, 79, 225, 233, 236

Elliott, Sgt P.L. RNZAF 243 Sqn 20, 108, 109, 225, 232

Farr, Plt Off L.R. RNZAF 488 Sqn 29, 152, 159, 225, 231
Fisken, Sgt G.B. RNZAF 243 Sqn 4, 16, 17, 20, 53, 59, 63, 67, 90, 112,
    119-121, 129, 137-141, 155-157, 161, 173-175, 181, 185-187, 191, 197, 216,
    223-224, 227, 228, 230, 233

Garden, Flt Lt M. RAF 243 Sqn 15, 20, 21, 53, 93, 101, 105, 107, 113, 119,
    120, 123, 126, 131, 133, 135, 141, 149, 155, 156, 169-171, 175, 179, 181, 191,
    216, 227, 228, 230, 232, 239
Gifford, Plt Off P.D. RNZAF 488 Sqn 27, 29, 95, 140, 141, 155, 167, 173, 186,
    188, 189, 231, 232
Gleeson, Flg Off P.G. RAAF 453 Sqn 188, 191
Godsiff, Plt Off J.C. RNZAF 488 Sqn 29, 107, 232
Gorringe, Sgt K. RAAF 453 Sqn 26, 37, 74, 83, 100, 125, 136, 137, 151, 179,
    227, 228, 232, 236
Grace, Flt Lt B.A. RAAF 453 Sqn 22, 37, 38, 63, 64, 74, 84, 85, 105, 109,
    125, 136, 137, 171, 203, 217, 227, 228, 230
Greenhalgh, Plt Off W.J. RNZAF 488 Sqn 29, 124, 152, 171, 227
Greenslade, Sgt M.A. RNZAF 243 Sqn 20, 113, 120, 121, 134, 135, 162-163,
    167, 174, 191, 192, 197, 228, 231
Griffiths, Sgt H.H. RAAF 453 Sqn 25-26, 37, 38, 77-80, 82, 83, 85, 96, 105,
    106, 193, 218-222, 227, 232, 233, 236

Halliday, Sgt W.R. RAAF 453 Sqn 37, 38, 100, 111, 136, 152, 193, 195
Harper, Sqn Ldr W.J. RAF 453 Sqn 22, 23, 37, 41, 70, 71, 74, 75, 78, 82, 84,
    85, 96, 99, 101, 110, 111, 114, 125, 129, 136, 151, 152, 158, 177, 188-190, 201,
    202, 215, 220, 235, 239
Harrison, Sgt G.T. RAAF 21RAAF/453 Sqn 36, 118, 232
Hastwell, Flg Off J. RAAF 453 Sqn 190
Henkel, Flt Lt N.F.V. RAF 4PRU 164
Hesketh, Plt Off G.L. RNZAF 243 Sqn/488 Sqn 4, 17, 20, 29, 95, 131,
    132, 225
Holder, Flg Off M.H. RAF 243 Sqn 15, 17, 19, 20, 35, 43, 47, 59, 119, 120,
    128, 137, 139, 141, 146, 149, 156, 216, 227, 228, 231
Honan, Sgt T.W. RNZAF 488 Sqn 29, 30, 115, 116, 232
Hood, Flg Off B. RAAF 21RAAF/453 Sqn 35, 50, 66, 74, 118, 131,
    171, 236
Hooper, Flg Off J.B. RAAF 21RAAF/453 Sqn 36, 44, 45, 69, 217
Howell, Sqn Ldr F.J. RAF 243 Sqn 39, 40, 56, 93, 94, 97, 105, 109, 113, 127,
    134, 135, 141, 199, 213, 228, 231, 236, 239
Hutcheson, Flt Lt J.H. RNZAF 488 Sqn 27-30, 90, 95, 97, 115, 117, 124, 144,
    148, 216, 228, 230, 232

Irving-Brown, Plt Off M. RAAF 453 Sqn 26, 225, 232

Johnstone, Plt Off F.S. RNZAF 488 Sqn 29, 140, 176, 185, 188, 230, 232